BOBBY BRADDOCK

A Life on Nashville's Music Row

BOBBY BRADDOCK

A LIFE ON NASHVILLE'S MUSIC★ROW

COUNTRY MUSIC FOUNDATION PRESS  VANDERBILT UNIVERSITY PRESS

NASHVILLE, TENNESSEE

Published by Vanderbilt University Press
and the Country Music Foundation Press

This book is printed on acid-free paper.
Manufactured in the United States of America

Jacket design by Bruce Gore | Gore Studio, Inc.
Text design by Dariel Mayer

Library of Congress Cataloging-in-Publication Data on file

LC control number 2015000677
LC classification ML410.B7787A3 2015
Dewey class number 782.421642092—dc23

ISBN 978-0-8265-2082-1 (cloth)
ISBN 978-0-8265-2084-5 (ebook)

I lovingly dedicate this book to my daughter,

Lauren Braddock Havey,

and to my grandson, Braddock James (Dock) Havey.

I also dedicate it to the memory of my friend and mentor,

the great Southern author John Egerton.

CONTENTS

ACKNOWLEDGMENTS

I was very fortunate to have a great author like John Egerton guide me through the writing of two books, and I honestly don't think I could have written either one without him. Each time I finished a chapter, I would drive to his home on Copeland Drive in Nashville—usually very early in the morning—and put the manuscript in his mailbox. Within a few days I would get a call, and John would ask in his western Kentucky drawl, "You wanna come over and talk?" Within fifteen minutes I would be sitting in the little office behind his house. Sometimes he might say, "Bubba, you're just not convincing me," and I'd go back home and read all his comments, written out by hand across each page, and take another shot at it. But there were times when he would sit at his desk, reading my chapter, then look up with that big squinty-eyed smile and tell me, "Damn, son, this is good." I always kinda knew how to write a song, but I had to be taught how to write a book. I couldn't have had a better—or nicer— teacher than John Egerton.

I got a lot of other good help on this book, which was originally titled *Hollywood, Tennessee*. Advice from the great Elvis biographer Peter Guralnick was obviously priceless. Feedback and copyedit suggestions from author Michael Kosser, journalist Sharon Cobb, and songwriter-proofreader Chapin Hartford were extremely helpful.

The long and probably incomplete list of first-readers of my manuscript, who often gave me constructive advice, includes Tami Jones Andrews, Martin Bandier, Carmen Beecher, Melissa Bollea, Kaci Bolls, Walter Campbell, Stanley Cox, Dixie Gamble, Peter Guralnick, Jim Havey, Lauren Braddock Havey, Tammy Jacobs, Kathy Locke, Barry Mazor, Shannon McCombs, Don Pace, Dolly Parton, Alice Randall, Bob Schieffer, Blake Shelton, Troy Tomlinson, and Terry Wakefield.

And when long-term memory, reference books, and the Internet failed, there was always Dale Dodson, who knows more about old country music than most people twice his age. Many times I went to Michael Kosser's indispensable book *How Nashville Became Music City, USA*. The late Wade Jessen's satellite radio show was steeped in country music history, and any conversation with Robert Oermann or Marty Stuart is an education. ASCAP's LeAnn

Phelan was helpful with contacts. My daughter, Lauren, has an amazing grasp of timelines. My son-in-law Jim Havey's PR skills are always an asset.

Before my large tome was ready for production, the photographer Dennis Carney was a tremendous help in making old snapshots look like professionally shot photographs. And I owe a debt of gratitude to those who granted us permission to use their pictures. Their names are mentioned in a separate place in these pages.

This book has two publishers. It is a joint venture between Country Music Foundation Press and Vanderbilt University Press. Country Music Hall of Fame and Museum Director Kyle Young got the ball rolling with CMF Press, and Jay Orr became my editor, relentlessly challenging me, but never forcing me, to make this or that little change. (Jay is an amazing fact-checker, and I swear if I were to misspell the middle name of Bill Monroe's bus driver's cousin's wife, Jay would catch it!)

The final destination, before hitting the stores, for *Bobby Braddock: A Life on Nashville's Music Row* was Vanderbilt University Press, where Michael Ames's very professional staff sprinkled their magic dust on my words, and Joell Smith-Borne's team gave my manuscript one final copyedit and proofreading. Others on the VUP staff are Eli Bortz, Dariel Mayer, Betsy Phillips, Jenna Phillips and several whom I never met but who worked on my project. Though I never met Bruce Gore, I must acknowledge the man who proved me wrong when I said there would be no book cover with my picture on it that I could possibly like.

To all those mentioned in these acknowledgments, I say a very big, heartfelt thank you!

And a big thanks to Sony Music Publishing's Troy Tomlinson for making it possible for me to obtain permission to use song lyrics.

I would like to add this. I can't believe that Judy Roberts, who has been a fixture at Sony Music Publishing since the Tree days of 1968, does not appear as a character in my story. She is a constant and important part of it, and I just wanted to mention her name and ask her to forgive the oversight.

Finally, I want the daughters of my late publisher Donna Hilley to know that my accounts of Donna and I sometimes butting heads over my financial neediness does not take away from the fact that I had enormous respect and affection for her, and I think that shines through in these pages. And I want Carolyn Killen, the widow of my original publisher, Buddy Killen, to understand that my occasional good-natured references to Buddy's little quirks pale when compared to my portrayal of him as a great man who helped my songwriting career more than anyone else in Nashville (with the possible exception of Curly Putman). This book is not some big puff piece. I tried to be honest and balanced, and the truth does not always paint a perfect portrait. If I wrote a book full of sweet, wonderful characters who were perfect in every way, it wouldn't be very interesting, and I don't think people would like it very much. I don't kick anyone around in this book nearly as much as I do myself.

BOBBY BRADDOCK

A Life on Nashville's Music Row

FOR A SONG

One night in the early spring of 1965, I sat watching TV with Sue, my wife of nine months, in a little, rented, red brick house on the southeastern edge of Nashville. Since February, I had been working a young musician's dream job, playing in the road band of a superstar. Marty Robbins was one of my favorite singers, so I felt fortunate to get the gig, especially only a few months after moving to town. And even better, he had taken a liking to some of my songs. He was doing a recording session that night, so I was keeping my fingers crossed. Sue urged me to relax and enjoy the TV show, but it was hard to concentrate. When the phone rang, I popped up off the couch.

"Hey, Bobby, it's *Ox*," hollered Don Winters, whose tenor singing voice was a perfect harmony blend on Marty's legendary gunfighter ballads. "The Chief says get on over here to Columbia studio, he's got somethin' he wants you to hear."

I was on Nashville's Music Row in about fifteen minutes. The musicians in the studio were a mix of some of Marty's road band and the in-demand, A-team session players. The Jordanaires, of Elvis fame, supplied the background vocals. Marty Robbins, the unusual-looking man with the extraordinary voice, motioned me over. "Hey, Bob, tell me what you think," he said softly. He then opened the door to the control room and asked the engineer to play "Matilda," a song I had written specifically for The Chief.

Though it was just a stereotypical cowboy song that would be merely an album cut unheard by many, I thought it was the most gorgeous thing I'd ever heard. No future radio hits or award winners would ever equal the thrill of listening to my very first "cut" coming out of the large speakers in Studio B at Columbia. I had been trying to decide whether I wanted to be a piano player or a songwriter. My mind was made up that night: I was going to be a songwriter.

I look back in amazement at those times. It was a different world, a different America, a different South, and, germane to this book, a different Music Row. In the 1990s I wrote a song called "Time Marches On" that has this line: "The only thing that stays the same is *everything changes*." Anyone who hates change is in for disappointment without end. The young guys are old, and the old guys are gone. But I can hear their echoes. Since I moved to Nashville in 1964, the traditional country songs have been replaced by whatever it was you heard on the radio or YouTube this morning.

Sometimes the Nashville new breed will ask me to tell them "the stories," meaning the *funny* ones, but I know plenty of sad ones too. For writing this epic tale of Nashville's music business, I've got something even better than my long-term memory: a closet full of journals, eighty-two volumes in all. I sat down every single night—for four decades—to record what was going on around me, often in great detail. No matter what the circumstances or the shape I was in, I always managed to write something down every night before falling asleep.

So through the pages of this book walk the great characters I've encountered over these many years: some of them famous, some of them infamous, and some of them unknown. And mixed in with all this is my own crazy life, as well as a running history of the newsworthy events that shaped our surroundings, and the popular music that colored our lives. I hope that everyone who enters here will leave knowing what it was like to be in this remarkable town in each unique decade. So as time marches on, I hear the big clock ticking away, as I try to get it all down before too many more characters bite the dust.

In looking back over the years and thinking about all I've seen, I feel as if I've been to the circus. And the ticket didn't cost me much at all. I got it for a song.

1

TWO CITIES

This is a tale of two cities, both of them called Nashville.

One, a municipality, had its beginnings in 1779, when a small group of white settlers built a stockade called Fort Nashborough on the banks of the Cumberland River, in an area known as French Lick, about thirty miles northwest of the geographical center of what would become the state of Tennessee. When my bride and I set up housekeeping there 185 years later, it was pronounced NASH-vul (rhymes with *bashful*) and referred to alternately as the Athens of the South, the Wall Street of the South, and the Buckle of the Bible Belt. With one of America's first combined city-county metropolitan governments, this state capital then boasted a population of 425,000.

The other Nashville was not so much a city as a name that people gave to an entertainment center or a destination or a dream. "I'm going to Nashville" didn't call up images of tall buildings or university campuses, but of cowboy hats and guitars and microphones. It was the country-and-western capital of the world, Music City USA; it was *Hollywood, Tennessee*. This Nashville had its beginnings in 1925 when seventy-seven-year-old "Uncle Jimmy" Thompson played his fiddle on a program broadcast by radio station WSM. When the Braddocks rolled into town thirty-nine years later, it was pronounced NASH-ville, with only slightly more emphasis on the first syllable. This is how it was said by practically everyone not born in the area. *This* Nashville contained few natives, most of its inhabitants coming from small towns and farms across America, particularly the Southeast and Southwest. These were the singers, songwriters, musicians, publishers, managers, and booking agents. *This* Nashville was the magnet that led me to quit a popular rock & roll band and hitch a trailer to my car, as my pregnant wife, Sue, hitched her wagon to my star. We left my native Florida for that magical musical Mecca in Middle Tennessee.

Nancy Sue Rhodes was from Fairfield, Alabama, a steel mill suburb of Birmingham. When I met her only a few months earlier, I saw a cute, engaging nineteen-year-old girl who weighed ninety-something pounds and stood barely five feet tall. I saw big blonde hair, which was okay in 1964, and effervescent sky-blue eyes. What I didn't see was a young woman who was looking for a husband and had decided that I was a prime candidate. She spun her web, and I flew right into it. What I also failed to see was a tortured soul with dark memories of an alcoholic family, memories that she would never share with me. I saw her many faces, some of them loving and lovable, but I would never see deep into her soul. She kept that part hidden.

Ironically, when I decided to move to Nashville, Sue was the only person I knew who was supportive of relocation, but for reasons of her own. My grandfatherly father, a Deep-Southern, Old-Florida character to his core, told me in his W. C. Fields–meets–Foghorn Leghorn voice, "Bobby boy, that's a long waayy from home. When you get ready to mooove back to Polk County, Flahrr-da, let us knowww, and we'll dooo everythinnng possible to help you out." My mom, who often smiled from ear to ear even when she wasn't happy, was dead set against the move, and smilingly told me so. Big John Taylor, a guitar genius who normally had a happy Andy Griffith-like country boy demeanor, was angry at me for quitting (and splitting up) his group, one of the best rock & roll bands in the state. My two best friends in my hometown of Auburndale admitted years later that they had thought I'd be back to Florida within six months.

"You're going to do so good in Nashville," Sue cooed in her Alabama drawl. She may have had confidence in my musical abilities, but she was also very eager to get away from Central Florida and my ex-fiancée, Gloria.

On "band wives' night" at the El Patio Club in Orlando, home base for our band, Big John's Untouchables, someone had told my bride that Gloria was still wearing the engagement ring that I had given her four years before. From that point on, Sue wouldn't let up. "Call her and tell her you want that ring back!" she demanded over and over—and to placate her, I did. Finally, Gloria showed up at our house in Orlando, with a letter from advice columnist Ann Landers, assuring her that the ring rightfully belonged to the former betrothed, and that she didn't have to return it to me. Sue's enraged reaction was to physically attack Gloria on our front steps. I felt that we were sitting on top of a nuclear arsenal and would have the shortest marriage in history if I didn't do something radical, so the next day I announced my decision to move to Nashville, much to my bride's delight (but she probably would have been just as happy if I had asked her to move to Albuquerque or Wichita or Youngstown). My notice that I was leaving caused so much acrimony within the band that the lead singer and I got into a fistfight onstage during a jam-packed performance.

"I just *know* you're going to do good up there, Daddy," Sue said. This woman was carrying my child, so I was determined that the marriage was going to work.

My dream was to be a songwriter, but I wasn't really sure if I had what it took. I felt confident that I was a good musician and could get a job in Nashville playing piano, on recording sessions or on the road, and that was fine. I would love that. I figured it would all fall into place when we got there. I had

Wedding day picture with Sue and my parents, July 20, 1964

only a couple of contacts in Nashville, and they were rather tenuous, so this was pretty much an exercise in blind faith.

One bright morning in early September, we took the big leap, loading up my 1962 Oldsmobile and heading north. I had a strong feeling that I would never live in Florida again. Though we had been residing in Orlando, my hometown was Auburndale (pronounced *Orbundale* by many of the locals). Polk County—where pendulous balls of gold adorned the surrounding countryside like weeds and wildflowers—was the leading citrus-producing county in America. My father was a citrus grower. This was pre-Disney Central Florida, and my neck of the woods was very Southern. Most of my classmates' parents were native Floridians or Alabamians or Georgians. This was not Northern-influenced Miami or Ft. Lauderdale. The white Auburndale classrooms were only that month enrolling the first black students ever, fully ten years after the Supreme Court had ruled that separate schools were unconstitutional. In fact, the 1964 Civil Rights Act that made it unlawful to turn black people away from public accommodations had been in effect for only two months, so the entire South was still in the baby stages of racial justice, and for the most part, had let go of the old ways grudgingly.

So this was the world we were living in as we began our new adventure. We drove through the grove-covered rolling hills of Central Florida past the little blue lakes, through the horse country around Ocala, through the flat tobacco land of North Florida into similar terrain in South Georgia, then turned westward into the sun, taking Alabama roads on up to the Birmingham area, where Sue would stay for a few days with her sister's family while I went on to Nashville to find a place for us to live.

After leaving my bride with her family, I headed north on the road to Nashville. Interstate 65 was far from completed, so most of my little journey was on US Highway 31. In those days, the first thing you saw when crossing into Tennessee was a billboard emblazoned with "WELCOME TO THE THREE STATES OF TENNESSEE." These signs would be taken down in the early 1970s, but in 1964 the state was still officially divided into three grand divisions: West Tennessee, Middle Tennessee, and East Tennessee. (The state being short and wide, her regions have never been referred to locally as north, central, and south.) The three divisions were a throwback to Civil War days when the mountainous eastern counties, having few slaves, remained loyal to the Union and joined up with the Federals rather than the Confederacy. The rest of Tennessee treated these mountaineers rather harshly during the early days of the war, but after the Yankees captured the capitol in Nashville, East Tennessee rejoiced, and sought revenge on the rest of the state. That sectional hatred from both sides was passed on down for a century, and though most of today's younger inhabitants may not know exactly why, to this day, people from that part of the state seldom say that they're from Tennessee; it's usually "I'm from *East* Tennessee."

My destination city of Nashville sat approximately in the middle of *Middle* Tennessee, a land of beautiful rolling hills, horse and tobacco country interspersed with pleasant old courthouse towns. As I drove around the square in the town of Franklin, I knew that I was only one county away from my destination. I neared the journey's end with country radio turned up full blast. My pulse quickened as I approached the city of country dreams.

Nashville got its big country music start in the 1920s when radio station WSM began broadcasting the Grand Ole Opry, so named because the old-time fiddling show aired immediately after a program that featured *grand opera*. Some people have said that Nashville had the perfect geographical pedigree to be the epicenter of American country music because it was located to the east of this or to the west of that, but in truth the music was popular all over the rural South, and it could just as easily have been headquartered in any number of cities in the Southland or, for that matter, to the north, where the popular WLS Barn Dance in Chicago preceded the Opry by a year. On the night that country came to town, Nashville was not a bastion of music, but a busy river city and a bustling financial center. The first big record stars in the field that we now call country, Jimmie Rodgers and Vernon Dalhart, were not Nashville connected, and it wasn't until the mid-1930s that the Opry featured a big-selling recording act, Roy Acuff. Though the hoedowns would remain popular on live shows, recordings of fiddle and dance tunes were being replaced by songs with lyrics, with words about Jesus and Mother and long lost love. These ballads, like the fiddle tunes, were nothing new; they were the rustic sound of the lower American heartland, from the mountains to the hills to the flatlands and the plains, brought over on ocean vessels from England, Scotland, and Ireland a century earlier, even more than two centuries earlier. Beginning in 1939, the famous Grand Ole Opry was broadcast nationally on the NBC radio network, but even then many of the country stars were not recording in Nashville, but in places like New York, Chicago, Dallas, and Atlanta—catch phrases like "The Nashville Sound" and "Music Row" were still quite a few years away. There were genres within the genre, and the sounds might include mandolins from the mountains or accordions from the bunkhouse. World War II spread this rural art form to all parts of the continent, and this American stew had some added ingredients stirred in by drifters on the High Plains, and polka-loving farmers in the Midwest. And even if some in the industry didn't like to admit it, there was a fair sprinkling of African hot sauce. An important part of 1940s country was the swing and honky-tonk from Texas and Oklahoma, which was finding its way to California. By the middle of the twentieth century, nobody knew whether to say hillbilly, country and western, or even folk and western. In great contrast to the bright-eyed, bouncy pop ditties of the day, here was something raw and realistic, with story songs about cold, cold hearts and back street affairs, sung by farm boys from the South who dressed like cowboys from the West.

When I was a kid, I generally disliked this hillbilly music that my big brother and his friends listened to—singers like Hank Snow, Webb Pierce, and Carl Smith. I said, "*I* could write *that* stuff," not knowing then that someday I would. When I got to junior high, I was drawn to rock & roll along with my peers. Hearing Elvis's "Mystery Train" was a defining moment. I felt that Johnny Cash was rockabilly just like Elvis and eagerly awaited each new release. After opening the country music door, I was drawn first to the crossover artists like Marty Robbins, then to Ray Price's traditional Texas shuffles, with the crying pedal-steel guitar and lonesome fiddle. This led me back to the music of my brother, which I listened to with new ears, particularly appreciating the genius of Hank Williams, the original Nashville singer-writer superstar. Though I was also into rock & roll (Everly Brothers, Little Richard) and rhythm & blues (Ray Charles, Jimmy Reed), I had come to love country music most of all. I would remain a fan of the genre for the rest of my life, but it would never move me as it did in the late 1950s when I was in my teens.

In September of 1964, country fans hadn't gotten over the marvelous voice of the late Patsy Cline, and Jim Reeves was beginning a posthumous string of hits that would last for many years. Jumping out of the radio were Buck Owens and his twangy Bakersfield sound, and Roger Miller's pop-country novelty hits. I had been loving a lot of the rock & roll, especially the Beatles, but now that I was no longer in Big John's Untouchables, I was starting my new life totally focused on country music. Rock & roll was the wild girlfriend; country was the wife you settled down with. And that's how I got to Nashville. Ever since my senior year in high school, I had fantasized about coming to this city to make music—to play it or write it—and here I was.

Once in Nashville, US Highway 31 became Franklin Road, a thoroughfare lined with lush, spacious grounds and large, handsome houses and mansions: red brick Georgian, Greek Revival, Colonial, and large ranch-style. I turned right onto Harding Place, and carefully followed my directions through some twists and turns to a middle-class suburban area and the small ranch-style home of Benjamin Joy Eidson, known professionally as Benny Joy.

I knew Benny through Big John Taylor, my former rock & roll band-leader—they had toured Europe together in the late 1950s. Benny was born in Atlanta but moved to Florida as a child. A talented rockabilly shouter with a frantic style, he became a local star in the Tampa area. He never had any national hits, even after he moved up from an independent record label to Decca, but for the past couple of years he had been having some success in Nashville as a country songwriter. He was tall and thin, with a pallid complexion, and his features were bat-like—big dark eyes, large ears, and a little pointy nose. Though only in his late twenties, he was such a nervous wreck that his entire head trembled!

"Well, hey there, Bobby, come on in. I want you to meet my mama." His mother's name was Verna. A good-natured woman of about fifty-five, she came from a rural area of Georgia and spoke with a country accent. When she laughed, her eyes twinkled and her torso bounced up and down. I would come to realize that Benny was a mama's boy and a control freak. She lived with Benny to wait on him hand and foot, and every little thing had to be just right, or he would give her hell.

"Man, I've found a place for you to stay, while you're lookin' for somethin' permanent," Benny said. "Hank Snow's rhythm-guitar player is on the road this week, and you can sleep in the guy's bed 'til he gets back in town. It's in a roomin' house over near Franklin Road."

Benny was congenial and helpful, taking me up and down Music Row the next day. He wanted to help me find a gig as a piano player. Several months before, I had sent him several of my songs, and he wrote back, informing me that my melodies were decent but my words were weak, and he would have to change my lyrics and share in the credits in order for the songs to be presentable. As far as he was concerned, I was in town to be a musician, so I didn't promote my songwriting aspirations when I was around him.

Music Row appeared to be no more than a leafy little neighborhood within the city, but the area, just southwest of downtown, was the epicenter of Nashville's music business. It was roughly three long avenues and parallel alleyways, corresponding cross streets, and a couple of circular side streets. With only three or four actual office-type buildings, it looked more residential than commercial. Old two-story houses sported signs that converted them into record labels, publishing companies, recording studios, and managers' offices.

"Hey, Hockey," Benny yelled to an acquaintance as we strolled down 16th Avenue South. He liked to call people "Hockey" for some reason, often spoken in the voice of his impersonation of the black character Kingfish from the TV show *Amos 'n' Andy*. "Uh, look heah, Hockey, this is mah friend Bobby, and hmmmm, he's a really *mean* piano player." Benny was trying to be helpful. We crossed the street and saw a thickset middle-aged man wearing sunglasses, walking out of the Decca Records offices.

"Hey, Owen, I want you to meet Bobby Braddock," he said to Owen Bradley, the legendary head of Decca's Nashville division, producer of multiple country superstars, and one of the founders of Music Row.

In 1954 the Bradley brothers—bandleader Owen and guitarist Harold—bought an old two-story house on 16th Avenue South and converted it into a studio for recording music and making films. They added what was called a Quonset hut, a large prefabricated structure that was a familiar sight to those who had served in the military in World War II. The prefab room became one of the two studios at that address, and the Bradleys got so much recording business—including all the Decca artists that Owen was producing—that they phased out the filmmaking. A couple of years later, in 1957, RCA Records opened the first new edifice in the area to be built for music. In 1962 Columbia Records bought the Bradley property, tearing down the house and putting up their Nashville offices, but leaving the popular Quonset Hut Studio B intact. When I moved to town, Music Row was already a clearly defined place that was home to most of the local recording industry. Owen Bradley was probably the most powerful man on The Row, followed closely by his friend and counterpart at RCA, guitar guru Chet Atkins.

Mr. Bradley was affable but not the kind of man one would slap on the back; only a fool would treat him with anything less than total respect. When Benny Joy introduced us, I asked Bradley if it was true that there was a clique of musicians who got all the studio recording work.

"Well, if there is, they have to keep on their toes to stay in it," the Music Row legend answered with a smile.

"In other words, they have to click to stay in the clique," I quipped.

"Very good," he laughed. "That's a good way to put it." I later learned that Mr. Bradley had been known to run and hide when he saw Benny coming. Benny meant well, but he could be overbearing.

The next night was Saturday night, and Benny took me backstage at the Grand Ole Opry. Located in the heart of downtown Nashville, the Grand Ole Opry House was also known as the Ryman Auditorium. Formerly the Union Gospel Tabernacle, it was built in 1892 by a riverboat owner who had gotten religion. Benny introduced me to country music stars such as Faron Young and Stonewall Jackson, and asked them if they knew anyone who needed a piano player, going way beyond what one would normally do to help a friend of a friend.

I found an apartment in a run-down little complex on Rains Avenue, next to the Tennessee State Fairgrounds, on Nashville's south side, in a working-class part of town known as Woodbine. The old-timers referred to this part of Nashville as Flatrock. I called Sue from a phone booth, told her I had a place for us to live, had gotten a job as a vacuum cleaner salesman, and would be in the Birmingham area the next day to pick her up.

At a convenience store, I bought a newspaper from a coin-operated rack. This was in the days before TV news had killed off afternoon newspapers, and most major cities still had one. The morning *Tennessean* was adamantly liberal, and the evening *Banner* was unyieldingly conservative, and the two papers gave Nashville and Middle Tennessee two distinctly varying points of view. Ironically, both publications were housed in the same building, under a joint printing and advertising umbrella that was called Newspaper Printing Corporation. In earlier days, the employees of the rival papers had been forbidden even to speak to each other.

The next morning, I drove down to Alabama to bring Sue back to our new home. We spent the rest of the day and part of the night moving into the little apartment that she didn't seem to care for. I was shocked to learn that musicians in Nashville could not get a telephone unless they paid a special deposit to the phone company! After a good night's sleep, we did the grand tour of our new hometown, as we listened to Roy Orbison sing "Pretty Woman" on rock & roll station WKDA, and Buck Owens sing "Together Again" on country station WENO. We drove downtown, heading east on Broadway past Union Station, a Romanesque Revival-style building that had been there since 1900, on past the bars and dives on "Lower Broad," then onto one of the bridges that crossed the Cumberland River into East Nashville, a multiracial multiclass section of the city, with its shotgun shacks and 1880s Victorian mansions. We swung back across the river and drove by the state capitol, built high on a hill a few years before the Civil War and modeled after a Greek temple. After driving through largely African American North Nashville, we headed west on West End Avenue to Centennial Park for a quick look at the Parthenon, a near-perfect replica of the original one in Athens. We continued westward through posh Belle Meade, where the old money resided (insurance, investment banking, etc.), and finally to the outskirts of town where we rode through Nashville's two huge city-owned recreational parks. We were too tired to head east of town for a tour of The Hermitage, President Andrew Jackson's mansion. Our only disappointment was there were not yet any suburban shopping malls, as there were in Orlando; the big department stores were still located downtown. But overall, we were impressed with what we had seen. With one of the silly little mispronunciations she liked to give certain words, Sue said, "I just love *Nashul*, Daddy."

She didn't love the dingy little apartment, however, so a change came quickly. We rented part of a house, a nice red brick one, in an upper-middle-class part of town called Crieve Hall, from a couple whose kids were away at college. Because we were occupying only two or three rooms, this enabled us to live in an upscale neighborhood at a cost that was affordable, and the change in atmosphere was uplifting.

I wasn't selling many vacuum cleaners, so we were living mostly on the money that my parents had given us for a wedding present. Door-to-door sales work isn't a good occupation for a bad driver with a terrible sense of direction who has a tendency to get lost all the time. Absent-minded in the extreme, I had a penchant for misplacing anything that wasn't nailed down. What brain I had seemed to work pretty well, especially the creative part, but a good-sized little chunk of it definitely appeared to be missing.

We opened a checking account at Third National Bank. The names on our checks read "Mr. Bobby Braddock or Mrs. Sue Braddock." I complained to the teller that I didn't want to have to sign my checks "*Mr.* Bobby Braddock." "Oh, we put 'Mr. and Mrs.' on *white* people's checks," the young woman explained. "That way we can tell if the person who signs the check is white or colored." This was late in the year, *after* passage of the Civil Rights Act of 1964. Sad to say, though, my problem wasn't the segregated checking accounts, but the prospect of having to use two extra letters when I signed my name.

There were Southerners who were ahead of their time on the issue of race, and I wish I had been one of them, but I wasn't, and to try to suggest otherwise would be a lie. Nashville was certainly quite Southern—anyone hearing the accents could never doubt that—but even with the bank's race obsession and the segregationist tone of the evening newspaper, my new hometown was certainly more progressive than my old one. Auburndale had its roots in Alabama and Georgia. I had a small-town, Southern white point of view. I would have told you that I loved "colored people" but just didn't believe in *forced* integration. Of course, had integration not been forced, there would have been no integration. It would be a few more years before I saw the light and gained enlightenment on this and other issues.

Living in Tennessee was an exhilarating experience, and autumn made it even more so. The broadleaf trees—oaks, maples, and dogwoods—were turning red and orange and yellow, quite different from Florida where trees waited until winter to make a slight color change, then stingily held on to most of their leaves.

I was crazy about Nashville, even finding magic in the street names, like Old Hickory Boulevard and Granny White Pike. I felt certain that good things were forthcoming, so there was excitement in the air. I would see some country music star stopped at a traffic light—often mistaken identity, no doubt—and couldn't wait to get home to tell Sue who I had seen.

Because of a lack of storage space, I kept my Hammond organ and Wurlitzer electric piano in our bedroom. I sat down on the edge of the bed to write a song at the piano every chance I got, even if Sue was asleep. I told her she needed to get used to it, that my career came first, and if that went well, then everything else would too. For some reason that philosophy didn't seem nearly so arrogant and selfish back then.

For a couple whose marriage had gotten off on the wrong foot, Sue and I were getting along pretty well. To be sure, there were clashes—even in the best of times, we were never far from being the cobra and the mongoose—but with her carrying my child (and not having a really easy time of it) and both of us in a strange new land with very few acquaintances, we became closer and closer. It was the two of us against the world.

There were a couple of rather strange aspects to our happy relationship. One was our cast of fantasy characters or alter egos. It was as though we had joint split personalities or a collective dissociative identity disorder. Altogether, there were several of these phantom entities populating our lives, with three standing out from the pack. There was Petunia Pigeon, a funny little bird that Sue portrayed by flapping her elbows against her hips as she "flew" around the house, squawking out insults; she was sort of a female Donald Duck. Pigeon, whose meanness belied her underlying sweetness, was the total opposite of Sue, whose sweetness belied her underlying meanness. There was my Homer, the dim-witted cow. Then there was Small Bobby, a three-year-old version of myself.

The other strange aspect of our relationship was the Ouija (pronounced WEE-jee) board, which I knew very little about until Sue told me of the experiences she had had with one when she was a child. It was a large wooden board with the entire alphabet and numbers zero to nine printed across it, along with the words "YES," "NO," and "GOODBYE" at the top. The process required two participants placing their fingers on a planchette that had a little window in the middle, from which one could see the letters the piece stopped on as it moved rapidly across the slate, answering the questions being asked of whatever spirit happened to be present at the time. The objective was to receive spiritualistic or telepathic messages. It may have appeared to an onlooker that the movable indicator was being manipulated by one of us, but I knew *I* wasn't moving it, and I didn't think Sue was. Sometimes the answers would be information Sue couldn't possibly have known, and I came to believe that we were actually communicating with the spirits of the departed. The question is, how reliable is a spirit who has nothing better to do than hang out playing late-night board games?

"Who do we have here tonight?" I asked.

"Woogie," the board spelled out, referring to the nickname for "Ouija."

"Where can I get a good song idea?"

"Turn on the TV and watch *The Red Skelton Show*."

I did as I was instructed, and within two or three minutes, someone on the show said a line that included the phrase "while you're dancing." I grabbed "Woogie" and shoved it into Sue's lap, and asked, "Should I write a song called 'While You're Dancing?'" As we placed our fingers on the planchette, it zipped to the upper left-hand corner of the board and landed on "YES." If I had a title I believed in, the rest of the song always seemed to fall into place. I ran to my electric piano, and within a half hour I had put together what would become, about a year later, my first song in the country charts, "While You're Dancing."

Despite our dalliance with witchy things, we still embraced traditional Christianity. Sue was Southern Baptist but went with me to the Church of Christ, a non-charismatic but ultra-fundamentalist group that was especially strong in Tennessee. I had been baptized into it three years earlier in my Florida hometown, scurrying down the aisle to answer the altar call because I thought for certain that I was having a heart attack. (I was then having panic episodes as a result of an amphetamine overdose.) The Church of Christ interpreted the Bible more literally than any group in all of Christendom, and believed that total immersion was essential to salvation, so I wanted to get into the water while I was still alive. Basically, they believed that *only* Church of Christ people were going to Heaven.

My political beliefs were just as far to the right as my religious ones. I had been reading *American Opinion*, the official organ of the John Birch Society, which believed that recent presidents from both parties—Eisenhower, Kennedy, and Johnson—were part of an international communist conspiracy. I was an enthusiastic supporter of the GOP presidential nominee, Barry Goldwater, so far to the right that he was scaring away mainstream Republicans.

Because I was away from the house so often, it was decided that Sue should have her own car. We didn't have much money, so we checked out some of the cheaper used cars around town. At Jessup's Best Buys Used Cars we found a green Chevrolet Bel-Air from the early 1950s that looked like it was in very good condition. The proprietor, Roy Jessup, assured us that the Chevy was the best car on the lot. We test drove it, and it seemed to run just fine. The price was low, so I wrote the man a check. "Pigeon" was circling around the car, flapping her elbow/wings, saying in her squeaky/squawky voice that it was her car, and Sue couldn't drive it. When the transmission fell out before Sue made it home, I called up Mr. Jessup who told me sorry, all sales were final. I ran by the bank and stopped payment on his check. Later that afternoon, someone from the bank called to inform me that there had been a mistake, that Mr. Jessup, who was also a customer there, had already brought the check in before I came by, so it was too late to stop payment on it. Certainly Jessup had more pull at the neighborhood bank than I did, and I suspected that I was being lied to. I had no choice but to go to the car lot and ask for my money back.

I walked into the office and saw the bookkeeper, a seemingly kind old gentleman who wore an old-fashioned green eye shade.

"S-s-sir, is Mr. Jessup around?" I asked.

"He knows you tried to stop payment on that check," the old man sighed, "and he's not very happy. I can give you the name of a good mechanic, but I suggest that you . . ."

About that time, Roy Jessup, his beefy bald head beet red, stormed into the office and shouted, "You little sonofabitch, I oughta make a mudhole outta your ass!"

I grabbed him and pushed him up against the wall. Suddenly I felt something cold pressing against my temple. It was the barrel of a pistol, in the shaky hand of the kindly old bookkeeper. He kept the gun on me until the police arrived several minutes later. My focus then turned to avoiding arrest, to be repentant rather than try to paint Jessup as a crook, which probably would not have gotten me any more help from the law than I got from the bank that made a "mistake" after stopping payment on my check. I would just have to hit my parents up for enough money to get the transmission fixed or buy a cheap rebuilt one. Things could have been worse. I left Jessup's Best Buys Used Cars a free man, with my brains still inside my head.

This experience with the bank gave me a bit of perspective on how the Nashville establishment then looked down on the music community. The city's paragons of privilege—the old money, the insurance tycoons, and the investment bankers—seemed to think of the music industry leaders as snake oil salesmen, and the singers and musicians as unwelcome country cousins.

The vacuum cleaner sales job wasn't panning out, but I heard about an opening at Hewgley's, a block-long downtown music store that sold school band instruments. I got a job in the basement, where a crew of people was doing repair work. It was like a body shop for horns. I was hired to polish the trumpets after the dents had been removed.

I had to wear an apron and operate the trumpet-polishing machine. One day I got my apron caught in the machine and nearly choked to death.

"It was just a freak accident, and I don't think it'll happen again," I tried to assure the store manager.

"We just can't take that chance, son," the boss man told me. "But I understand some of these parking lots are hiring folks now, and I'll be glad to give you a letter of recommendation."

Benny Joy lived about a mile from us. Benny was helpful to me and called Sue his "little sister," but he could wear you out, too. "Benny is no joy," Sue often quipped. His mama, Verna, who had taken Sue under her wing, was best friends with Grace Rainwater, the mother of pop singing sensation Brenda Lee. Grace, who talked constantly about "Bren"—and was rightfully proud of her—looked like an older version of her daughter. Sometimes Sue hung out with the two moms, and sometimes she and Verna shopped at Kmart together while I checked out Music Row with Benny.

Benny put together a little group and got us a four-nights-a-week gig, and the pay was peanuts. I rented a U-Haul, and we transported my organ to a dumpy little club in a semi-rural area north of town. The drummer in the band was Randy Scott. Randy's wife came to our gigs and made him terribly jealous when she danced with assorted male patrons at the club. One night, in the middle of a number, he threw his drumsticks in the air as he jumped up and screamed at his wife, "SIT DOWN!" Everyone on the dance floor went quickly to their seats.

Sue and I soon acquired some more friends. Lance Carpenter, a singer-writer who was about my age, had been a regular customer at the El Patio Club in Orlando when I played there with Big John's Untouchables. He moved to Nashville with his girlfriend, Donna Anderson, big sister of future country star John Anderson. I was fond of both Lance and Donna, but Sue self-righteously disapproved of them living together unmarried, which was odd because Sue certainly wasn't chaste while *we* were dating. It was through Lance that we got to know another Orlando transplant, Decca recording artist Wilma Burgess, who was living with her mother. Wilma was romantically involved with Ginny King, who had worked for Jim Reeves, the pop-country giant who had died in a plane crash a couple of months earlier. (My theory of why Sue was more tolerant of Wilma and Ginny than Lance and Donna is that lesbians were not even on her radar; homosexuality was such a taboo subject that she may not have even heard it condemned from a pulpit.) A chubby girl with a beautiful velvety voice, Wilma would have three hits within a year or two. As a perfect example of "life ain't fair," when she died in 2003 she was managing a BP gas station and didn't even rate a mention in the country music industry's unofficial newspaper of record, the *Tennessean*. But in 1964, they were like family to us, and we spent many pleasant nights playing Scrabble with them. Lesbianism wouldn't have been a big career boost for Wilma, so she and Ginny did not flaunt their relationship. We saw our first Tennessee snow at their little house near the upscale Green Hills area, and by the time we got home, it was a winter wonderland, like nothing this Florida boy had ever seen.

Sue was all about fantasy. She liked to play the role of a high-class Southern belle, but sometimes her blue-collar mill-town roots gave her away when she pronounced *wash* as "warsh," or *humiliate* as "hu-MULE-iate." There was that darkness in her background that I wouldn't know about for decades, and had I known, I think I would have been more understanding of her. I think our gallery of "characters" gave her a sense of family. She was witty, she was smart, and Longfellow could have been thinking of her when he wrote:

> *There was a little girl,*
> *Who had a little curl*
> *Right in the middle of her forehead*
> *When she was good,*
> *She was very good indeed*
> *But when she was bad she was horrid*

She could be such a loving person, sometimes carrying it too far, like tell-ing me, "Him just a big old baby" while spoon-feeding me my supper. But who am I to say she was on the weird side, when I was only a couple of years removed from living in a mental landfill myself?

And besides, I *looked* crazy. I had Tourette's syndrome. I didn't shout out expletives, which most people associate with Tourette's, but more typically I made a grimace or blinked my eyes—mine was one eye at a time, like a turn signal—and had a strange stutter, a sort of quick doglike panting sound that I made before speaking. In my book dialogue, I have myself t-t-talking like this b-b-because it's just easier to characterize my stutter that way.

So a lot of our arguments could have been avoided if I had simply said "I'm sorry" or walked away when I first saw her folding her arms, huffing and puffing, and rolling her eyes up toward the ceiling. But when she got that way, my little streak of mischief couldn't resist saying some little something that would push her buttons, causing her to go so berserk that I would have to hold both her hands until she calmed down, to keep her from beating the daylights out of me.

But basically we were having a good time, playing games, watching TV, going to movies, and listening to music. I continued to write songs, but I was writing in a vacuum, with no one to sing them to but Sue, who was no coun-try music authority. I was getting no professional feedback and had no idea if I was any good at it or not.

"Honey, that thing at the Palms Club seems to be winding down," I said. "Why don't we go down and see your mama and sisters the day after Christ-mas, then on down to Florida to see my folks?"

"I don't think your mother likes me. She always seems to have some little criticism."

"That's ridiculous," I told her. "Besides, we won't be down there very long. I have to be back here to play a gig New Year's Eve."

We got to my parent's house on my father's eighty-second birthday. He looked frail and every one of his years. The twenty-five-year gap between my parents seemed even wider. But he was in good spirits, talking on and on about his citrus groves. ("They're the prettiest ahhran-ges in Polk County, Flahrr-da," he often said.)

"Well, Dad, what do you think about being eighty-two years old?"

"Well, Bobby, you knowww the Bible says that man's allotted tiiiime is threeeee scooore and ten years."

"You're twelve years past your allotted time, so I'd say you're doing pretty good."

He laughed and said, "You know, the man worthwhiiile is the man who can smiiile when everything else goes dead wronnng."

We visited with my older brother and his family. Paul Braddock Jr. was my opposite in every way—athletic, outdoorsy, mechanical, not musical, not a big reader. We went to see my mother's brother, Uncle Lloyd, a talented, beetle-nosed man who showed Sue his paintings. Sue wasn't too happy when I went out for a couple of drinks with my best friends, Don and Stanley.

Before we returned to Nashville, Mom sat me down for a heart-to-heart talk.

"Well, honey, you know you're going to be a daddy pretty soon."

"I know Mom, in May, just a few months away."

"Well, you've been in Nashville for three months and haven't really gotten anything going," she said with her big smile and nervous laugh. Then my eyes glazed over as she told me about different job opportunities in Polk County. "Maybe we could help you out, and you could go back to college." She didn't understand that when I moved to Nashville, I moved my heart and soul up there as well. Polk County was right in the geographical center of a beautiful subtropical paradise, but I had no desire to live there anymore.

In January of 1965, I got a week-long gig in a club along Nashville's tourist strip, Printers Alley, with former pop star Mark Dinning. I also got my first road job, riding a bus down to Keesler Air Force Base in Biloxi, Mississippi, with Cousin Wilbur and Blondie Brooks, a cornball country comic and his attractive singer wife. I had seen them perform at the Auburn Theater in Auburndale when I was ten years old.

One night Mom called and said that my father wanted to talk to me. He had heard Billy Edd Wheeler's outhouse song, "Ode to the Little Brown Shack Out Back" and asked me if I could find him a copy of the lyrics. He thought it was very funny, and I told him I'd do that right away. The next day my mother called to tell me that Dad had apparently suffered a stroke and wasn't expected to live.

Only the desire to see my father alive once more time could get me on an airplane. I was twenty-four, and it was my very first flight. In the earliest part of my toddler memories I'd had a recurring nightmare about blowing up (in a plane, I thought—past life experience?) and at three years old I saw the wreckage of a military plane right after it had crashed into a tree in my uncle's backyard. So I was a white-knuckled nervous wreck in the air from Nashville to Orlando.

As it turned out, my father didn't die, and would not for several years. He wasn't paralyzed, but he had lost most of his mental faculties, was able to speak only a few words, and was not recognizing people. When he came home from the hospital, my mother chose not to put him in a nursing home and would not for quite some time—"Look at all that he's done for *me*," she said. There would be nurses, but the brunt of the caretaking burden would be borne by her. My mother had a baby at age fifty-seven—an eighty-two-year-old baby boy.

When we got back to Nashville, I felt that I should find a *real* job. We were running low on money, and a child was on the way. I went to an employment agency and filled out some papers. When I got home, Sue was standing at the door. "Randy Scott wants you to call him. He said it's important."

This was the drummer who screamed at his wife from the stage of the Palms Club. He had done some road work with a major recording star and played on recording sessions now and then. Maybe he had a gig for me. I called him back immediately.

"Hey Randy, it's Bobby Braddock," I practically yelled into the phone.

"Hey, man," he said, "do you want a job that could last forever?"

2

SINGING THE BLUES

When I was a sophomore in high school and falling in love with country music, one record that particularly excited me was the Marty Robbins rendition of "Singing the Blues," a slightly up-tempo song with a somewhat bluesy melody. Marty was not the stereotypical "singing through the nose" hillbilly. He sang with an understated intensity, blessed with a rangy, near-perfect voice that slid effortlessly into a sad falsetto. He was a great crooner but fully capable of belting one out, too. Known as the man with the teardrop in his voice, he acquired the nickname "Mister Teardrop." He spent over thirty years on the country charts, enjoying his greatest success from the mid-1950s through the 1960s. Many of his recordings were double-barreled country and pop hits. Like Elvis and the Beatles, he had a repertoire consisting of a wide range of styles and genres, most of them his own compositions. There were the teen ballads like "A White Sport Coat (and a Pink Carnation)" and the gunfighter ballads, a genre that he practically invented, epitomized by one of the best story songs ever written: "El Paso." The first record to have the distorted guitar sound known as "fuzztone" was not something by the Rolling Stones, but Marty Robbins's "Don't Worry." He was equally at home with traditional country, rockabilly, and Hawaiian music. I loved it when he would drop in unexpectedly on Ralph Emery's legendary all-night radio show on WSM in Nashville, *Opry Star Spotlight*, clowning around with the host, then strumming on his small Martin guitar or sitting down at the studio's grand piano, accompanying himself on song after song, Ralph's phones lighting up with requests from all over the eastern half of America. Marty was my favorite country singer, and needless to say, I was thrilled at the opportunity to audition for his road band.

Randy Scott put me in touch with Marty's piano player at the time, Joe Babcock, who was quitting the road so he could concentrate on songwriting and singing back-up on recording sessions. "All you need to know for this job is the piano intro to 'Don't Worry' and 'Ruby Ann,'" said Joe. Actually, I would have to learn an entire catalog of songs and sing some harmony parts as well. I spent a couple of days practicing the two piano intros, making sure I copied the licks exactly as they were played on the records.

The audition was at the office of Marty Robbins Enterprises, on 18th Avenue South. The converted two-story house had an Asian look—I thought of
an American embassy in some medium-size Japanese city. Marty and his
band were awaiting my arrival. Not a towering man, he had slightly curly
sandy hair, small eyes, a broad nose, and a wide grin. He had a unique combination of Polish features from his father's side and Native American from his
mother's. His legal name was Martin David Robinson (his father had changed
the last name from Maczinski to Robinson). Marty spoke softly in the accent
of Old Arizona, not quite Southern like Texas, but not Northern either. In
today's world of video-friendly young country hunks, I'm not sure he would
have become the superstar that he was in his day. He had his first hits in
his late twenties, and on this audition day he was thirty-nine. He was fifteen
years my senior, and I remember thinking he was a little old. He gave me a
friendly welcome and quickly got down to the business of seeing if I was any
good.

I saw the look of relief on the faces of Marty and his musicians as I played
the bluesy intro to "Don't Worry" and the rockin' intro to "Ruby Ann." He
then ran through his current #1 hit, Gordon Lightfoot's folky "Ribbon of
Darkness." Two of the guys supplied great close harmony on his western
songs, but he needed a third voice for his doo-wop pop, and that's where
I came in. Gathered around the little piano in his office where everyone
could hear everyone else, I hit the parts smoothly and on key, though that
wouldn't always be the case in some of the big echo-y auditoriums we would
be playing.

"Well, Bob, you've got the job," Marty said softly with a big grin as his
small eyes twinkled. I would later learn that those little eyes turned into tiny
slits when he was angry (fortunately, usually not at me).

The events of this day made me feel almost as though I were part of a
weekly TV show, watching one well-known character after another walk on
to the set. In the front door appeared fabled songwriter Vic McAlpin (who
had been Hank Williams's fishing buddy), closely followed by country music's
most famous deejay, Ralph Emery himself.

"What the hell's going on?" Ralph asked in his six-o'clock-news voice.

"This is Bob, my new piano player," Marty said. I was walking on air.

Good morning to yooooou
Good morning to yooooou
We're all in our places
With bright shiny faces

I awoke from a deep sleep in my bunk on the Marty Robbins touring
bus to the sound of "The Chief" singing his wakeup call as he walked up
and down the aisle. We were approaching our hotel in Austin, Texas. "Okay,

With Marty Robbins at Manhattan Holiday Inn in New York City,
December 1965

boys, get your stinkin' asses outta bed. Wake up, Bob, time to get up and get
dressed."

It wasn't a spectacular bus, even by 1965 standards. It was a converted
1948 model originally owned by Greyhound. There were comfortable seats
up front, a restroom in the middle, several bunk beds in the back half, all of
them small and narrow except for the star's big draped one, and in the back
of the bus was a large poker table.

Marty and most of the band had been up late the night before, playing
poker. He had a mischievous sense of humor, but he could also be a bit petty
and get in a nasty mood if he lost at poker, so I would stay out of the ongoing
card games and managed to get along with him quite well.

Marty's buddy in the band was drummer Louie Dunn, a short flat-topped
guy about Robbins's age. Whenever Marty chose to fly instead of riding the
bus with us, he took Louie with him. Nobody in the band ever crossed Louie,
and he's the one who gave all the band members their nicknames—everyone except himself. Louie didn't have to observe me very long—I would be
"Blinky" (and, at twenty-four, the baby of the band).

This first tour with Marty took us to Texas and Louisiana in early February. In those days, promoters often booked several superstars into big city
auditoriums on what were called "package shows." This tour was headlined
by Robbins and the Cherokee Cowboy, Ray Price, whose big hit "Crazy Arms"
had spent an incredible twenty weeks in the #1 spot on the *Billboard* country charts a few years before. His traditional Texas shuffle songs continued

to be popular despite the pop/rock influence on country music. Price was a rather serious man who reminded me of a stoic Indian chief. In a backstage restroom, I heard some guy tell him, "The way things are goin', the federal government's liable to start telling you that you gotta hire a colored guy in your band."

"Well, he'd better be able to cut it," Ray deadpanned.

Another big star on this first tour was Sonny James, known as the Southern Gentleman, and he was indeed old-fashioned and chivalrous. Marty had told him that I was a "nice boy," so Sonny asked me if I would hang out with his wife, Doris, who was traveling with him. "I don't know about some of these folks that are hangin' out here, and I'd feel better if you'd sorta look after her while I'm onstage."

When Marty wasn't out on the road, he always played the Grand Ole Opry in Nashville on Saturday nights, another great thrill for me—to be backstage with all the legends and lions. The Opry was broadcast live from downtown Nashville over 50,000-watt station WSM and drew a packed house made up of people from all over America, especially the South and Midwest. The back door of the building was just across the alley from the rear entrance to Tootsie's Orchid Lounge, which was filled with a mix of stars, musicians, and fans. Tootsie Bess was the plumpish, congenial proprietress, who had no compunction about jabbing a rowdy drunk in the butt with a hatpin.

Marty's hobby—and passion—was racing, which he often did on Saturday nights at Nashville's Fairgrounds Speedway against the big-name pros like Richard Petty and Bobby Allison. In the years ahead, when the last Opry show of the night was reserved for Marty, it would become a common sight: Marty Robbins speeding through the city streets in his racecar, trying to get to the Grand Ole Opry in time to close the show. The Opry was supposed to segue into Ernest Tubb's *Midnite Jamboree*, but when Marty was on, it usually ran late. In a local nostalgia newspaper, *Nashville Retrospect*, Robert Chaffin wrote that Marty "was famous for calling for his own applause by doing a come-hither motion with his arm and bringing the audience to a crescendo." The Opry staff was trying to end the show, but Marty kept encouraging the crowd to demand more encores.

Soon after I completed my first tour, Marty's guitarist, Jack Pruett, invited Sue and me to have dinner with him and his wife and two children. Jack and Jeanne were from rural Central Alabama. Jack had a slow, country drawl (an oft-told story was about the time he told some people in Minnesota, "Y'all sure do talk funny up here") and because his Native American heritage manifested itself with an Asian look, Louie Dunn had nicknamed him "Bandy Wong." Jeanne was outgoing and outspoken, and a good songwriter and singer—years later and in her forties (though many sources say she was thirty-six) she recorded a mega hit called "Satin Sheets." While we were on our way up, Sue had a knack for ingratiating herself with those who were higher up in the pecking order, and so it was with the Pruetts. The next time we went out on the road, Jeanne insisted that Sue stay with her and the kids.

I always looked forward to the times when Marty traveled on the bus rather than by plane. I got a kick out of his wisecracks ("Doing these shows is like robbing Wells Fargo; you ride into town, get the money, then ride out") but I especially loved it when late at night he would get out his little Martin guitar and start singing—the man *loved* to sing. He sang Mexican songs that he learned in Arizona as a child; he sang Hawaiian songs that he learned in Hawaii as a sailor; and he imitated some of the classic pop singers of his time. He told me he liked my songwriting and to try to write him a Western song. I had heard him say "I've never known a man who disliked his own voice who could sing worth a shit," and I should have paid attention.

"I think you sing pretty commercial, Bob, and I'm thinking about doing a record on you."

"Aw, I'm not all that good," I said modestly, stupidly.

"Oh, okay then," he said, and never brought it up again. (A year and a half later, when publisher-producer Buddy Killen said the same thing to me, my answer was, "Great, let's do it!")

Marty and I shared the same political philosophy: ultra-right-wing conservatism. That kind of ideology in 1965 had nothing to do with abortion or gay marriage or even religion; it supported a strong military and espoused a fierce anti-communism. As with today's conservatives, government was seen as a bad thing, and too much government was seen as socialism or communism. Marty gave me some literature on the extremist John Birch Society and asked me to read it for him and give him a report, tell him what I thought about it.

A very interesting guy in the Marty Robbins troupe was Okie Jones, the bus driver. A tall, lovable guy in his mid-thirties, he'd had his own brush with a music career a few years earlier. Okie was very smart but raised dirt poor and could neither read nor write. So instead of playing poker with the guys, I rode shotgun with Okie, reading the map and the road signs for him.

We soon discovered that I was good at making an accurate ETA (estimated time of arrival), on two occasions looking at the map from hundreds of miles away and correctly guessing within minutes the time we would return home. So Marty decreed that it would be my official duty to figure out what time we would get back to Nashville, and all the band wives would know what time to be at Marty's office to pick up their husbands (in that era of one-car families). I made my ETA for the next night's arrival, and Marty called his secretary from the bus phone (twenty-something years before cell phones) and told her to call all the band wives and tell them what time to be there. The bus came rolling in four hours after the wives got there, and I lost my job as time estimator.

For some reason, Marty didn't like to confront me, so if he had a problem, he would usually pass his displeasure along to Okie, and let Okie tell me. I loved to do impersonations, and one person I enjoyed imitating was Ernie Ashworth, who had a loud, high voice with a lot of vibrato. Sometimes I would obnoxiously belt out my version of Ashworth singing "Talk Back Trembling Lips" and get quite a few laughs out of the guys. Okie told me one night, "I wouldn't do that anymore, The Chief doesn't like it."

One night the band guys were laying more than cards on the poker table. I guess you could call their show-and-tell game "may the longest man win." I stepped up and participated and won, quite proud of myself. Then The Chief came out of his large, black-velvet-curtained bunk bed and said, "What's going on here?" He whipped out the evidence that he was The Chief in every sense of the word. That ended my short-lived long victory and put me to shame. I can attest that Marty was a legend in more ways than one.

As the time drew near for Sue to have the baby, we decided that we needed more room. I looked through the classified section of the paper and read about a fairly decent-sized house with affordable rent. It was at 3338 Paragon Mills Road, in a semi-rural area called Bakertown, on the southeastern outskirts of Nashville. The cute brick house was on a street with homes that were not built too close together—in fact we could look out the window from our plywood-paneled living room and see a working farm with a barn in the back. The main drag in Bakertown was Antioch Pike, a winding road that seemed to meander through some rural county rather than within the city limits of a major town. There was a very ominous presence in the neighborhood, and that was the nearby state mental hospital—Central State—that had a large unit for the criminally insane. We were told that from time to time there was an escape, causing people to lock their doors and load their shotguns.

One night Sue and I got into a major argument; I don't know if she was angry because I was drinking or if I was drinking because she was angry, but in drunken frustration, I left the house and just started walking into the night. There was enough moonlight that I could see all the landmarks. I walked from our street onto Antioch Pike and headed to the right, going about a mile. I saw Meads Chapel Church of Christ, which we had been attending and walked up the steep hill behind the church into the cemetery, the highest point in the area. From there I could see it, like an ugly behemoth slumbering beneath the rising moon, a block wide with three stories of dimly lit windows: Central State Hospital.

Three years later, long after we had moved away, they built I-24 from Nashville to Chattanooga right through the middle of Paragon Mills Road and the spot where we had lived. They also extended one of Nashville's busiest streets, Harding Place, to become the access street to the new Interstate, cutting through that once semi-rural area, and running between the cemetery and the state hospital. That building has been replaced with another one, housing a branch of Metropolitan Nashville's Sheriff's Department, and the country roads that I once staggered down are now part of a busy commercial area in what has become a heavily Hispanic part of the city.

But in the spring of 1965, the neighborhood was bucolic and blissful, and there was general contentment at home as well. Sue had been adopted by several of the band wives, all of them considerably older than her twenty years. When I was in town we often went to the movies (mostly innocuous things like *Shenandoah* or Disney's *That Darn Cat!*), and when we stayed home, her Pigeon character would flap her elbows-for-wings and order Sue out of the house so she could play Scrabble, Monopoly, or the Ouija board with "Daggy." We weren't delusional, we knew we were play-acting, but we truly seemed to love each other's characters more than we loved each other. And my Homer character was a no-brainer; whenever I did something stupid, it was never me, it was Homer who had done it.

However, when we played with the Ouija board, Pigeon turned back into Sue, and it all became very serious. A very bizarre thing that happened with the board was the time it said, "Sue, go ahead and tell Bobby about it."

"Tell me what?" I asked.

She pushed the Ouija board away, gave me a sad little smile, and spoke softly, as she did whenever she wanted to open up her heart to me—or give the *impression* that she was opening up her heart to me. She spoke of her ex-boyfriend. "Warren's been calling me."

"What does *he* want?"

"He wants me to come back to him," she said, shrugging her shoulders as she rolled her sky-blue eyes. "He was *begging* me, said he would help me raise the baby."

"How dare that sonofabitch say that he'll raise my child! Who the hell does he think he is?" I roared. I was furious beyond description, glaring at her as though I were daring her to even consider such an absurdity.

"Well, I want our number changed so he'll leave me alone," she said with finality as she took my hand. I didn't think to ask her how he always managed to call when I wasn't home.

When I left on a tour of the upper Midwest around April 18, I was in a good frame of mind. Marty had just recorded my song, "Matilda," and our firstborn was due to arrive a few days after we were to return to Nashville, around May 1.

However, right after we finished a show in Grand Forks, North Dakota, on the night of April 22, someone said that a party in Nashville was trying to reach me. When I got back to the Stardust Manor Motel, I was finally able to get in touch with Wilma Burgess. Sue had been staying at Wilma's house and started getting labor pains. Wilma and her partner, Ginny, took her to Vanderbilt Hospital where the baby was safely and successfully delivered. I was the father of a baby boy, Brian Rhodes Braddock! I immediately sat down and composed a letter to my son.

Parenthood is a life-changing event, or it *should* be. Immature couples mature overnight as young men become protective and young women become nurturing. The paste that holds a relationship together is replaced by super glue. I came home to a tiny little boy who everyone said looked like me; I doubt that he did, but I liked to think that was the case. My make-believe character "Small Bobby," mispronouncing many words as three-year-olds often do, said "Brownie" for Brian, so that became the baby's nickname (my mom couldn't understand why we were calling our son the same name as my childhood dog). On the next Marty Robbins tour, Sue and the baby stayed with the wives of Jack Pruett and Don Winters while I was away on the road.

In June, we headed south to show off the new little Braddock to Sue's family in Alabama and mine in Florida. We drove into Auburndale with him all decked out in a cowboy suit.

"I'll swannee," said my mother as she bounced him on her knee, "he looks just like his daddy."

"Mom, d-do you really think he looks like me?"

"He looks like you did when you were this age."

"Hey there, dahlin'," my father declared with a rare smile, as we held up the tiny tot for him to see. Sitting there in his platform rocker, he sometimes called the baby Bobby, sometimes called him Paul. He was confused as to who we were and what was going on.

On our way back to Nashville, Brian seemed to have a touch of a cold. Our regular pediatrician in Nashville was Dr. Eric Chazen. For some reason, we had decided to start seeing another doctor, so we took the baby to the new guy, who seemed to think the cold was confined to the head. A couple of days later, I was sitting in our parked car with Brian while Sue was grocery shopping. The baby had been sleeping for quite a while, so I decided to wake him up and interact with him a little. When I was unable to arouse him from his sleep, I started freaking out, and ran into the grocery store and yelled at Sue, "I can't get Brownie to wake up!" She left the groceries in the buggy as we dashed to the car and headed toward Vanderbilt Hospital. Halfway there he woke up and started crying. The office of the new doctor was in the vicinity, so we drove by there to see if everything was all right. The doc took our little boy's temperature, looked at his throat, and listened to his chest with a stethoscope, finding nothing out of the ordinary but offering no explanation as to why we had trouble waking him up.

Everything seemed fine that night when we went to bed as usual, with the baby bed pulled up next to ours. Sue had experienced milk problems, so Brian was not a breast-fed baby. In the middle of the night he woke up crying; she gave him a bottle, then put him into bed with us to get him back to sleep. A little past dawn I was awakened by a blood-curdling shriek. Sue was screaming before she even woke up and saw little Brownie, whose face was a terrifying shade of blue. My first thoughts were that one of us had rolled over on the baby in the night and suffocated him. I phoned for an ambulance as we passed him back and forth to each other, trying in vain to revive him, holding a mirror in front of his mouth to see if there were any signs of breath.

As the siren wailed, the ambulance driver slowly and diligently wove us through rush hour traffic, while the other paramedic tried giving little Brian oxygen but offering us very few encouraging words. The hideous Friday morning nightmare continued as we pulled up in front of the closest hospital: ugly, gothic Nashville General, the charity hospital. The place itself looked like death.

The attendants raced him into the emergency room, but I could tell by the look on everyone's faces that it was the end of the road. The ER physician said the words that we didn't want to hear—*refused* to hear.

"My f-family has money," I frantically pleaded. "I can get you money. I'll pay you whatever you want if you can just *do* something!"

"You wouldn't have to pay me any money. If I could do something, I would, but it's too late. Your baby's gone. There's no pulse. The eyes are fixed and dilated. The body's cold." He had still been warm when we first woke up.

The county coroner arrived, examined the baby, and said that he had choked on his milk. An elderly man, he wrote on the death certificate in a shaky hand that the immediate cause of death was suffocation, and that it was due to "aspiration—uncertain."

We called Brownie's original pediatrician, Dr. Chazen, who was there within a half hour. He refused to believe that the baby had aspirated his milk. "I'll go back to Philadelphia and work in my father's clothing store before I believe that." He ordered an autopsy, which disclosed fluid in the lungs. The diagnosis was viral pneumonia. It was also referred to as crib death which is incorrect, because that terminology is the forerunner to SIDS—sudden in-fant death syndrome—which applies to infant deaths for which there is no known cause. There *was* a known cause for our baby's death, so it was neither crib death nor SIDS. No matter why his seemingly clear lungs filled with fluid in a few short hours, that knowledge won't bring him back, that baby of less than two months who would be, at this writing, middle-aged.

When I called to give my mother the tragic news, she said early that morning my father had told his attending nurse, "I can hear the baby crying, and I can hear the angels singing."

A few hours later, several friends—new ones but good ones—gathered at our little brick house. Jeanne Pruett told Sue, "We'll help you through this, mama."

"I'm *not* a mama!" Sue screamed.

"Now Sue, there ain't no sense in that. I didn't mean nothin.'" Jeanne had been calling her "mama" ever since the baby was born.

I followed my grief-stricken wife to the sliding glass door, slid it open, and led her outside to the backyard.

"I lose everything I love," she sobbed. I assumed she was referring to her father who had died in his forties four years before, and now little Brownie. It would be long after she and I parted ways before I learned that there was another loss that she had never told me about. Several months before we met she had given birth to a baby fathered by the same boyfriend who she told me was calling her before Brian was born. Though they were not married, she used his last name on the birth certificate. The male child was born prematurely in a hospital in Bessemer, Alabama, and died two days later. I would be totally in the dark on this little bit of history for thirty years.

We had the visitation at Roesch-Patton Funeral Home, just off Music Row. Brownie was dressed in his cowboy suit. We had recently been going to a Church of Christ close to our home, but before that had been attending Franklin Road Church of Christ, which was in the far-right wing of that ultra-conservative body. The Franklin Road minister, a man named David Claypool, smiled as he looked down at the little departed one, "Look how innocent! You should feel good that he's totally without sin and is guaranteed a place in Heaven." I was having a hard time feeling good about it.

The room was packed with members of both congregations, mostly women. My mother, who had flown in earlier to be with us, was typically giving some kind of advice that Sue took offense at, and Sue had begun to raise her icy voice to my mother. It was more than I could take, and I shouted at the top of my voice, "*STOP IT!*" It may have been the quickest exodus in history; within two minutes the viewing room was completely empty save my mother, my wife, and me. And our poor dead baby. Within a couple of minutes, one of the mortuary staff told me I had a phone call. It was Marty Robbins.

"Hey, Bob, this is Marty. I was just wondering if there's anything I can do."

"Oh thanks, Chief, I really appreciate you asking."

"Do you need for me to pay for the funeral?"

"Oh no, no, I can take care of that, but I sure appreciate it."

Still relatively new in Nashville and not yet having a map of the city in my head, I let the funeral-home folks talk me into having the burial (and ceremony) at Spring Hill Cemetery, in the Madison area, fifteen miles away from our house, while there was another cemetery only about five miles away.

I was touched to see Benny Joy and his mother, the band members and their wives, Marty Robbins's secretary, and Wilma Burgess with her little group, at the graveside service. There were also several church members there, despite the scene at the funeral home the previous day. That night Sue told me that Pigeon flew above the cemetery during the entire service.

As soon as we took my mother to the airport the next day, we ran by our place and threw some stuff into the car and left town. People would talk about how weird it was that we went on a vacation the day after our baby's funeral, but we didn't care. We didn't want to go back to the house where we had found our tiny son blue-faced and still. We wanted to escape and leave behind the horror show we had unwittingly starred in. We just wanted to move and keep moving. We went to the Smoky Mountains, then drove down to Florida, to Daytona Beach. In the same town where I had gotten my wife pregnant on our honeymoon, I impregnated her once again.

For the next couple of months, whenever I was in town, Sue and I were at Spring Hill Cemetery every single day. And every single day we went to the same florist and bought fresh flowers for the grave. We were a pitiful sight, and I don't recall ever seeing more sympathy than on the faces of the people who sold us all those sad bouquets. They stood there as if in pain, commiserating through misty eyes. I think they were probably relieved when we stopped coming.

Joining a band is like acquiring a group of instant friends and family. They constituted a support group that was comforting in a time of loss. Besides Marty's band members, we would also become close to Joe Babcock, the piano player I had replaced, and his wife, Carol, in a friendship that would last for many years. They were a few years older than us and were very religious people, so we acted a bit differently around them than we did our other friends. It was something like being around your parents; you didn't let them see you drink or hear you cuss.

Marty was publishing my songs through one of his companies, Mariposa Music. His musicians, all of whom wrote songs for Marty's publishing companies, would back each other up on the demo (demonstration) sessions—demos are done to record the songs to make them presentable for consideration by recording artists, their producers, and record label people. This quid pro quo arrangement kept Marty's demo costs close to zero. So when recording time rolled around, it was convenient and profitable for him to do songs from his own publishing company—written by Marty or the boys in his band. In fact, he had recently recorded my "While You're Dancing," the song inspired by the Ouija board and the TV show, and the rockin' midtempo tearjerker was slated for release as a single in the coming fall.

I was doing quite a bit of songwriting. My sometimes collaborator was Marty's steel guitar player, Bill Johnson, nicknamed "Bluto" by Louie Dunn, after the big sailor in the Popeye cartoons. Bill, a few years older than I, had been married and living in Miami when at age nineteen he discovered that his wife was cheating on him. In devastation and disbelief, he poured out his heart and soul into a song that he wrote in just a few minutes, "A Wound Time Can't Erase," which would become a country classic and the only hit he ever wrote. But most of my writing was alone and basically pretty unremarkable. There were a lot of too-clever titles like "The Broken Heart Club," "Mr. and Mrs. Fool," and "What You Don't Know Won't Hurt You (But It Hurts Me)." There was one particularly bad song, weighted down with clichés and bad metaphors, titled "Shot Out of the Saddle" that went like this:

Is there a doctor in the house
Would you call him to my side
I just got shot out of the saddle
And I'm wounded in my pride

My friend, journalist Michael Kosser, would write about me years later, "When you reach for the stars, sometimes you land in the garbage heap." I was aiming at the stars all right, but sometimes I was finding myself in the dumpster. But most of the songs weren't terrible—at least they were original—and I was getting a lot of encouragement from Marty.

We went out on a long summer tour, Sue staying with either Wilma Burgess or the band wives, *anything* to get away from that house of sad memories.

Marty was a great entertainer and had the audiences in the palm of his hand. Performing looked like an exercise in joy for him. He was joined by singers Don Winters and Bobby Sykes on harmony for his Western songs and often cracked up the guys *and* himself up while they were singing, which the audience loved. When I describe Marty as odd looking, I don't mean to say that he didn't appeal to women, because he did in spades. He was a super-charismatic man. I can still picture him in his well-tailored, pinstriped suit standing there after a song, grinning from ear to ear, yelling and gesturing, leading the cheers for himself, the crowd eating it up. Young women loved him, as did the older ones who were always bringing him homemade cakes and pies, which he wisely threw away when they weren't looking.

One time Marty's fifteen-year-old son, Ronny, joined us on the tour. Being the "nice boy," I was officially designated by his father to hang out with and watch after the son, who was then and remains to this day a super-nice guy, sweeter in temperament than his father. One night, about a half hour before time for Marty to go on, Ronny told me, "I wanna see my dad," so we started weaving through the circuitous route in the large auditorium that I thought would take us to the backstage area. When we finally found it, there was The Chief sitting on a stool, cozied up next to a sexy young woman. Quickly moving away from the girl, my boss' eyes turned to angry little slits as he glared a hole through me. Nothing was ever said of it, however, because after all, I wasn't doing anything that I had been told not to do. A secretive man, and also fiercely private where his family was concerned, Marty was married to a beautiful and devoutly religious lady named Marizona, whom he placed high on a pedestal. Marizona was thought to be the inspiration for his hit song, "My Woman, My Woman, My Wife."

I thought there was a plethora of available women when I was playing rock & roll clubs in Florida, but that paled in comparison to traveling on the road with a superstar. Some of the guys in the band took full and constant advantage of this. My roommate must have had a testosterone level of three thousand and ran girls in and out of our room like it was a toll gate, practically every night. I was unable to get much sleep, and Marty complied when I asked for another roomie.

Sue and I may not have been the perfect match, and I had known other women to whom I was more attracted, but she was my wife and I was committed to her. Upon learning that she was once again pregnant, the bonds of commitment strengthened. However, that is not to say that I wasn't tempted. One night I met a pretty girl in Lima, Ohio, who rode with us on the bus to the next show, and we sat together, holding hands and kissing. But when we reached our destination and I had the opportunity to go all the way, I wouldn't go through with it. In fact, I was eaten up with guilt that I had even kissed her and had considered going to bed with her. This is why Marty considered me a "nice boy." A reformed alcoholic, The Chief didn't allow booze on the bus and frowned on any drinking while on the road, so he never saw the rowdy drunk side of the nice boy.

From the moment that we lost Brownie, Sue and I were determined to get out of the house on Paragon Mills Road and leave behind the memories of that hideous morning. We were finally able to buy a house, and we moved in on one of those beautiful Tennessee October days. The 1965 cost-of-living index was about one-seventh of what it would be just before the big financial slump of 2008, but the cost of *housing* was less than one-tenth of what it would be just before the slump, so in other words, housing was then more affordable. The price of that house would barely buy one night in the Royal Suite at New York's Ritz-Carlton Hotel today. But it was a nice brick three-bedroom ranch with a garage converted into a den, in a fairly new and pleasant middle-class neighborhood in the southern part of town. The address was 624 Whispering Hills Drive, a hilly street that ran off Edmonson Pike, which at that time was a suburban road that turned rural within a mile or so. The area was part of what had been a huge plantation before the Civil War. The owner had left the land to his freed slaves, and when we moved to the neighborhood there was an old established black community about a mile away. Atop the little hill in the woods behind the house were the remains of an African American cemetery. There were tall maple trees in our back yard that whispered loudly when the night winds blew, hence Whispering Hills Drive.

A gravel driveway ran up to the garage, which was no longer a garage but a converted den, with a large sliding-glass door, a den that we would initially use as my music room. To the left was the living room where we placed bright red furniture—it was a good-size room with one large window and a smaller one. Behind the living room were the dining area and another sliding door. To the left of the dining room were the kitchen and a hallway that led to the future baby's room and the master bedroom on the left (front) side, and the one bathroom and a little spare bedroom on the right (back) side. Our new home was typical 1960s suburbia, and we were able to afford the down payment only with the help of my mother. But we loved it and were glad to be living there.

Even after living in Nashville for over a year, I could still feel the magic. Sometimes the magic was coming from my little car radio, and it would have been magic no matter where I was. One day I was driving down 8th Avenue South toward the Nashville Public Library when I first heard my first major single, the mid-tempo "While You're Dancing," and it sounded wonderful. Marty was in top form; Bill Pursell playing major-seventh chords with a pounding, gospel piano rhythm was unique; and the song, *my* song, was . . . a rip-off! I didn't have enough sense to realize it when I wrote it, but the melody was very close to the big Drifters R&B/pop hit, "Save the Last Dance for Me." Marty's record would only get to the teens in the charts; if it had been a big hit, I might have been sued.

Although I was focused on country music—it was becoming my job, the factory where I worked—there was pop and rock stuff so good that I couldn't (and didn't want to) escape it, whether it was the Rolling Stones' "(I Can't Get No) Satisfaction," or the beautiful new Beatles record (a side of them we had never heard before). How can those who have heard "Yesterday" all of their lives understand how it sounded when it was brand new, in the fall of 1965? That beautiful melody, Paul McCartney's intimate vocal, the rich strum of the acoustic guitar and then that sad string quartet. Was there anything I was hearing on country radio that moved me that much? No, but this was the "country" that I had pledged my allegiance to; I had come here to work in the song factory. If I didn't love all the country music I was hearing (and I did *not* love it as much as the country music I had fallen in love with in my teens), then I needed to try to *write* music that I loved.

I was enjoying the road less and less, and absolutely *hated* trying to sleep on a bunk bed on the bus. Two comedians, billed as Quinine Gumstump and His Cajun Buddy Buck, were traveling with us, making the bus all the more crowded. In Nashville, I was getting booked playing piano on quite a few recording sessions, but I wasn't making enough money at that to justify quitting the road. Despite my wanting to stay in town, there are powerful scenes that play in my mind from those road days that in retrospect seem pretty glorious. Moments of Super Twang: Buck Owens and his rockin' Buckaroos, the hottest country act of the day, driving wild a usually subdued crowd of Canadians in London, Ontario. Moments of Rock-&-Roll Magic: a package show we played at an outdoor stadium in Birmingham, featuring Marty along with pop giants like the Beach Boys, the Turtles, and Roy Orbison. Moments of Great Country Gossip: a young flat-topped George Jones backstage, talking freely about the secret affair he was having with a well-known female singer (pre-Tammy Wynette).

One really indelible memory is of Johnny Cash, in his darkest drug-addicted days. He was not yet in his mid-thirties but looked fifty, was emaciated, and his voice was barely more than a whisper. But when he stepped on the stage, I have never seen anything like it, before or since—a scene that no movie actor would be capable of portraying. He had more electricity than anyone. When he stepped up to the mic, that audience belonged to him, and they remained in captivity for every moment that he stood before them.

I also fondly remember Marty's big sense of humor, even when it was a bit haughty and at my own expense. One day I was standing outside an auditorium we had just played in the Chicago suburb of Hammond, Indiana, talking to my mother's brother, my Uncle Paul, who like many Southerners of his generation had moved north to work in the steel mills. Marty's bus drove by and Marty yelled out the window, "Hey, that's my *nephew*; he plays piano for *Marty Robbins*." My uncle, who had a nervous tic similar to mine, stood there as embarrassed as I was, both of us wildly blinking our eyes like a couple of neon signs.

When we were playing in large auditoriums, I sometimes had trouble hearing my harmony part and unknowingly sang flat. One night, when Jack Pruett kicked off the intro to "A White Sport Coat," I jumped up from the piano to head for center stage and do my do-wop harmony. Marty turned around abruptly, pointed at me, and shouted, "Don't sing! *Ever!*" I thought, uh-oh, that's it, I've been fired. As it turned out, he wanted me to stay on as his piano player, but no longer as a harmony singer.

Even more humiliating was a recording session of Marty's that I played on. He had used me before to play on a session that he produced on Don Winters and decided that I was good enough to use on his own records. He was slated to record a song Jeanne Pruett had written, "Count Me Out." I had developed a piano style that emulated a pedal steel guitar, but did it quite differently than the Floyd Cramer "slip-note" method, so I was eager to show it off. The song was in C, my very best key. When we were running through the song at the session, I played my solo and blew everybody away. Veteran players Harold Bradley and Ray Edenton were telling me how amazing it sounded, asking how I did it. Then Marty said, "This is a bit high for me, boys. Let's drop it down to B-flat." So we went from my very best key to my very worst one. I played the solo, and it was just awful, the last few notes actually going "clunk clunk." Marty's producer, Don Law, insisted that it was fine and should stay on, possibly to teach Marty a lesson to discourage him from bringing his own musicians to perform on his record sessions. It should have been recorded again, either giving me a second chance in that unfamiliar key or having another instrument play the solo instead. Marty said that the song was the "B-side" of the record and nobody would hear it anyway, so my bad piano playing stayed. It was perhaps the most amateurish thing ever heard on a major label.

As luck would have it, "Count Me Out" wasn't the B-side after all; it was the A-side and became a hit. When it started getting heavy radio play, people would come up to me at shows and ask if that was me playing piano on "Count Me Out." I lied and told them it was some guy from California.

I started out 1966 a happy young man. We had experienced terrible tragedy a few months before, but everything else in my life seemed good. I had been to places I'd never been, met people I stood in awe of, even played Carnegie Hall in New York. "While You're Dancing" had been a modest hit. Instead of cooling on me for flat singing and clunky playing, The Chief started paying me extra to come into his office when we were in town, to pitch his catalog, to get songs in his publishing company recorded. I was playing more and more recording sessions. I had been hired to back up several country stars in a movie called *Music City U.S.A.* and in another movie, produced by and starring Marty, *The Road to Nashville*. Marty had always wanted to be a singing cowboy like his childhood idol, Gene Autry, so he started filming a TV series, *The Drifter*, and Sue and I wrote the scripts for several episodes.

I lay close to my wife, feeling her pregnant stomach. Unlike some men, turned off by pregnant women, I felt that bearing a child was an ultimately feminine condition, making one not less but *more* attractive.

"Okay, Daggy," she said, using Pigeon's word for Daddy as she often did, "you'd *better* be around here when *this* one comes."

"I've already told Marty that I wasn't going to leave you alone. W-we've got that Republican dinner pretty soon, then the California tour that should be over before the end of March. That would be running it pretty close, wouldn't it?" I asked, as I made little circles on her bulging belly button.

"I don't think you'd better go to California," she giggled.

Marty felt uncomfortable, maybe a bit insecure, around those who held high office. In Baton Rouge, the governor of Louisiana, John McKeithen, came backstage after the show and told Marty he would be honored to have us all come to the governor's mansion for breakfast the next morning. Marty thanked him and told him that we had to leave town that night, but later said to me, "I just don't know how to act around governors and people like that."

Marty and Opry legend Roy Acuff were the entertainment for a Republican fund-raising dinner in Nashville. The guest speaker was the man who had almost won the presidency six years before and would indeed win it two years hence—Richard Milhous Nixon.

During our little segment of the entertainment, Marty heaped so much praise on Nixon that the former vice president got up from the head table and bounded across the big hall straight for us, stopping the show to shake Marty's hand. I suppose guests of honor have the right. Marty squatted down so he could talk to Nixon from the stage. I could hear the conversation.

"Do ya stay pretty busy?" Nixon asked in his deep resonant voice.

"Oh, yeah, we stay out on the road quite a bit," The Chief replied.

"What did you think about the article on country music in *Look* magazine?" he asked.

"Well, I didn't read it," said Marty.

After Nixon returned to his table, Marty suddenly started going on and on about his fellow Arizonan Barry Goldwater, what a great man he was, and what a great president he would have made and would still make. This dinner was supposed to be all about Nixon, and Marty was making it all about Goldwater. You could see the discomfort at the head table among the people around Nixon, who sat there in his brown suit wearing a forced grin. Afterward, Marty told me, "Yeah, I think I'd like to get involved in campaigning for Nixon if he runs next time around," not realizing that he had probably squandered the goodwill he had gained in his initial flattery of Nixon.

When Marty and his boys rode off to the Golden West, where I had never set foot but which I dearly wanted to see, I stayed behind because I didn't want to be in some Stardust Manor Motel again when my wife was back in Nashville having a baby. Marty seemed to be completely understanding about me not making the tour.

Sue had enjoyed a pretty good pregnancy compared to the first one, experiencing very little sickness. On the night of March 28, 1966, we were watching the Monday night episode of the TV serial *Peyton Place*, perhaps the hottest show of the year, when Sue started getting labor pains. They were coming pretty close together, and I suggested that we get on to the hospital immediately.

"Not until *Peyton Place* is over," she insisted.

On the way to Vanderbilt, we speculated about the gender, in that presonogram age. One of us said—and I can't recall which one of us it was—"We could call the baby 'Jeep' and that would fit either sex." I got Sue checked in and sat in a waiting room for what seemed like forever. In those days, fathers didn't participate in the process; they were kept as far away as possible. There was one guy in the waiting room who was walking around in circles. Since the floor seemed to belong to him, I just sat there and worried in one spot. After what seemed like several hours but was probably several minutes, a nurse came and told me that Dr. Sarratt would see me.

I stood in a doorway as the tall, handsome, aristocratic obstetrician, Houston Sarratt, walked slowly down the hallway with what I perceived to be a grave look on his face. I stood there expecting the worst until he held out his hand and said, "Congratulations, you're the father of a fine, healthy girl." Thus was born Lauren Anese Braddock, having given her mother just enough time to finish watching *Peyton Place*.

I remember standing there so proudly looking through the glass at baby Braddock who seemed to be making a fist. Fellow band mate Don Winters, nicknamed "Ox" probably because of his short stature, stood next to me, proclaiming that the baby would be called "Oxetta." *Oxetta* didn't stick, but *Jeep* did.

Having lost our other baby, Sue and I were fanatically overprotective with this one. For the first few weeks, checking on the baby meant checking to make sure she was still breathing, still alive. In time we would learn that this healthy, hearty girl wasn't going anywhere, except deep into our hearts. Of all the things I would create—songs, whatever—nothing would come close to this, my greatest accomplishment.

I had made up my mind that I wanted to stay at home with my family, and on the next tour would tell Marty I wanted to quit the road. I was making a decent amount of money in town, especially playing piano on sessions for a guy who had an independent record company. Sometimes there were several sessions a week. Whenever we went to the Musicians Union to get our checks, we then headed straight to this employer/producer's office to give him a kickback of half our earnings. I would have been expelled from the union if this had been found out.

I had also been doing a lot of songwriting. There was no exclusive contract with Marty, so I was not obligated to show him every song I wrote. I had some songs that were unusual for their day. There was one about a fellow who happily commits suicide and no one is able to wipe the smile off his face, and one called "Insane," about a guy who finds his wife in bed with another man and blows them both away, but doesn't quite remember it. Another was inspired on that last tour with Marty. I was standing outside the venue and could hear Ray Price's steel guitar player, the great Buddy Emmons, tuning his instrument, using a nice chord with beautiful descending notes: ding, ding, ding, ding, ding. "What a beautiful melody that would make," I thought, and turned "ding ding ding ding ding" into "Before the Bird Flies," a song that I would finish as soon as I got back home. I've often wondered if I should have offered Buddy Emmons a piece of the song.

I had been told that Marty would not take it very well if I quit the band, and he would not let me have back any of the songs he had published. I spent the entire tour trying to get up the nerve to break the news, then when the bus pulled up in front of his office, after we had gone the last mile of the way, I said, "Marty, I'd like to quit the road and be home with my family and try to make it in town as a songwriter."

"Okay, Bob, if that's what you want to do, that's fine with me," he said pleasantly.

"Uh, c-can I have any of my songs back?"

"Any songs that I haven't put any money into, you can have back, sure."

Not only were there no hard feelings, but he asked if I would mind continuing to play with him when he was in Nashville, appearing on the Grand Ole Opry, and I told him I would be happy to. This would go on, in fact, for a year, until he finally found a permanent replacement for me.

So that night while little Jeep was sleeping in her baby bed, Sue and I were discussing what my next move should be. I had recently read that Tree Publishing Company had surpassed Acuff-Rose and Cedarwood, and was now the #1 publishing company in Nashville and country music. I had also read that Tree's #1 writer, superstar Roger Miller, had moved to the West Coast.

"Where should I go?" we asked the Ouija board.

It spelled out, "T-R-E-E."

I put in a call the next day to Buddy Killen, well-known producer, and executive vice president of the company that he had built up from a little cubbyhole office business into the biggest, most aggressive publishing company on Music Row. I was afraid I would have to talk to some intermediary, but I actually got Killen on the line. I always felt that the first thing I said to him was, "I want to write for Tree," but I'll defer to what he would say for the rest of his life—in fact he would tell me just a few days before he died that I had said: "I've always wanted to write for Tree."

3

A TREE GROWS IN NASHVILLE

On a sunny day in May of 1966, I stood and gazed into the bathroom mirror to make sure I looked presentable for this very important meeting at Tree Publishing Company. Though only twenty-five, my hair had already started thinning—I thought about bald-headed uncles on my mother's side—so I was starting to comb it forward, Caesar style, to cover up the early stages of a receding hairline.

Having just gotten baby Jeep to sleep, Sue transformed into Pigeon, flapping her elbow wings, telling me I was going to make a whole lot of money on a publishing deal. "You and me and the little *baby* bird are gonna get alllll the money, Daggy. *Sue* can't have any of it," she exclaimed in a high squeaky voice.

I whispered goodbye to the sleeping baby. As I opened the front door, our two adopted feline friends, Tarzan and Jane, darted inside (back in the days when dogs and cats typically roamed the neighborhoods). I got behind the wheel of our '62 Oldsmobile, backed out of the driveway, and began the seven-and-a-half mile trip that I would make many times over the next few years, heading west, then north, and finally hanging a left on South Street, which dead-ended at Music Row's main street, 16th Avenue South. A car racing out of control down South Street would have crashed head-on into the two-story house that was Tree Publishing Company. Emblazoned with big cursive letters across the building's imposing concrete front (made of geometrically designed blocks) was the company's name, along with its tree logo.

I had done my homework. I knew that in 1954, Jack Stapp, the dapper co-owner of Tree, had hired Buddy Killen, a twenty-one-year-old bass player from northern Alabama, as *songplugger*. With little knowledge and no experience in music publishing, Buddy learned fast and worked hard. A songwriter himself, he developed a good ear for recognizing a hit. He soon turned a little one-room operation into a competitive enterprise. In 1956, he talked a writer named Mae Axton into letting Tree publish her part of a song that was about to be recorded by an up-and-coming young singer, and before long Elvis Presley's first pop mega-hit "Heartbreak Hotel" made both the plugger and his publishers look pretty good. When Stapp bought out his partner, Lou Cowan, in 1957, he gave 10 percent of the company to his loyal secretary, Joyce Bush, and 30 percent to Buddy.

On this day, when I first met Buddy Killen, he was a thirty-three-year-old millionaire. Though he owned less than one-third of Tree and was only vice president, everyone in town knew he was the driving force behind the organization's success. Stapp was a genial ambassador, but Buddy had two great talents: a knack for business and a genius as a music man, not only as a publisher but as the producer of artists like rhythm & blues star Joe Tex, on the Stapp-Killen record label, Dial. So it was with both hope and apprehension that I walked through the door of the firm that had just replaced Acuff-Rose as the biggest music publishing house in Nashville.

Buddy was a nice-looking man with bright eyes and a big smile. His dark hair had begun to thin, a couple of stages more than mine. Unlike many people who worked on Music Row, he wore a coat and tie and always would. Brought up a poor country boy, he had a poor boy's deep appreciation for nice things. If one were to imitate Buddy's voice, the tone would not form deep in the diaphragm, but as a round sound way up in the throat. I know of no other way to describe his voice than Bullwinkle J. Moose with a Southern accent.

"You know, I don't usually meet with aspiring writers myself," he let me know. I think I got his attention on the phone when I told him that I wrote "While You're Dancing," which he had heard on the radio a few times. He took me to a little studio in the back of the building and introduced me to his sole country songplugger (besides himself), another Alabamian, Curly Putman, a tall man in his mid-thirties, already highly respected as the writer of the Porter Wagoner country hit "Green Green Grass of Home." (Tree's pop department consisted of John Hurley and Ronnie Wilkins, writers of the future Dusty Springfield hit "Son of a Preacher Man.") Buddy then directed me over to the piano and asked me to sit down and sing him some of my songs. I did "Insane," "Smile on My Face," and "Before the Bird Flies." He seemed more than a little impressed that these songs of murder, suicide, and noncommitment were totally different from what he was used to hearing. I told him I felt that country music was supposed to reflect real life.

"Let me listen to the other songs on your tape, and I'll call you in a few days and let you know what I decide," he said.

After a few days, I hadn't heard from him and gave him a call. "I haven't had time to listen to them yet, but I've been thinkin' about you," Buddy said. "Come on down here and let's talk."

He introduced me to Jack Stapp, his partner and Tree's president, a sweet-natured man in his early fifties who wore a hairpiece and horn-rimmed glasses. Joyce Bush, who had become Tree's secretary-treasurer, was a pleasant woman in her early thirties, also wearing horn-rimmed glasses. She and Mr. Stapp seemed to be cut from the same cloth; she could have been his daughter.

Buddy ushered me into his office and said, "We *want* you to write here,

Jack Stapp, founder and president of Tree Publishing Company in Nashville

Buddy Killen, executive vice-president of Tree Publishing Company in Nashville

but I'm only going to be able to advance you forty dollars a week (make that $280 today). Now, if we start gettin' your songs cut, I'll raise that to a hundred a week ($700 today). Don't be asking me for a raise, I'll tell you when I think it's time." Then he flashed his million-dollar smile, "Does that sound okay to you, Bob?"

"S-sounds fine to me. I hope you can get 'em cut."

"Oh, I think we can."

Long before coming to Nashville, I knew that a music publisher's role was to collect royalties from the record labels (and from people who put out sheet music, songbooks, etc.), and then split the receipts with the writer. The rationale behind not doing your own publishing, especially as a new writer, was that an established publishing company employed people who knew how to do all the paperwork and deal with complicated foreign administration of copyrights, and major publishers like Tree had the connections to play your songs for the right people. The publishers collected money from sales, which were called "mechanicals." The performance organizations like BMI (Broadcast Music Incorporated) and ASCAP (American Society of Composers, Authors, and Publishers) collected money from radio and television stations for airplay, called "performances," and split that between publishers and writers. I was already a BMI writer before coming to Tree.

The forty dollars weekly advance, of course, wouldn't be enough to support my family. Fortunately, I had become the regular replacement piano player at WSM-TV for both the early morning and afternoon country music

Curly Putman, emerging hit songwriter and Tree's sole country
songplugger

My MGM publicity shot, 1967

TV shows, filling in whenever the regular pianists weren't able to make it.
I was doing occasional recording sessions, too, but unlike most musicians
whose session work starts to build as their reputation gets around, with me
it was the opposite. Sometimes on recording sessions, I would start thinking too hard about *meter* and would end up playing *out of meter*, and conse-
quently my sessions were dropping off. For some reason, I didn't experience
this problem when playing the live TV gigs.

In order to get someone to cut a song, a decent demonstration recording
has to be presented. In 1966, unlike in later years, it wasn't unusual to get as
many as twelve songs on a three-hour demo session. You ran down the song
with the band, and they played it once, maybe twice, and that was it. In the
recording studio, I stood in line with several songwriters who were waiting to
sing their songs: Red Lane, Don Wayne, Autry Inman, and the great recording artist Dottie West. Within a week, I was back in the studio to demo more
songs (in Nashville, *demo* is also a verb).

Buddy and Curly Putman were pitching my songs successfully. Every few
days I was getting one recorded. Fifties rock & roll star Jack Scott cut a country record, and I had both the A-side and the B-side. I wrote a bouncy little
song called "Ruthless" (about a guy losing his girlfriend, Ruth) that a teenage
Hank Williams Jr. sang.

Curly was an anomaly in that he was a songwriter who was able to be an
objective songplugger, and just as apt to pitch someone else's song as his own.
He was a low-key, likable country boy. One day I walked into his office, and

he introduced me to a twenty-year-old shapely blonde named Dolly Parton. She was getting a lot of attention for her harmony singing on the Bill Phillips hit "Put It Off Until Tomorrow," which she had written. Dolly was signing with Monument Records, and her first single was going to be a song of Curly's: "Dumb Blonde" (it would be one of the few songs in her career that she did not write herself). It was during her pre-wig days, and she was spirited and friendly. She asked us if we wanted to hear a song she had just written about a girl who was in love with a rich Texas oilman. It was called "I'll Oil Wells Love You, I'll Oil Wells Be True." Hey, I thought, a gorgeous punster, an amazing combination! What a sight she was to see before her journey to the top; as fresh as a mountain breeze, as beautiful as a young man's best dream.

It just seemed natural that Curly and I would write together. Though "let's write" hadn't yet become the Nashville equivalent of "let's do lunch" as it would in the twenty-first century, more and more country hits were being co-written—about 40 percent in those days, as compared to nearly 90 percent forty years later. Classic pop collaborators like Rodgers and Hammerstein were partners, one being the composer and the other the lyricist. In rock & roll and country, however, collaborators were more likely to be two or three people brainstorming, strumming their instruments in search of a hit groove, and throwing lines at each other, maybe one being a little stronger on lyrics but writing some melody, too, and vice versa. I sometimes found co-writing to be a painfully awkward experience—two people just sitting around looking at each other blank-faced—but sometimes it was a situation that was comfortable and, every once in a while, exhilarating. A lot of country writers built successful careers as co-writers, while others wrote most of their big ones by themselves. I was capable of going both ways, but always felt a little prouder knowing that I had written something alone. I think Curly was more adept at co-writing than I was, more able to be creatively compatible with a wider range of people, though he certainly wrote some of his best songs solo. Nashville co-writers are a lot like lovers: sometimes they have a committed relationship; sometimes it's a one-night stand; sometimes it's somewhere in between. And they come together like lovers do: sometimes randomly and carelessly, sometimes because they have good rapport, and sometimes because circumstances throw them together. Curly and I started doing some collaborating because we had that good rapport and because we were both hanging out at Tree. It wasn't a one-night stand or a committed relationship, but somewhere in between.

We wrote a song that we both liked, and Curly promptly placed it with a fairly big artist. The next thing I knew, I was in Buddy's office with Curly and the artist, who suddenly, without contributing one note or one word, had become the third writer on the song. Buddy passed around the contract and the pen and we all signed our names. I promised myself that I would never again let anyone, no matter who it was, put his or her name on a song I had written unless that person had contributed, too. Happily, it was a dilemma I was never faced with again. I had gotten caught up in an old Music Row custom that was going out of style. Back in the 1950s, for instance, superstar Webb Pierce had his name listed as co-writer on many of his big hits, but it was commonly believed that he didn't really do any of the writing. So I was starting my career on Music Row at the end of an era, and it didn't matter much about the song; it wasn't a big hit. I don't mention the artist's name simply because this is a nice person who was merely engaging in an old way of doing business, and who probably hasn't given the transaction any thought for a very long time.

Buddy was especially taken with my novelty songs. Some of them may have been clever, but in retrospect, they seem pretty corny to me, like throw-backs to 1920s vaudeville. One of the better ones was "Country Music Lover," a song about a guy whose girlfriend knew so little about the genre that she thought "Ernest Tubb was a sincere place to take a bath" and "Johnny Cash was money you find in a commode," and, lo and behold, it got recorded by Little Jimmy Dickens, who was having a lot of success with that type of song. *Cash Box* magazine wrote, "Since signing his writing pact with Tree, Braddock has had seven songs recorded, an average of better than one a week." Unfortunately, I was becoming spoiled, thinking it would always be this easy to get songs cut.

Having experienced gigantic success with a brilliant writer, Roger Miller, and having secured him a recording deal that catapulted him to both country and pop superstardom and his own network TV show, Buddy somehow got it into his head that I was the next Roger Miller. In *Music City News*, Buddy was quoted as saying that I had "the promise and potential of Roger Miller. Bright, fresh and fantastic are mild adjectives to describe this young man's capabilities." I got my advance raised to $100 a week.

"Valentine," Buddy said (he had started calling me that since learning that my full name was Robert Valentine Braddock), "I think I'm gonna be able to get you on MGM." *Billboard* wrote, "Bobby Braddock, exclusive writer for Tree Music, recently signed a recording contract with MGM." It was pretty heady stuff.

Jim Vienneau was MGM's director of A&R (artists and repertoire) in the days when that title was synonymous with being a producer, before the days of independent production, when "producer" and "A&R man" would become separate entities. Basically, a producer is to a recording session as a director is to a movie. Jim was a friendly guy of about forty who had come to Nashville from New York, where he had produced pop acts such as Connie Francis. He was a big fan of my songwriting, but I don't recall him ever saying anything about my singing.

I went into the recording studio on November 3 and recorded "Ruthless," "I Know How to Do It," and "Gear Bustin' Sort of a Feller" ("I'm a double-clutchin' scale-jumpin' mile-makin' tail-gatin' cop-dodgin' line-crossin' coffee-drinkin' pinballin' jack-knifin' fog-timin' wind-jammin' late-runnin' gear bustin' sort of a feller," most of the terminology being supplied by my

Music Row, circa 1967: RCA Studio B, 17th Avenue South

truck-driving brother-in-law in Alabama). Shortly after that, I went back and recorded two more of my songs. From that point on until nearly the end of the decade, MGM would release several singles on me, produced by Jim Vienneau and often co-produced by the witty and talented Norro Wilson. Most of these records would make the country charts, but just barely, which would make me fall way short of being "the next Roger Miller." I sang in a breathy style, and had made as my trademark a sort of "eefing" sound, a vibrating guttural noise that I must have thought was funny. My idea of hell is spending an eternity listening to those awful records that I made for MGM. But after all, I came to Nashville to be a songwriter, not a recording artist.

Nineteen sixty-seven would become my first successful year in the music business and the last decent year Sue and I would have as a couple. There were times when she would fold her arms and impatiently roll her blue eyes upward, as if she were looking at something ugly on the ceiling, and there were even times when she would scream at me (much more likely to happen when I was drinking), but for the most part we were having a good time together and thrilled to have a healthy baby. Pigeon and Small Bobby and Homer still showed up often. Sue would have gallbladder surgery in the early part of the year, but other than that, we would enjoy good times, see our first decent income, and begin the crazy pattern of spending more money than I made.

Sue became friends with Curly Putman's wife, Bernice, who was a few years older than she. Curly and I had hit it off immediately and were already friends. He was ten years my senior, a tall, curly-headed North Alabama boy who was raised on Putman Mountain, where his father operated a sawmill. Curly was slow-talking and low key, wrote with a lot of depth, and had a sing-

Music Row, early 1970s: Sixteenth Avenue South at Division Street.

ing style that sounded about as lonesome as he looked. He had a certain sadness about him that I think was innate. His "Green Green Grass of Home" was recorded a few months earlier by Tom Jones and not only had become a big pop record in America, but was turning into a major hit around the world—there were already recordings in numerous languages. The Putmans were moving from their house in our part of town to a larger one that had a swimming pool and spacious grounds with a lovely river view.

"I went shopping with Bernice," Sue said, "and I was embarrassed; Bernice buying nice things that I couldn't afford."

"Why should you be embarrassed?" I asked. "She knows I don't make the kind of money Curly does. A year ago, Curly didn't either. Just be patient."

One night Sue and I went to a little gathering at the home of Joe and Carol Babcock. There was an affable, intelligent guy there, about three years older than me, John Hartford, a deejay at local radio station WSIX. He had recently signed a recording contract with RCA. He gave me a copy of his new single record; he had written it and was pretty excited about it. He asked me to give it a listen and see what I thought. When I got home, I put it on the turntable, played the fast-paced banjo-oriented folksong, then turned it over and listened to the flip side. It was a song called "The Good Old Electric Washing Machine Circa 1943" which featured him imitating the hum of the new washing machine and then the chugging, sloshing sound of the old one that he sorely missed. That was the side that I loved, and I called him up right away.

"J-John, this is Bobby Braddock. I just listened to your record, and the washin' machine song is the hit. That's the one."

"Hmm-m-m, I dunno," he said in his flat St. Louis twang, "the record label's really high on the other side."

"Oh no, it's the washin' machine song that's the hit."

The "other side" that the label was really high on was "Gentle on My Mind," which went on to be recorded by Glen Campbell and many others, and would become one of the most-played radio songs of all time.

Congratulations Valentine," Buddy Killen beamed as I walked into his office one fine spring day, "You've got your first Top Ten record." Little Jimmy Dickens had crossed that psychological threshold in *Cash Box* magazine with "Country Music Lover." Music historians generally consider *Billboard*'s popularity chart to be the definitive one, but there were three major trade papers: *Billboard, Cash Box,* and *Record World.* If I made the Top Ten in any one of these, I considered it a Top Ten record. The Statler Brothers were about to cut my oft-recorded "Ruthless," a song I had written the previous year in about ten minutes, my most quickly written song ever, and one that would soon become my first one to make the *Billboard* Top Ten.

I'd had a recent cut and forthcoming single by a long-time favorite, Ferlin Husky, "You Pushed Me Too Far," a dark comedy about a guy who pushes his unfaithful wife off a mountaintop. The first song I ever played for Buddy Killen had been about a man who barges into his bedroom and opens fire on his surprised wife and her lover. In my third release on MGM, "I'm a Good Girl," the protagonist discovers that his love interest is actually a "bad" girl and proceeds to blow her away. I, who never knowingly harbored murder in my heart, seemed to have a propensity for the execution of promiscuous female song characters.

I had made it a practice to take my records around personally, whether they were my MGM recordings or something I had written for someone else, to the five country radio stations in the metropolitan Nashville area. I would go to 50,000-watt WSM to visit Ralph Emery's late night *Opry Star Spotlight*, probably the single most popular country radio show in America. His show reached half of the continental United States, and was very popular with truckers. Ralph was a true professional. Having gotten rid of his small-town Tennessee accent, he had that classic radio/TV voice; deep, booming, resonant. His *Nashville Now* would be the top-rated show on cable TV in the 1980s, and he would be called "the Johnny Carson of Country Music," but because Ralph wasn't a comedian, I think "the Ed Sullivan of Country Music" might be more appropriate. Ralph could be a bit of a smart ass, but, perhaps because I had been such a diehard fan of his since high school, he was very nice to me. He was fond of my parody songs and started having me sit down at the studio's grand piano, generally reserved for Marty Robbins, and lampoon the hits of the day. One of my parodies was about the Jewish guy who was in love with the Christian girl, "*Gentile* on My Mind;" another was about the high esteem in which an auto mechanic was held by his family, "The Grand Grand Grease of Home."

Then I would go to Nashville's other 50,000-watt station, R&B earlier in the night but pure country at 4 a.m. when Bob Jennings played music for farmers, milkmen, and other early birds in the eastern half of America. A publisher and songwriter by day, Bob was more down-to-earth and less urbane in his style than Ralph. Ralph, not yet in his mid-thirties, seemed to like playing the celebrity role a little bit more than Bob, who was about a decade older. Both men were very nice to me back when I was a newcomer.

Both Ferlin Husky's "You Pushed Me Too Far" and the Statler Brothers' "Ruthless" hit the Top Ten, as did their follow up, a song I wrote with Curly, the up-tempo "You Can't Have Your Kate and Edith Too." I got the idea from a radio comedy show that I had heard as a child. Over three decades after the Statler Brothers hit, a successful young Nashville writer would call me up and say, "I have a title I've just got to write with you. You've got to hear this title, it's your kind of song." It was "You Can't Have Your Kate and Edith Too." The writer was too young to have heard our song in 1967 and thought she had come up with a new idea.

Lauren—or Jeep—was a vivacious little girl. At the year-and-a-half mark, she was saying a few words and really starting to get around. Though she was loathe to be confined in any enclosure, whether it was her baby bed or her gated room, basically she was a happy and sweet-natured child. I have an old home movie of her dressed up in her Sunday best for some Church of Christ service, getting the daylights spanked out of her by her mama, who was wearing an expression of irritation rather than anger, as though the butt-swatting was some kind of an inconvenience, a chore that had to be done. Sue was passing it on; both of us were. Both Sue's parents and mine had believed the old adage, "spare the rod and spoil the child," and apparently we did, too.

The best thing I ever created, Lauren Anese "Jeep" Braddock

We didn't break the chain. These acts of violence are passed on; spankers beget spankers. In that era, most parents administered some degree of corporal punishment—perhaps a majority still do, particularly in the South. In some instances, such as a kid hitting a parent or running out in the street, a spanking may work best, I don't know. I just know if I had it to do over, I would run life's movie backward and take back every one of the spankings I gave Jeep. I feel that I was being cowardly, inflicting pain on a tiny person incapable of defending herself from a big grownup. I'm proud that Lauren grew up to administer forms of discipline to her own child that are more civilized and just as effective. She broke the chain. I wish that we had done it first.

Jack Stapp, the founder, major shareholder, and president of Tree, had a distinguished history in broadcasting, having been an official at CBS radio, program director at WSM and the Grand Ole Opry, and general manager of Nashville's popular rock station, WKDA. He had been given co-writer status on Red Foley's 1950 monster hit "Chattanoogie Shoe Shine Boy" as a business favor, but he didn't write a lick of it and was not really a music man. He knew the *business* end of music, and behind the scenes he was a hard-nosed businessman who sometimes had sharp differences with Buddy Killen. He was gifted at motivating people. "Bobby boy," he often said, "you're like old man river, you just keep rollin' along with those hits." This classy and congenial bachelor, brimming with Old South charm, always looked as if he had just stepped out of *Gentleman's Quarterly*. Though fifty-four years old, Jack had a penchant for very young women—as young as the law allowed. I once heard him say that he had no interest in women over thirty.

By that standard, Tree's secretary-treasurer Joyce Bush was two years too old for Jack (and very married), and though attractive, she was more the girl next door than glamorous. Not to say that there was anything shady about Jack or Buddy's business practices, but Joyce, a devout Baptist, was Tree's moral compass and kept everybody honest. She always seemed to have a kind word for all, big or small. It became a running joke around the office that, as my luck would have it, whenever I said a cuss word or started a dirty joke, Joyce always seemed to pop up, graciously acting as though she hadn't heard a thing.

While Jack would wear expensive tailor-mades, Buddy preferred nice but more casual suits, sport coats, and blazers (but always with a tie). Never lacking in self-confidence or self-love, Buddy Killen was a very proud, even vain, man. I don't think he had a lazy bone in his body. He was energized and energizing, never content, always wanting more.

Buddy liked to tell the "rubber ball story," about him sitting in their little one-room office back in the mid-1950s, agonizing over not being able to get anything going, and in frustration, throwing a rubber ball across the room. The ball hit the wall and bounced right back to him, and it dawned on him that "for every action there's a reaction," which spurred him on to call up everyone he knew to announce that he had some songs to play for them. The man single-handedly made Tree country music's biggest publishing company. And nobody ever believed in me as much as Buddy Killen did.

Although Curly Putman's reputation was growing as one of Nashville's best songwriters, he continued to pitch songs for Tree. Some songpluggers applied the hard sell, but Curly's style was low key and homespun. Producers and artists knew they wouldn't be high-pressured by Curly and were aware that he was representing perhaps the best song catalog in town, including some of his own songs. (Over the years, songpluggers would sometimes be called "professional managers" and "creative directors," but nearly a half century later "songplugger" is still the title of choice.) Although I doubt that my oddball writing style was influenced by anyone at Tree, if I had a songwriting mentor, it was Curly. He was in charge of the demo sessions, and sometimes we butted heads because my production ideas didn't conform to his more conventional ones. I enjoyed having a few beers with Curly at a bar next door to Tree called Kountry Korner, often joined by other Tree writers such as Don Wayne ("Saginaw, Michigan" and "The Belles of Southern Bell") and the songwriter's songwriter, Red Lane. Curly was a great *singer*, with a sad mournful style, and was once asked how he'd like to be raking in some of the big bucks that the super singers were getting. "Well, if a man could, a man would," he drawled philosophically. I once heard him say, not about beer but a cold glass of milk, "If the Lord made anything better than this, he must have kept it for himself." Though still in his thirties, Curly was a wise old sage.

One fall day, after hanging out around Tree and getting home about four o'clock in the afternoon, I sat down at my piano and played around with a song idea I'd had for a few days, "I L-O-V-E Y-O-U," (*do I have to spell it out for you?*). I wasn't loving the way it was coming together (that song would have to wait another ten years to be written), but I liked the concept of spelling out words, and hit on the idea of parents shielding their four-year-old child by spelling out the damning evidence that their marriage was falling apart. I called the song "D-I-V-O-R-C-E."

> *Our little Joe is four years old, and quite a little man*
> *So we spell out the words we don't want him to understand*
> *Like T-O-Y and maybe S-U-R-P-R-I-S-E*
> *But the words we're hiding from him now tear the heart right out of me*
>   *Our D-I-V-O-R-C-E becomes final today*
>   *Y-O-U and little J-O-E will be going away*
>   *I love you both and this will be pure H-E double L for me*
>   *Oh I wish that we could stop this D-I-V-O-R-C-E*
> *Watch him smile, he thinks it's Christmas, or his fifth birthday*

And he thinks C-U-S-T-O-D-Y spells fun or play
I'll spell out all the hurtin' words and turn my head when I speak
But I can't spell away this hurt that's drippin' down my cheek
Our D-I-V-O-R-C-E becomes final today, etc.

Curly liked the song and thought we should do a demo on it, which we did. Both he and Buddy pitched it to several people with no positive results. I thought it was a pretty good song—despite lyrics that today might be considered a bit corny—and had high hopes that it would prove successful.

Ironically, about the time that I wrote this very traditional country song, I was abruptly pulled into the late sixties counterculture a little bit without even realizing it. I was impacted musically in a way that I hadn't experienced since high school . . . and by a Beatles album. I loved the Beatles from the beginning. The British invasion took place back when I was in Big John's Untouchables in Florida. I loved us playing early Beatles hits; it was rock & roll with more than the typical three chords. I enjoyed their music from that time on, occasionally buying their singles but not really keeping up with the famous albums like *Rubber Soul* and *Revolver*, probably because I was focusing on my new career as a country songwriter. One day I was at the home of Marty Robbins's harmony singer, Don Winters, when his teenage son, Donnie, started talking about *Sgt. Pepper's Lonely Hearts Club Band*, the Beatles album that had taken the world by storm. I had heard a lot about it but, because none of the tracks were being released as singles, I was unfamiliar with the songs. Donnie sang "With a Little Help from My Friends," which I loved, and on the strength of that, I bought the album.

That night I woke up sometime between midnight and dawn and, unable to go back to sleep, took the shrink wrap off *Sgt. Pepper's* and drove out to the huge city-owned Percy Warner Park on the edge of town. I was driving a new Mercury Marquis that had an eight-track player (blasting through big speakers that I'd had installed on the car doors). As the sun came up, I drove through the park's hills and hollows to the amazing sounds of the title tune, then the enchanting "With a Little Help from My Friends," the emotional "She's Leaving Home," the exotic "Within You Without You," the happy "When I'm Sixty-Four," the riveting finale, "A Day in the Life," and all the wonderful songs and tidbits in between. I fell in love with this revolutionary new music at first listen. By mid-morning I was low on gas but still driving through the park, held captive by what has often been called the first rock concept album. With all the tasty ear candy panned hard left and hard right, half of it was coming at me from one door, and half of it from the other. Just as my writing had been affected by hillbilly hero Hank Williams and blues guru Ray Charles, my future work would be influenced by the Beatles, though in age they were my contemporaries.

About the time that I was drawn to the psychedelic Beatles, Sue and I saw the film *Bonnie and Clyde*. Though not prudish in our everyday lives, we were

Birthday celebration at the old Tree building, late 1960s

initially put off by profanity in the movies until we saw *In Cold Blood*, based on the Truman Capote book that we had read two or three times. Then *The Graduate* brought us to accept sexuality in the movies. I had read a couple of books about the bank-robbing sweethearts Bonnie Parker and Clyde Barrow, and upon learning that their lives were being portrayed in a movie, I was eager to see it. *Bonnie and Clyde* had not been heavily promoted and had just opened at the downtown Tennessee Theater. I found great excitement in the juxtaposition of slapstick comedy and cold-blooded murder, and in mixing Depression-era authenticity and a hint of mod fashion (with some bluegrass music thrown in). The famous final scene, in which Warren Beatty and Faye Dunaway are riddled with bullets in slow motion, was like nothing seen on the screen before. There were about thirty people in the theater, and at the movie's end they filed out of the theater in a kind of stupor, as if in a state of shock. Two weeks later, crowds were wrapped around the block waiting to get in.

It's ironic that I had been drinking and fighting since high school days, was a "speed freak" in my late teens, and a male whore in my rock & roll band days, yet I was initially offended when I saw these topics depicted on the screen. Years later, when I described this irony to my friend, the great Southern author John Egerton and told him how *Bonnie and Clyde* suddenly had become my new favorite film, his take was that I had been converted to a willing voyeur of sex, violence and "dirty talk" by one powerful movie drama—truth ramped up to glamour by Hollywood—while still holding on, unquestioning, to political, religious, and social beliefs and attitudes that would not bear scrutiny. The movie made me think, he said, but in those other areas I was not conditioned to think.

So I was open to the counterculture but only through the arts, i.e., *Sgt. Pepper's* and *Bonnie and Clyde*. I would remain politically and religiously conservative for almost another two years.

Autumn left and winter came, a new calendar went up on the kitchen wall, then late winter's first warm breath heralded the coming of yet another season. Still there were no takers for "D-I-V-O-R-C-E." Both Curly and Buddy had pitched it all over town with no results. I couldn't understand why nobody would record it.

"I think the melody's too happy for such a sad song," said Curly.

"Y-you think it needs a new melody?" I asked.

"Well maybe just on the last line of the verses and the last line of the chorus," he replied. He was right. Those were the saddest parts of the song, but my tune sounded a bit like a soap commercial, too bouncy.

"What would *you* do?" I asked. He picked up his guitar and sang it through, and on the lines in question he sang it plaintively, mournfully. "Let's put it on tape just like that," I said. We did a simple demo, Curly singing and playing guitar, and me playing piano with the left-handed low-note licks that would become the song's signature.

I thought his melody changes, though confined to a small area, made a significant difference in the commerciality of the song and suggested that he take half of the writing credit. Curly argued that because he was better known than I was, he might get all the credit if he shared the copyright with me. We finally compromised, Curly having his name appear as co-writer but taking only 25 percent of the song.

That night at a Recording Academy banquet, I saw Tammy Wynette's producer, Billy Sherrill. I told him about the song and he asked me to get it over to him. The next morning, Curly and I went by Sherrill's office; he wasn't there, so we left the tape with his secretary. The next day, Curly told me Billy had called and said they were going to do the song. Many years later, Billy would tell radio interviewer Laura Cantrell, "When I heard it, I threw my stuff in the garbage can, so that was it. It was a hit before we even walked in the studio—before Tammy even heard it, I would have bet money that it was a #1 record." He told me, "We pulled out all the stops on that one."

It was still early in Tammy's career, but she already had a small string of hits, so there was a little bit of pressure there; you sure don't want to write an artist's first bomb. But when I heard the recording I knew it wasn't going to be a bomb. Billy had the good sense to change "our little Joe" to "our little boy," and now that it was a female song, "Y-O-U and little J-O-E" became "*me* and little J-O-E," bad grammar notwithstanding. Music Row's great young producer and the girl with the wonderful little catch in her voice created a great moment in country music.

One night in May of 1968, Sue and I were having dinner at a little meat-and-three restaurant on Nolensville Road with two couples roughly our age, who lived on our street. Someone played "D-I-V-O-R-C-E" on the jukebox. I said, "That's my song, and I think it's going to be a big, big hit." And it was. The spelled-out title would become a catch phrase over the years, often showing up in headlines about someone's divorce. It went to #1 for three weeks, made the pop charts, became Tammy Wynette's biggest record at that time, and my first song to top the charts. Later in the year the folks back home would see Sue and me decked out in formal wear, sitting in the audience at the CBS broadcast of the CMA Country Music Awards, when "D-I-V-O-R-C-E" was one of the five contenders for Song of the Year.

"D-I-V-O-R-C-E" was almost recorded by pop star Connie Francis. I say *almost* because someone at Tree denied her request to change one of the lines in the song, apparently never thinking to check with the one who wrote the words—a major violation of protocol. Connie was in town from New York looking for material, so I called my producer, Jim Vienneau, who was also her producer, and asked if he could get me a couple of minutes with her. I expressed to both my co-writer (Curly Putman) and my publisher my wishes to tell her that it was okay to change the lyric. Her real name was Concetta Rosa Maria Franconero, and when Jim introduced me to the dark-eyed Italian-American beauty, my heart skipped a beat as I remembered how sexy I thought her singing voice was when I was a teenager. I told her I was a fan and had no problem at all with her changing a few of the words. "I'm sorry, Bobby," she said sweetly, "but it's too late, I've already picked the material. But I do think you'll have a big pop record on that song someday." Her prediction would come true, sort of, when a spoof version of the Tammy Wynette hit topped the British charts several years later.

We made frequent family excursions to the Great Smoky Mountains or to Panama City, Florida, the Gulf beach of choice for Sue and many other Alabamians. We often saw her family in Alabama and mine in Florida. Though Sue and I were having difficulty getting along at this point, the beach was usually a respite from all of that, and we did well when visiting her family. The trouble always began when we went down to my hometown. Sue didn't seem to like my friends, and she clearly had problems with my mother. My feeling was if you love someone, you love their family, period. Sue's mother Louise, recently remarried, was pleasant but a little distant (perhaps shy), had a weakness for beer, and if she ever cooked a meal, I never saw it. But I never made critical comments about her, because she was Sue's mother. Sue didn't extend the same courtesy to me. On the way to Auburndale, she talked about how she dreaded visiting my mother, and constantly put her down after we left. Granted, Mom could be a little annoying with her bits of advice laced with nervous laughs, but Sue took great umbrage at it. And I constantly had to hear about how my mother favored my brother's daughter over Jeep, which if true, was understandable to me because they lived in the same little town and saw each other daily.

Sue and I had become friendly with two couples who lived on the other side of Whispering Hills Drive. Sue was particularly close to one of the young women. I liked them all just fine; the guys talked a lot about the stock market, which I found boring, but in retrospect I think I should have paid more attention. One night we all went out to a bar. When it was closing time, the bouncer took away the girls' unfinished drinks. I was drunk enough to think that I could order a big, beefy bouncer around, and when that didn't work, I shoved him up against the bar. I recall seeing a fist coming at me like a jet flying out of a 3-D movie screen, and the next thing I knew, I was lying on the floor with two women bending down over me, both of them screaming, "Are you all right? Are you all right?" I soon realized that both of the women were Sue, surrounded by little stars and comets and meteor showers.

Our friendship with all these folks came to an abrupt end one night when Sue and I got into an intense discussion with one of the guys about the condition of some of the beef that he had sold us from his family's farm. Sue lost her temper and told him she knew who he was screwing around with, and threatened to tell. We became persona non grata to everyone in our age group on Whispering Hills Drive.

There was a couple who lived two or three streets over whom we once visited—Dan and Annie Holder—and I think Sue became acquainted with Annie because our babysitter, Mrs. Sorrow (an older lady who lived up the street from us) also took care of their child. Dan was a solid-citizen type, several years older than I was, a ten-year Air Force veteran who was now an airline pilot. While we were at their house I invited them over to dinner the next Friday night. Granted, I should have consulted with Sue in private, but she seemed to be on board, and the Holders readily accepted the invitation. When we left, Sue told me she didn't want to fix dinner for them.

"Why?" I asked. "You're a great cook," which she was.

"I just don't want to do it," she said, folding her arms—never a good sign. "He's really picky, everything at their house is so perfectly in place, I just don't want them to come over."

"What do we tell them?"

"*You* think of something, *you're* the one who invited them."

Looking back, it all seems so simple; I should have called the Holders and said, "I'm *so* sorry, but Friday's not going to work. Maybe we can reschedule soon?" Instead I was convinced that I could get Sue to change her mind, yet every day she dug her heels in deeper. I begged her, tried bribing her, but nothing worked. I was too embarrassed to call them up, but what ensued (no pun intended) was even more embarrassing. By late Friday afternoon, when the house was still messy and there was no activity going on in the kitchen, I came to the stark realization that there would be no dinner for the Holders. I had decided to go ahead and call them, but when Sue got into her car and left, I realized that I didn't have their unlisted phone number. I had two or three drinks to muster up the courage to meet them at the door and explain what had happened, but when I saw them pulling in the drive, I totally lost my nerve and told Jeep, "We're playing a game. We're going outside and hiding under the house."

"We play?" asked little Jeep with the pixie haircut.

"Come on with Daddy," I said, picking her up and heading out the back door. We had no basement, but there was a large crawl space under the house, large enough for Jeep and me to hide. "Shhh-h-h, we can't talk, okay?" Though only two, she seemed to get it, and put her hand over her mouth.

There was ringing and knocking, knocking and hollering, and then I could hear them walking through the house. I was wondering if they would ever leave, then heard a police siren. Dan, a retired Air Force officer and a very take-charge type of guy, was concerned because my car was there and the house was unlocked. He suspected foul play. I can think of no moment in my life more humiliating than being discovered by a search party, having a policeman's flashlight shining on me and little Jeep, crouched down underneath the back of our house, sheepishly looking up at the cop and Dan and Annie Holder. The crazy Braddocks' bad reputation was no longer confined to Whispering Hills Drive but now spread through the entire area.

This was about the time when I learned that we didn't have a bank balance of several thousand dollars, as I had thought, but *zero*. At first I believed the bank had screwed up, then I suspected forgery, but after several meetings at the bank, all roads led to Rome, and all fingers pointed to the other person on the joint account, my wife. Sue's first explanation was that she took the money out of the bank and buried it but had amnesia and couldn't remember where it was.

"You're not *that* crazy, and I'm not crazy enough to *believe* that you are," I told her.

She took my hand, gave me that sad little smile and spoke softly, as she did whenever she wanted to open up her heart to me—or give the *impression* that she was opening up her heart to me. She talked about her shopping trips with Curly's wife, Bernice, and Jackie Peters, wife of Ben Peters who the year before had enjoyed a huge Eddy Arnold crossover hit. "It just made me feel so bad, them being able to afford all those nice clothes. I wanted to have nice things too. Honest, I didn't realize I was spending that much money."

This was coming from the woman who sometimes beat up on me and kicked me between the legs (and when drinking, sometimes I would slap her back), but I was always a sucker for atonement and regrets. When someone is mean and yells at me, I'll yell right back, but when someone apologizes, I don't know what to do but accept it. So even though I wasn't sure that her wardrobe was worth several thousand dollars, I let it go. I went to Tree and got an advance on the forthcoming "D-I-V-O-R-C-E" money, though I was already into them for a substantial sum. I would never again have a joint checking account with anyone.

When I look back at old home movies, I see a very attractive young woman with a sexy body, but there was so much bad energy between us back then that I didn't see her that way at the time. I think it was mutual. Intimacy between us became rarer and rarer. But I remained faithful, and I assumed she was doing the same. There was one time I was tempted, and if the door had been open I think I would have run right through it.

One night, with record in hand, I went to radio station WSM, to Ralph Emery's show, *Opry Star Spotlight*. There I met someone who I thought was the most beautiful girl I had ever seen. Her name was Cheryl Poole, a twenty-one year-old singer from Tyler, Texas. She had long dark hair and beautiful brown eyes. We talked for a long time, and I was thunderstruck. I was never around her again. I later heard she was seeing Roger Miller in California, and I once saw her on TV singing "D-I-V-O-R-C-E," though she was barely old enough to be singing about a four-year-old son. I would fantasize about her and dream about her for a long time to come.

I was unhappy in my marriage, and just as unhappy about my receding hairline. I heard about a method of hair replacement used by African Americans called *wefting*. "Wefts" of hair were woven into your own hair. I made an appointment with a Mrs. Gorman in Atlanta, and was very pleased with the results: it actually looked like I had a full head of hair. But I knew this would work only as long as I had something there to weave the wefts into.

Nineteen sixty-eight is a year that will resonate as long as there are history books and history channels. There were the assassinations of Martin Luther King and Bobby Kennedy, the race riots in America's big cities, and the anti-war riots at the Democratic National Convention in Chicago. President Lyndon Johnson, who earlier in his term persuaded Congress to pass an unprecedented amount of major social legislation, by 1968 had fallen into disfavor because of his role in the war in Vietnam. America turned against its pro-war Democratic president, a Texan, just as it would turn against a Republican president from Texas forty years later for his support of an unpopular war.

In the 1968 presidential race, America had to choose between Hubert Humphrey—a liberal Democrat who was tainted by Johnson's war, and Richard Nixon—a conservative Republican who didn't say much about the war and was actually drawing some support from the war's most strident opponents (to their everlasting regret). Add to this mix . . . George C. Wallace, a feisty little man, who spoke out angrily against a lot of things but basically was motivated by just one thing: race.

Of all the confessions that I make in this book, this may be the hardest of all: in 1968 I voted for George Wallace for president. He had been elected governor of Alabama in 1962 as a hardcore segregationist, and in the fall of 1968 he would carry several Southern states in his attempt to win enough electoral votes to deny any presidential candidate a majority. That would have thrown the election into the US House of Representatives where he hoped to play the role of kingmaker.

I knew that Wallace attracted riffraff and racists. He was not my hero. One of the reasons I voted for him was simply that he was more conservative than the Democratic or Republican nominees, and I still held on to the tenets of Goldwater conservatism and the Henry David Thoreau motto, "That government is best which governs least." But, regretfully, another reason I voted for him was because of the remaining vestiges of being born and raised in a white-dominated segregated South. Though I had seen some light—I no longer believed in slavery's ugly offspring, racial segregation—I still had not had an epiphany. I needed to learn that to love history, you don't have to live in it. And most of all, I needed to learn that whatever was supposedly noble and honorable about the Old South never found its way to the black people or even the poor white people of the region. "Noble and honorable" was a myth. When I let go of the myth, it was like releasing a helium-filled balloon and watching it disappear into the sky. That would happen about a year later, but in 1968 I voted for George Wallace. You can't take back a vote, but you can denounce it.

George Wallace created an atmosphere that encouraged violence in his state. During the same week that four little black girls were murdered in the 1963 bombing of a Birmingham church, George Wallace's state troopers were busy keeping other little black children out of a Birmingham elementary school. Birmingham became known as "Bombingham," and the image of children being assaulted with fire hoses and attack dogs is forever burned into America's guilty consciousness. Businesses stayed away, which is why states just as Southern—such as Georgia and South Carolina—prospered in the years ahead, and Alabama did not.

The rock & roll band I was with, Big John's Untouchables, was playing a Birmingham venue called Pappy's Club throughout most of that troubled summer of 1963. Though we were appalled by the violence, not a one of us had much sympathy for the Civil Rights movement. In time, the attitudes of so many of us white Southerners would change, and in fact George Wallace himself would eventually apologize to all African Americans for his segregationist days, graciously acknowledging that he had been wrong. Alabama isn't the only state with a checkered history. A new study of lynching in the South from 1882–1930 has found that blacks were more likely to be lynched in . . . Mississippi? Surprisingly, no, but in my home state of Florida, which led the nation in the most lynchings per capita. I think of this memoir as a view of the world through my eyes as I share what was going on around me and how I was affected by it. My last rebel yell, in 1968, is a part of that.

I am also guilty of committing the musical equivalent of voting for Wallace. Curly Putman informed me that John Wayne was interested in recording a patriotic song. "Why don't *we* write him one," Curly suggested. We wrote a spoken-word piece that we titled "Ballad of Two Brothers," in which one brother goes to Vietnam, and the other is a student demonstrator against the war. We threw every bad stereotype imaginable into this recitation piece, then Buddy Killen came into Curly's office and threw in some more. This was possibly the most pro-Vietnam War song ever written. Autry Inman, a marginally successful country singer in the early 1950s and a struggling songwriter in the 1960s, ran across our demo and took it to Billy Sherrill, who was not only a top producer but the head of Epic Records in Nashville. Billy's friend and co-writer Glenn Sutton agreed to cut a record of it on Autry, and did. I was there at the session, and it came off well. Billy was helping out, conducting the musicians at the end of the piece where the psychedelic music slowed down and segued into "The Battle Hymn of the Republic." Two days later, Inman stormed into Tree and told Buddy that Glenn Sutton was taking his voice *off* of the tracks and replacing it with the voice of Bob Luman, a more successful and contemporary singer.

"Bob Luman's down there in the studio right now. They're puttin' *his* voice on it!"

"Well, Autry, I hate that," said Buddy in his Southern Bullwinkle voice, "but there's nothing much we can do about it."

"There damn sure *is* something *you* can do about it. When you first came to Nashville and didn't know anybody, I took you in and fed you and let you live at my house. By God, go over there and tell them it's my goddamned record, not Bob Luman's!"

Buddy did exactly that. Sherrill and Sutton agreed to issue the record in Autry's name, but they kept Bob Luman's voice on as the soldier, and Autry's as the hippie protester. Autry was a good singer and writer but his talking voice was that of a nasal, country-accented forty-year-old man. To hear him say things like "out of sight," "baby, I'm beat" and "I'm sorry, Dad, but this God-and-country bit just isn't my bag" was downright comical. He sounded like anything but a college-age hippie.

The record was released in the late fall and made the *Cash Box* country Top Five and got well up into the pop charts. From the beginning, I thought it was not a very good piece of material, and by the time it reached its peak, I was already having a change of heart about Vietnam. The song would eventually win a BMI Award (for heavy radio performance) which I would hang on the *inside* of a closet door. I eventually had my name officially removed from the song, leaving Curly and Buddy's names as the writers.

It had been a good year. Besides "D-I-V-O-R-C-E" and "Ballad of Two

Brothers," there were a couple of fairly big ones by a guy Buddy produced named Jack Reno. The new year, 1969, started out with "Joe and Mabel's 12th Street Bar and Grill" by Nat Stuckey, and with my biggest record as an artist, "The Girls in Country Music," which was about as bad as the title suggests.

Looking at old home movies from this era, one sees on the surface a happy family: a smiling guy with a full head of hair, a pretty and petite blonde wife, an adorable little girl with a pixie haircut, and a comical basset hound (Cleo) chasing two cats up the tall fort-like wooden fence that barricaded our maple-shaded back yard. The movies would not show Sue and me screaming at each other as the animals scattered and little Jeep covered up her ears.

So we had our fun, and we had our horrors. Our imaginary characters didn't show up very often, except for Homercow, whom Jeep got a kick out of. It wasn't a good marriage, but I would never regret it, because from this union came the most wonderful daughter that one could ask for. Had I known about the alcoholism and violence in Sue's childhood, maybe I would have been more understanding and sympathetic. She certainly wasn't all bad; she loved Jeep very much, and she was witty, funny, could be quite charming, and she was extremely bright. And good looking. *I* was surely no prize. Perhaps because of her alcoholic parents, Sue drank very little. But I drank more and more, often came home late, and was obnoxiously silly when drinking in public. And I was too protective, in a controlling kind of way, insisting that she not drive outside a certain area because I was afraid if she crossed busy Nolensville Road she might be in an accident. My guess is that we loved each other, but were not very much *in love*. We definitely got on each other's nerves. But still, there was this facade.

One morning I woke up a lot earlier than usual, and walked into the kitchen where Sue was talking on the phone, a wall phone, and she was standing there with her back to me, talking to a girlfriend. She had no idea that I was anywhere in the world but in bed, sound asleep. What I overheard would set in motion the wheels that would eventually change our lives forever.

4

CHEATIN' SONGS

Sue wasn't exactly speaking *sotto voce* as I stumbled into the kitchen all sleepy-eyed that morning in 1969. Neither was she shouting into the phone, but she didn't seem to be taking a lot of precaution—after all, she had her back to me, and she wasn't facing the hallway and master bedroom where she could have spotted me as I approached. Apparently this was not the first such conversation she had had, and she was pretty confident that she could count on me to be sound asleep at that time of morning. There was a conspiratorial tone to her voice as she talked to some confidante—possibly someone I had never met.

"He took off in his patrol car, peeling rubber all over the parking lot," she said into the receiver. "I just stood there dumbfounded for several minutes, then here he comes back again. *God*, I was glad to see him! I couldn't stand him being mad at me."

In just those few words, it was obvious that Sue was having an affair with a cop—either a Metro Nashville police officer or a Tennessee State Trooper. Apparently this was taking place about a mile away off Nolensville Road at Harding Mall, sometimes called "hardly a mall." She had girlfriends I barely knew who worked at a hair salon there. If I had been smart or cool, I could have quietly stood there in the kitchen and let the whole story unfold, but I was too emotional and couldn't stand it any longer.

"Okay, what the fuck's *going on* here?"

Sue hurriedly told her friend that she had to go and hung up. Trying out one excuse after another, she finally settled on an admission of a "flirtation" but assured me that it had gone no further than that and vowed to stop seeing the guy immediately. I knew from experience that her word didn't mean much. But being dishonest is one thing; committing adultery is another—I wasn't expecting it, and I was shocked and saddened. Had she made a serious effort to seek my forgiveness, I think it would have been my nature to give it, especially to keep the family together. But later that day when I called her from Music Row, she turned icy cold and told me she didn't even care if I came home. I told her I wanted to speak to Jeep and was told, "She doesn't want to talk to you. She's busy." She was talking about the light of my life, the little buddy who often went to Tree Publishing Company with me, tagging along behind me—the wee angel who loved to sing with me, belting out, "Who's afraid of da big bad woosh, da big bad woosh, da big bad woosh." I was upset and paranoid enough to believe that "Daddy's lil' gull," who was nearly three years old, didn't love me anymore. I wanted to die.

Before driving home to Whispering Hills Drive, I headed out of town, down to neighboring Williamson County. A couple of miles to the south of the town of Brentwood stood an extremely tall hill—almost a mountain—an area that has long since been covered with assorted "McMansions" on two-acre tracts. But in those days it was isolated and uninhabited and my favorite place to go to collect my thoughts. I turned off the main road and drove to the top of the steep grade.

I got out of the car and found a nice soft, grassy place to sit down, meditating beneath the towering pines and birches. I wasn't madly in love with Sue but had loved her as a family member and, though tempted, had never run around on her. I won't say that all my love for her disappeared that day, but all trust and respect was buried like a dead animal high on that hilltop beneath the trees. Now my main concern—I was horrified at the prospect—was losing little Jeep or her love. Sue, or anyone else who threatened a rift between that child and me, was the enemy. Worse than committing adultery, even worse than turning a cold shoulder after making me feel so vulnerable, was her cruel attempt to make me feel that my child was turning against me.

After about fifteen or twenty minutes of calmly looking down at the beautiful rolling hills and Highway 31—the road that had brought me to town a few years before—a feeling of peace and serenity came over me. As I drove down the slope, my mind was made up about several things. I knew Jeep wasn't going to stop loving me overnight, and I wasn't going to let Sue make me think otherwise. I would not leave the marriage until I knew that my little girl was too old to be brainwashed and turned against me. And the only way my male ego would survive this blow would be to get *revenge*. I was going to hop into bed with some woman—*any* woman—as soon as possible.

When I got home I hugged Sue with my arm (if not my heart) and that's about what I got in return. When I tucked Jeep into bed, she was more precious to me than ever before. "I love oou, Dick Duck Daddy," she said, using her almost-three name for me.

The next morning I was scheduled to go to Atlanta for the periodic tightening of the tapestry of wefts that were woven through my diminishing hair. The beauty salon proprietress who did this, Mrs. Gorman, was a regal African American woman of middle age, possessing a keen intellect and a great sense of humor. My visits to her were always a delight. When she got through with my hair, I wrote her a check and bade her goodbye. Her next customer came in—an attractive young black woman who was attending a nearby college. I shook hands with her as we were introduced, and as I left I said, "I appreciate it, Mrs. Gorman." As I hit the front door, I realized that I had left my briefcase in a chair outside the enclosure where I had just had my "hair" tightened. As I picked up my attaché, I could hear the young woman on the other side of the thin wood partition doing an imitation of me. "Oh, I *'preciate* it Miz Gorman, I *'preciate* it. That's so cute, he sounds like Andy Griffith." We white Southerners used to imitate black dialect, never realizing that blacks were poking fun at *our* honky accents.

That night I was staying at the Atlanta American Hotel, hell bent and determined to find female companionship. I took a shower, put on some sporty clothes, and took the elevator down to the hotel lounge. All I could see were couples. Then I was approached by two African American females, a big-boned smiley one and a gorgeous young unsmiling one, with much emphasis on young, probably about twenty years old. It didn't take me long to realize that the older, larger woman was the business agent for the younger, smaller one. Never before had I paid for sex—at least not directly—but I was a man on a mission. It was 9:00 p.m., and I didn't want to run around Atlanta looking for women. I had a demon to kill, and the sooner the better. Twenty dollars was a lot of money then, but I didn't bat an eye as I said, "Let's go."

This seemed to be a good combination, Denese for friendly conversation and her little friend Ruth for sexual pleasure. Denese sat down in a chair and turned on the TV as I led Ruth to bed and gently undressed her. Everything was going great until we had been at it for about five minutes. Ruth looked up at me and uttered the first words out of her mouth since we'd met. Noticing my nervous tic, from my Tourette's syndrome, she asked, "How come you blink yo' eyes?" The effect was instantaneous. It was as if a drill sergeant had told my good soldier, "At ease, private." But that was okay. I had gotten my revenge. Now I was ready to go back to Nashville and my family, to coexist with Sue the best I could.

One of the most easygoing people I ever knew—and one of the most talented—was a tall, good-looking man who did janitor work at Columbia studio. He was a sweetheart of a guy and had bright blue eyes that twinkled with curiosity. About four years older than I, he had been a Rhodes scholar and an army captain, but decided to come to Nashville, start at the bottom, and try his luck. Whenever I demoed my songs at Columbia, he would often put down his push broom and ask me questions about songwriting. Women up and down Music Row were gaga about the guy, and when he started having some success with songs he'd written, there was talk about him getting a recording deal. I remember telling someone that he would never make it unless he changed his name, because I felt it was a name that no one would be able to remember: Kris Kristofferson.

One day when Kris was at Tree, he asked if I would listen to a new song he had written. I told him sure. We went into a vacant office where he took his guitar out of the case and sat behind a wooden desk as I sat across from him on a couch. I listened to him sing this majestic story ballad in his gravelly voice. When he finished he asked, "Well, whaddaya think?"

"I think it's a really good song," I said, "but I don't know if it's commercial. I don't know who would record it." Ray Stevens did, and so did Johnny Cash, who had a big hit with it. It was called "Sunday Morning Coming Down."

Song ideas come from everywhere, and I doubt that I would have ever written a song about man landing on the moon if not for my publisher. I went with my family on a weekend trip to the Smoky Mountains. On the way home I was playing dashboard drums to the Beatles' "Get Back" which was blasting from the car radio, when Sue suggested that we stop off at a motel and watch live on TV Apollo 11's moon landing and the historic walk of the astronauts. It was July 20, 1969, which also happened to be our fifth wedding anniversary. When we got back to Nashville, Jack Stapp told me that he had gotten word from a friend at NBC-TV that the network's nightly news program—the top-rated *Huntley-Brinkley Report*—would include a segment on songs from Nashville about the moon landing. "Bobby boy," Jack said, "if you can write a moon song and be here tomorrow morning at 5 a.m., I can get you on network TV." They would be taping the piece at Tree's little studio in the back of the building.

I sat down at the piano in the studio, fooled around for a few minutes, and came up with a dumb little thing that I ran by Jack. It was very unusual to play a new song for Jack Stapp instead of Buddy Killen, but this was a very unusual situation because Jack had strong connections with the networks in New York. The song went:

> Oh the moon will never be the same again
> I'm proud of what my country's done, please don't misunderstand
> But the days of moon and June and spoon are gone for good my friend
> And the moon will never be the same again

"I love it, Bobby boy. Be here at five o'clock tomorrow morning."

Sue and I had agreed to go out with Curly and Bernice Putman that night. After dinner at a place called the Jolly Ox, we went to see a show at the night club that sat atop the King of the Road Hotel. I proceeded to get very, very drunk. I have a vague recollection of running down Whispering Hills Drive in the wee hours of the morning, wearing nothing but a necktie, and Sue running after me, screaming, "Stop, you damned fool, you have to sing on the *Huntley-Brinkley* show." I managed to somehow get to Tree by 5 a.m., still drunk.

At 5:30 p.m. we turned on the *Huntley-Brinkley Report*. For the end-of-the-show story, there they were—the country songwriters in Nashville who had written songs about man walking on the moon. First came a guy singing "I'm Gonna Build Me a Honky-Tonk on the Moon," then another, singing

"Big Old Moon Baby Me." Finally there was this very relaxed, somewhat disheveled young man playing a piano and singing, "The Moon Will Never Be the Same Again." As they cut away from me, on came wry David Brinkley in Washington, then solemn Chet Huntley in New York, delivering their routine goodnights to each other. Chuckling, Brinkley said, "Goodnight Chet." Huntley, with a look of utter disgust, sighed and said very quickly "Goodnight David."

There were a lot of interesting perks that came with writing for a well-connected publishing company. Buddy gave me the opportunity to do some collaborating—and have a few beers—with Jack Palance, famous as a bad guy in 1950s western movies, and a future Oscar-winner for 1991's *City Slickers*. In real life, Jack was definitely a good guy.

It was a lazy, hazy summer in my little corner of Music Row. Curly had started his own publishing company, Green Grass Music. The songplugger who replaced him, Hap Wilson, was a good-natured old Music Row fixture, but not as effective at getting my songs cut. My main activity was making my final record for MGM: "The Trash Man."

It was the summer of '69. Johnny Cash—already a legendary music veteran and still in his thirties—was hotter than ever with his own network TV show and a big hit, "A Boy Named Sue" playing on both country and pop radio. The hottest rockers were the Rolling Stones with "Honky Tonk Women." The most talked-about movie was the cult favorite *Easy Rider*, and the most talked-about crimes were the grisly murders committed in Los Angeles by the followers of Charles Manson.

As soon as Jeep had performed in her summer dance recital—the first of many that she would be in over the years—the family embarked on a long car trip that took us first to Florida before heading north. While half a million hippies were converging on Woodstock in upstate New York, we were taking a Gray Line tour down in Manhattan. When we got back home and had our movies processed, Sue was furious when she realized that the eye of my camera couldn't stay off a lovely young Chinese woman to whom I had given more frame time than St. Patrick's Cathedral, the Empire State Building, or the Statue of Liberty.

It was a very uneasy truce between us; a cold war that often erupted in battle. In her mind, I was playing around with every female who worked at Tree. One night we went out to dinner with a couple, and when Sue thought the young woman and I had been engaged in too much conversation, she exploded, pounded the table with her fist, then jumped up and said she was taking a cab home. In truth, except for the tit-for-tat in Atlanta, I didn't run around at all. I was taking her at her word that it was over between her and her policeman boyfriend. But something had changed in us both. I didn't feel nearly as close, and I think she was just plain mad that she had been found out. So I had forgiven her but not really, and she was sorry but not really.

The war of the Braddocks was nothing compared to the war in Vietnam, the one that I missed. Six years earlier, a letter from a psychiatrist citing my mental instability—due to amphetamine overdose—had kept me out of military service. When the war started going full force in 1965, I fully supported it but felt guilty and hypocritical because I was sitting it out. I remained strongly pro-war until June of 1969 when a *Life* magazine edition featured the week's war dead, all 242 of them, with individual pictures like a high school yearbook. It put a human face on the war and impacted me greatly. Then when the story broke in November that, in March 1968, American soldiers had been ordered to murder several hundred unarmed Vietnamese citizens—many of them women and children—that did it for me. The infamous My Lai Massacre turned me totally against the war.

And there was another war going on, deep down in my soul. On one side was the part of me that believed the Bible was the inspired word of God, the roadmap to Heaven. On the other side was the part of me that was constantly asking why, why, *why*! *Why* did the Bible indicate that the world was only a few thousand years old, depicting modern-day animals but ignoring the prehistoric ones (which weren't uncovered and discovered until the nineteenth century)? *Why* did the Bible teach that God invented the rainbow as a sign that there would be no more great floods, when any kid could see that spraying a garden hose in the sunlight would create a rainbow? *Why* would God cause people to suddenly start speaking different languages, rendering them unable to understand each other as they attempted to build a tower to Heaven, when surely God would have known that a lack of oxygen would have stopped the men by the time the tower was a mere few thousand feet tall (as though they could possibly have constructed a tower hundreds or thousands or millions of miles tall, or however far up into the sky that Heaven was supposed to be)? *Why* did the Bible speak of angels at the four corners of the earth, when God the creator would have known that his own world was round? *Why* did God say "I the Lord thy God am a *jealous* God?"—*why* would God, surely much more evolved than we are, be jealous? *Why* would He, of a higher moral order than the rest of us, stoop even lower than Hitler and burn people alive, not for just a little while, but forever? I was torn between believing in a loving God who exceeded earthly mortals in every way, and God the big, jealous baby who made people scream and writhe in hideous pain, not for hundreds or thousands or millions of years, but forever, just because he had gotten his ego bruised. I agonized over it more and more.

In the midst of this personal turmoil, early in 1970, I wrote a song that painted a picture of a soldier in Vietnam seeing a flashing light, a lady in Belfast asking her neighbor, "Missus Clancey, what was *that*?" In Memphis, Tennessee, a teacher raised the window closest to the river; the children in her classroom swore they heard a choir singing down the street. "In Washington DC a White House secretary's lips began to quiver . . . the president just put aside his papers and rose quickly to his feet." Then the protagonist says, "I lay in a cheap motel in the arms of someone else's woman when a loud explosion rocked the room and turned the morning into night. I jumped out of bed and ran into the street with hardly any clothes on. As the sky lit up my heart stood still and I could feel my face turn white."

> *All at once the clouds rolled back and there*
> *stood Jesus Christ in all his glory*
> *And I realized the saddest eyes I'd ever seen were looking straight at me*
> *I guess I was awakened by the penetrating sound of my own screaming*
> *It didn't take me long to stumble out of bed and fall down on my knees*
> *As tears rolled down my face I said "Dear God,*
> *I'm thankful I was only dreaming*
> *And if I never go to hell Lord, it's because you scared it out of me"*

When I had finished the song, I did something I didn't typically do: I sat there at my piano and cried like a baby. I'm not sure if it was because I thought I had written a great song, or because I was overcome with love for Jesus, or if I knew this was my swan song to religion as I had known it. But all that little-boy fear in me—all those times as a child that I lay in bed scared to death that Jesus would come in the night, always relieved to wake up and see the light of the next morning—it all exploded in my psyche in one gigantic spiritual orgasm. I named the song "Revelation." Buddy Killen twisted Billy Sherrill's arm and talked him into recording it on me and putting it out on Columbia. Several artists, from Waylon Jennings shortly thereafter to Joe Nichols thirty-five years later, would record it.

I had been having what may not *seem* like a nightmare, but to me it was. For weeks, almost every night, I dreamed there were two full moons shining in the sky, and I would wake up in a cold sweat. Then, after writing "Revelation," I dreamed again of the two moons, only this time they slowly melded together, merged into one. The fusion of the two moons gave me great relief, and I would never have the dual moon dream again. The conflict was over. I woke up at peace and knew that I was changed forever. My belief in God would remain strong, but not based on fear.

One day I was planning to take Jeep to a movie but couldn't find my billfold. I got down on my knees to look behind the living room couch and noticed a bulge in the carpet and what appeared to be the edge of an envelope poking out. I reached inside the carpet and pulled out approximately two dozen letters, all addressed to Sue.

"Jeepy, Daddy's going to lie down for a little while," I said. "I promise we'll go to the movie later." I no longer slept in the master bedroom with Sue, but in a little hideaway off my music room, next to our swimming pool. I locked the door and dove into the letters.

They were all postmarked Birmingham, Alabama. Most of her mail was from a Rex Wordsworth, whom I gathered was an intern at a Birmingham hospital. While a lot of his dispatches were newsy, it was undeniable that he and Sue were lovers and that he had to be as secretive as she; so my assumption was that he had a wife. Sue was having an affair with the guy, but she wasn't even being faithful to *him*. There were three letters from a man who was a deputy with the Jefferson County Sheriff's Department, making references to the times he had been with Sue and his deputy buddy had been with Darlene, a Nashville girl who Sue had started running around with. My wife was having affairs with men that little boys wanted to be when they grew up: policemen, doctors—was there also a fireman or cowboy or astronaut? Now I knew why Sue had been going to Alabama so often "to see her mother." The young doctor and Sue seemed to be having a very serious love affair, but her relationship with the deputy seemed to be just sexual high jinks.

I told Sue that something urgent had come up that I needed to discuss with her. Our part-time African American housekeeper, Jennie Lake, had just arrived, so I asked Jennie to play with Jeep in the backyard while I had a talk with her mother. Sue was worried.

When we walked back into the house, I said, "Sit down."

"What in the world is going on?" she asked.

"I w-want you to know that I've f-found your letters."

"What letters?"

"Come on."

After a few seconds of silence she said, "Those are my letters, by God, and I want them back! *Where are they?*" she demanded, raising her voice.

"Well, I'm a better hider than you are. You'll get those letters back when you sign this paper I've made up for you."

I WAS THE FIRST IN THIS MARRIAGE TO COMMIT ADULTERY, AND SHOULD ROBERT V. BRADDOCK AND I EVER DECIDE TO SEPARATE OR DIVORCE, I WILL NEVER MAKE ANY ATTEMPT TO TAKE OUR DAUGHTER, LAUREN ANESE BRADDOCK, AWAY FROM HER FATHER.

NANCY SUE RHODES BRADDOCK
MAY 3, 1970

"Sign this statement and the letters are yours," I said. "If you don't sign it, the letters are mine, and I have no intentions of keeping them all to myself." I had her over a barrel. Expressionless, with no sign of emotion, she took the paper, found a pen, and signed it. I went to my music room to get the letters. She had hurt me for one very bad day the year before but was incapable of hurting me ever again. Looking back from another century, I think of her as an unstable, emotionally scarred person rather than a bad one, and I obviously didn't make her very happy; but at that moment I was thinking of her as the enemy—and thoroughly amoral. I would do anything necessary to protect myself and to keep from losing my daughter. So with the door locked behind me, I pulled the letters from the pocket of an old bathrobe way back in my clothing closet, all except for two from the young doctor and one from her good-ol'-boy cop, whom I would refer to as "Deputy Dawg." The next morning I would put these in a safe deposit box.

Sue's commentary ran the gamut. She claimed that the letters were an exaggeration, and she had never actually been unfaithful to me, which I didn't believe at all. When she said the cop meant nothing but she *had* gotten close to Rex—however, she was willing to give him up—I was skeptical. When she suggested, "Let's have an open marriage," I told her that might be a good idea and that I needed to get away and think things over.

I knew who I wanted to have an affair with. Seven years before, when I was playing with Big John's Untouchables in Orlando, there had been a strong mutual attraction with a girl named Charlotte Jones. Charlotte then had a very jealous husband, so I got involved with someone else. But I never forgot Charlotte—the attraction and the compatibility. She was intelligent, sophisticated, very funny, and looked like Vivien Leigh as Scarlett O'Hara, with Bette Davis eyes. A Florida hometown friend, Stanley Cox, had mentioned to me the last time I saw him that she was remarried and had become Charlotte Taylor, but she wasn't very happy. I called Stan and asked him to see if she would be interested in hooking up with me for lunch sometime in a couple of weeks. He called back and told me she said yes. He gave me her work number. I called her and we had a great conversation. We worked up an elaborate plan for meeting at her girlfriend's house.

I drove down to Florida to my parents' home, nervous with anticipation. I put on a nice blazer. I had just recently taken my first baby step into having long hair by combing my hair down over the tip top of my ears. I drove to Lakeland, the metropolis of my native Polk County, and found the address. As I was ringing the doorbell, I recalled Charlotte's sensuous mouth, which always bore just a hint of a smile; her cute little ears, her dark hair, big blue eyes, creamy complexion, and a tiny smattering of freckles across her nose. I wondered if she was still a knockout. She came to the door, and the only significant change I saw from age twenty-two to age twenty-nine was that she had developed some very large breasts.

"Well hello," she said in her soft, low voice, "you look very Nashville." I didn't know what that meant, but she was smiling so I took it as a compliment. We drove thirty miles west to Tampa's old Latin community, Ybor City, which was settled in the 1890s by people who came there to make cigars. We went to a great old restaurant, Los Novadades, which had beautiful mosaic tiles on the walls and specialized in Old World Spanish and New World Cuban cuisine. We had a great time eating yellow rice and chicken, drinking sangria, catching up, making each other laugh, kissing, then running through a thundershower to my car. I took her to a motel—though she said we weren't going to have sex, and she kept her word. I saw her again the next night (she had red braided ribbons in her hair), and I took her to a motel where she once again said she couldn't have sex with me.

I drove back to Nashville not in love with Charlotte, but "in lust" with her. I was painfully attracted. I liked her a lot, as I had years before. She was a great conversationalist, and no subject—or word—was taboo. But she wasn't an easy make.

The first night I was home, I wanted to tell Sue—who had, after all, suggested an open marriage—that I was going to be having an affair. This was very important to me. I had a strange moral creed: if someone else were unfaithful to be with me, that was between her and her husband or significant other, but *I* would not be unfaithful to someone I was committed to. I felt there was no longer any commitment between us—sex with Sue had practically become a thing of the past. There was someone I wanted to be with, and I didn't want there to be any deceit.

"There's nothing physical between you and me anymore; you've been going elsewhere for that. So I just want you to know that I'm going to be seeing somebody from time to time," I announced.

"You are *not* going to have a fucking affair, by God," she screamed, slapping and kicking.

"But *you* . . ."

"You sonofabitch!" she screamed.

It didn't matter about *her* affairs. She was totally devoid of any sense of fair play. I had Sue's signed confession, so why did I let her bully me so? My rationale was that I wanted to keep the family together if possible, for Jeep's sake. So even though Sue had at least a couple of boyfriends, I could see that I was going to have to sneak around to be with Charlotte. The next day, I went to the downtown post office and rented a box.

Charlotte was the ultimate pen pal. Her letters were clever, often hilarious. We both drew cartoons (hers were better because she was a real artist) and we devised a code to write the most confidential things. We joked that we were like a couple of spies. We met in Atlanta a few weeks later (my excuse: getting my hair wefted), and I met her down in Florida again a few weeks after that (excuse: going down to visit the folks).

I was in a happy mood on my way to the Nashville airport to pick her up in late November. I had a good record out for the first time in a year-and-a-half, "Something to Brag About" by Charlie Louvin and Melba Montgomery. The song seemed to be symbolic. At the age of thirty, I think we both crossed a threshold. I learned something I should have known before: the best sex you can have is when you focus on how good it is for your partner. Charlotte too experienced something that she had never had before.

I was attracted to her, on a scale of one to ten, a ten. I loved her just

Sue, Jeep, my mom, and me in Auburndale, Florida, June 1970

enough that being with her made me smile all over, but it was not that crazy, helpless, out-of-control love. That's not what I needed. It was definitely the sanest relationship I had ever been in: great sex without losing my mind.

In early 1971, Jack Stapp and Buddy Killen hired two new songpluggers at Tree. One was Larry Henley, a short, blond-headed guy in his early thirties, formerly a member of the NewBeats of 1964 "Bread and Butter" fame. It was Larry's high falsetto that sang "I like bread and butter, I like toast and jam." The other new plugger was Johnny Slate, a guy who was as tall as Larry Henley was short. Buddy Killen took Johnny over to meet impish producer genius, Billy Sherrill. Billy, suspecting that the new janitor at Columbia had been stealing his liquor, had filled a liquor bottle with cleaning fluid earlier that day and apparently had forgotten about it, because after a few minutes of late-afternoon socializing, the toxic chemicals inadvertently ended up in the stomach of Johnny Slate. Sherrill and Killen were horrified, but probably not as horrified as Slate, as they rushed him to the emergency room.

This was around the time that I met Michael Kosser. We struck up a conversation in the Tree reception area one afternoon. He was a year younger than I, a New Yorker whose background had included being an army lieutenant, a newspaper reporter, and a law school student. He came to Nashville by way of Chicago, where he had been singing in a country bar. Kosser had the wild and wooly Dylanesque hair that sometimes adorned young Jewish heads, often referred to as an "Isro" (rather than an "Afro"). He knew my name and my catalog. I told him a tasteless joke. We became fast friends and began a decades-long routine of long phone conversations about current politics and old music. (Sue, with her disdain for the ones she thought of as my less famous friends, accused Kosser and me of being "queer" for each other because we talked on the phone a lot.) I thought he was a political junkie and music hound like me. The fact was, he had other people with whom he carried on long conversations about other topics, with the same enthusiasm; subjects out of my area of expertise such as military science, economics, and spectator sports, particularly baseball. I won't call him the wisest man I've ever known, but one of the most intelligent and definitely the most well-rounded and well-informed. He went back to Chicago shortly after we met and returned to Nashville with a wife. Curly signed him to Green Grass Music where he wrote a few hits, but he would ultimately make his mark as a journalist and author.

Jeep and I sometimes went to the Kossers' apartment for homemade pizza. Mike and I would talk politics while his wife, Carolyn, played with Jeep. Though Sue, Jeep, and I often did things together—like picnics with the dog by a creek in the country or kiddie rides at a place called Fair Park—more and more, Daddy's little girl was Daddy's little companion about town. She went with me to Tree, where she lit up the place like a ball of sunshine, and to movies, where she whispered a hundred questions. In her 2009 childbirth memoir *A Journey to the Son*, a grownup Lauren/Jeep would look back at these days with her daddy:

> *My daddy, the "piano player," wore a hairpiece at the time, smelled of Old Spice cologne, chain-smoked Kent cigarettes and chain-chewed speckled Certs breath mints. Sometimes there was the added sweet aroma of Bacardi rum and Coke. My dance teachers said that he had "bedroom eyes" ("What does that mean?" I wondered). Like his piano, the timbre of his personality resonated throughout the house. There were storms when his combs,* TV Guides, *and peace were lost (I would counter his "I'm going to FIRE that damn maid!" with "Please Daddy, don't put Jennie on fire!"), then calm when they were found. He was fun and funny, though, and did "Do-Things" with me—our term for our special time together before bed when we would read books or play games or draw pictures. We were nocturnal buddies; he would let me hear the intro of the Johnny Carson theme music and at "Here's Johnny" send me off to bed. He was everything to me.*

Sometimes Jeep accompanied me to the big post office downtown, where I checked my long-distance-relationship box for mail. Sue and I learned about each other's post offices from Jeep's chatter. I already knew about Sue's PO box, of course, and she must have suspected that I had one, too, but it made her angry at me anyway. One day she walked into the downtown post office and caught me red-handed, standing by my box reading a letter from Charlotte. She started screaming and crying, attracting a lot of attention in the busy facility.

Sue and I often went our separate ways—she to concerts and parties with girlfriends, I to the bars around Music Row or an occasional stock car race. On March 8, 1971, I saw one of the great fights of the century on closed-circuit TV—the contest between two undefeated heavyweight champions, Muhammad Ali and Joe Frazier. I don't deny that boxing is barbaric or even that it should be banned, but in those days I liked it a lot. The event was shown on big screens in selected theaters and auditoriums across America, and the only venue in Nashville that had any seats left was Tennessee State University, a largely black institution. My two friends and I were among the very few white people there. Though both Ali and Frazier were black, Ali was the hero of most African Americans, many of whom called Frazier the "white man's champion." There was a lot of anger in the building when Frazier won in a closely matched bout, and we could feel the hostility as we calmly but quickly made our way to the front door, avoiding eye contact with other people as much as possible. When I got home, Sue asked me if I had gotten any dirty looks. I told her that I had in fact gotten some dirty *words* from a guy in the crowd, to whom I had responded, "Don't be mad at me, I was bettin' on Ali," which was the truth.

One time when Sue knew I was "getting away" to Atlanta for about three days, she was uncharacteristically kind, considering the circumstances, and even offered to pack my clothes that I had laid out on the bed. I thought perhaps she had recently had a nice experience with her boyfriend or was anticipating one; at any rate, I appreciated it.

When I picked up Charlotte in Atlanta, we headed straight for the Airport Hilton where we checked in and hopped into bed, having our great fun and intermittently drinking rum and Coca Cola. Charlotte had taught me, at the age of thirty, the brain-cell-killing joys of smoking marijuana (because of what "speed" had done to me at nineteen, I had resisted any other drugs for years). We had this game we made up in which one of us came up with synonyms for the sounds and syllables of someone's name, and the other had to figure out who the subject was. For instance, she said, "Okay . . . magician, Jamaican for 'man,' and fish egg." I played with it for a while and finally got it, Merlin mon-roe—Marilyn Monroe. Sometimes the slight mispronunciation made it even more fun.

"Okay," I said, "breast, and something a lion jumps through." She was saying "titty hoop," "knocker hoop," then "boob hoop."

"That's it," I confirmed.

"Who's Boob Hoop?" she queried.

"The guy with the ski-jump nose who was in all those movies with Bing Crosby."

When she realized that my subject was Bob Hope, she spewed a mouthful of rum and Coke all over me. Stoned out of our minds, we laughed ourselves even sillier. Every few minutes one of us would say "Boob Hoop" and once more we'd convulse with laughter.

Eventually, I got up and opened my clothes carrier so I could hang up whatever I might wear when we went out for a bite to eat the next day. I then realized why Sue had offered to pack my clothes for me. Instead of the outfits I had chosen to bring, she packed the ugliest mismatches I owned. I had told Charlotte earlier that Sue packed for me. "Oh look," she laughed, "she packed your clown clothes." We decided the joke was on Sue because we spent the whole weekend in bed, calling room service whenever we were hungry. Who needed clothes?

A couple of months later I drove down to Lakeland where I picked up Charlotte and continued southward to Miami Beach. This was long before the days of South Beach—back in the days when the residents were oldsters from New York, and the beach was brownish from oil slicks. But it was a tropical paradise; not the redneck Florida where Charlotte and I were raised. We had great fun.

The first time I called Jeep from Miami Beach, Sue got on the phone crying, begging me to come home. The next time I called, Sue got on the phone screaming at me, *demanding* that I come home. I had recently started keeping a journal and wrote in it, " . . . told Sue that I would come home a day early. This upset Charlotte, but she's a damned sight more tolerant than Sue. We went to Vizcaya Gardens, then saw movie *Summer of '42*." "Drove back to Lakeland, laughing all the way."

When I got home and started to bring my stuff in, Sue looked in the trunk and saw the birthday gifts that Charlotte gave to me. She ripped the pages out of a couple of books, busted a bottle of wine against my rear bumper, and threw a nice silver wine goblet onto the driveway and started stomping up and down on it.

I don't know why I felt a need to qualify the word "love" with Charlotte, but I wrote her a letter in which I stole a line from a Willie Nelson song that I liked. I wrote her, "I love you in my own peculiar way." Two or three days later I got a telegram; it was from Charlotte. The telegram was written in the code that we had devised. After about twenty seconds, I deciphered the code and got her message: "Fuck you in my own peculiar way."

When autumn's first cool touch caused our maple trees to blush as they whispered little secrets in the wind, Sue and I had to face the inevitable. We were badly in debt. Preventive medicine was never administered around the Braddock house; only emergency surgery. It was my idea to sell our house (much improved with a swimming pool and adjoining room, and a big Alamo type fence around the back yard). That would give us money to pay off our two mortgages, the IRS, and recent Tree loans—with enough left over to get by awhile and *rent* something somewhere. That may have been a fairly rational emergency plan—until Sue found the house she wanted us to rent. We were in debt from living beyond our means, and the house she had in mind was on Curtiswood Lane, just a few houses down from the governor's mansion! There were two professors—man and wife—who were going to England for a year, and they wanted to lease their very large stone house, furnished. What they were asking was a lot of money in 1971, but quite reasonable for such a nice, large home. I felt that in order to keep the marriage together for Jeep's sake and to continue seeing Charlotte, it was a good idea to go along with Sue on everything else. I said yes.

The owners must have had family money to afford such a nice house on professors' pay. Their friends who were overseeing our moving in were condescending, and it wasn't always easy bargaining with them about what we could bring in. I didn't feel very much at home in a house we were leasing that was full of other people's furniture, books, and personal effects. Hoping that we would be able to sell our place on Whispering Hills Drive very soon, we moved into this large dwelling where the lights wildly and repeatedly went off and on each time we left—upstairs and down, like a big light show—as though there were ghosts celebrating our being out of their house.

Jeep got one of the highest scores on her "entrance exam" for kindergarten at Franklin Road Academy, a private school. It was so important to me that the family stay together that I cancelled plans for a weekend with Charlotte when Sue threatened to leave me if I left town (and assured me that she and Rex Wordsworth were over). Apparently Rex hadn't gotten the word, because one day I saw some letters poking out of Sue's purse. I removed the epistles from their casings just long enough to see that they were from Rex, and to feel the warmth and smell the smoke. So I called Charlotte and told her I would see her if she could come to Nashville instead of Atlanta. But I would have to be very careful; telling Sue that I knew what she was up to wouldn't work. If I had said, "You're still having an affair, so I am, too," she probably would have been ready to leave. I had a signed confession from her in which she admitted to being the first to commit adultery, and made a pledge that she would not try to take Jeep away from me. Why didn't I just let her go? I must have cared more about her than I wanted to admit. I remember thinking that my career hadn't been going as well as the year before, and for that reason she would be more likely to leave.

Then suddenly from out of nowhere came a big overseas hit, "Did You Ever," that had been a moderate country success for Charlie Louvin and Melba Montgomery earlier in the year. It was inspired by a TV commercial that showed a filling station customer trying to tell the attendant what he wanted, but every time he got out half a sentence, the filling station guy finished it. I thought the ad was pretty funny, so I started the song like this:

(male) *Did you ever?* (female) *Not so much that you could notice*
(male) Could you estimate how many? (female) Eight or nine

(male) *Will you do it anymore?* (female) *As soon as you walk out the door*
(male) *I just wondered, did you ever?* (female) *All the time*

Lee Hazelwood, Nancy Sinatra's producer and sometimes duet partner, heard it on a Los Angeles country station and immediately recorded it as a duet with Nancy. The record did nothing in the United States but exploded suddenly in Britain, becoming a big hit and selling several hundred thousand copies. It was a strange feeling, knowing that I had a big hit going but never hearing it. Nobody in Nashville knew I was hot again except my family, friends, and publisher. Though we still wanted to sell our house across town, this big record took some of the pressure off.

The current crew of pluggers at Tree were not getting many of my songs recorded, but I enjoyed hanging out with them. One night Johnny Slate, Larry Henley, and Curly's songplugger at Green Grass, "Indian Jim" Bowen, threw a party in the huge entertainment room at an apartment complex where one of them lived. This was the biggest and wildest party I had ever been to. There must have been 300 people there. I started out drinking my usual, rum and Coke, then switched to wine. There was a crazy vibe to the gathering from the beginning. Jeannie Seely was there with her husband, songwriting genius Hank Cochran, who had penned her career song, "Don't Touch Me," a few years before. As they slipped into an apartment just off the party room, I could hear them arguing, then Jeannie loudly shouting, "Don't touch me!" as life imitated art. People at the party were getting so drunk that they started sliding off the chairs onto the floor.

I met a girl who was standing off in the corner by herself. She was very pretty, had small features, a sweet smile, and beautiful green eyes. She told me her name was Sue Lawrence and that she was separated from her husband (I would later learn that this was a regular off-and-on pattern for them). She was a twenty-year-old Alabamian who had lived in South Florida since she got married at fifteen, and who spoke in a soft voice with the accentless accent of Miami. Despite her background as a child bride from the rural South, she seemed worldly-wise and very easy to talk to. I liked her. She was there with some guy from Huntsville, Alabama, who was caught up in a big poker game across the crowded room.

Willie Nelson, not yet a superstar but already a legendary songwriter and highly respected singer, was there.

"A Ouija board once told me you were lying in bed in a hotel," I told Willie. "It said you were s-s-staring at the ceiling, thinking 'I'm crazy' and th-that's where the idea for "Crazy" came from," referring to Patsy Cline's most famous song from about ten years earlier.

Willie, not a man of many words, looked at me and said, "Hmmmmm."

"Is that true?" I asked.

"Yeah," he softly said as he nodded.

Willie had some hashish that I smoked, and it was so powerful that it was almost hallucinogenic. On top of the alcohol, it was making me practically crazy. Suddenly deciding that I wanted to go swimming, I ran to the pool, got on the diving board, and was about to dive in.

"Stop," a female voice screamed, "there's no water in there." It was Sue Lawrence. I looked more closely into the bone-dry pool.

"You saved my life," I told her. We continued to talk. "I think I need to go home," I said, remembering that my wife was out for the night and Jeep was with a babysitter.

"You're not able to drive," she said. "Let me drive you, and the guy I'm with can follow us." So that's what we did. She had to stop a couple of times for me to throw up. She ran into a filling station and brought out wet paper towels to wipe my face. When we finally got to Curtiswood Lane, I was too hammered and stoned to know where my house was. Sue Lawrence's friend, fifteen or twenty years before cell phones, had a mobile phone in his car (the kind they had on ships and in presidential limousines). I gave him my number and he got Sue Braddock, who had just gotten home. When he asked for directions, she told him, "Keep the sonofabitch."

About 10:00 a.m. a warm, unfriendly sun rose over an oak tree, waking me up as I lay in the front seat of my car, pulled over to the side of the road a few houses down from where I lived. I was wondering what kind of hell I was going to catch when I got home, and I was also wondering: who was that angel, that pretty Florence Nightingale who saved me from a broken neck in a drained swimming pool, and who wiped drunken puke off my face with Texaco paper towels.

5

THE TACO BELL BUILDING

If you had headed south out of Nashville on Franklin Road on a fall morning in 1971, in sight of traffic humming gently along on the still-new Interstate 65 over to your left, and if you had then hung a right on Curtiswood Lane, driving past the governor's mansion, you would have come to the big leased house where the Braddock family was foolishly living over its head. The stately neighborhood would have been lush with trees: dogwoods, oaks, maples, and elms, leaves ablaze with flaming red and bright yellow. If you had paused at our place, you might have seen our cat Jane chasing squirrels and chipmunks on the leaf-covered lawn. Jeep most likely would have been in kindergarten, her mother probably off to points unknown, and I might have been climbing into my light blue Mercury Marquis for the morning drive to Tree Publishing Company.

I would have turned on the ignition and the radio and pulled out onto Curtiswood, maybe glancing to see if I could spot the new governor, Winfield Dunn, the first Republican to occupy the mansion since the state purchased the property in 1948. Then I would have turned left on Franklin Road, still called Franklin Pike by old-timers—a throwback to the previous century when major routes into Nashville were dirt toll roads called turnpikes. (It was along the Franklin Pike that General John Bell Hood's Confederate Army retreated south in disarray after the Battle of Nashville in 1864.) By the 1920s the road was paved, and around 1930 it became part of US Highway 31, one of three major cross-country routes that intersected at Eighth and Broadway in downtown Nashville.

As I drove north that long-ago morning, watching the leafy, suburban scenery give way to storefronts and stoplights, I might have noticed where Franklin Road became Eighth Avenue South. Then, when I was within sight of the city's skyline (dominated by the L&C Tower), I would have turned left on South Street and driven the remaining few blocks to Music Row.

Tree had just moved into their new location, two blocks north and one block west of the old one. They bought a three-story Spanish mission-style building with arched doorways, balconies, and tile roofing. The place was strikingly different from anything else on Music Row. A few years later, when

The "Taco Bell Building"

the Taco Bell restaurants came to town, Tree's offices would sometimes be referred to as the "Taco Bell Building."

The ground floor was a parking garage that was being replaced with a reception area and writers rooms. The second floor housed the songpluggers and their assistants, the little demo studio, and the tape copy room. The executive offices were on the third floor.

After five years I had fallen into a routine of going to the office almost every day, even though the writers on staff were free to work at home. I would play my new songs for Buddy Killen ("That's good, Valentine, just make sure that you don't get too far out.") and the songpluggers. I would do simple little *work tapes*, with just me and the piano; the songs that passed muster would get full treatment with a band.

Quite often I would go hang out at the old building, too, because that was where Curly Putman had opened up his offices for Green Grass Music (which was half-owned by Tree). I longed for the days when Curly was plugging for Tree and getting a lot of my songs recorded, and I still occasionally co-wrote with him. I had started going to lunch with my new friend Michael Kosser and another of Curly's writers, Steve Pippin, who was in his mid-twenties and enjoyed trying to out-pun me. Sometimes Eddy Anderson—Tree's twenty-year-old tape copy boy and assistant sound engineer—went along with us. I liked Eddy because it didn't take much for me to make him laugh.

Often I got home in time to watch old *Twilight Zone* reruns with Sue and then go on a family picnic. But occasionally I would do some afternoon drinking. The kind of drinking I did depended on who I was drinking with. With Curly, it usually involved going to Kountry Korner for a beer or two. With recording engineer Tommy Cassasa, I typically would go to Bandy's, a lounge-type bar off West End Avenue where there were usually a lot of folks who were in "the business," and I would get half-drunk on rum and Coke. But if my drinking buddy was songwriter-session musician Joe Allen (three-eighths American Indian and a year or two younger than me), we would go from bar to bar and usually smoke pot, too; I would end up totally wasted, late for dinner, and in serious trouble with Sue.

Though I could go several days in a row without a drink, when I drank I had a problem cutting myself off; I had a tendency to keep putting them away until I was intoxicated. Eventually—many years later—I would learn to become a moderate social drinker. There are many who would say that is clear evidence that I was not an alcoholic. There's an old spoken-word recording called "Ten Little Bottles" in which Johnny Bond tells the difference between alcoholics and drunks when he says "Us drunks don't have to attend all those danged old meetings." Without a doubt, AA has been a great force for good and has helped rehabilitate millions of people, but there is a point of view today that some alcoholics *can* make the transition to social drinking (my definition of a social drinker being someone who doesn't drink past the point of a warm glow or first buzz). I honestly don't know if I was an alcoholic, though my binge-like behavior leads me to consider it a strong possibility. Whether I was or not, I sometimes came home drunk to an empty house, finding my cold supper on the kitchen floor where Sue had thrown it before taking Jeep to a Holiday Inn for the night. Whatever it was—this drinking thing—I probably inherited it from my dad.

I have no recollection of a hard-drinkin' father because he quit when I was two. He was mayor / city manager / municipal judge of our little Florida town, and did all his drinking at home (though legend had it that he once drove into town with part of our garage hanging from his car). When a lady came to our house one day and saw Mayor Braddock through the screen door, passed out on the living room floor in his underwear, my mortified mother decided to take action. She got syrup of ipecac, which induces vomiting, and started pouring it into Daddy's liquor bottles. One day he told my mother in his Old Florida drawl, "I just cannn't keep that stuff on my *stomach* anymooore." For the rest of his life, he would tell people that was why he quit drinking, never suspecting it was Mother's sweet manipulation that got him on the wagon.

"The rest of his life" came to an end on October 16, 1971. My sister-in-law called from Florida and said, "Your dad passed away at 5:30 this morning." Although my reaction was to say, "Oh, no," it was not so much despair as it was the shattering of the notion that he was somehow immortal. I can't honestly say that I was overcome with sorrow, because I had done my grieving for my father over the past several years, seeing this dignified old gentleman live out his final years as a helpless adult baby. I had hated that, and I think I was relieved that he could have his dignity back and move on to whatever awaited him.

Easily old enough to be my grandfather, he was a classic nineteenth-century man—it was as though there were several generations separating us. He was a different kind of Floridian, pronouncing Miami as Miam-uh, calling land turtles gophers, and firmly believing (even as the state became urbanized, suburbanized, and tourist-dependent) that "evvveery person in the state of Flahrr-da is deee-pendent on and affected byyy the citrus industry." As long as he was able to wash his own white hair, he shampooed it with the same product he had used since childhood: a black bar of pine-scented Packer's Tar Soap that came in a tin container. (As a child, I liked to use the containers for lizard caskets whenever he was through with them.) In the very old Southern tradition, he tipped his hat to every lady, stood erect when "Dixie" was played, and kissed all of his children on the mouth—his two little boys as well as his two grown daughters. He sang songs about plantations, mules, and possums that he had learned from former slaves. He was honest to a fault with everyone but himself, because he had all the prejudices one would expect from a man of his time and place.

His prejudices did not end with African Americans, to whom he never spoke harshly but treated as children that were to be taken care of. Black people were familiar to him and he loved them paternalistically like *Gone with the Wind*'s O'Hara family loved Mammy, Prissy, and Big Sam. But he had a distrust of all things foreign and different. I remember, as a child, hearing him explain to a neighbor why he could not support the mayoral candidacy of one Joe Lombardi (an Italian American who had moved from his native California to Auburndale after being stationed nearby during World War II), even though "Joe is a niice boy, and I like him verry much." He went through an imaginary conversation between himself and someone passing through our little town, in the event that Joe were to be elected.

"Nice little townn you have."

"Thank you, thank you very much. Weee like it heah."

"Whoooo's your mayor?"

"Joe Lom-barrrr-deee."

"Ooooh, Eye-*talian*, huh?"

I inherited some of his prejudices which, thankfully, I had mostly gotten rid of by the time of his passing. But I got more than his prejudices, bad temper, and taste for alcohol. I also inherited his penchant for puns, his love of animals, and his dedication to opening doors for "the ladies"(whether they liked it or not). For years I had missed him very much. I felt that he had died years before, and they were just getting around to burying him.

At eighty-eight, P. E. Braddock had outlived a majority of his peers, but the former mayor's reputation in Auburndale was rock solid and still intact, and Kersey Funeral Home (directly across little Lake Stella from my father's house of thirty-four years) was filled to capacity for the funeral.

Shortly before his first stroke, Dad—a lifelong Baptist—had converted to the Church of Christ (I think mostly to please my mother) and was rebaptized by Thurston Lee. "Brother" Lee was a tall, swarthy, well-fed man who wore a villainous little mustache and parted his black hair in the middle, making him look like the guy who tied girls to the railroad tracks in the old silent movies, or perhaps the head of a Mafia family.

Mom chose Thurston Lee to officiate at the memorial service. The Church of Christ was even more conservative than the Baptist Church and believed that the Old Testament was important history but the New Testament was *law*. Dad never really understood that there were any major differences between the Church of Christ (who in those days believed they were the only people going to Heaven) and the Baptists, so Thurston Lee seemed a little puzzled when my mother told him that Dad loved the Twenty-Third Psalm and had wanted it read before he was buried. At the graveside gathering, the big preacher in the olive-colored suit, said, "Brother Braddock AH *requested* that the Twenty-Third Psalm AH be read at his funeral. I don't know *why* AH he wanted it, but here it is." Then he proceeded to read, "The Lord is my shepherd, I shall not want . . ."

After the casket was lowered into the ground, there was a hymn and a final prayer. I saw my lifelong friends Don Pace and Stanley Cox standing a few feet away, and I walked toward them. Stanley and I were both raised in the Church of Christ and had been doing our imitations of Thurston Lee since childhood. Stan pulled me close and said, "Brother Braddock AH wants the Twenty-Third Psalm, and AH *by God he's gonna get it!*" People probably wondered why I was laughing out loud just after my father's funeral.

That night Sue, Jeep, and I were at my parents' house, along with my brother, Paul, and his family, and my two half-sisters, Louise and Lucille. The two sisters, (approximately my mother's age—early to mid-sixties) knew and appreciated my mom's devotion to their father in his last years. Though Mom finally gave up on trying to care for Dad at home, she spent most of her waking hours at the nursing home with him, bringing him her home-cooked meals, patiently feeding him like a one-year-old, and changing his diapers— no easy feat. I only heard her complain once, when she sighed and whispered, "I'm a widow without widow's privileges."

Louise, a year older than my mom, was a merry widow, looking cute and youngish in her size six dresses, with her facelift and blonde hair. "Lavonia," she said to my mother, "we both love you like you were our sister."

Younger sister Lucille, once the beauty of the two but by the 1970s looking older than Louise, agreed with what had been said, and added, "Lavonia, I loved my mother, but she had a jealous streak and never made Dad happy the way you did."

Of all the things my father left behind, the most appreciated was the one thing I always seemed to need the most—not because I was greedy but because I never seemed to be able to hold on to it—money! He had some money in the bank, a tiny bit in the stock market, and a few government bonds that he had put in our names. But most of the money would come from the citrus crop, from the groves that we were to decide among ourselves how to divvy up, since Dad didn't specify that in a will. Although my father always liked to talk about how he didn't have much and how people in agriculture never knew for sure if they were going to have a good year or go broke, as the son of a citrus grower I always knew that money did indeed grow on trees.

When we returned to Nashville, we decided to move back into our house on Whispering Hills Drive. (The opening of I-65 would make my daily ride to Music Row a few minutes quicker.) The house had failed to sell for the asking price, but we were feeling financially secure for the moment, so getting revenue from the home sale was no longer essential. We managed to get out of the lease on Curtiswood Lane—I think they were only too happy to be rid of us. Back to the old neighborhood came the Braddocks, their two cats, and a new basset hound, Lightnin,' who replaced the old one, Cleo, who had disappeared a couple of months earlier. It took more than just one moving van; I had to get piano movers to transport a baby grand that I had recently purchased after hearing that Ray Charles really loved it when he played it on Johnny Cash's TV show.

I was hoping to get another recording contract. Buddy Killen informed me that Chet Atkins, the world's most famous guitar player and head of RCA's Nashville division, was listening to my tapes and considering signing me to the label. Chet, one of the most laid-back people I ever met, was at Jack Stapp's birthday party at Tree. He paid me big compliments on my songwriting.

"I imagine you were bored to death, listening to all that junk of mine," I said in my typical self-effacing, self-destructive manner.

"No," he softly drawled, "I enjoy your work very much." As I left, he wished me good luck and said he would be talking to me. But that was the last I heard of Chet signing or producing me. I was learning that while modesty is an endearing trait, self-condemnation can undermine people's confidence in you, and there is a happy medium. Sometimes I had to learn lessons over and over before they finally sank in.

The ongoing drama of my personal life kept me from focusing on my songwriting career as much as I should have. Sue and I were into a pattern of playing cat-and-mouse games.

Woody Allen (or Carol Burnett or Charlie Chaplin) said, "Comedy is tragedy plus time." Looking back from another century, I find a lot of humor in what we were doing, but it wasn't very funny while it was happening. Often Sue would swear that she was no longer having an affair, prompting me to call Charlotte to tell her I needed to work on my marriage and couldn't see her anymore. Then I would find a love letter to Sue from Rex Wordsworth, or I would get a Mobil credit card bill for a set of tires she bought for Darlene, her partner in crime, and I would invariably contact Charlotte about a rendezvous, and she would be ready and willing to take me back as her lover. Why she put up with my wishy-washiness, I don't know. Only once did Charlotte indicate that *she* wanted to break up with *me*, and I agreed that we should. A few days later I got a letter from her, expressing her disappointment that I didn't put up any resistance. I replied, "Oh, I thought you meant it. Good! Let's get together!" Though I often wondered if I'd ever find Sue Lawrence, the sweet and lovely girl who saved my drunken life one night and washed my face with filling station towels, I was very attracted to Charlotte, and she was a great diversion from my unhappy marriage. One day, near Franklin, Tennessee, we got carried away in broad daylight on hallowed ground at the Confederate Cemetery, putting our clothes back on just before a group of Mississippians came along looking for the graves of their ancestors. One night in Florida, I convinced her that it was safe to have sex because I was certain that my big, funny friend Don Pace was totally passed out on the motel room floor—not telling her until later that in the midst of things I had glanced over and seen that he had one eye wide open.

One rainy Atlanta afternoon we sat in a McDonald's booth next to two cops, both of us getting drunk as we sneaked a bottle of rum back and forth to each other. Not wanting to part company, we decided to cancel her flight so she could ride back to Nashville with me the next day, then take a plane back to Florida from there. A bit hung over, we overslept while the sun rose high over Atlanta. As we pulled out of the Airport Hilton, I told her if we averaged seventy-six miles an hour, I could have her at the Nashville airport in time for her flight. The traffic was sluggish, but at Marietta, Georgia, I told her if we averaged eighty miles an hour, we could still make it. By Chattanooga, I realized we would have to average eighty-nine miles an hour. At Murfreesboro, Tennessee, I announced that I could have her there on time if we averaged 495 miles per hour! We had fun all right, but it usually wasn't fun when I got home from what Sue called my "whoring around," and the old double standard isn't much of a talking point when you're being physically assaulted.

But there were times that we were okay, especially on vacations. Jeep said she wanted us to go to Florida for her birthday, so we did. As we cruised down the highway, she said, "I wish I could freeze at the age I am now—I wish I could always be six years old." She crawled into the backseat with her mom to take a nap, then, always considerate, started crying, "I'm afraid Daddy's feelings will be hurt 'cause I'm not sitting up there with him anymore." I didn't know whether to laugh or cry when she said, "Daddy, I hope when I grow up I can be as good as you and Mama." When she referred to something that happened "back when I was in my late fives," I wrote in my journal: *I've never loved anyone or anything as I love this child.*

When we got back to Nashville, I finished up an album I had been work-ing on. It was produced by Tree's songplugger Johnny Slate and engineer Tommy Cassasa, and arranged by me. The group, made up of some of Music Row's best session players, was called Raspberry Bathtub Ring, but I was the lead singer and the songs were mine—covers of hits like "Ruthless," "Some-thing to Brag About" and "Did You Ever," but also new ones, all novelties. One, "X Movies," speculated on what it would have been like "if there had been X movies back in the good old days," with a bit of prophecy in the line "If Ronald Reagan had performed without his clothes, he might be president today, who knows," eight years before the California governor was elected Commander-in-Chief. The project was pure hybrid: psychedelic ragtime bluegrass. If that sounds like a bunch of people stoned out of their minds, it's because that's what it was. It was a spec (for speculation) session, the music business equivalent of a TV industry pilot. I liked it far better than the stuff I had cut on MGM, but nobody picked it up.

There were two new songpluggers at Tree. One was Jimmy Gilmer, who was my age, a big pop star several years earlier with "Sugar Shack" and "Bottle of Wine." Gilmer was a sweet guy and I liked him very much, as did every-one else. The other plugger, holding the position of creative director, was Jan Crutchfield, brother of hit producer Jerry Crutchfield. Jan spoke gruffly but he had a solid reputation as a songwriter, having penned Jack Greene's powerful hit "Statue of a Fool." Jan seemed to enjoy playing my comedy songs to people for kicks, but when it came time for serious pitching, he got out the Joe Allen songs.

I got so depressed about not getting songs cut anymore and about the failure to find a label home for the Raspberry Bathtub Ring project, that I went to a tall building that stood across the street from my beloved Nashville Public Library (where I would eventually check out everything that F. Scott Fitzgerald ever wrote). I stood in front of the library and stared at the sky-scraper for about half an hour, seriously thinking about going to the top floor and taking a leap. Then I happened to remember that Jimmy Gilmer had told me a couple of days before that he would like to start listening to anything in my catalog that I felt good about, because he wanted to start getting me some cuts. I drove back to Tree and played Gilmer about an hour's worth of songs, including several that he really seemed to like. He took them upstairs and played them for Buddy who said, "Way to go, Valentine." That made me feel better, but I was really wishing that I was signed with Curly Putman's com-pany, Green Grass Music; Curly was getting Michael Kosser and Steve Pippin cuts just as he had done for me at Tree in the 1960s.

One night Sue and I went to the King of the Road club with Curly and Bernice Putman to see a popular West Coast rockabilly act, Larry and Lorrie Collins, who had recorded in the 1950s as the Collins Kids. Sitting alone a couple of tables away was Andy Griffith. Curly and Andy had met in Holly-wood on the set of Andy's top-rated TV show, through Curly's good friend

George "Goober" Lindsey. Curly invited Andy to join us at our table. "This is a friend of mine," Curly said, "Bobby Braddock. He wrote 'D-I-V-O-R-C-E.'" Andy made such a to-do over the song that I was too dumbfounded to explain that Curly was the co-writer. "I've admired your husbands for a long time," he told Sue and Bernice. Of course, he'd never heard of me before, only the song. A very nice man.

Not long after that, when my mother was up for a visit, I saw George Lindsey getting out of a car, about to go into an office. I asked, "Mom, would you like to meet George Lindsey, who plays Goober on the *Andy Griffith Show*?" She said she sure would. So we parked the car and followed George up the sidewalk to the door of the office he was about to enter.

"George," I said, "I'd like for you to meet my mom."

"Well, hello there, Miz Braddock," George said, with all his natural friendliness.

She put her hands on her hips, reared her head back, and said with a big smile, "Why *Goober*!" There before our eyes, my mother had turned into Aunt Bee.

When my mom was visiting, there was the usual tension coming from Sue, and when she left, there was the usual relief. Sue had more alcoholic genes than I did, but had only recently transformed from near teetotaler to social drinker, so after Mom's departure, my wife joined me in having a rum and Coke. Our basset hound, Lightnin' (like all basset hounds) was totally sweet and nonaggressive—and dumb. I poured a little rum in a water dish to see if the dog had any interest in it. He did; he loved it. I gave him an entire bowlful, and he lapped it all up and started woofing for more. (*Don't do this!* I've since learned that it could be dangerous.) He got so drunk that he kept trying to jump up on the couch but couldn't make it. After laughing at him for quite a while—I was pretty happy to have a dog that would drink with me—I put him outside in our fenced-in back yard. During the night, our drunk hound got all the magazines and newspapers from the crawl space underneath the house, ripped them to shreds, and scattered them everywhere. When we awoke the next morning and looked out the sliding glass door, there was the biggest mess I'd ever seen. It looked like there had been a ticker-tape parade, plus a ton of confetti. There in the middle of all this was long-eared Lightnin' lying on his back, feet up in the air, passed out cold.

I was not happy about the lack of activity with my songs. According to Sue, Bernice Putman had recently said that Curly really wished I could write for his company. One afternoon I saw Curly in Buddy's opulent office, on the third floor at Tree. I hung around awhile, and when he left I rode the elevator down with him, and we walked out to the parking lot. I told him that I really wanted to write for Green Grass. Did he think it would cause any hard feelings between him and Buddy?

"Bobby, you know I'd sure like to have you," he said, "and no, I don't think it would cause any hard feelings on Buddy's part. But I think you oughta tell him that *you* approached *me*, and not the other way around."

Neither Curly nor I was aware that another Tree writer, Red Lane, had recently told Buddy that he too wanted to leave Tree for their subsidiary. Buddy's answer to me was a resounding "NO!" "I can't let all our good writers go over to Green Grass!" he fairly shouted. This may have been the straw that broke the clichéd camel's back, because Tree would soon buy out Curly's half of Green Grass and get him back as a writer, giving him a nice big office. He would agree to pitch the songs of certain writers, which included me.

Tree was my home away from home, and Jeep was practically raised there. (Though Sue played up to all the Tree big shots at social events, I have no recollection of her ever setting foot inside the building itself.) In looking back at old journals, many of the entries have to do with Tree and what was going on there. One journal passage referred to bookkeeper Ann Kosloff, about whom I wrote "she has a great-looking body for a thirty-three-year-old," as though she had reached senior citizenship. It was at about this time that Dixie Gamble, a part-time model from North Carolina, came to work there and I (and many other guys) developed a crush on this extremely good-looking young woman who would become a lifetime friend and great achiever. There was a secretary in her early twenties, Bridget Flye, who looked like a movie star. Of course, Sue thought I was having sex with all of them. I was being monogamous with Charlotte, but sometimes wished I were half the Romeo that Sue thought I was.

At the annual BMI Awards banquet at the Belle Meade Country Club, Sue was enjoying herself during the cocktail hour, cutting up with sixty-something *Nashville Banner* country music columnist, Red O'Donnell, who often published puns that both of us sent him. Sue had a knack for playing up to older men and winning them over. The awards presented by the three performance societies (ASCAP and SESAC were the other two) were given for the songs that had received the most airplay during the previous year. My award was for "Did You Ever." By the time we got to our table, I was drunk and having fun, which meant that Sue was having none. When the director of the Nashville office, Frances Preston, solemnly announced that BMI President Ed Cramer was seriously ill in New York and unable to attend, I stood up on my chair and shouted at the top of my voice, "LET'S HEAR IT FOR ED!" Bernice Putman gave me the evil eye and scolded, "Bobby, I think *you'd* better sit *down*."

As I staggered to the stage to receive my award, Kris Kristofferson yelled out, "Blink those eyes, Braddock!"

Sue was very angry with me all the way home. Never wanting a party to end, I decided that I'd drop Sue off at the house and go to WSM and visit with Ralph Emery on his all-night show. I took Sue home and off I went, driving drunk into the rainy night. Halfway there, I took a curve too fast and faced an oncoming car, running into it head-on. BAM! Both cars were destroyed.

I had a goose egg on my knee, and the guy in the other car, just as drunk as I was, had one on his head. I begged him to go to the hospital to have it checked. He finally agreed to when I told him he might die if he didn't. If this happened today I would probably get jail time, but all I got was a ticket and the responsibility for two totaled cars.

I got a scolding from Buddy Killen—not for my behavior at the BMI Awards but for losing the second single in a year because of my big opinionated mouth. A few months before, I had told Jim Vienneau at MGM that I disliked singer Billy Walker changing my "She Told Me So" to "Baby Told Me So," which resulted in their throwing the song out. Then at the BMI Awards the night before, singer Jan Howard had told Buddy that she recently played me her cut of "Sweet Song of Love," and after seeing the look in my eyes, called Owen Bradley at Decca and said, "Please kill 'Sweet Song of Love;' the writer hates it. Don't put it out." "Valentine," Buddy sighed, "will you *please* stay away from artists after they've recorded your songs?!"

Sue and I, ever the antagonists, did share in our love for Jeep, and there were still things that we enjoyed doing together. We actually liked the same TV shows: *All in the Family*, *The Mary Tyler Moore Show*, and *The Bob Newhart Show*. We still saw a lot of movies—1972 was the year of my new all-time favorite, *The Godfather*. Whenever we went out, we had two babysitters to choose from: Mrs. Sorrow, the pseudo-grouchy but loyal old lady from down the street; and our part-time housekeeper, Jennie Lake, whom Jeep adored and I liked—despite the fact that she covered up for Sue and spied on me. I forgave her because she was so good to Jeep. Sue and I could be friends and have fun, but the antagonism was always close by; the hostility was always just one careless word away.

Sue hadn't moved in the same political direction as I, but we never argued about it. In the Democratic presidential primary earlier in the year, she voted for George Wallace, and I voted for Hubert Humphrey. In my journal, I wrote:

> In 1969, I started moving leftward, but that gave me a long way to go before I reached the "center," where I think I've been stationary for the past few months: to the left on some issues (a clean environment, legalization of marijuana, equality under the law) and to the right on others (pro-free enterprise, a strong defense, and no easy abortions). I probably average out in the "middle of the road."

I didn't trust President Nixon but worried about Democratic nominee George McGovern's blind idealism. I was torn. I agreed with McGovern's strong stand against the war in Vietnam. A few days before the election, I was saying that I would vote for McGovern, but when I walked into the booth I pulled the lever for Nixon.

It was my religious transformation that upset my mother. I never doubted that there was a God, but indeed did have doubts that the Bible was God's inspired word. Mom mistook that for agnosticism or atheism, which was far from the truth. In a letter from November 30, 1972, she wrote:

> *The only reason I mentioned your views on religion (or lack of them) is because I do love you and am greatly concerned about your "hereafter." Call it atheist, agnostic, infidel or whatever. Who do you think would ever have the intelligence to write anything like the Bible, or what reason for doing so, if it wasn't the inspired word of God? And the only reason I mentioned about Lauren saying church was boring was because I thought you might tell her that church is a duty, and not intended to be entertaining . . . simply because I love her and am concerned about her "hereafter."*

And then she added this sad note that made me feel very bad for her:

> *I can really understand why so many wives and husbands die so soon after their mates do. They get so darned lonely, with no one to confide in, to discuss problems or pleasures with. No matter how busy one is, they need someone who cares, and when they have no one they lose all desire to live. I bet I could die and the buzzards would be the first to know. There are plenty of widows here my age that like to get together and go out to eat or to a show or concert, etc. but that just doesn't take the place of family.*

Despite the end-of-the-road tone of her letter, my mother would be around for another twenty-five years.

I had long ago gotten Sue to quit her habit of trying to impress people with name-dropping, by yelling, "Oops," and cradling my hands underneath her, just above the floor as though to catch the name she was dropping. But she never got past her pretensions of being rich, which we certainly were not. We were usually in debt (I wrote a song about us called "Split Level Poverty"). So whatever the rationalization was for us to sell our house and get a nicer one farther out—it seems that we decided a better alternative to splitting up was *moving on up*—Sue said, "You don't have to do a thing; I'll scout out houses; all you'll need to do is look at the ones I find and tell me what you think." I don't think we looked at many before I saw the one on Newsom Station Road, in an area of suburban homes on two-acre lots in an otherwise rural area about seventeen miles west of downtown, with interstate access most of the way. The two-story house, high on a hill, was brick Georgian by design but had white columns that gave it a colonial look. Though it was only a three-bedroom, two-bath house, it was built and situated in a way that made it look like a little mansion. I think I said yes the minute I saw it. It was priced at $46,000—equivalent to nearly $400,000 in 2008 real estate dollars before the big plunge. The builder had carelessly blasted away too much of the surrounding woods before constructing the house, but that environmental indiscretion would eventually be fine with Jeep and me when we started discovering slabs of petrified wood and broken-up rocks imbedded with prehistoric invertebrates and insects. We would get new trees planted and have a large vegetable garden. Jeep would have kids on both sides to play with in our hilly yards or in the highly elevated woods behind us.

Our poor hound, Lightnin,' had somehow gotten into our swimming pool on Whispering Hills Drive and drowned. So along with cats Jane and Brother, we would be bringing along our new German shepherd, Pussycat, who loved us dearly but terrorized everyone else (cutting short her residency in the new neighborhood). Across the street from the house was a creek filled with crawdads, turtles, and little fish. Less than a mile down Newsom Station Road was the Harpeth River—and the remains of an old grist mill and partial dam, built in 1862. Our future here would include Sue's absence on many nights when she supposedly was staying in an apartment with friends close to where she was going to school. I would come to look on this residence as the house where Jeep and I lived; a very special place that would hold many fond memories.

Not long after we moved in, Joe Allen was driving me home from a night of drinking and smoking weed, probably because he was not quite as screwed up as I was. As we exited the interstate about three miles from my house, Joe deadpanned, "Evil spirits. Evil spirits around here." Joe's dark complexion and high cheekbones revealed his Native American ancestors from the Southwest plains, one of his parents being one-half American Indian, and the other being one-fourth. Joe was a likable guy and my favorite roaring buddy, though he could sometimes lapse into bitterness. He was probably my favorite of the new breed of songwriters around Tree.

One night Joe and I were at a bar, and I made some comment about cheating. Joe said, "Man, you've given me a great idea for a song." He told me, and it went right over my head.

"When I'm putting on my coat and tie," he repeated, "I'm putting on the one who really loves me." It was about a guy getting dressed up to go cheat on his woman. He asked me if I wanted to write it with him, but it continued to go over my messed-up head. Joe wrote the song alone. Producer Billy Sherrill changed it to "When I'm putting on my makeup, I'm putting on the one who really loves me," and "The Midnight Oil" became one of Barbara Mandrell's biggest early hits.

Joe, like Red Lane, was thought of as one of the "cool" songwriters. Although I had written my share of deep, serious songs, the ones that got recorded seemed to be my comedy stuff, and even the serious "D-I-V-O-R-C-E" had a bit of novelty to it, with the play-on-words lyrics. I think that was how I was perceived when I was thirty-two years old: the guy who wrote the far-out songs, the ones with the Alfred Hitchcock endings. So the night that Joe took me to Hank Cochran's house I felt some trepidation, and when we got there the marijuana only made me feel more paranoid. Hank Cochran was a legend, famed for songs such as Eddy Arnold's "Make the World Go Away" and a couple of Patsy Cline's biggest hits. He wore a little goatee and had a strong sense of self that probably came from leaving Mississippi for California on his own, when he was still a child. Hank had a cult following, a lot of guys who tried to be just like him, calling everybody "cousin" as Hank did. In the not-too-distant future, he would treat me with respect and affection—and those feelings would be mutual—but in the spring of 1973, most of my Hank Cochran experiences had not been good ones. Hank's little house, set in the country several miles southeast of Metropolitan Nashville, was sort of a love nest for him and his girlfriend, Ruthie. When we walked in, someone was there giving him a B-12 shot in the butt.

After we had been there for a while, Hank and Joe started writing a song. When they got hung up on a line, I threw one at them that they both liked.

"I'm not trying to get in on the song," I said.

"Oh *yes*, you are," quipped Hank.

Later on Hank's girlfriend, Ruthie, surveyed me very carefully. While Joe's coal-black hair hung over his collar, and he had on scruffy jeans and a jeans jacket, my toupee-covered hair came down over the top of my ears but wasn't really long, and I was wearing striped 1970s-style pants and a paisley shirt. "You look too clean cut to be a picker," she said as she looked me over. "And you don't have enough shit behind your eyes to be a songwriter." No, I'd only gone crazy for two years back in 1960 for taking too much speed, I had lost a baby son when I was twenty-four, and I struggled each day with not enough marriage and too much alcohol. No, even though I had written one of the biggest country hits of the past few years, I didn't have enough shit behind my eyes to be a songwriter. I wasn't one of the cool people.

One songwriter who treated me with great respect was the king of them all, craggy Harlan Howard, sometimes called the Irving Berlin of country music. Harlan was in his mid-forties and had a string of hits that was unmatched. To this day no writer has surpassed the success of his catalog. He had started using me as a piano player on his demo sessions back in the late 1960s, and we developed a good friendship. He called me "juvenile," but he addressed most anyone younger than himself that way. Whenever Harlan said something, I listened, because it was usually great advice or great fun. He said bad relationships were excellent songwriting fodder. He also said, "My problem is that I always treated my wives so good that they never wanted me to leave the house." Oh, definitely, he had a big ego, but he also had a way of making other people feel good about themselves. I think Harlan loved life more than anyone I ever knew. Though named after his ancestral home of Harlan County, Kentucky, he was born in Detroit and brought up in an orphanage there, and he had that Detroit accent (saying "God dammit"

Nashville BMI head Frances Preston, yours truly, BMI's Roger Sovine, Tree's Joyce Bush, Jack Stapp, and Buddy Killen, at the 1973 BMI Awards banquet

like "Gyod dimmit"). One night (he was on either his third or fourth wife) Harlan got very drunk at a party at Curly Putman's house and brought me on to sing "Revelation."

"This is the most underrated songwriter in town," he bellowed. "If only he had just half the publicity of _____" (I won't say who). "Gyod dimmit, he's out-writing _____ right now. I *love* him!" He was comparing me to a songwriter whom I greatly admired, and though I didn't believe what he was saying, I did believe that both he and Jim Beam meant every word of it.

One of the most legendary stories to make the rounds on Music Row took place at one of Curly's parties. Curly always got warm, red-faced, and lovable when he'd had a few drinks. His wife, Bernice, a good woman by all means, always made sure that Curly—and everyone else—behaved. The Putmans lived in a beautiful mansion on a giant, fenced-in piece of land outside Lebanon, Tennessee. They decided to have a huge festive get-together, inviting their music business friends *and* the cream of Lebanon society—an interesting mix, to say the least. Curly, a little tipsy, got up and said, "Now we're goin' 'round the room, and when it comes your turn, stand up and say who you are and what you do."

"Well, when you have something wrong with you, I'm the one you come to see," said a dignified-looking, white-haired man.

Legendary Hank Cochran   Dave Kirby: . . . a bear for the FBI

"That means he's a doctor," Curly said, and went on to say the man's name.

After a banker and a home builder got up, I stood and said, "My name's Bobby Braddock. I wrote 'D-I-V-O-R-C-E' with Curly, and also a few other things you might have heard on the radio."

Over in a corner sat a tall, skinny, blond-haired guy named Dave Kirby, who played guitar on a lot of recording sessions and had written some hit songs. Dave was known to say things for shock value—he even had Beatle Ringo Starr going, on one session—and on this party night, he had a little sly grin on his face, as though to say, "This is a silly formality; what can I do to liven things up?"

After a couple more people announced their names and professions, Dave got up, surveyed the crowded room, and said, "My name is Dave Kirby, and I once fucked a bear for the FBI." You could have heard a pin drop. There was dead silence—for about three seconds. Then the room erupted in laughter, and then mass howling. It went on for several minutes, and everyone was in hysterics—everyone but Bernice.

If anyone "discovered" Curly it was Roger Miller. Roger had met him at a shoe store where Curly was a salesman in the early 1960s. Curly was a few years older than the "Music Row wild man," but Roger recognized the power in the songs that Curly played him, and called the Thom McAn employee to the attention of Buddy Killen.

Roger had been one of Tree's hot writers since 1958, and he enjoyed limited success as an artist on RCA, but when he signed with Smash Records in 1964, he exploded across America with his unique novelty songs, becoming an overnight superstar in the worlds of both country *and* pop. The first time I saw Roger, Buddy Killen was introducing him to a deejay who was so starstruck that he tripped on a step as he was about to shake hands and fell flat on his face. Without missing a beat, Roger quipped, "Enjoy your trip?" He had an amazingly quick wit, and anyone who tried to keep up with him did so at their own peril. Right after the deejay took his trip, I was introduced to Roger who said, "Man, Buddy's been telling me great things about you."

He was always fun to talk to, and whenever our paths crossed, he would often tell me, "Let's get high and write something sometime." According to Roger, all of his hits ("King of the Road," "Dang Me," etc.) had been written when he was high on pills, one exception being "You Can't Roller Skate in a Buffalo Herd,"—not one of his most memorable efforts. One day I got the opportunity to co-write with Roger. Red Lane had the idea "In Love with Love," and thought it would be fun to see how many people could co-write one song; so a total of fourteen of us wrote an okay ditty that was eventually recorded by a guy named David Rogers. My sole contribution to "In Love with Love" was the line "'Cause love's been good to me."

Buddy enjoyed the glamour and glitz of superstars and was responsible for the careers of many of them. He produced the big pop hits of R&B funnyman Joe Tex. A current monster song was "Ramblin Man" by the Allman Brothers Band, and it dawned on me that I had known these guys when Buddy had them hanging around Tree a few years before (billed as The Hour Glass, they had recorded a soulful version of "D-I-V-O-R-C-E"). I used to give rides to a talented young guy from Indiana who Buddy had signed—John Hiatt—who would go on to make many albums and attract a large loyal following around the world. Buddy even produced an album on movie star Burt Reynolds, who one day reminisced with me about his football days at West Palm Beach High and the time they beat my two-year undefeated little hometown team, the Auburndale Bloodhounds. Probably, though, the most memorable of all the luminaries from this period was the old boy from Texas whose earlier records Buddy had played bass on and sometimes produced: George Jones, probably the most renowned traditional country singer since Hank Williams.

Sometime after George married Tammy Wynette, her producer, Billy Sherrill, persuaded the already legendary Jones to sign with Epic Records and become another one of the super producer's artists. Billy had a reputation for making records that were "slick," because he liked to use a lot of orchestration (which is ironic, because today it is acknowledged that he redefined traditional country and made some of the most enduring recordings in the history of that genre). Billy was not one of those producers who just sat in the control room and waited to see what the musicians came up with—he ruled his sessions with an iron fist and often came up with the arrangements himself. He had an acerbic sense of humor and never went out of his way to be the most beloved man on Music Row. At first, George didn't quite know how to take him or his production ideas, but eventually Billy won George's trust, which would result in the great star shining brighter than ever and ascending to even greater heights.

A wisecracking little guy with dark blond hair, Sherrill was either an introvert or just didn't like most people. It was a good thing that he had the ability to write and co-write monster hit songs himself, because there were only a few songpluggers and songwriters whom he would admit to his inner sanctum. Fortunately for me, I was one of those few. There were rumors on Music Row that Billy had a deal with Buddy to cut a certain number of Tree songs. I always seriously doubted that because I think these two proud men cared more about the quality of their work than making some kind of side deal. Both were tremendously successful with their talents, and they used them to accumulate huge wealth.

One day Curly had an appointment with Billy. I urged him to play "Nothing Ever Hurt Me Half as Bad as Losing You," an uptempo song that had about as many words as I could cram into it. Curly was a little reluctant because he knew that Billy's publisher, Al Gallico out of New York, would be there, and Billy had a tendency to turn into Don Rickles in the insult department when he had his little group around him. It was only at my insistence that Curly played this goofy song, although he was afraid people would make fun of it. Luckily, both Billy Sherrill and George Jones liked it.

> I've had a splittin' headache from my eyebrows to my backbone
> Arthritis, 'pendicitis, Bright's disease, and gallstones
> Bleeding ulcers, ingrown toenails, swollen adenoids
> The Asian flu a time or two and inflamed vocal cords
> I've had a toothache so severe my jawbone split in two
> But nothing ever hurt me half as bad as losing you
>
> I've had the lit end of a cigar pressed against my belly
> Whupped on with a crowbar 'til my eyeballs turned to jelly
> Accidentally nailed my index finger to the wall
> Cut off half my toes and soaked my foot in alcohol . . .

. . . and much, much more. A masochist's delight and another silly song by Braddock. But it was a hit silly song. The words were so fast and furious that George barely got all of them out, and on the fadeout of the recording, you can hear him miss a couple and yell out "Wa-hoo!" Although it was a Top Ten record, he never once sang it on a personal appearance. Shortly after its release, I met him for the first time, and he said, "So *yore* the sumbitch who wrote that thing. Ah was *wonderin'* what you looked like."

Several months later, he showed up at Tree and wanted me to hear his recording of a much more serious song I had written, "She Told Me So."

> There's roses blooming in the Arctic Circle
> Icebergs in the Gulf of Mexico
> There's not one star in Heaven
> Or a sunrise every morning
> I'd believe it if she told me so

George was telling me it was going to be his next single (it wasn't). He wanted to hear some more songs. Over the years, I think it would finally sink in with him that most people considered him the greatest country singer of all time, but in the early 1970s, he was self-effacing and lacking in self-confidence.

"Uh, I don't wanna *bother* y'all down here," he said.

"B-b-bother us? You're *George Jones!*"

I took him up to Buddy's office and one of the new songpluggers, Judy Thomas—an attractive, somewhat masculine blonde—was running back and forth to the tape room to get songs that Buddy and I wanted George to hear. Finally George said to Judy, "Hey booger, y'all got any *whiskey* around here?" Judy managed to come up with a bottle of J. W. Dant. Then he asked for a guitar and serenaded us for about two hours. As night fell on Music Row, we had one very drunk George Jones on our hands. Buddy said he had to go home and put me in charge of taking care of George.

Then I got a call from Billy Sherrill, who asked me, "Is Jones over there?" Most people called him George or Possum (because he looked like one) but Billy called him "Jones."

"Yeah, I'm with him right now."

"Is he drunk?"

"Definitely."

"Does he think he's supposed to be recording tonight?"

I told him he hadn't said anything about it. Tammy Wynette was recording, and I got the impression that Billy and Tammy didn't want George around if he was drunk.

George agreed that he wasn't able to drive and would let me take him home. As we sat in the Tree parking lot, he started talking about Tammy.

"Here, feel this knot here on my head," he said. I felt a little egg on the lower part of his skull. "Tammy put it there," he lamented, "but *damn*, I love that woman." (Those of us who knew and loved Tammy would tell you if she put a knot on George's head, she probably had good reason.) Then suddenly he jumped out of my car and headed for his long Lincoln, insisting that he was able to drive.

"George, you really shouldn't be driving. L-l-let me take you home, and I'll bring you back here tomorrow to get your car."

"Yore writin' great songs, chief," he yelled as his big car took off across the parking lot, "and I'm behind you all the way."

I was starting to get a few song cuts again because Curly was back at Tree. There was one called "Moontan" by singer Jerris Ross that Jeep danced to at her annual recital; Johnny Carver had a fairly big hit with "Tonight Someone's Falling in Love," which I co-wrote with Jimmy Gilmer; and there was Cal Smith's recording of "Bleep You." Radio was a bit resistant to that one, and it didn't make it too far up the charts. In 2007 Jack Ingram had a clever hit song titled "Love You," in which the singer/character invokes the word "love" in place of the f-word. That's what I did with "Bleep You," in 1973, but I don't think the world of country was ready for it back then. My "bleep" was a substitution not just for the f-word, but also the s-word and the GD word.

Bleep you old woman, it's my turn to speak
I'm really leaving and if you think I'm teasing, then you're full of bleep
Your bleeping around and your bleep-bleep lies
Are driving me crazy, so bleep you old woman
Bleep you, goodbye

One day Jeep was with me when "Bleep You" came on the car radio. Excited that it was my song, she started singing along with it. Though well aware that the child had heard many foul-mouthed arguments between her mother and me, apparently I wasn't thinking of that when my curiosity prompted me to ask, "Jeep, do you have any idea what that song means?"

Looking straight ahead, and without hesitation, she innocently replied, "Fuck you, old woman?" If I had been wearing dentures, they would have fallen out of my mouth.

In the late spring, the family took another Florida vacation. On the way down, we switched back and forth between country radio (Charlie Rich singing "Behind Closed Doors" and little Tanya Tucker singing "What's Your Mama's Name") and pop radio (The O'Jays' "Love Train" and Stevie Wonder's "You Are the Sunshine of My Life").

We hit several Florida beaches, meeting up with the Putman family in Miami Beach, then going to St. Petersburg Beach with my mom and my brother, Paul, and family. Before heading back to Nashville, we visited a place we'd never been to before, a barely inhabited little island off Florida's southern Gulf Coast, Captiva. It was a seashell goldmine, so Jeep and I spent the afternoon collecting some unusual ones. That night I got into my books. My favorite fiction was by American writers of the 1920s, having read everything by F. Scott Fitzgerald and Sinclair Lewis. I was then reading what would become my favorite fiction of all time. Thomas Wolfe's *Look Homeward Angel* was based on his own life. Wolfe, who died at thirty-seven, was not only a literary giant but a physical one, writing out his manuscripts on the top of a refrigerator. After reading awhile, I started drinking rum, and made a half-drunken entry in my journal:

A tiny sliver of an island, little cabins. My first impression was that
the bay seemed too marshy, the Gulf too calm. But like many women,
it becomes truly lovely in the night. Gentle crashing of small waves,
wind whistling low through the Australian pines, occasional shutting of
someone's screen door. The island is now bathed in the light of a full moon.

Jeep was happy to get back to Newsom Station Road. Her favorite play-mates were two brothers, Reb and Todd Moorer, who lived next door to us. Their parents, Lewis and Carol, were members of the Church of Christ, conservative in politics as well as religion, and great neighbors. One day I approached their home just as the ladder Lewis Moorer was standing on started to fall backward from their two-story house, where he was doing some work on the edge of the roof. I caught the ladder just in time and pushed it back in place. He said it was as if the hand of God had reached out and saved his life.

I loved the street where we lived. Jeep had a lot of playmates, but probably didn't have a bigger one than her daddy. We enjoyed going up the steep hill behind the house and exploring the woods. Never giving up on the hope that we would find a basset hound that would survive, we got another one, this one named Hot Dog. Whenever the hill got too steep, I had to pick up Hot Dog and carry him.

When entering our house from the back, the first room was the den (we never used the living room up front). To the right was a large rec room that I used as my music room, to the left were the kitchen and dining room, and then Sue's bedroom with a big round bed. Jeep's bedroom, which Sue had had decorated in a dark motif with spooky black and white wallpaper, was upstairs. My bedroom was across the hall. Every night Jeep and I would read each other stories or make something up. I liked to tell her a scary story in a happy voice, which cracked her up, or a sweet, innocuous story in a scary voice, to which she would squeal, "Daddy, stop!"

Jeep had attended first grade at a public school. First- and second-graders shared the same classroom at the public school nearest Newsom Station Road. I thought that would be regressive, so for grade two we enrolled her in a private school, Harding Academy.

Sue and I continued to live our separate lives. I still had to be discreet about mine to escape Sue's wrath, and it was her choice to be discreet about hers. I saw clear evidence that she was still seeing the doctor in Birmingham, who by this time must have completed his residency, but I also suspected that she was not being true to him. I once picked up the phone when it rang, and I seemed to have some drunk guy on the line; Sue, who had picked up the extension, started giggling. There was some cute little joke going on between them. She later apologized. I honestly didn't care.

Charlotte was a respite from my unhappy marriage. I was still very attracted to her, but I was never sure how deep it went for me. Once she came to town and got so drunk at a bar that she embarrassed me, and I told her I wanted to split up. When she started crying, I took it back. I should have considered myself fortunate to have her in my life; her temperament was so much better than Sue's. She was never mean to me, and I never caught her in a lie. (Ah yes, I know, she *was* lying to her *husband*.) I would never forget the twenty-four-hour period when Sue and I were under the mistaken impression that Jeep had been diagnosed as probably having leukemia. During that dreary, slow-moving day, Sue was as devastated as I was, but we couldn't seem to bear being around each other. Luckily, Charlotte was in town, and being with her calmed me down and gave me the strength that I needed at that horrible moment.

Bad financial decisions, poor money management, and overspending led me to sell my brother the orange groves that I had inherited from my father. All that land in Central Florida would have been worth a fortune in the twenty-first century, when Polk County was becoming known as Orlampa.

Jeep loved being a little girl, and if there were a lot of seven-year-olds who suspected that there was no Santa Claus, she was not among them. Our first Christmas at Newsom Station Road was a nice one. I said yes when Sue said she wanted to buy me an organ, replacing the one I'd had to sell a few years before. This was a Hammond T-series with set rhythms (which I loved.) I appreciated the gesture. So Christmas was great until Sue saw a Christmas card I had received from Dixie Gamble, addressed to me, rather than both of us. She became so furious that she threw hot soup on my pants and left for the night.

Always drama. But as 1973 came to a close, things were looking good in many respects. Billy Sherrill had loved a song of mine called "We're Not the Jet Set," ("we're the old Chevro-let set") and recorded it on George Jones and Tammy Wynette. It would be a good record; then decades later—in 2007—it would be used in a major Chevrolet TV commercial debuting on the Super Bowl show. I also had a song about good race relations in the future South, "I Believe the South Is Gonna Rise Again," ("but not the way we thought it would back then") that would be recorded and charted as singles by both Bobby Goldsboro and Tanya Tucker.

One cold January night in 1974, Woodward Maurice Ritter, known to millions as Tex Ritter, died of a heart attack a few days before his sixty-ninth birthday, while posting bond for one of his band members at the Metropolitan Nashville jail.

Tex, schooled in both law and drama, spoke in the Deep South accent of East Texas where there were few cowboys, but he'd had a lifetime love for cowboy lore and cowboy songs. There were three major milestones in Tex's career. In the 1930s, he starred as a singing cowboy in dozens of B-grade western movies and became known as "America's most beloved cowboy." In 1952 his voice became associated with the Oscar-winning title song for perhaps the most acclaimed western film of all time, the Gary Cooper and Grace Kelly classic *High Noon*, with Tex's deep voice crooning throughout the film: "Do not forsake me ohhhh my dah-lin.'" Then in 1961 came a country-pop smash, "I Dreamed of a Hill-Billy Heaven," which showed his prowess at delivering recitations.

Tex moved from Hollywood to Nashville in the early 1960s and became president of the Country Music Association. I came to know him when he was playing the excellent role of air personality sidekick to Ralph Emery and other hosts of the late night WSM *Opry Star Spotlight*. He was always a gentleman and always nice to me, even when I was just a new kid in town. When he was on a plane that was hijacked and forced to land in Cuba, Curly and I wrote "A Funny Thing Happened on the Way to Miami," which Tex recorded and charted. He liked another song of ours—"Wichita"—and when he recorded it, I stood at his studio microphone and helped coach him and coax him. In 1970 he ran for the Republican nomination for the US Senate, as a moderate against the conservative winner Bill Brock—though I had a hard time imagining Tennesseans electing someone named "Tex." No doubt he would have been proud to see his son John Ritter become one of the hottest TV stars of the 1970s and 1980s.

It all seemed so apropos; America's most beloved cowboy dying after riding in to get one of his boys out of jail.

One of the biggest thrills in my life was when Buddy Killen told me that Chet Atkins wanted to record one of my instrumental songs, "West Memphis Serenade." My Hammond organ had a built-in recorder that allowed me to track the rhythm pattern, then separately play along with it, utilizing my steel-guitar style, pulling the drawbars in and out with my left hand while playing the melody with the right—a sad tune with a beat. The thrill wasn't so much that the world's most famous guitar player wanted to record my song, but that Chet wanted me to play on his session. He rented a T-series Hammond like mine, so it would sound just like what I had done on the home demo.

At the recording session, Chet played the melody, of course, on the guitar, and he did it beautifully. After we had tracked that, I was overdubbing some steel guitar-like sounds on the organ. The other musicians were hanging around the studio while Chet sat in the control room with Buddy (they were co-producing the album). There was something that Chet wanted me to do differently, but rather than tell me over the talkback, where everyone would hear it, he walked out into the studio and sat down next to me and said, almost in a whisper, "Why don't you do that thing just half as much? Maybe do it every other time. What do you think?" Of course, I agreed with him. Then he went back into the control room, and I played it again, the way Chet had asked me to play it.

"Hey, I like that," he said over the talkback, "let's do it that way." It was *his* idea, but he was making it sound as if it were *my* idea. In the future, when I was a producer, I would remember that kind gesture. Always leave a musician feeling good about himself or herself, and never do anything that might embarrass a musician in front of his or her peers.

When the album came out I looked at the musician credits and my heart sank. Because the keyboards on all the other songs were played by Bobby Wood, the record label had made a mistake, and under "West Memphis Serenade," it read: Organ: Bobby Wood.

A musician from my home county in Florida, Jim Stafford, had been a seventeen-year-old kid back in 1961 when I predicted that he would someday be a famous guitarist. But thirteen years later he was finding a different kind of fame. One of his Polk County cohorts from those days, Gram Parsons, had already gained fame as "the father of country rock," then died of a drug overdose in 1973. Soon after, Stafford was having a string of rock novelty hits like "Spiders & Snakes." In the spring of 1974 he was in town, and I spent a few hours at his hotel room smoking weed with him and his road manager, Gallagher (who would within a few years become a nationally known comedian). Stafford got me a couple of prime seats for his Nashville concert a few nights later. Back in the days when he was calling me from Florida, Sue would say, "Why doesn't that Jim Stafford leave us alone?" and refused to hang out with him and his then-wife whenever they came to town. But backstage after his tremendous performance, Sue was about to eat him alive. "You are *so* great. Bobby always said you would be a star, and I thought so too. Please come over to the house tonight."

"When you're hot you're hot, when you're not you're not," as Jerry Reed said in his song. Don Wayne, who had a tremendously successful catalog at Tree, was thought of as a very traditional writer. One of the newer songpluggers told him, "Folks don't wanna hear about the frost on the pumpkin." Normally an easy-going, soft-spoken man, Don felt a little resentful about that remark and maybe just to prove a point to the guy who said it, he decided to use that as a line in a song—a song that told of a sophisticated lady meeting a country guy in a bar. "She said hello country bumpkin, how's the frost out on the pumpkin?" The two would fall in love and marry, and she would continue to call him her country bumpkin. The song tells of their baby, "the soft and warm and cuddly boy child feeding at her breast." He too becomes her "country bumpkin." In one of the most powerful moments in country songwriting, it concludes:

> Forty years of hard work later, in a simple,
>   quiet, and peaceful country place
> The heavy hand of time had not erased the raptured
>   wonder from the woman's face
> She was lying on her death bed, knowing fully
>   well her race was nearly run
> But she softly smiled and looked into the sad
>   eyes of her husband and her son
>
> And she said so long country bumpkins
> The frost is gone now from the pumpkin
> I've seen some sights and life's been somethin'
> See you later country bumpkins

Shortly after Don turned in this song, Buddy Killen and Jack Stapp agreed that he had become pretty cold as a writer, and that they would probably continue to have difficulty getting his more traditional songs recorded. So they dropped him; that is, his contract was up, and they elected to cut off his advances, making it pointless for him to re-sign with the company. "Country Bumpkin" was soon recorded by Cal Smith, and Don Wayne's swan song at Tree became a monster hit. At the annual BMI awards dinner, it was honored as the song receiving the most radio airplay for the entire year. Jack and Buddy ran up to the stage and embraced Don as he graciously thanked his former publishers and posed with them for pictures.

Moral support is the lifeblood of a songwriter. My little girl, my mother, my girlfriend—they all seemed to be cheering me on in my creative endeavors more than my wife. I admit that I wasn't transmitting much love to her, but I certainly wasn't receiving any that I could detect. When she was giving me hell about taking a trip, I said, "Who are *you* to talk? You do it all the time." "I wish I *was* doing it all the time," she retorted. Once she even glared at me and told me that her boyfriend was a much better lover than I was. I didn't doubt that he was better than I had been. Charlotte was certainly better than Sue had been. We weren't a match—not physically, not mentally, not spiritually. We were the perfect match for only one little second, when fate mixed my DNA with hers and made the most wonderful daughter in the world.

There was a great piece of music by Crosby, Stills & Nash, "Suite: Judy Blue Eyes," that was obviously "Sue's song." She played the record a lot, and I supposed that Rex Wordsworth had told her that it reminded him of her, because of her blue eyes. There was one period—I guessed that they had broken up—when she moped around in an obvious deep funk for days, sometimes putting on "Suite: Judy Blue Eyes" and playing it over and over as she sat and stared out the window. I felt sorry for her. I wanted her love life to be good. I wished there were someone that *I* loved that much.

It was about this time that I got a phone call at Tree from a girl who told me her name was Sue Lawrence. It almost rang a bell but not quite. Then she mentioned meeting me at a party—over two and a half years before—and it all came back to me. She was the girl who kept me from jumping head-on into an empty swimming pool and who nursed me through my sick drunkenness. I had thought about her for a long time after that until she gradually faded into my mental archives. She said she was coming to town with a girlfriend and asked if I would like to get together. I remembered then how good-looking and sweet she was and told her I'd love to see her. I got a guy for her girlfriend, and we all ate steak and biscuits at a place called Ireland's, then split off. It was Sue's twenty-third birthday. She was wearing a fall, which I thought made her resemble Barbara Mandrell. Sue Lawrence: sweet, easy to talk to, lovely, sexy. We had a great time together and agreed to do it again soon. That night, in code, I referred to her in my journal as "the new Sue."

The next day, I called Charlotte at her work in Florida and told her I had been with someone. Both of us being married, there was not a real commitment between us, but not to tell her would have felt wrong to me. She didn't love hearing it but seemed to appreciate the honesty.

Having a wife (though in name only), a regular but uncommitted relationship (with Charlotte), and a new acquaintance to whom I was very attracted (Sue Lawrence), I think it's fair to say that I was not at that time a one-woman-man. I had wandering eyes, and those eyes had seen a gorgeous waitress at a restaurant I sometimes patronized. The girl's name was Sunnybrook. I was thirty-three, and she was a Vanderbilt student of about twenty. I thought she was a knockout. I asked her out, and she said sure, she would love to go. She gave me her phone number and told me to call the next day. The next day was a Saturday, and I was so excited that I called her fairly early in the morning. She asked me to call back in a half hour, so I did. Another girl answered the phone and told me Sunnybrook was gone. When I asked when she would be back, the girl said, "In the fall. She's gone home to Ohio for the summer."

If Tree had a moral compass, it was Joyce Bush, secretary-treasurer and 10 percent owner of the company. She was a savvy businesswoman, but consistently kind and constantly positive. It was Buddy and Jack who made the major decisions, and, knowing Joyce's heart, it probably broke when they let Don Wayne go, but her effect on the company was always present, always good. A couple of years before, Joyce had been diagnosed with breast cancer. She fought it hard and continued to be the happy workaholic. A typical early morning scene was Tree's maintenance man, Sonny McCullough, driving up with Joyce, then slowly walking alongside her, leading her, making sure that she didn't fall as she made her way into the office to do a hard day's work. One pleasant night she was able to leave her hospital bed to go to the dedication of the Joyce Bush Piano Laboratory at Belmont College, attended by hundreds of friends from Music Row. In her last days, she begged to be taken to Tree, saying she wanted to die there. No one took her there to die, of course, but she passed away at age thirty-nine in June of 1974. Jack Stapp, for whom she had worked since she was a senior in high school, was so grief-stricken that he was unable to attend the funeral and had to be admitted to a hospital.

Jack and Buddy always made sure that they had the best help possible, including legal representation. Instead of using a Nashville attorney, their official lawyer was Lee Eastman in New York, father of Paul McCartney's wife, Linda. In the summer of 1974, the McCartneys decided they wanted to spend a few weeks in the Nashville area. Paul wanted to check out the music scene, so he talked to his father-in-law about setting something up through Tree. Buddy Killen, who after all his years in the business still had a tendency to be a bit starstruck, was elated. It was decided that Paul, Linda, and the members of their band, Wings, would stay in Curly Putman's mansion near Lebanon,

Paul and Linda McCartney and their band, Wings, during their stay at the Putman residence, "Junior's Farm"

paying today's equivalent of a few thousand dollars a week in rent. During that time Curly and Bernice would take a trip to Hawaii and Japan. Dixie Gamble was in charge of taking Linda's huge grocery list to the store, and I remember that not everyone in the group was at that time vegetarian, because several pounds of sausage were included.

I encountered the McCartneys in the downstairs hallway at Tree one day, but all of their attention was focused on their toddler who had just gotten poop on the carpet. I later told Buddy that the Beatles were very important to me, and it would mean a lot to actually get to meet Paul and hang out. He told me that on the following day Paul and Linda were to meet him at Tree, as they had plans to go to dinner with Chet Atkins at the Loveless Cafe, a country cooking mainstay about ten miles from downtown. He said he would ask them to come by early so we could chat awhile in the parking lot.

About five o'clock, they drove up in a small rental car. They got out smiling, Paul wearing a dark leisure suit and Linda wearing a simple but pretty "peasant" dress.

"Paul, this is Bobby Braddock," Buddy announced.

"Oh, you're Paul Smith, the bluegrass guy, right?" I said for God only knows what reason.

"The bluegrass guy, very funny," Paul said as he playfully punched me on the arm.

Although he had just turned thirty-two, I noticed little crow's feet around his eyes. His hair was short for a Beatle's.

"Bobby's one of our better writers, and consistently has songs in the charts," Buddy said reeling off titles that I could tell Paul didn't recognize. Then I mentioned "Did You Ever," a big hit in Britain three years before.

Paul raised his eyebrows with a look of surprise, "BO-bee, you wrote that? Wow. Way to go," bopping me once again on the arm. I was thinking, Paul scratches his head and songs bigger than "Did You Ever" tumble out. He was being nice. I told him I was not only a Beatles fan but a Wings fan, and loved the *Band on the Run* album. I could tell he wasn't used to talking to people in country music who listened to Wings albums. I mentioned how much I loved a song called "Picasso's Last Words."

"You have good taste if you like 'Picasso's Last Words,'" Linda said. I had seen her pictures many times, getting the impression that though she wasn't movie-star glamorous, she was naturally attractive. But in person, I thought she was beautiful, inside and out. She had a radiance, and she had a kindness. Both Paul and Linda were peppering me with questions about country music. I asked Paul if the *Sgt. Pepper's* album was actually recorded on only four tracks, and he said it was.

Finally Buddy said it was time to go pick up Chet, and he started to climb into his Cadillac. Paul said, "BO-bee, you're going with us, yes?" Buddy looked as if he was about to have a stroke. He didn't want one of his songwriters getting in the way of megastar elbow-rubbing.

"Oh no, I just wanted to meet you guys. It's been a thrill for me."

"We *will* be seeing you again, won't we?" asked Linda, with sincerity that I didn't doubt.

"I hope so," I said. I never saw them again.

They recorded two sides for the next Wings album at Buddy's SoundShop studio: "Sally G" and "Junior's Farm" (Paul referred to Curly—whose name was Claude Putman Jr.—as "Junior"). The McCartney family left Nashville not on a jet, but in a big camper, wanting to see America up close, as a family. Curly and Bernice were proud to point out the stray cat that Paul and Linda had named "Sally G.," but they weren't happy about the lingering smell of marijuana around Junior's Farm.

My track record—a big country hit, a big British hit, and a few semi-hits— seemed like nothing compared to this man who was part of a band that had turned the music world upside down, a songwriter whose compositions were already considered among the most memorable of all time. I was a flea, and he was an elephant. Meeting him made me realize that I needed to get my butt in gear. When the history of country music was written, I didn't want to be a mere asterisk, I wanted to be at least a small paragraph.

6

OMEGA AND ALPHA

As surely as cicadas live out the last stages of their lives by swarming into Nashville every thirteen years, old country music fans used to do it every year. After the Opryland theme park opened in 1972, they came in even larger numbers, usually by highway, often bringing along their children and grandchildren. This was especially true in the summertime when the reception areas of the music publishing companies got a steady stream of folks who were thinking heck, since they were in town anyway, why not drop by one of those places and see if there was somebody who would give their songs a listen?—the answer usually being "I'm sorry, but our policy is . . ." As the tourists were heading into Nashville, the music business people were heading out because the summer has traditionally been a slow time on Music Row—sort of like the Christmas holidays, only longer.

The Braddocks were no exception in the summer of 1974, spending a few days in New Orleans and also at our favorite Tennessee vacation spot, Watts Bar Lake Resort, just west of the Great Smoky Mountains, where Sue liked to sun by the pool while Jeep and I searched the woods for arrowheads. This was the summer that Jack Nicholson got his nose cut in *Chinatown*, the summer that I was reading Philip Roth's *My Life As a Man*, and turning up the radio every time they played "Band on the Run." I was feeling positive about the future—not Sue's and mine, but mine. It was nothing I could put my finger on; it was more like something that was in the air. I was writing what I wanted to, and hopeful that if I kept doing enough of that, I would have a lot of hits that weren't carbon copies of everything else. Ah, carbon copies. Ah, 1974.

This was the year of Watergate. There was no escaping the alleged crimes of the Nixon administration, and even the apolitical were aware. The Senate Watergate Committee had created new American heroes on the nation's TV screens. By the summer of 1974 the spotlight was on the US House of Representatives, upon whom the responsibility of impeachment would fall.

That summer, when not on the road with my family, I spent a lot of time watching the Watergate hearings. When the hearings weren't on, Sue was often home watching her soap operas, and Jeep was maybe watching *Brady Bunch* reruns. When I wasn't watching the hearings, I was usually at Tree—

or Tree International, its official name in the 1970s—often having lunch with my regular noonday crowd: Mike Kosser, Steve Pippin, and Eddy Anderson. These lunches would often turn into something of a larger scope, such as composing the longest sentence in the world—we went into a studio to record it for posterity—or practical jokes, such as me being led out to the car wearing shades like a blind man, then watching the passersby gawk as I attempted to drive. The day that I would grow up was still many years away.

I had become close friends with nineteen-year-old boy wonder Rafe Van Hoy, formerly one of Curly's Green Grass writers before signing with Tree. We made each other laugh a lot. Rafe was a super-talented songwriter, singer, and guitarist, and I had never met anyone whose successful future I was so certain of. His parents had moved to Nashville from East Tennessee two years before, when Rafe was still a senior in high school, so he could pursue a music career.

Those summer days, I thought a lot about Sue Lawrence, and we wrote each other occasionally. Charlotte and I continued to see each other and keep in touch between visits. Once, when I told her that she owed me three letters, she immediately sent me three. I wrote her back that I had received two long ones from her, then commented, "I don't know if 'Christ, I'm horny' counts as a letter, but I was glad to get it."

Charlotte flew into town to see me on the day that President Nixon resigned. For some reason we had trouble finding her a room farther out, where she usually stayed, so I got her accommodations at the Hall of Fame Motel, which was next door to Buddy Killen's recording studio, SoundShop. Buddy happened to be in the motel lobby as Charlotte was checking in, so I introduced them. Charlotte and I were glad to see Nixon going, and were looking forward to watching his farewell speech on TV.

"Hey, are you guys going up to a room? Are you going to be watching Nixon on TV?" Buddy inquired. Oh no, I thought, we're going to have to watch this long-awaited historic moment with a diehard defender of Nixon. Buddy wasn't a political partisan, because twenty-four years later he would side with Clinton when *he* was threatened with impeachment; Buddy just seemed to empathize with any president who was in danger of being brought down. He was a very powerful man in his world, and I think he identified with the preeminently powerful. So Nixon was on the tube making his pitiful speech, and Buddy was telling us how Nixon hadn't really done anything wrong. I was keeping my mouth shut out of respect for my publisher, but after we'd all had a few drinks, Charlotte started to challenge him, and she didn't stop at politics. I cared a lot about Charlotte, but she had a tendency to embarrass me when she'd had too much to drink, and this night was no exception.

"You're really a very insecure man," she told Buddy. Twice he stood in the doorway about to leave, then came back inside to discuss it further, asking Charlotte why she thought that. It really bothered him.

The next day at Tree, Buddy asked, "What's the matter with that girl? Is she *crazy*?"

I was sporting a beard, something I had wanted to do for a long time. Looking back at old pictures, I want so badly to write a "letter to me," as Brad Paisley did in his song, but in my letter I would tell the 1974 Bobby, "The beard is cool, but *please* get rid of that awful *rug*. Just pull it off now, the sooner the better." It would take someone in my future to tell me to toss the hairpiece.

I was beginning to think that nothing could save Sue and me. She had her life, I had mine, and we no longer had any mutual friends other than Curly and Bernice Putman. One thing we consistently had in common was Jeep. We had discussed the possibility of her going to Peabody Demonstration School, which was affiliated with Peabody Teachers College. I had a Florida cousin, Clayton Braddock, who had become press secretary for the Tennessee Department of Education, and he said the Peabody School had a very good reputation. It was a progressive school where a lot of college professors sent their children, and it was highly favored by the local Jewish community. There was a long waiting list, and it appeared that Jeep wouldn't be able to get in until 1975. But when the Demonstration School announced that it would operate independently of Peabody Teachers College (which was about to merge with Vanderbilt University) there were suddenly some openings. Jeep made good scores on her "entrance exam," and we were able to enroll her after all. The facility was located just off Music Row, so it would be easy for me to pick her up after school, often taking her back to Tree with me. She would soon become the little girl going around the building showing everyone her pet hermit crabs.

As Sue and I walked through the doors of the white-pillared country club where I would pick up BMI honors for "Nothing Ever Hurt Me Half as Bad as Losing You," Dolly Parton grabbed me like a long lost friend. After networking around the large room for a few minutes, I realized that Sue had disappeared. I finally found her at one of the banquet tables, plopped down next to Dolly who was trying to eat her salad. Sue was slurring her words and talking to Dolly about an interview for a book she was planning to write. I had embarrassed Sue at the BMI Awards a couple of years before, so I guess it was payback time.

I knew I had to perform a major balancing act around Sue the following week because Sue *Lawrence* was coming to town one day, then I was getting with Charlotte for a couple of days after that. Sue Lawrence and I got together for a wonderful afternoon at a motel in Franklin, about twenty miles south of Nashville. She lived with her husband in the Miami area and also had a regular boyfriend there. She often visited her parents in northern Alabama. The Lawrences seemed to be in a constant state of separation. Though only twenty-three, Sue had a seven-year-old son. I kept telling myself that this very good-looking girl was not someone I should be involved with. "Beware," I told myself, "you could get pretty foolish over this girl." Charlotte was safer.

Soon after Charlotte left town, I attended a meet-and-greet that Curly Putman had put together for Lamar Alexander, Republican nominee for governor. Curly had written and recorded the official campaign song. Only a couple of months older than I was, Alexander was unusually young for a gubernatorial candidate, and I thought he was bright and personable. However, I was tired of voting for Republicans so I supported the Democratic nominee, Ray Blanton, a former congressman from rural West Tennessee. Jeep wrote a campaign song for Blanton, just our own little private one, with a tune like a marching band football fight song.

> *Ray Blanton, Blanton, Blanton*
> *For our state, state, state*
> *Don't be late, late, late*
> *For he won't make Watergate*

Blanton was elected and, unfortunately, he *did* "make Watergate." His administration was the most corrupt in Tennessee history, and he ended up going to prison. Alexander would be elected the next time around, then re-elected four years later, and even Democrats would consider him one of Tennessee's best governors.

After election day, with scents of burning leaves riding on the wind and visions of sugar plums dancing in our heads, Music Row tended to relax a little, but I still spent much of my time there. One day Dixie Gamble showed me the lyrics that a Japanese songwriter had written in English, and all the plurals were missing their "s," and I thought that was very funny. It inspired a song full of singulars called "My Better Half."

> *I kick my shoe off, I pull my sock off, and take my pant off*
> *Then I find my pajama and put it on*
> *Then I crawl into the bed and cry my eye out*
> *Now that my better half is gone*
>
> *I just lay there, and as I lay there, my arm feels so empty*
> *And my lip longs to kiss her all night long*
> *If I had the gut I'd blow my brain out*
> *Now that my better half is gone*
>
> *I was a whole man when I was with her*
> *Now I'm a plier, I'm a scissor*
> *I'm half this, half that*
> *Half slow, half fast*
>
> *I've got the blue, and I'm up to my elbow in heartache*
> *Now that my better half is gone*

It would never become a hit, but it would be recorded several times, twice by me.

The 1974 holiday season holds an abundance of vivid memories: Thanksgiving at "Junior's Farm" and all of us getting to hold Curly and Bernice's baby granddaughter, a future Tree employee; Jeep being upset when she found her new parakeet, Eggbert, missing from his cage, as our Siamese cat, Brother, slept contentedly on the floor with a feather sticking out of his mouth; Sue trying to convince Jeep, and Jeep trying to convince herself, that there was a Santa Claus; and me buying a Christmas present for myself, a Minimoog synthesizer.

I used the Minimoog, along with other keyboard instruments, to stack tracks—that is, to play the various parts one at a time—for demos of my songs. A few years before, Tree had decreed that no songs could be demoed unless the writer was supervised by one of the songpluggers. I felt that the pluggers didn't have production skills any better than mine, so I rebelled and started demoing my songs with nothing but my vocals accompanied by myself on piano. After a year or two of this, I started overdubbing Moog synthesizer bass and a "string machine," becoming a one-man-band, fortified by engineer Eddy Anderson playing drums while he was rolling the tape. (This kind of hands-on recording would help me years down the road when I was producing.) Amazingly, these bare-boned little makeshift demos included a lot of songs that got recorded and became hits. If Tree hadn't been so shortsighted, and I hadn't been so obstinate, I wonder how many more hits I would have had with better-sounding fully staffed demo sessions. In time, I would start using Rafe Van Hoy on guitar, and gradually add other instruments, until finally I had gone full circle, and my lone-wolf demos had turned into full ones. I got my way by gradually sneaking in the back door.

I was writing plenty of songs and getting a few of them recorded. Anytime someone released a single that I had written, I got extra copies of the records and sent them to my family and friends in Florida. I knew they were proud that I was having some success in the music business. My mother, who had always associated country music with the drunken hoedowns she recalled from her youth in rural Georgia and Alabama, started liking country music when I became a part of it. She was a great press agent, keeping the *Auburndale Star* supplied with headlines. My father used to say "Fools' names, like monkeys' faces / Often appear in public places." But anyone on Music Row who said that he or she didn't like publicity wasn't telling the truth. I had been fortunate in getting a lot of it, in various articles in the papers of Nashville and other cities, and occasional profiles in publications like *Country Song Roundup* and *Music City News*, and articles in music trade journals like *Billboard*. *Time* magazine had called "I Believe the South Is Gonna Rise Again" the "anthem of the New South."

Red O'Donnell was a good media contact for me. A delightful man, he was a Nashville institution, renowned for his music biz columns in the evening *Banner*. Red was born into Nashville's Irish Catholic community, in the old days made up, in large part, of railroad workers. He was sort of a Southern leprechaun: red hair turned white, big smile, and rosy cheeks enhanced by a little alcohol. His columns were extremely popular with readers who loved tidbits about the stars, but Red's writing style was more entertaining than seriously journalistic. I also learned that he liked to invent his own dialogue for his interviewees.

I was happy that Red was going to do a big feature story on me for the front page of his paper's weekend entertainment supplement. When I opened up the paper and saw the picture of Jeep and me looking in a mirror, I was pretty excited. And then I read the article. Although Red had interviewed me, what he wrote never came from my mouth. He had me saying things in baseball metaphors. I didn't use baseball lingo when talking about *baseball*, much less music.

"I'm a .100 hitter," he had me saying. "During 1974 I wrote about 65 songs and about 10 were recorded." It got worse. "If you want more statistics on writer Bobby Braddock," he had me saying in the third person, "I've been writing for approximately 10 years. I've written, say, 800, and 70 of them are on record. You can be a professional writer, but until they are on wax, you just *ain't* a writer." I, who had made an art out of sounding modest, came off like a slick-talking egomaniac. I was livid. Donna Hilley, Joyce Bush's hand-picked successor at Tree, had a background in PR. She told me any publicity was good publicity. I asked her, "Then how about murder?" Red was a sweet old guy, so I let it go. But years later, on two occasions, I would call newspapers demanding corrections on misquotes far less severe than what Red had done. I may say dumb things, but I want them to be *my* dumb things.

The most powerful effect that opening a newspaper ever had on me was on February 27, 1975, when I saw, on the front page, a large picture of nine year-old Marcia (pronounced MAR-sha) Trimble, who had left her home two evenings before to deliver Girl Scout cookies to neighbors across the street. She never got there. Maybe it was because she was one year, to the day, older than Lauren, but it hit me very hard. I didn't normally think of myself as psychic, but I was so overwhelmed with sadness that I closed my eyes and saw several images, one of a room full of lawnmowers. I told the head of the Metro Police homicide division what I had "seen," though I think he thought I was nuts.

The Trimbles lived on Copeland Drive, in a comfortable neighborhood between the areas known as Green Hills and Belle Meade. The normally quiet street was suddenly filled with police cars, news vehicles, and curiosity seekers. (One of the first on the scene was a fledgling TV reporter from Nashville's Channel 5 named Oprah Winfrey.) People throughout the county were asked to search nearby woods and creeks. Little Marcia's body was found several days later in a garage (that had been thoroughly searched on the night of her disappearance), visible from the Trimble home through a little patch of woods. The garage was full of lawnmowers (and objects that *looked* like lawnmowers, such as vacuum cleaners) just as I had "seen" after reading the newspaper article. It was reported that she had been sexually assaulted. A man named Jerome Barrett would be convicted of her murder on compelling DNA evidence—*thirty-four years later.*

While the Trimble family's nightmare went on, our lives went on. *Godfather II* became my new all-time favorite movie, Tanya Tucker's cut of my "I Believe the South Is Gonna Rise Again" hit #12 in the charts, Jack Stapp—at sixty-four—quietly married a young woman still in her twenties whom he had "mentored" since she was a teenager, and singer-songwriter Dick Feller recorded a live version of a song of mine called "Sing Me a Shitkickin' Song."

Then came the Great Flood of 1975. On the morning of March 13, the Harpeth River started overflowing its banks, and by late afternoon our house was on a tiny island in a giant lake, with the water almost to our door. We were lucky. Most of the houses on our street were partially submerged, and one had totally disappeared from sight. One of our neighbors owned a grocery store and brought food and supplies in a boat. On the final day of the flood, Sue and I were getting along so badly that I thought it best to leave. I knew the waters were receding and that Jeep was safe, so I waded in water up to my neck to Highway 70 and caught a ride into town.

I got drunk and blew up the house. April Fool!" I wrote in my journal. In reality, things weren't quite that crazy. I had gotten into the habit of drinking liqueur as a bedtime sleeping potion—sweet, fruity, creamy, even chocolate-flavored liqueur—not enough to get drunk on, but enough to give me a good sleeping buzz. Sue still slept downstairs on her big round bed, while I slept upstairs across the hall from Jeep, who was going through a daddy's-girl phase and often went to sleep clinging to one of my shirts.

One fine spring day, after Jeep and I returned home from exploring the old grist mill at the river, Sue told me that Jim Stafford had called. When I reached him, he said in his TV evangelist-type voice, "Hey, Bobby, I'm gonna be tapin' a Timex TV special from Opryland in a few days, and I'd love t' have you come hang out."

"Do you m-mind if I pitch you a couple of songs?" I asked.

"Man, I want you to play me a *bunch* of your songs," he said in his homespun drawl.

(I once told Stafford that sometimes people would ask me if I was from Texas, and he said he got that a lot, too. I think it's because our native Polk County, Florida—like Texas—was settled mostly by Southerners but with a sprinkling of Midwesterners thrown in.)

A few days later his road manager, Gallagher, called me and said if I would come to Opryland around 11:30 a.m., Jim would be taking a break, which would give him time to listen to my material in the dressing room. I got a portable tape machine and headed for Opryland. The show was being taped at the new Grand Ole Opry House, which opened at the park in 1974.

Jim was behind schedule, but that gave me the opportunity to hang out for about an hour with Dennis Weaver, who was then the star of the popular TV show *McCloud*. I best remembered him as the limping sidekick Chester from *Gunsmoke*, which had been the longest-running series in TV history. Weaver mistakenly thought that I was rolling in money (royalties from "D-I-V-O-R-C-E"). A vegetarian and yoga enthusiast, he gave me a stern lecture about smoking. "You really ought to think about giving it up," he said.

Suddenly Stafford barged in the door and said, "Hey, Dennis, they're ready for you. Bobby, let's go eat some lunch before we listen to songs. Lunch is on Timex." He was driving a high-speed golf cart. His record producer, Phil Gernhard, rode next to him as I hung on in the back, sitting next to a nervous reporter from *Country Music* magazine who was there to do an interview. Stafford was fully relishing the star role—buzzing across Opryland, people jumping out of the way as he went from paved road to grassy lawn to gravel trail. After leaving the cafeteria, we raced back to the dressing room trailers, on the same kind of wild joy ride.

Stafford liked several songs that I played him. His favorite was a suite I had recently written, "Mary Ann, Catch Me If You Can," which chronicled an off-and-on relationship over a period of many years. There was one line, "I'm back from the battle of South Vietnam" that Stafford's producer, Phil Gernhard, went ballistic over. "That was the stupidest goddamned war in history. I don't even want to *hear* about that war." I explained that it wasn't a pro-war line, that I, too, had been against the war; the line was simply a marker along the highway, on the protagonist's journey through life. He didn't care, he thought the line needed to come out.

Ironically, this is what I wrote about that war in my journal, the war that had just ended, the war that America had pulled out of two years before: "South Vietnam is now 'liberated' and Saigon is now Ho Chi Minh City. From a corrupt, rotten-to-the-core capitalist government to a ruthless, take-over-by-force communist government. Which is worse? There have been thirty-five years there of one war after another. Thank God that's all over. Our big tragedy: 50,000 Americans died. For what?"

Sue had thrown herself into becoming active at Jeep's school in the PTA, as leader of the Brownie troop, and as editor of the school newsletter. She was proud to be getting in the spotlight, and I was glad to see her doing it. I think there must have been a permanent break between Sue and Rex Wordsworth, because she had started playing up to several men in the music business, all successful and all ranging from several to many years older than I. At one gathering, I bent down to tie my shoe and looked under the table and caught a glimpse of her holding hands with a Music Row executive who was sitting next to her. At a big party, she and a legendary songwriter left the room at the same time, through separate doors, then returned at the same time an hour later, through separate doors. Many years later I would ask still another music business veteran if he ever went to bed with Sue. *"No,"* he exclaimed, visibly upset, then added, "but if I did, I wouldn't tell you."

I received a letter from the *other* Sue, Sue Lawrence, telling me she would be coming to town in three weeks. She wrote, "I wanted to be with you again this year on my birthday. Remember last year? WOW!!!!!" So I had my lovers and felt that my wife deserved to have hers.

When I saw Sue Lawrence get out of her car at a motel in Franklin, I almost jumped out of my skin. Her blonde hair was in an Afro and she wore a tight floral print dress. Her looks took my breath away. We had a wonderful time, though we only had from late morning until mid-afternoon to be together. This "new Sue" and my "old Sue" were like night and day, but their biographies were eerily similar. Both blonde Sues were Tauruses born in May, and both were from northern Alabama, but there was more. Both had five-letter, two-syllable first names; Sue in the middle; and one-syllable six-letter maiden names ending in "s." Nancy Sue Rhodes and Wilma Sue Sparks. I didn't need two Sues in my life. I told Sue Lawrence that I was going to start calling her *Sparky*, for her maiden name, Sparks. She loved it.

The "old Sue" and I weren't arguing as much, perhaps simply because we had drifted far apart. There was still an occasional crazy fight, though. I wrote in one journal entry "Sue and I had significant differences this morning, and I commenced to slap her hand with my face, then kick her in the foot with my balls."

I was proud of Sue for shedding all vestiges of any earlier Southern racism. Southern whites and blacks socializing in the twenty-first century would get scant attention, if any, but this was 1975. I had voted for the race-baiting George Wallace for president in the general election only seven years before, and Sue had voted for her fellow Alabamian in the Democratic presidential primary only three years before. One of Jeep's best friends at school was an African American girl named Michelle Bahner. We had spent a couple of enjoyable evenings with Michelle's parents, her father a jovial pediatrician who liked to keep me well supplied with rum and Double Cola while I played the piano. Jeep had spent the night at their house, so Sue suggested that all four of the Bahner children spend the weekend with us. We took them to dinner and then to Fair Park, Nashville's traditional year-round fun place for children in those days. A young black man who said he had just arrived from Milwaukee asked me if we were some kind of church group. When I told him that the children were my daughter's friends, he said, "Man, this is a pretty cool introduction to Nashville."

But I was far from being the coolest guy in Nashville. True, I was thought of as being friendly to everyone, but every once in a while my hair-trigger temper would present itself to some rude guy. There was a new songplugger at Tree named Tom Griggs. He didn't exactly win my undying affection when he started making fun of my novelty or comedy songs. Meetings with him were difficult because he stayed on the phone most of the time, and I just felt that he never showed me much respect. One day he asked if I had something for Johnny Russell. I suggested "Ruby Is a Groupie (With a Cosmic Cowboy Band)," and he waved his hand and said, "No, it's too short." I could feel my face changing color. The song was about two minutes and ten seconds long— short but not unusual for 1975—and if an artist and producer thought it was too short, they could always arrange it in a way to lengthen the recording. I felt there were plenty of legitimate reasons for not pitching my song, but "too short" was not one of them. I should have just calmly told him what I thought, walked out, and asked another plugger to pitch it to Johnny Russell; or I could have pitched it myself. But his little peccadilloes had been building up, and this was the straw that broke the legendary camel's back. I exploded and leaped across the desk at Tom Griggs. "You sonofabitch," I yelled.

"Bobby, Bobby, Bobby, Bobby, no, no, no! I'm sorry. Calm down."

I climbed down off his desk and left in a huff. "Asshole," I muttered, as I stomped out the door.

The next day, I felt bad about the way I had reacted, and went to Tree to apologize to Tom Griggs. I walked into his office and discovered that it was bare; everything had been removed. Buddy Killen was standing nearby.

"Wh-where's Tom?" I asked.

"I fired him," Buddy said.

"You fired him? Wh-why did you do that?"

"I'm not gonna have anyone around here who doesn't treat you with respect, Valentine," he replied with resolve. I tried to talk him out of it, but he said his mind was made up, that Tom was already out of there permanently. I never wanted to do anything that affected anyone's job, their livelihood. But I must say, I was deeply touched by Buddy's loyalty. I had my occasional differences with Buddy, and friends had heard me imitate his Bullwinkle voice, but in those days I never doubted that Buddy truly cared about me and believed in me.

Tammy Wynette's seven-year-old "D-I-V-O-R-C-E" was suddenly a big hit in England. And on the strength of some of my novelty songs like "Ruby Is a Groupie," "My Better Half," and the one about the nearsighted snake falling in love with a garden hose, "The Snake Song," Buddy had secured me a record deal—my third recording contract—this time with Mercury. I thought it would be nice to have success as an artist, but I don't think I gave it much thought beyond that, or asked myself what my day-to-day life would be like if I were to accidentally record a hit. It bothered me that no one seemed interested in me as an artist unless I was doing my comedy songs.

As a kid I loved the Spike Jones hits—serious music that would suddenly switch to sped-up voices, whistles, sirens, hiccups and burps—and when our family had company, I amused them with my a cappella versions of those songs. The comedy that tickled me the most in my childhood, whether on records or the silver screen, was the silly stuff; Lou Costello could make me fall out of my theater seat laughing. My favorite comic in 1975 was this new guy, Steve Martin, who I thought was the funniest person on TV. I had seen Martin several times on Johnny Carson's *Tonight Show* and loved his balloon depictions, happy feet, and "Excuuuussse ME!" When Curly Putman told me he had become acquainted with Steve Martin at a club in Reno, and that he and Bernice were going to catch his show at the Exit/In in Nashville, I jumped at the chance for Sue and me to go with them. Steve sat and visited with us for a while before the show, and when Curly invited him to go to dinner with us afterward, I got the feeling that Martin was making up excuses and giving us country yokels the brush-off. But I thought his act was hilarious. Like the Pied Piper, he led the audience out into the parking lot where he hot-wired a car and took off in it. It was great seeing him in those days when he would work a small club like the Exit/In. Within two years he would be the hottest act on TV.

Jim Stafford had also done well on national TV, and in fact had gotten his own summer show on ABC. When the season ended, he was in Nashville and gave me a call, inviting me to come to a little party at his suite at the Spence Manor, a fashionable Music Row residence hotel. I was met at the door by his girlfriend, a beautiful brunette named Deborah Allen. She had been a singer in the Opryland theme park and met Stafford a few months earlier when he was doing the Timex special at the Opry House there. He invited her to be part of his summer TV show, and they became an item. I thought, Stafford, you lucky so-and-so. She was twenty-one and ultra-friendly, the total extrovert. Deborah was extremely animated; when repeating a conversation she had heard, she would adopt the voices and mannerisms of the people she was quoting. She was a first-rate musician, but impressed me most when she sat down in the middle of the floor and sang an a cappella song about her mother and daddy, in a beautiful, earthy, haunting voice. Deborah Allen would one day become a star, and also one of my very closest friends.

Danny Davis, of Danny Davis and the Nashville Brass, was one of the guests in Stafford's suite. The moment Danny left, Stafford—perhaps seeing the well-known bandleader as a father figure—breathed a sigh of relief and yelled, "All right, bring out the weed." As these words are being written here, Danny Davis is gone and so are some of the others; the younger people in that room are now the older people in other rooms, Jim Stafford spent over twenty-five years as a star in his own theater in Branson, Missouri, and has now returned to our Florida home county, and the Spence Manor hotel suites are now condos. The only thing that stays the same is everything changes.

September of 1975 was the beginning of a new era at Tree International. Jack Stapp took the less active title of Chairman of the Board and relinquished his presidency to Buddy Killen. And Jan Crutchfield was replaced as creative director by Don Gant.

When Donald Wayne Gant came to Tree, he was a month shy of his thirty-third birthday, but already a music business veteran. He was nice look-

A great mentor of
songwriters, Don Gant

ing, unselfconsciously balding, and though slender, had a teddy bear quality
about him. A tough kid from East Nashville, he had learned the publishing
business inside-out at Acuff-Rose while still a teenager. He had sung with the
Everly Brothers and had been a motorcycle-riding pal of Roy Orbison. In his
mid-twenties he had a pop hit as vocalist with the Neon Philharmonic, singing "Morning Girl" with a fake British accent. He then had success as a producer, recording Jimmy Buffett on the hit "Come Monday" and the infamous
"Why Don't We Get Drunk and Screw." So by the time Don Gant came to
Tree, he had experienced practically every facet of the music business.

"Gant" would impact Tree in a way that can be compared only to that of
Buddy Killen himself. In fact, Buddy would come to envy Gant's magnetic
pull on the ones who wrote the songs—from the start, there was a mutual
love between this song man and the songwriters. He had the charisma of an
evangelist or a superstar or a dictator. Writers would start gathering after-
hours in Gant's office to sip wine, smoke pot, and listen to each other's songs.
Writers from other publishing companies would start showing up—legends
like John D. Loudermilk, Mickey Newbury, and Guy Clark. An enigma within
an enigma, Gant was laid-back around music, a raving maniac on the golf
course, lovable and funny, sexist (though he liked many women), and racist
(though he liked *some* blacks), bluntly honest, totally unpredictable, devoted
if he loved you, cruel if he didn't, super talented, and he respected songs and
songwriters more than anyone I ever knew. His politics were right wing, but
he would love the most liberal song in the world if it was well-written. I never
heard him use the word "commercial," because if he thought a song was great,
he'd go to hell and back to get it cut, whether it was perceived to be salable or

(*From left to right*) Harlan Howard, Curly Putman, Joe Allen, Red Lane, and me (far right), mid-1970s

not. Though Gant would one day have serious differences with Buddy Killen, he would also throw someone out of his office for putting Buddy down: "You can't talk that way about him in this building."

Gant immediately hired a short, stocky, thirty-ish, wisecracking, well-liked womanizer named Dan Wilson who would soon be recognized as one of the best songpluggers on Music Row. Buddy made Tree what it was, and Gant and his followers would take it to the next level.

At the BMI Awards banquet, where I won awards for "(We're Not) the Jet Set" and "I Believe the South Is Gonna Rise Again," Buddy had arranged for Sue and me to sit with Charlie Fach, the head of Mercury Records in Nashville. Charlie told me that the Mercury people in New York were excited about me as an artist. He also talked about the high regard he had for Buddy, and asked me if I was going to the Buddy Killen Day festivities down in Alabama.

There was a Tree bus going down to Buddy's hometown of Florence, Alabama, but Sue and I decided to drive down in our car. We hadn't been there long until Sue was mad about me sharing a joint with a pretty blonde.

"I'm driving back to Nashville," she snapped, "and if you don't leave right now, then you can come home on the damned Tree bus." I did exactly that. It was a bus full of happily stoned people, proud to have been a part of honoring Buddy Killen on his day. On I-65 near Franklin, several miles south of Nashville, we stopped when we saw a car that had left the road and landed upside down alongside the opposite lanes. From the looks of it, it had probably rolled over several times. There were several people trapped inside the car, and a woman pleaded that we help her little four-year-old daughter, who was unconscious and appeared to be badly injured. The doors were all jammed and the squashed top had made all points of entry inaccessible except for a portion of one window. The ambulance had just arrived and the paramedics said it was urgent that the child be removed and taken to a hospital. Only one of our entire group, Rafe Van Hoy, was small enough to fit into the opening, and it wasn't an easy fit even for him, but he managed to get inside the car and hand out the little ebony-skinned girl whose clothes were soaked in blood. She was rushed to the nearest emergency room, where she was pronounced dead on arrival.

That shook me up terribly. I could only imagine the mother's agony. It made me think of how precious Jeep was to me. She had started back to school at Peabody Demonstration School, which had undergone a name change: University School of Nashville, soon known to all as USN.

In November Sue and I attended a party at which I was drunkenly flirtatious. She said it was the last straw, so I moved out. We had split up very briefly a couple of times before—in other words I took some clothes to a motel room for two or three nights—but this time I actually rented an apartment, in the Melrose area of South Nashville. The floors were covered with cheap shag carpet, which I called "hairy linoleum," and it had a stale urine odor that the landlady assured me would be gone within a few days. I called a well-known attorney, Jack Norman Jr., and Sue found *her* high-priced lawyer—the Braddocks weren't going to do anything cheaply if they could help it—and we started making plans for our D-I-V-O-R-C-E.

Appropriately—art imitating life—the song "D-I-V-O-R-C-E" was the gift that kept on giving, but in ways that I had never expected. A few years before, Sheb Wooley had recorded a parody called "D-I-V-O-R-C-E #2" under the name of his alter ego, Ben Colder, and it was all playing out in the late fall of 1975.

Sheb was a very funny man who had enjoyed a well-rounded career. He was in several famous 1950s western movies, such as *High Noon* and *Giant*, and played Pete Nolan in the hit TV series *Rawhide*. In 1958 he wrote and recorded one of the biggest novelty hits of all time, "The Purple People Eater." In the 1960s, he moved from Hollywood to Nashville and had success in the country field, a #1 record—"That's My Pa"—and several hits credited to his drunk parody-singing alter ego, Ben Colder. Many years later, he would play the high school principal in the popular film about basketball, *Hoosiers*.

Sheb and I wrote several songs together for his Ben Colder albums. Though he was nearly twenty years older than I, we had the same warped sense of humor and had fun collaborating. We wrote one called "Astrology" with Sheb's hilarious line (which he swore to everyone that I wrote):

> *You mean I can't see Uranus*
> *'Til Neptune crosses Venus?*

So when Sheb told Curly and me that he had written a parody called "D-I-V-O-R-C-E #2," we thought that was great until he asked for a piece of the song. When you write a parody of someone's song, you can have a piece of it, but only if the writer or writers of the original song are on board. Typically, it's not done. Curly and I talked it over. Sheb was a good guy and would be the only person ever recording that version, so okay, what the hell, let's cut him in on it. But because I had 75 percent of the original, and Curly had 25 percent, how would we do a three-way split? After much pondering, I said, "Aw, it's not going to make that much money anyway, why don't we just split it three ways evenly, each of us taking a third." My own generous words had taken me down from three-fourths of a song to one-third.

A very popular Scottish comedian, Billy Connolly, was a big sensation throughout the British Isles, a kind of Steve Martin of the United Kingdom. So when we were told that he was having a British hit with "D-I-V-O-R-C-E" we were pleasantly surprised. We had never even heard the record since we didn't live in England, but we were elated when it became #1 in the UK. My elation quickly evaporated when Buddy Killen obtained a copy of our monster hit and played it for us. It was the Ben Colder "D-I-V-O-R-C-E #2." I would make less than half as much as I had thought. Sheb had done absolutely nothing wrong; he had just been a smart businessman in asking for a piece of the pie. "It doesn't hurt to ask," as the saying goes. The next time I saw him, I said, "Hey, Sheb, we sure had us a big hit together in England, didn't we?" He seemed embarrassed and changed the subject. But if he hadn't written the parody, we wouldn't have had the Billy Connolly hit. And if we hadn't cut Sheb in on a song that became a hit, it would have been the other way around: *we* would have felt embarrassed.

The day before I fell head over heels in love, there was a chill in the air, typical for a Tennessee Thanksgiving. I picked up Sue and Jeep at Newsom Station Road, and we rode into downtown Nashville to have Thanksgiving dinner at the revolving Polaris Restaurant atop the Regency Hotel. Sue and I were still separated, but we were not moving forward on the divorce. I had been dating a very young woman who sang in clubs around town, Carla Watson. Buddy Killen had recently produced my first session for Mercury and was excited about "Ruby Is a Groupie." On country radio, Waylon Jennings was asking, "Are You Sure Hank Done It This Way?" and on pop radio, the Silver Convention was chirping to the new dance beat "Fly Robin Fly." The whole world was watching to see which Democratic presidential candidate was going to rise to the top and oppose Gerald Ford. And my world—and Sue's and Jeep's—was about to change.

On November 28, 1975, I drove down to Athens, Alabama, just over the Tennessee line, where Sparky's sister Fay dropped her off to meet me at the post office. Sparky was more beautiful every time I saw her. She had gorgeous emerald eyes, a sweet, friendly face, and a body that I couldn't keep from touching.

That night while we were high and in the midst of everything, I told her that I loved her. I immediately hated myself, telling myself that I'd told a damned lie. I knew I liked her a lot and was wildly attracted, but *love*?

On the way back to Nashville, it was as though she crawled up inside my brain like some romantic tapeworm. When I got home and Sue bitched at me (for barely getting there in time for her to leave for a couple of days), all I could think about was Sparky. When I went to bed, I heard Sparky's voice, saw her penetrating eyes, smelled her perfume. I woke up missing her, reliving the day and night before. I felt that I had put a curse on myself, telling her that I loved her, and now loving her was my punishment for lying. I had never fallen this hard before, and I was scared to death. Sparky and I were to get together again in a couple of weeks. I could hardly wait to see her, but I was also freaking out.

One thing that grounded me a bit was that Sue had gone to Hawaii (my Christmas present to her), which enabled me to have complete charge of Jeep for about a week. This gave us some good quality time together, and I felt that we had a lot to talk about. One afternoon I was taking her home from a magic class that she took every week at the Jewish Community Center. We were discussing magic, and the talk turned to Santa Claus. She began quizzing me relentlessly. How could he get that many toys in one sleigh? How could he visit that many homes in one night? She was nine years old and in the fourth grade, and most of her friends had quit believing. The previous Christmas she told me that one of her classmates had stated adamantly that there was no such thing as Santa Claus. Jeep's response was, "I *know* there's a Santa Claus because my daddy said so, and *he wouldn't lie to me!*" That broke my heart. And here one Christmas later, she was trying to convince herself of something she didn't really believe anymore. I could identify; I believed in Santa until I was *ten*. As long as she had been willing to believe, I guess I had been willing to feed the fantasy, but now she was searching for real answers. I always felt a little guilty fooling her anyway, so I told her the truth. She cried and cried. Now my heart was *really* broken. I took her to the mall and bought her a stamp collection set, and that put a smile back on her face.

So I was staying with Jeep at the house on Newsom Station Road. I told Sue on the phone that the stale urine stench was still in my apartment, and I was going to try to get out of the lease. Then after she returned from Hawaii, I could get another place. She suggested that we stay together until after the holidays, and I said that would be fine. Splitting up may have been advisable and desirable, but it seemed like such a hassle having to leave the nice big house where Jeep lived, and since I spent so much time going back and forth to stay with Jeep when her mother was away, living at home was just easier. Why couldn't Sue leave, why did it have to be *me* moving out?

I drove down to Alabama with diamond earrings (for Sparky) and a racing heart (for Sparky). Sparky seemed thrilled to see me, but she wasn't thrilled to hear me going on about being scared and wondering if she was going to disappoint me or hurt me. After I got back to Nashville, she was hard to reach on the phone, and when I finally got her she didn't seem to be as enthusiastic about me.

Right after the New Year came in, at the dawning of America's bicentennial, I drove down to Alabama on pins and needles, compulsively eating one Certs breath mint after the other. As I crossed the Alabama line and sped past the wintry landscape—the cotton fields without cotton—I was wondering if I had completely blown it with Sparky. I was resolved to be confident and cool when I pulled up to the Athens Post Office. But as I watched her get out of her sister's car, it was like my finger was in a light socket! I ran to her and we fell into each other's arms, just like in the movies, both saying "I love you" in unison. We headed for a motel in Huntsville, far enough away from where she lived to be relatively safe. How we made it there, I don't know, because I couldn't keep my eyes or my hands off this beautiful girl sitting beside me, and the car swerved all over the road as if a twelve-year-old were at the wheel.

Sparky and I both had spouses, and that wasn't going to change overnight, but our *lovers* would go out of the picture immediately. Sparky said she was going to bid farewell to her "boyfriend," a traveling musician she had been seeing occasionally for some time, and I knew I had to tell Charlotte right away that it was over between *us* too, but I wanted to tell her in person.

I went down to Atlanta the day before Charlotte was to arrive, so I could already be settled into a room at the Airport Hilton and have a good night's sleep. I had loved our five-and-a-half-year relationship, and she had brought sanity to my crazy life with Sue. Charlotte had a dignity about her, and I would never intentionally do or say anything to rob her of that. I wanted us to leave this motel the next day with our friendship intact.

I picked her up at the airport in mid-afternoon, and after putting her suitcase in the room, I suggested that we go down to the lounge and have a drink. I don't recall Charlotte *ever* saying, "Nahhh, I don't feel like drinking today."

As we sat in the semi-dark lounge, sipping our rum and Coke, I tried to work my way into the message, starting off by telling her what a great girl Sparky was, and that we had gotten pretty close lately. Instead of commenting on my comments, she changed the subject, and started talking about my songwriting. I had no idea if I was a better lyricist or melody writer—I would have guessed that it was about equal—but being a musician, I liked to think that the melodies I wrote were fairly decent. From out of nowhere, Charlotte said, "I think you write really good lyrics, but frankly, I don't think your melodies are all that great." She was hurt, so she was trying to hurt me. Instead, she pissed me off and made this whole breaking up business a lot easier.

Just about that time I heard it coming from the jukebox: rat-a-tat-tat-tat, rat-a-tatty-tatty-tat. It was the unmistakable marching drum cadence that was the intro to Paul Simon's major hit, "Fifty Ways to Leave Your Lover."

"Charlotte," I said, "I've been trying to tell you something. Listen carefully to these lyrics—that's what I've been trying to say." Three decades later I would be able to amuse Paul Simon with this story about letting his words end my relationship, but the day that it happened I didn't feel so good about it. We went to our room and became characters in a Kris Kristofferson song, like "For the Good Times," "Help Me Make It Through the Night," or perhaps "holding Bobby's body next to mine." I was sort of like an outlaw having one last shootout before riding into the sheriff's office and turning himself in.

I started a routine of going to Alabama to see Sparky every Monday—that was our day. Because she and her husband were still together, it was always a one-day clandestine operation. Her sister Fay would take her to meet me at the post office in Athens, and we would go to a motel, usually in Huntsville. The natural high I was on got my creative juices going like never before. I wrote a medium-tempo boom-chick song about our affair called "Her Name Is," in which there would be a musical instrument playing licks in place of the girl's name and other pertinent information. The coming summer, it would be a hit for George Jones.

> *Oh I love her and I just can't live without her*
> *And I've got the urge to tell the world about her*
> *But our love's a secret that can't see the light of day*
> *But I went and wrote this love song anyway.*
>
> *Her name is da-da-da, her eyes are daaa*
> *Her hair is just like da-da, and she measures da-da-daaa*
> *Oh someday I'll fill in the lines, when she and I are free*
> *And we'll walk in the sunshine, da-da-da and me*

Coincidentally, no sooner had I written this song than Sparky separated from her husband and moved in with her sister and brother-in-law. I'm sure she would have liked it if I had left Sue, but she didn't pressure me. Instead of picking her up at the post office in Athens, Alabama, I started picking her up at Fay's apartment in nearby Decatur, and often, when we went to a motel, we would spend the night. Sparky's three sisters and two brothers lived in or near Decatur. Her parents lived in a small town south of there. I hit it off with her mother, but Sparky didn't want her strict Pentecostal father to know about me as long as she and I were still married to other people. Sue was away from home three nights a week, so what could she say about me being gone *one* night? Plenty. But I went anyway.

One beautiful spring-ish day in late winter, I was making my two-hour trip to Decatur, listening to Nashville's WSM-AM, which at the time had a middle-of-the-road daytime format. They played a song that I thought was a little cheesy, but I fell in love with it. It was "Afternoon Delight,"—WSM would play this song for several weeks before it started to hit nationally—and word-for-word it was about Sparky and me, and our delightful, sexy afternoons.

There were a couple of instances, usually within a few minutes after getting together, that Sparky told me she had thought about going back to her husband, "because I feel sorry for him," but after an hour or two she was her old self.

We were great playmates, and I don't mean this in a sexual sense, but like two kids who delighted in playing together. I don't think she had a black belt, but she had studied karate and was very strong, and one of our favorite games was getting on the floor, where I grabbed this petite girl's wrists and tried to keep her pinned down. Usually I couldn't.

There was a lot of partying with her family and friends. One night I got very drunk and rode a tricycle all over the parking lot outside her sister's apartment. Sometimes we went to a club in Huntsville, Alabama, and sat in, me playing the piano while Sparky sang (she was sort of a soft-voiced version of Tammy Wynette).

Sparky's best girlfriend from Florida, Gail Creel, came up to stay with her for a while, so I took Rafe Van Hoy down to Decatur with me, and the four of us went to a night club. Rafe was driving my car as Sparky and I sat in the back seat in a trance, looking into each other's eyes, transfixed for several minutes, not saying a word. Months later, I would write about it in a song called "We Said I Love You with Our Eyes."

> *I won't say we were stoned because*
> *Being stoned's against the law*
> *I'll just say we were stoned in love*
> *Anyway that's true enough*

One day, though it was hard to tear myself away from Sparky, I had an appointment back in Nashville to write with New York lyricist Hal David, who, with Burt Bacharach, had written some of the biggest and most enduring pop hits of the era. Bacharach and David had the same impact in the 1960s that Rodgers and Hammerstein had two decades before. Hal was in town to co-write with several Nashville writers. I had already collaborated with him a couple of times. He wanted to hear songs I had already written, and in each case wanted to keep my melody but replace my lyrics with his; he thought he could top them, and he was probably right. That wasn't the case with Rafe's "Spring Flower in Bloom" that Hal changed to "Don't Lie Me a Love," which Rafe and I thought—when sung—sounded like "Dumb Limey in Love." None of the things I wrote with Hal were ever recorded, though his time spent in Nashville wasn't in vain. He and Archie Jordan wrote what would be a monster hit by Ronnie Milsap: "It Was Almost Like a Song." On our third and final co-writing date, I was late by about twenty minutes. Hal normally had a sweet disposition, but he was very unhappy with me. "You should never be late for a writing appointment. That shows disrespect for your co-writer."

I was effusive in my apology, then opened up my briefcase and showed him some pictures of Sparky. "I know th-there's no excuse for being late, but she's the reason I was," I said.

"My God, what a beautiful young woman," Hal whispered as he perused the pictures of the girl with the penetrating green eyes, straw blonde hair, and perfect white teeth. This from the man who saw Ursula Andress on a movie screen and immediately wrote "The Look of Love." Then he handed the pictures back and scolded me once more, "But you're right, there is *no* excuse for being late."

I was inspired and doing a lot of productive writing. I knew that George Jones and Tammy Wynette were about to record, and I wanted to write something that felt like an old-time country gospel song, thinking that would be a real switch for country music's most famous divorced couple. I got the idea for the lyrics from a TV show about the "biography" of a handgun, following its history and all the people who had owned it. I thought: why not use that angle with a wedding ring. I had the title "Golden Ring," the melody, and the story, but I was stuck. I went to Tree and called Curly Putman, to see if he would like to come in and write it with me, but he said he wanted to hang around his farm. Then Rafe Van Hoy walked through the front door. We sat down and wrote it in a few minutes. It was everything I wanted it to be: slightly uptempo and churchy, an old-fashioned melody with contemporary lyrics, and a country feel in an urban setting. (I envisioned a couple from the South or Appalachia who were living in Chicago). It was Friday and I was going down to Decatur to see Sparky the following Monday when the studio was available, so I asked Rafe if he would put together a demo on it. He stacked everything, playing a couple of guitar tracks and singing all the parts for an entire vocal group. Within a few days, Billy Sherrill cut a great record of it with George and Tammy, and within two weeks it was playing on the radio. Some songwriters refer to their songs as their children. If that's the case, this was the quickest trip from conception to the delivery room in my career. In the twenty-first century, a writer would be lucky to get a song on the radio a *year* after it was written. "Golden Ring" would hit #1 by summer.

I had read about playwright Charles MacArthur, sitting on a bench in Central Park with his bride, actress Helen Hayes, back before they were famous. He had a bag of peanuts, and as he poured some into her hand he told her, "I wish they were diamonds." That gave me the idea for a waltz titled "Peanuts and Diamonds." Although it wasn't quite finished, I played it for Bill Anderson, and he said he loved it and wanted to record it. Bill was known as Whispering Bill and recorded one country hit after another—almost all of which he wrote—throughout the 1960s and early 1970s. His career had cooled for a couple of years, but he was enjoying a comeback, with Buddy Killen producing him. I had become well acquainted with him a few years before when he was the narrative voice for a documentary on the lives of three Nashville songwriters, and he came out to our house on Newsom Station Road, where they were to film me. In the film, he turns into our driveway, and little Lauren yells, "Hi, Bill," and Bill yells back, "Hi, Jeep." I had to pick up Jeep at USN on the afternoon Bill was to record "Peanuts and Diamonds," and take her to the studio with me. While Bill was singing another song with the musicians, I was in the control room trying to finish my song, and Jeep sat on the floor working away in her coloring book. Bill liked what I had, but felt that the song needed a chorus. He came up with two lines: "Peanuts and diamonds, sawdust and satin / Lone Star and sparkling red wine," and in putting them before two of my verse lines, "Cowboys and rich girls don't live in the same world / but they both cry 'I wish you were mine,'" the four lines became a chorus. He recorded it immediately, and it would become a Top Ten record. He should have taken a piece of the song because of his contribution to it, but for some reason neither one of us ever brought it up.

Still another 1976 hit would be one I wrote with Sonny Throckmorton, "Thinkin' of a Rendezvous" which would spend two weeks at #1 with one of Billy Sherrill's artists, Johnny Duncan. Sonny Throckmorton was a tall, pot-smoking, loud-laughing son of a Texas Pentecostal preacher. This mid-tempo cheating song with sort of a calypso beat would kick off Sonny's hot songwriting streak, one of the hottest in the history of Music Row. Many of Sonny's hits would be songs he wrote alone. He had already written two verses and a chorus on "Rendezvous," and I thought it needed a third verse. That's all I wrote—that and a suggestion that the cheaters' motel be called "the Family Inn"—so I took only one-third of the song

Sparky and I continued to get closer and closer. It was no longer just the sexual attraction; she was sweet and gentle and funny and easy to be around. I brought her to Nashville occasionally, but because I was still living at home, we always had to get a motel room—which we could do just as well in Decatur, rather than make the extra four-hour round trip to Nashville. I wrote Charlotte, who had remained a good friend, "Wife still stays away on her three school nights, that is she spends the night away. Monday and Wednesday are my days (to be away). Saturdays and Sundays are the only times we're both here together, and even then, sometimes one of us is away, such as tonight. For all practical purposes, we're already separated." Sparky wrote me, "Each time I'm with you, I love you even more. It seems like I can't live without you, so maybe someday we can live together, but only if you want that."

When she celebrated her twenty-fifth birthday on May 2, I thought how young Sparky was to have an eight-year-old son. Allen was a very handsome little guy, a combination of both his parents' good looks. He was close to both his mom and dad, and spent as much time with one as the other. He and I hit it off from the start.

Jeep had heard about my "girlfriends" for years, from her mother. Because her mother and I were estranged and practically separated, and because Sparky and I were so close, I decided to tell Jeep about her. She was excited to find out that Sparky had a son two years her junior, and was eager to meet them both. Late one night Sparky and some friends were in Nashville and dropped by Newsom Station Road (obviously Sue was away that night), mostly because she wanted to tiptoe upstairs and take a look at a sleeping Jeep. I thought it best to hold off from introducing them until I was no longer living at home.

I think the event that gave me the courage to finally and officially leave Sue was when I drove Sparky into Nashville, and we were cruising down Music Row. Sue was on her way to USN to pick up Jeep when she saw us stopped at the light. She slammed on her brakes, jumped out of her car, ran up to mine and climbed up on the hood. She pressed her face up against the windshield on the passenger side, with the wildest look in her eyes, breathing heavily, causing her chest to heave up and down quickly like a frog. Sparky burst out laughing. Sue screamed something, then slid over to my side of the hood, once again pressing her face up against the glass. People started blowing their horns, and she finally climbed down.

I immediately started scanning the classified section of the paper, looking for a place, not extravagant but decent, in the Music Row area. I found something I really liked not far from there, on Oakland Avenue, in a pleasant older neighborhood near Belmont College. The brick house was built in 1912, and the downstairs area was for rent. It was furnished with nice wicker furniture. I took Sparky by to take a look at it—after all she would be my most frequent guest. When she said she loved it, I made my decision to leave home. Sue went nuts. She begged me to stay, and even brought back Pigeon, flapping her elbow wings and squeaking "Daggy, please don't go," which I must admit did make it difficult for me. But I had made up my mind.

Sparky and I were having dinner at a Polynesian/Asian restaurant. One of the entrees on the menu was called "The Empress Dowager," and Sparky, cutting up, pronounced it "Doo-wagger." So I nicknamed her "The Empress of Doo-wagger" and the rental house would come to be known as "Doo-wagger." Allen would many times say, "Mama, I wanna go to Doo-wagger."

When Sue was away I had movers load up my stuff from our home in the country, and made the big move to my bachelor pad. When they closed the big trailer doors and pulled away from my new place on the afternoon of June 1, 1976, I had an incredible feeling of freedom. I called Sparky and told her I had moved into the house.

"Baby, I can't wait to be there with you this Monday," she cooed.

"I feel so *free*," I said, as I gave the girl a box with my heart in it, then handed her the key.

7

A MAN OBSESSED

The young man stood banging on the large glass window overlooking the church auditorium and the wedding of the girl he loved. "ELAINE!" he screamed over and over, at the top of his lungs. He had raced across the California countryside at speeds exceeding 120 miles per hour, attempting to get to the First Presbyterian Church of Santa Barbara while there was still time, and when his car gave out, he ran the rest of the way. He was going to do everything humanly possible to get this girl and take her away. It worked. "BEN!" she screamed back at him, leaving the groom standing at the altar, running to the determined young man as fast as she could. The scene is from a movie I had seen several years before, *The Graduate*, and the young man played by Dustin Hoffman, was named Benjamin Braddock. *This* Braddock *also* believed that wanting something badly enough could make it so, but in June of 1976, I had never had the opportunity to contemplate the fine line between steely determination and obsession. Nor had I had any cause to pay much attention to that old adage, "Be careful what you wish for—you might just get it."

This was my summer of love, and the farthest thing from my mind was that my girlfriend might be hard to hold on to. Sparky had been working a road gig as a back-up singer for Grand Ole Opry star "Jumping Bill" Carlisle, but that was usually on weekends, so Mondays and Tuesdays became our days together. When her work played out, Monday continued to be the day I drove down to Alabama. Typically, after spending some time with her family or friends, we headed back to Nashville.

The minute we walked into "Doo-wagger," we would start drinking and partying. Our favorite beverage, a sweet white wine called Beameister Liebfraumilch, looked more like it came from a pottery shop than a liquor store, and before the summer was over, the decorative German vessels adorned the mantle and tabletops and lined the living room walls.

We were like children, without a care in the world. She was something of a contortionist, and could twist her body into a pretzel and hide from me in cabinets and dresser drawers. Though she weighed only about 110 pounds to my 160, she loved to pick me up and carry me around when we were out in public. One day, as we came out of Baskin-Robbins, I pulled off the wig she was wearing and threw it in a dumpster; she retaliated by grinding her ice cream cone into my face. More than once at the movies, I handed her what she thought was a fountain Coke, just so I could see her spew it out when she discovered that it was Dr. Pepper. Though she spoke in the unsouthern accent of Miami, where she had lived for several years, she was raised in the hills of northern Alabama and knew how to talk that way. Often we drew attention as we tried to out-hillbilly each other while loudly conversing in a restaurant.

When Sparky and I had Rafe Van Hoy along, it got even worse. One night Sparky drove my white Mercury Marquis down an alley off Nashville's Belmont Boulevard as Rafe and I ran naked in the headlights, stopping to knock on a friend's back door, realizing we had the wrong apartment when a Music Row secretary opened her door and stood face-to-face with two nude songwriters. Another time, Sparky and I swapped clothes in the front seat of my car as Rafe and his date did the same in the back seat; then we drove crossdressed down busy Broadway until a cop appeared in my rear-view, and Rafe frantically removed his dress, saying he would rather be arrested in the buff than meet the Metro Jail inmates in a frock. Sometimes Rafe or I would gently slam into the other's bumper at a traffic light to generate a fake fight, then jump out of our cars yelling and cussing, and rolling around in the street, as Sparky screamed for help. Rafe was twenty-one, Sparky was twenty-five, and I was . . . thirty-five! All of us going on seventeen.

I think it was an exciting time for both Sparky and me. I was enjoying more success than I'd ever had. Because I had two current hits by George Jones—one solo and one with Tammy Wynette—we decided to go see him perform at his own night club, Possum Holler. As we walked in the door, George was on stage singing "Her Name Is," and after his set, I introduced Sparky as the girl I had written the song about.

One day Sue dropped Jeep off to stay with me for the afternoon, unaware that Sparky was there. I wanted my little girl and my girlfriend to meet. Ten-year-old Jeep was at her most hyperactive, hop-scotching around the living room as she talked to Sparky. They connected immediately. Occasionally, Sparky and I brought her son, Allen, along to Nashville with us, and Jeep was already envisioning him as her little brother.

Despite her zaniness and physical strength and human-pretzel maneuvering, Sparky was soft and gentle, like her voice. If she loved attention, she was also attentive to others. If she had a smart-aleck sense of humor, she also had a lot of compassion. She told me she had cried when she heard Martin Luther King was assassinated—not a typical reaction of the white Southerners I had known in 1968.

Her good nature was tested a lot. One day Sue called me up and asked to speak to Sparky. "I know some people who can take care of you," Sue said in her icy voice. "Hey, lady," Sparky laughed, "I may know some people myself."

A few days later, the florist delivered a funeral wreath to my place, in memory of Sparky.

Sparky also had to endure seeing me upset over deeds that Sue had done, such as calling the phone company and having my number changed just to give me a hard time (and I couldn't find out what my own new number was). Or the time she saw me emotionally demolished, as I listened to Jeep wail on the other end of the line because the phone had just been snatched from her hands, her mother screaming, "You're NOT talking to your father while he's with his WHORE!"

I was so caught up in Sparky that I couldn't generate my usual enthusiasm for politics in that election year. This would be only the second time I voted in a presidential race, and the first time (of many times) for a Democrat. This would be the last time that the South, Democratic since the Civil War, would solidly support a Democratic candidate for president: Jimmy Carter of Georgia. When I took Jeep trick-or-treating, she wore a rubber mask of the nominee's face, going from door to door toting her brown paper bag that read PEANUTS, shaking hands, saying, "Hi, I'm Jimmy Carter."

It's hard to make memories in adult life that are as magical and mystical as the ones from our youth. As long as there is life (and a functioning brain) in me, I will be able to relive, and be haunted by, the dissonant harmonies of the crickets, rain frogs, and alligators around the little lake in front of my Florida childhood home, the comforting sound of a late night train echoing across that lake, or the moaning and sighing of the mighty Atlantic, lulling me to sleep as I lay in bed in a little summer cottage. Nineteen-seventy-six, when I was in my mid-thirties, had that kind of magic for me—as magical as the Walt Disney films I had seen in my very early days, or the rock & roll songs I had heard in my adolescent years. It was a thrill when "Golden Ring" went to #1, but more than the music, it was Sparky who topped the charts. She seemed to be a hit with my friends; Don Gant loved her singing, and Rafe thought she was a first prize. One night she and I went out with Rafe and my Tree friend, glamorous Dixie Gamble, who was by that time divorced. The next day Dixie told me that when Rafe and I went into a convenience store to buy some beer, Sparky turned to her and said, "I love him so much." More and more, marriage was enthusiastically discussed. It all seemed so perfect.

Then around Thanksgiving, Jeep and I drove Sparky down to Alabama. We stopped, just before dropping her off at her sister's apartment, to eat at McDonald's. As I looked across the table at her, I was overwhelmed by a feeling of profound sadness.

"Sparky, I've got the saddest feeling. I hope you're not going to break my heart."

She took my hand. "Baby, I would never do anything to hurt you. Don't you know how much I love you?"

Two weeks later, as we headed toward Nashville and passed the barren winter cotton fields, she told me that Troy was begging her to come back to him, and she said she couldn't help but feel sorry for him. It had happened two or three times before, but after being with me for a few minutes, she seemed to put it out of her mind. This time, I resented it, wondering if his ghost would ever go away for good. "Then wh-why don't you go back to him? I think you should," I said, wanting her to say no, of course.

"Okay," she said, calling my bluff.

For the next two days, it was like we were both in mourning, sitting around in stunned silence, often clinging to each other. But I wasn't going to ask her not to go. If she didn't love me enough to stay without my urging, then she didn't love me enough. I wasn't going to fight for her. For a very long time, I would consider it the biggest mistake I ever made.

I couldn't bear the thought of the sad ride down to Alabama, then the lonely ride back home, so Sparky called her sister to come get her, and I watched them drive off into the dark December night.

I went into the deepest of deep funks. There was no solace in having another #1 country hit, "Thinking of a Rendezvous," because it was a song that Sparky had loved, and whenever I heard the pop group Chicago's then-current hit "If You Leave Me Now" (not my song), it thrust the knife deeper into my heart.

Nashville had turned extremely cold and would remain so, with record-breaking days of ice and snow on the ground, for what would seem like eternity. The landscape that happy eyes may view as a winter wonderland, sad eyes see as Siberia.

I thought life without her didn't seem worth living. But rather than feeling suicidal, I was determined to get her back. I sent her a letter in care of her sister Fay making an impassioned plea.

Sue was relieved to hear that Sparky had left me and used the opportunity to present the good Sue, the compassionate listener. But she couldn't hide her anger when she found Jeep's diary and read about how close her daughter had gotten to Sparky and how sorry Jeep was that Sparky and Daddy had split up. The house on Newsom Station Road was up for sale, and Sue was leasing an upscale condo at Jefferson Square in the Green Hills area of town. When she urged me to move in with her and Jeep, I politely told her that it probably wouldn't be a good idea, but in my mind I was thinking *no damned way*. I took Sue with me as my date to the annual Tree Christmas Brunch, encountering people who knew Sparky but didn't know Sue, and several who later told me that my wife and I just didn't seem like a match (someone used the term "odd couple").

Buddy had produced two more of my songs on Bill Anderson, "Velvet and Steel," inspired by words someone used to describe president-elect Jimmy Carter's wife, Rosalynn, and "Head to Toe," which I had written about Sparky.

I had a single out—"Big Black Telephone"—that I had recorded for Mercury earlier that year when Sparky was working the road with "Jumping Bill" Carlisle. The song was about me sitting around trying to send her a telepathic message: "Call me, call me." Dixie Gamble had added a sexy "hello" to the recording, and Sue felt certain that it was the voice of Sparky. Now Mercury was working the record hard at country radio, but I couldn't have cared less. The only thing I cared about was getting Sparky back.

A major blow came when I called Sparky's sister Fay, who told me she never had the opportunity to give Sparky the letter I had mailed. In my journal, I wrote:

> They LEFT FOR MIAMI Saturday! Fay said she would read
> (my letter) to her over the phone. Sparky told Fay she would
> call me sometime this week, and to tell me that she loves me.
> Wonder if she knows or cares how much she has hurt me.

Poor Jeep! When she came to spend the agreed-upon three days a week with me, she was subjected to what may have been the most boring time in her life. I almost never took her anywhere, because in the days before voice mail, cell phones, and text messages, I didn't want to be away if Sparky called. But she didn't complain much, and kept the lonely vigil with her daddy, constantly giving me encouraging words and positive thoughts on those cold, bleak nights. I was grateful that I had her love and support, but I was concerned about the growing chasm between her and Sue, and often told her, "You've got to love your mother."

As Christmas drew nearer and there was still no phone call from Sparky, I was so fed up with my own dedication and determination that I left my lonely lair and went out in the Tennessee arctic morning. But I still hung around Doo-wagger as much as possible, waiting for that call.

Several days later I was having one of my many phone conversations with Sparky's sister Fay. "I hate to tell you this," she said, "but I talked to Troy's aunt, and she said they're getting along real well." Fay left word for Sparky to call her at 4 p.m., at which time she said she would urge her to call me. About 4:45 she called.

"You crazy man, what's the matter with you?" Sparky asked.

"Crazy man is right. Me without you equals crazy. Are you happy?"

"I'm making it, but I'm not happy, because I'm not with you. Don't you know that I love you?" Then she told me that she thought she would eventually have lost me to my wife.

"You *told* me to leave," she said softly, sadly.

"And that was stupid. I've learned my lesson," I replied with great resolve.

After a pause, she took a deep breath and said, "*Please* don't stop loving me, and hang on."

I hung on all right, across the many miles, and began several days of alternately cajoling, enticing, manipulating, guilting, seducing, and begging. I had to have her back right then. I couldn't stand her being with him and not me.

As the Nashville temperature plummeted, as new snow fell on top of old snow, I persisted and she resisted. She was asking for time to work things out, time that I wasn't willing to give her. After keeping on for days without letup, I finally wore her down, and she unenthusiastically agreed to come back to me. I told her I could fly to Miami or meet her and Allen in Tampa at her girlfriend Gail's house. She said no, she would come alone, and she would drive straight through that night.

As soon as I hung up, I felt like shit. After I called the Alabama Highway Patrol, I grew panicky—ice storms were forecast for the entire state, and the path would continue across Georgia. There was no way she could safely drive from Florida to Nashville.

When I heard from her that night, she sounded like she was in the midst of an emotional collapse. She said Troy was screaming at her not to go and threatening to call me. Allen was crying. She said there had been a big fight, and that she fainted for the first time in her life.

"Sparky, I've been so obsessively crazy. L-let me take all the pressure off you. The roads aren't safe to drive on tonight, and you're clearly not ready to come. Let's give it a rest. I'm so s-sorry you're upset, and I'm sorry Troy and Allen are upset." I had never felt such an outpouring of relief and love and gratitude. She swore she would work things out in time regarding Allen, that she would make everything up to me and show me how much she loved me. "I would have married you a *year* ago," she declared. She said we could talk, we could write occasionally, and she even asked if I would come and see her for a rendezvous, so we made plans for me to go down there in two weeks. I was relieved that the long vigil was over at last. I had fought a valiant fight. In the month since she left, I had lost fourteen pounds, developed dark circles under my eyes, and wrecked my body—I had a pretty bad case of prostatitis. I was ready to heal and I was ready to be happy.

My big motivation for getting Sparky back was love, so I was joyous in the knowledge that my ship was probably coming in; it seemed to be sitting there on the horizon. But I think my sense of urgency stemmed from jealousy, knowing that she was sleeping with Troy after I'd had her exclusively for a year. I wanted that situation to change as quickly as possible. And until she was all mine again and we were being true to each other, I felt a need to have female company, to level the playing field, so to speak. I called up Dena Boehms, a beautiful college student who had sold me her Minimoog keyboard a couple of years earlier, and she said she would love to go out with me when she got back from Hollywood where she had a role in a major dark-comedy film, *Kentucky Fried Movie*. I called Charlotte in Florida, and made plans to get with her on my way down to Miami in two weeks.

Since coming to Tree sixteen months earlier, Don Gant had already made a significant difference there. But there was tension in the building because Buddy Killen and Don Gant had one volatile thing in common: they were both powerful forces, bigger than life. One day when I had trudged through the eternal snow of the winter that kept on giving and struggled into the Tree lobby, I saw Buddy walking swiftly down the hallway toward me with an angry look on his face. He grabbed me by the arm and said, "Come have lunch with me at the Peddler, I need to talk to you." What in the hell have I done, I wondered. When we got to the restaurant, Buddy put both hands on the table and looked me in the eye. "I don't think I can work with Don anymore," he said sternly.

"Don G-Gant?" I asked, really quite puzzled.

"Yeah."

"What has he *done*, Buddy?"

"He walked into my office this morning and said, 'Hey, Buddy, your hairpiece is lookin' good.' Carolyn was there, and she didn't even know that I *wore* a hairpiece."

Carolyn was Buddy's lovely young girlfriend (and future wife). I was about to bite my lip off to keep from laughing. "*He* said *that*?"

As soon as I got back to Tree, I went to Gant's office. "You scoundrel," I teased. "Did you really tell Buddy that his hairpiece was lookin' good?"

Gant defiantly jutted out his jaw. "Damn right," he said.

Tree wasn't big enough for the two of them, but a parting of ways would have to wait. Gant (along with Donna Hilley) had recently been given the title of vice president, a high-salaried position. And Buddy needed him.

The next day there was a lot of ice and snow, but I wanted to go in to Tree. Dixie's car was a better snow dog than mine, so she took Jeep and me to Music Row with her. When I got tied up there doing some co-writing, Dixie took Jeep to her house, where there was an adult sitter, to play with her two boys. At the end of the afternoon, as I walked across Tree's parking lot to get into Dixie's car, I did a little dance on the ice, just to show that I could. "Way to go, B." she laughed. Then, as I proceeded on my way to her vehicle, *swish, pow*! I was down on the ice in a split second. I tried to get up, but my leg, which was turned inward, was numb and immobile. It was a "ski break," broken completely in two at the lower tibia, or shin bone.

If I ever had a living nightmare—and I say nightmare because so much of it is blocked out that it seems like a dream—it was lying on a gurney at Vanderbilt Hospital while two interns tried to fit the two broken parts of my bone back together, as though my leg were a jigsaw puzzle. Dixie heard me yelling from down the hallway, and came in there and told them to stop. She also advised them that I would probably sue.

My dear old publisher, Jack Stapp, pulled strings and got me a nice suite atop Baptist Hospital. Sue, back from nursing her wounds in Alabama, was there with Jeep. As soon as they left, Dixie gleefully told me that she had just talked to Sparky (she got in touch with her through Gail), and Sparky said since she had decided to come back to me anyway, she would just move up the timetable and come right away. There was a room next to mine where she could stay. The last thing I remember before being wheeled away to surgery was Donna Hilley telling me that a NO VISITORS sign had been posted down the hallway, and that she had showed the security guard a picture of Sue, who had just told me on the phone that she was going to come to the hospital and run Sparky off.

Mike Kosser picked Sparky up at the airport the next morning and brought her to the hospital. That night, as I lay there with about as bad a broken leg as one could get, I scribbled in my journal, "I'm the happiest man in the world."

Two whole weeks later, Rafe Van Hoy came to take Sparky and me to Doo-wagger. She had not left my side since arriving, and was probably about as stir crazy as I was. The ice and snow that brought me down still covered the ground. Mindless of my leg, we made love as soon as Rafe left. And drank a bottle of Beameister Liebfraumilch. And went to my piano, where I sang her favorite song, "Colour My World," and she sang "Standing Room Only." Not surprisingly, my leg began to swell very badly, and I was in great pain. She continued to wait on me hand and foot. For five days. On the fifth day she was missing Allen and feeling guilty about going off and leaving him. This time she didn't give me the chance to tell her to go. She had made up her mind to leave and proceeded to call a cab to take her to the bus station. As she walked out the door, I threw my crutch at her.

Several days later, she called me, and said that she and her sisters had gone to Florida to get Allen, but by the time she was back in Decatur she was feeling guilty about taking the eight-year-old away from his father. The fact that Troy's girlfriend had moved in with him probably added to her general bad feelings. She said she went into seclusion at her parents' house and sort of went crazy.

"I'm seeing a lawyer on Monday, to get the divorce started. If you still want me to, I'll come up with Allen in a couple of days, put him in school, and when we're both divorced, we can get married like we planned," said Sparky, but not with a great deal of enthusiasm.

When she didn't call the next day, I called Fay, who said that Troy was in Alabama and that Sparky had lit into him in a jealous rage. She told Fay that she did love Troy after all. A few days later, Fay told me that Sparky and Troy were back together, were staying in Alabama, had gotten "saved," and had never been happier. Somewhere along the way, Sparky had gotten saved and I had gotten lost. I was ready to start finding my way again.

One pleasantly cool early spring afternoon, on my first trip to Music Row since breaking my leg, I dropped by Tree where I talked for quite a while with the king of country songwriters, my friend Harlan Howard. When I told him what had happened between Sparky and me, he said, "Well, Gyod dimmit, kid, you oughta get a few good songs out of that one." If Spencer Tracy, a shorter but more glamorous version of Harlan, had come along after him instead of before, Tracy would have been the perfect actor to play the craggy, gray-haired songwriting genius.

I had recently been elected to a two-year term on the Nashville Songwriters Association board of directors, and went from Tree to a board meeting where I met for the first time the biggest female pop singer of the 1960s, Brenda Lee, a sweetheart of a lady whom I would come to adore over the years, and Felice Bryant, who along with her husband, Boudleaux, wrote country standards like "Rocky Top" and many Everly Brothers hits like "Bye Bye Love" and "Wake Up Little Susie." Since the board meeting was at the Hall of Fame Motel, and this was my first major activity in the outside world in some time, it's not surprising that I ended up at the bar.

If I had met Lorene Williams a few drinks sooner, I probably wouldn't have picked her up and taken her to my place. I was very drunk, and I thought she looked okay. Maybe she was sitting (and lying down) more than she was standing up that night, but somehow I overlooked the fact that she was a giantess. A couple of days later, I remembered her as a pleasant lady, two or three years older than me, a successful businesswoman who wore tinted glasses. I knew that I had a date with her, and her address and the directions were written on a Hall of Fame Lounge napkin that had been wadded up in my pocket.

I hopped up Lorene's front steps on my crutches, expecting to see a woman who was not petite but probably my size. I was shocked when an Amazon opened the door. I was intimidated by taller women and this one was towering, big-boned, and gushing. "Well, hiiii there sugar. Great to *see* you," she squealed as she squeezed me tightly, almost raising me up off the porch.

"Uh . . . L-L-Lorene," I stammered, looking up into her tinted glasses, almost in the throes of a panic attack, "I'm. . . . I'm s-sick, and won't be able to go out tonight. But I didn't want to call you up and tell you that, I w-w-wanted to show you the respect of telling you in person."

"Wellll, honey, aren't you sweeeet. I'm so sorry you're sick. You go home and get you some rest and call me when you're feeling better."

They say nature abhors a vacuum, and so did Sue; she immediately tried to fill the void, coming over to cook meals for Jeep and me. Occasionally, she would stay at my place on one of my "Jeep nights." I know she disliked me going out with various women, but she wanted to get in my good graces, and didn't say much about it.

I had been dating a lot of girls to help get Sparky off my mind. (Charlotte came up from Florida one weekend; it was good to see her, but her hanging out with me and my friends just made me miss Sparky.)

One night Sue came over to keep Jeep, and they watched Rafe and me perform on a televised writers show, for a local charity. After our performance, as we packed up and headed toward the front door, I could see several men and women—business people and civic leaders—lined up near the studio entrance. "Oh, my God, there's this woman I went out with one night," I said, spotting Lorene, the Amazon who freaked me out.

"I bet she's beautiful," said Rafe.

"No, trust me, she's not."

"I've *never* seen you with a girl who's not good looking," he replied.

"Well, you're about to see one."

"You're exaggerating," he laughed.

"Well, I'll tell you what," I said. "When we go through the line, I'll put my hand on her shoulder, so you'll know she's the one."

"Okay," he said, "but I bet she's at least a decent-looking girl."

As we walked through the line, the towering woman's eyes lit up behind her tinted glasses, as I put my hand on her shoulder and said, "Hi, Lorene."

From behind me, I heard Rafe, loud and clear, "You've got to be *kiddin'*!"

Another night I went out with Rafe and his friend Don Cook, a bass-playing Texan in his mid- to late-twenties whom Don Gant had signed to Tree as a writer. Cook was one of the funniest people I had ever met. We picked up Cook's fellow Texan friend, ace guitarist Mark Casstevens, and went to a bar called the Gold Rush for a few drinks. I had never been to the Gold Rush when there was not some kind of agitation going on. My theory was that the place had been built on Indian burial grounds, awakening the spirits from their peaceful sleep. Some guy bumped into Cook as he attempted to get past our table and muttered something about moving out of his way. Cook looked up at him and said, "You son of a bitch." When the guy jumped on Cook, I started beating him with my crutch. Realizing that he was outnumbered four-to-one, the antagonist soon took leave.

I was writing more and more songs, many of which were about Sparky or inspired by her. One day I had an idea that came from out of nowhere and told Curly Putman about it. The concept was about a man who was so obsessed with the woman who left him that only death could quiet the demons that had haunted him over the years. I don't know if I was projecting into the future, imagining myself still hung up on Sparky, or if the song had absolutely nothing to do with her; I recall no epiphany. "He Stopped Loving Her Today" would become a very important part of my life and Curly's. We wrote some of it that afternoon; I took it home and worked some more on it that night; then Curly and I knocked it around the next day. We decided to give this melancholy ballad a rest for a few days, but several months would pass before we revisited and completed our song. To be continued.

When Tree had bought out Curly's part of Green Grass Music a few years before, Jack and Buddy gave Curly a permanent office, a nice large room on the first floor. Sometimes when I dropped by Curly's office, Eddie Miller would be there. Eddie was a congenial guy from Oklahoma who was best known for his song "Release Me," a country hit for Ray Price in the 1950s and an international pop hit for Engelbert Humperdinck in the 1960s. One spring night, Eddie died of a heart attack at the age of fifty-seven. Rafe Van Hoy, Mike Kosser, and I, all fond of Eddie, agreed to meet at Tree and go to the memorial service together, at Roesch-Patton Funeral Home, which was just off Music Row.

The funeral officiant, a Pentecostal minister with a televangelist voice, made an undoubtedly well-intentioned remark that came out rather strange: "Eddie Miller was *not only* a personal friend of our Lord and Savior *Jesus Christ* . . . he was also a personal friend of *the head waiter* at the *Belle Meade Cafeteria*." Rafe and I almost lost it. I was biting my lip not to laugh. Kosser, sitting to our left, was understandably embarrassed and slid several feet down the bench to disassociate himself from Rafe and me, who, despite our best efforts, weren't able to hold in every snicker.

Then, if that weren't enough, the preacher started to deconstruct Eddie's name, letter by letter. "E is for *excellence*, and this was a man who took such great pride in everything he did, and who certainly had a standard for excellence. D is for *dynamic*, and ohhhhh, Eddie Miller was truly a dynamic man—the energy that man had when he was hot on an idea! And *another* D . . ."

Rafe and I were both biting our lips, snickering through our noses. At this point, I think both of us decided to just turn away and not look at each other. This was getting serious.

"D is for *daring*. Eddie Miller dared to pursue his dreams, and to make those dreams come true, and he dared to defy those who discouraged him. I is for *interesting*. Eddie Miller was one of the most interesting men . . ."

I think Rafe and I had both almost straightened up by this time, but I couldn't resist it, I just had to say something about this alphabetical light show, this acronym avalanche. "I'm sure glad this isn't Kris Kristofferson's funeral," I whispered. Rafe's body lurched forward as he mouth-farted and blew air out of his nose, and I followed suit. We both sat there with our shoulders shaking and had no choice but to cover our faces and act like we were crying. After a minute, I glanced over to my left and saw that Kosser had moved to the very end of the pew. Rafe and I decided later that Eddie Miller had probably been looking down from Heaven, laughing with us.

Spring is a gloriously beautiful season in Middle Tennessee, except for those days when a nasty storm system rolls in, like a mean old boy riding in from somewhere to the west, threatening to drop a tornado or two. After the worst winter of my life, April was like Heaven. The dogwoods were in bloom, and life was beginning to have a sweet scent again. And there was the great music, the songs that live in the RAM of the brain and keep memories alive:

Kenny Rogers was telling "Lucille" that she'd picked a fine time to leave him, Glen Campbell was singing about those "Southern Nights," Abba had a monster hit called "Dancing Queen," and Fleetwood Mac had an exciting new record, "Dreams."

I was lucky to have a lot of friends, male and female. My rental house on Oakland Avenue was in the middle of a little Tree colony. Rafe was renting a small house half a block away on Belmont Boulevard; Dixie lived about a block down the street from me; and Don Cook and his gorgeous little doll-faced girlfriend with big beautiful eyes, Charmaine Denney, lived in a large house across the street from Dixie.

One night Cook, Charmaine, Rafe, and I were sitting on my front porch, talking. My wrestler-like neighbor from across the street, a giant of a man named Johnson, came over and told us we were too loud and to hold it down. His wife taught school while he sat around their house all day drinking beer. As he left, I said, "Mr. Johnson, I would feel more neighborly if I knew your first name." He muttered, "Asshole, my name's Asshole." From that moment on, he became Asshole Johnson to all of us. Cook, who with his slightly round face, mustache, and long hair, reminded me of the cowardly lion in *The Wizard of Oz*, went into the street and hurled some little insult at Asshole Johnson, who came charging back, jumping on Cook, and landing on top of him as they both fell to the pavement. Little Charmaine immediately made a punching bag out of Johnson's head until he removed his massive body from Cook. As Asshole went back to his house, he told us that we hadn't heard the last of him, and indeed we hadn't.

Rafe was a really close buddy. He had a girlfriend from nearby Madison, in her late teens, whom he occasionally brought to my place. He and I often went to Don Cook's house where we drank and smoked pot with Cook and a couple of his young professional friends. One night we danced in the street with some girls from Belmont College, then partied with them at Rafe's place.

I was doing okay, writing quite a bit, some of the songs being about Sparky. Barbara Mandrell's beautiful younger sister, Louise, was singing demos of female songs for us around Tree. Cook and I got her to demo a song we had written titled "Getting Under You, Then Getting Over You." I asked her if she had any compunction about doing a song with such a title—she was a very religious girl—and she said no. Cook and I weren't sure if she was being broad-minded, or if it just went over her head.

I still loved and missed Sparky, but I was no longer obsessed with her. I had heard nothing directly from her since she had gone back to Troy a couple of months before. Her little sister Debbie—who was close to Jeep's age—had sent a birthday card to Jeep, upon which was written "HI JEEP . . . LOVE YOU BABY . . . SPARKY."

I had recently called Fay, and she told me that Sparky had finally gotten around to reading a letter that I had sent her after she left—it was a nice letter with no coercion, no attempt to talk her into coming back. She said Sparky broke down and cried and then showed the letter to their mama, who also cried. But Fay told me that Sparky didn't want to talk to me, because she was trying to make her marriage work and was afraid of what might happen if we had a conversation. But I was okay with all that. Did I accept her being gone? Yes. Was I okay with the fact that I might never see her again? That was hard to say, because I had a strong feeling that I *would* see her again, that she *would* come back.

On Monday, April 25, 1977, Sparky called me at Tree and invited me down to see her on her twenty-sixth birthday, one week from that day. I didn't hesitate for a second when I told her I would be there.

"I don't guess you'd believe me if I told you I love you," she said.

I laughed and said, "Well, just how much do you love me, Sparky?"

She gave me what had always been her stock answer, which was music to my ears. "A whole big old bunch."

I wrote in my journal "I don't trust her, but I don't guess I need to."

The next day, I sat down in a Tree writers' room to attempt to write something with Sonny Throckmorton, the tall, charismatic, high-voiced, pot-smoking, songwriting genius who referred to everyone as "Puddin.'" I got another call from Sparky, and after our conversation I told Sonny that I had a song idea, "I Feel You Coming Back Again," thinking, of course, of Sparky. We wrote it quickly, and the chorus ended with:

> *I feel you coming*
> *I feel you coming*
> *I feel you coming back again*

The next day Sonny told me that his wife felt certain that nobody would sing something that sounded that risqué, and she had suggested that we change it to:

> *I feel like loving*
> *I feel like loving*
> *I feel like loving you again*

It would take four years, but eventually T. G. Sheppard would take this ballad to the #1 spot. Harlan Howard was right! Sparky was a veritable song garden.

Over the next few days, Sparky and I talked quite a bit. She gave me a long list of reasons why she went back to Troy (none of them being, of course, that she loved him). Things didn't seem to be going so well between them, however, and I could once again feel what felt like her love for me, across the miles.

When I met her in Alabama on her birthday, we had a wonderful time, and she asked me playfully, "Can I come back to Nashville?" She wanted to come that summer, only a month away. But, of course, I wanted her to come back *immediately*. Once again I became obsessively and possessively impatient. After a couple of weeks, I could see that I was on the verge of losing her again and backed off. "Baby, I love you, but you love me *too much*," she blurted out.

I didn't deny it, and she gave me her solemn oath to come to me the next month. We talked on the phone almost every day for the rest of May, making plans for her to move into an apartment. Gail would come up from Florida to be her roommate. At summer's end, Allen would move to Nashville to start school.

One fine summer day, I was both walking on air and scared half to death as I left my place to drive down to Alabama and get the love of my life. As I left, I scotch-taped the lyric of a new song onto the storm door, for Sparky to see and read when we got back. "Come On In" would become a Top Ten record for Jerry Lee Lewis the next year. My dream was coming true, but instead of letting myself relish the sweet victory, I had to analyze it—just *had* to know for certain that she was coming to me because she really, really loved me. A part of me thought that her big problem with Troy was his girlfriend, and that she may have been coming to me on the rebound. That apprehension manifests itself in the lyric.

> *If you're here 'cause you love me*
> *And not just because*
> *Things didn't work out with him*
> *If you've had sweet dreams of me*
> *And where we left off*
> *Come on in, come on in*

Sparky kept her word. She filed for divorce and left Troy in June. We decided it would be best not to live together until both divorces were final, so we found her a decent apartment in a complex on Murfreesboro Road. Her friend Gail moved to Nashville with her eight-year-old son, Tommy, to live with her and Allen. I would be paying for Sparky's half of the rent. Gail immediately found a job as a waitress at a nearby restaurant. I didn't want Sparky to have to take a job; I would rather that she be free to play and make music with me. Of course, had she *wanted* to work, I wouldn't have stood in her way. But the only job she seemed interested in was "country music star."

Initially, Sparky was filled with love and enthusiasm. It was a whole new world, and it tickled her fancy. "Head to Toe," which I had written about her, was a current hit by Bill Anderson. Also, she seemed to be angry at Troy about something. So for several reasons, she was ready for change, and a relationship with me looked good and so did Nashville.

Though Allen was spending the summer with his father, he spent some of the time with his mom. Late one afternoon, Sparky was at my place; it was a weekend, so I had Lauren (Jeep), and she had Allen. Though close to downtown, my neighborhood was a quiet, shady old area near Belmont College with little traffic, so it was safe for the kids, ages nine and eleven, to play in front of the house. They rushed up the steps, a bit upset, and told us that the man who lived across the street had rudely ordered them to stop petting his cats. It was Asshole Johnson, who had attacked Don Cook a few weeks before, only to be counterattacked by Cook's girlfriend, Charmaine. Asshole had warned us that we hadn't heard the last of him. I had discarded my crutches but was still wearing a cast on my leg. I hobbled quickly across the street and reprimanded him for being impolite to the children. Within a minute or two, we were fighting, and I ended up on the pavement with a big sumo wrestler on top of me. Sparky and the kids were immediately in the street, on the scene.

"You get *off* of him, his leg's in a cast," Sparky said loudly. Johnson continued to try to hold down my hands as I struggled to grab his neck. Jeep was demanding that he stop sitting on her daddy.

"I said get *off* of him!" Sparky shouted, as she got down underneath Mr. Johnson and tried to pry him from atop my body. As she let out a loud shriek, this small woman suddenly picked up the gargantuan man and sent him tumbling onto the pavement. It was a sight so stunning that it was almost surreal and brought to mind stories about the mother who summons up supernatural strength and lifts a burning bus off her child. For the second time in recent history, Asshole Johnson scurried into his house in disgrace, bested by a petite female.

"Sparky," I said in amazement, "I can't believe you d-d-did that for me."

"Well, to tell you the truth," she laughed, "he had this horrible green snot coming out of his nose, and I panicked and knew I had to get him off both of us, *quick*!"

I won't dwell too long on the biggest superstar of all time, as all of the major events of his life have already been thoroughly chronicled in Peter Guralnick's dazzling biographies, but when I walked into Tree International one warm August day in 1977, and Judy Littlefield, the front desk receptionist, asked, "Have you heard that Elvis died?" it was the equivalent of learning about the death of a good friend or head of state. Although I had never met the man, I felt that I knew him. I first heard him on the radio singing "Baby Let's Play House" when I was fourteen, and a few months later the host of a local teenage dance show on an Orlando, Florida, TV station announced, "*Here's* a record that's causing a lot of controversy—some people say this guy's *pop*, and some say he's *hillbilly*. Tell us what *you* think." The record was Elvis's "Mystery Train," and I was a gone goose. Just as the automobile had been invented before Henry Ford, but Ford was the first one to put it across successfully and mass produce it, so it was with Elvis Presley and rock & roll. There had been several country-meets-black recordings, but it was Elvis who fully exploited the combination and defined it as the new music of the youth of the world. Some believe if it hadn't been Elvis, it would have been this one or that one. Some say it would have been Carl Perkins and "Blue Suede Shoes." If there had been no Elvis, there may have been *several* artists whose music would popularize rock & roll—after all, Bill Haley and the Comets had already introduced it to a receptive audience. But Elvis had it all: the right voice, the right sound, the right look, and the right *schtick*. And, probably above all else, he had the right timing.

Years later, I would, in a way, know Elvis vicariously by sleeping with a woman with whom I knew he had slept. She would describe him as a gentleman and one who was sexually normal (contrary to what some others said), and would tell me that her only complaint was the difficulty in having alone-time with him, because his Memphis Mafia was always hanging around. I got to know one of his guys, Lamar Fike, a good-natured man who years after Elvis's death would become so large that he would tumble from his seat onto the floor at a party, and it would take four of us to get him back on the couch. I learned great stories from the musicians who played with "The King" on the road and on his sessions—a drummer at an Elvis recording session took a pickle off a tray in the break room, between songs, and one of the sunglasses-wearing mob grabbed his hand and growled, "Those are *Elvis's* pickles!" I knew songwriters who gave up a piece of their song in order to get an Elvis recording—it wasn't a perfect world, this Elvis world; after all, he died at only forty-two, with from nine to seventeen drugs (depending on which account you believe) in his system. But someone doesn't become *the biggest* by accident; there is a reason. Music, the centerpiece of my life, would not have been the same without Elvis Presley. And his strong ties to country music were many. Muddy Waters sang, "the blues had a baby and they named it rock & roll." That's true, and I think the daddy was a hillbilly.

In August, the cast was finally removed from my leg, after seven months of imprisonment. My heart wasn't doing as well as my leg, however, because Sparky was wavering once more. Small wonder that I was writing songs with titles like "She's Changing Her Mind Again" and "When One Falls Out and One Stays In." She admitted to me that she wasn't happy, and that she didn't love me as much as she once did. I went to see her at her apartment one day, and she seemed pretty frazzled. She had been attending to Allen, who wasn't very happy in Nashville, and her roommate Gail's eight- year-old son Tommy, a cute and funny little boy who had the energy of about ten normal kids. She told Allen, "I need to go outside and talk with Bob." I remember a futile, heartbreaking conversation with her in the parking lot, my heart dragging along on the pavement as she walked back up to her place, and I sadly walked to my car.

Sparky's divorce was coming through more quickly than mine, because hers was uncontested while Sue and I were waging war. Then, as summer turned to fall, Sparky's divorce became final but she seemed to only grow sadder, saying that she loved Troy more than me. "I'm not going anywhere yet," she told me, "but sometimes I feel like I'm a plane circling the airport." Once she told me that if she left me, she would probably "go to Africa."

But the more we hung out at Tree, partying with friends, the better she seemed to get. Her spirits seemed to lift further when I took her to buy something to wear to the BMI Awards banquet in October.

At the banquet, I won four awards, tying with Billy Sherrill and Bob Mc-Dill for first place. As I went to the stage to pick up one of the awards, Billy Sherrill yelled out, "Next year 'Womanhood,'" referring to a song of mine that he was planning to record on Tammy Wynette soon.

Tammy, maybe the best traditional country female singer of all time—the girl with that wonderfully sad little catch in her voice—approached me and gave me a congratulatory kiss for my award for "Golden Ring," which had been a very big record for her and George Jones the year before. She was with a new George—her boyfriend George Richey—songwriter, pianist, and producer.

"We're having a party at my place afterwards," she said. Then turning to "her man," she grabbed Richey by the arm and said, "Please get them to come to our party." I told them that we would be there.

After putting in a quick appearance at Don Gant's party, we went to Tammy Wynette's fancy home on Franklin Road. Tammy was kind and gracious, as always, showering Sparky with compliments when I told her it was she who sang the demo of "Womanhood." But for all her graciousness, Tammy seemed to defer to her boyfriend to be her spokesperson. There was a song of mine that she loved (but was afraid to record) and wanted me to sing, but instead of asking me, she said, "Richey, get Bobby to sing 'I Like Pain.'" We heard talk among the other guests that Tammy and Richey were going to be married soon. We eventually headed back to Don Gant's party and familiar faces.

The Gants lived in a spacious old house in the West End area, Nashville's first suburbia, which had built up around the extended streetcar lines in the early 1900s. Lynda Gant was an outspoken woman who was totally without pretension, a tall, thin girl who Gant sometimes called "Olive Oyl," the beanpole girlfriend of the cartoon character Popeye.

At Gant's party we listened to Rafe's wonderful baritone voice, laughed at Cook's hilarious stories, and were entertained by the bizarre antics of songwriting legend John D. Loudermilk, who with his business-suited girth and little mustache, reminded me of the father in some 1930s movie comedy. Gant seemed to love everyone around him and told Sparky that not only did he plan to produce me but also planned to produce *her*, because he thought she was a star. If Sparky's problem had been depression, she was getting good medicine for it on this night.

We dropped by my place before I drove Sparky to her apartment, and I

On the fashion page of the morning *Tennessean*: "Rug Head" Braddock, Waylon "The Outlaw" Jennings, and super writer Bob McDill

later wrote in my journal about "Sparky in my bed, looking like a movie star." "I'm still here," she said.

The next day there was a picture of me, of all places, on the fashion page of the morning *Tennessean*. I was shown standing with two other men, and it was an article about country music "fashion statements." There was the great maverick singer Waylon Jennings in his outlaw clothes, crackerjack song-writer Bob McDill wearing a nice tux, and me with ruffled shirt and bow tie, sporting a jeans jacket and a full head of someone else's hair.

Sparky called me up and told me what a wonderful time she'd had the night before. From then on every time we were together, she seemed more and more like her old self, or the old self that I liked. Then on one cool night we had a nice meal at a restaurant that we liked called Houston's, saw Bar-bra Streisand and Kris Kristofferson in *A Star Is Born*, came by my place and sang, then hung out together for a couple of hours. As we left for her place around 5 a.m., she said she needed to go back inside and get some-thing. When I got back home and started to get ready for bed, I saw the big letters Sparky had written across my bedroom mirror in lipstick: LOVE YOU BRADDOCK. From that moment on, the issues of her loving and missing

Troy, not being happy, not loving me as she once did, seemed to evaporate and disappear.

On the night of October 18, 1977, I finished—or *thought* I finished—the song Curly and I had started several months earlier, "He Stopped Loving Her Today." This song, which would become far more famous than its writers, got an initial rating of seven from me, on a scale from one to ten. In my journal I wrote "Dunno," meaning "don't know" as in I didn't know what to make of it. Curly thought that I deserved a larger slice of the song than he did, and as I've stated, we were more apt to divvy up songs that way back then. Had it been written today, it probably would have been an even split, fifty-fifty. Surely without his involvement it would never have been written. This was the song that was never in a hurry, and the world of country music would not be hearing it for another two-and-a-half years.

A sad and funny twist is that this song, which was about a man who loved a woman so much that only his death got him over her, was not consciously written about anyone—and most certainly not about Sue. The only charted song I wrote about Sue was the obviously unflattering "Bleep You." Yet when "He Stopped Loving Her Today" became a major hit, she would tell a lot of people that she was the inspiration for it.

A couple of months earlier, Sue had filed for divorce for the second time, at my insistence. But when I decided that she was asking for way too much money—alimony in the guise of child support—I filed for divorce myself, giving her the opportunity to challenge it and counter with her own terms. I thought she was using Jeep as a bargaining chip in a money game.

While Sue had never set foot inside Tree International, Sparky was there all the time. If we weren't demoing songs in the studio, we were partying in Don Gant's office, and the party would sometimes continue at Doo-wagger or at Gant's house. Because Sparky was more outgoing than I was, and seemed to experience some kind of crowd-stimulation high, I think I had more friends during this period than I would have had otherwise. There were a large number of cohorts, but the core group seemed to be Don and Lynda

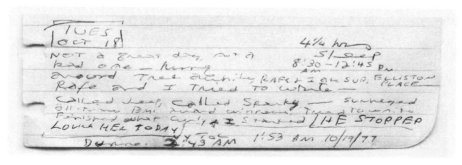

Journal entry about writing "He Stopped Loving Her Today," dated October 18, 1977

Gant, Don Cook and Charmaine, songplugger Dan Wilson and his wife Donna, Tree employee Terry Choate and his wife Wanda, and Rafe VanHoy, who rarely took his regular girlfriend around the Tree crowd. All of us drank, most smoked marijuana, and a couple did cocaine (though I never used cocaine because of my harrowing late-teen experience with speed, which made me wary of all "uppers").

Then Deborah Allen came back to town with the impact of a small earthquake. There was something about Deborah and her personality that demanded and got attention. A beautiful brunette with big doe-like eyes and a hearty, penetrating laugh, she was a first-rate singer-songwriter. We were all Fleetwood Mac fans, and at first her singing reminded me of Stevie Nicks, but that wasn't fair because Deborah was just as original in her own right, and had a voice that was equally at home singing torch, pop, rock, soul, or country.

At first, Sparky was a bit jealous of Deborah and all the attention she was getting. If there had been no Sparky, I probably would have charged after Deborah like a Mexican bull. As it was, she was in the process of breaking up with Jim Stafford, and there was an almost immediate connection between her and Rafe. As Rafe would later say, "I met Deborah and followed her off down the street." They wrote a couple of songs together that blew me away, and the first time I ever heard them in the recording studio together, where she was singing harmony with Rafe on an album that he was recording, I thought it was a musical match made in Heaven. While Deborah came from the far southwestern corner of the state in the hot, steamy Delta, Rafe's home was over five hundred miles from there in the northeastern corner of the state, in the cool mountains—about as far apart as you can get in the wide state of Tennessee—and they met in the middle, in Nashville. It looked like destiny to me.

It didn't take long for Sparky and Deborah, who were both very funny, to become best friends, and the four of us started hanging out. Deborah, who rarely participated in drinking or smoking grass, didn't always care to party with the larger crowd (Rafe often showed up without her), so Sparky and I split our time between the big group and just Rafe and Deborah.

Sparky and I took some time off for a wild, fun trip to New Orleans. Upon returning home, I wrote a song inspired by a beautiful dancer I had seen in the Crescent City, a dancer who turned out to be a guy in drag. The song was about an old boy who picked up such a "he," thinking he'd gotten himself a "she."

> *Shame shame, Sherree*
> *For not telling me*
> *The one and only thing that would have mattered*

With her eye on being awarded the big bucks, Sue wanted as much custody as she could get, so she called a moratorium on discipline—clearly a tactic to win Jeep over, I thought. This made it harder for me to keep my eleven-year-old in line. "I can't stop being a father to Jeep and start letting her have her way about everything, just to compete with her mother," I wrote in my journal. "A year ago she had nothing but contempt for her mother. I kept saying, 'Jeep, you've got to love your mother.' I hope it doesn't backfire on me."

But when the Christmas season arrived, Jeep saw the old Sue emerge. There was a tug of war going on because Jeep wanted to have Christmas Eve dinner with me at Sparky's apartment, then be at her mother's by 10 p.m., but her mother insisted that she be at her place "not one minute later than six." The dispute came to a head a couple of days before Christmas when Sue ordered Jeep out of her house and threw the Christmas presents Jeep had brought her out the door behind her, screaming, "Give them to your father's whore!" Sparky decided to play peacemaker and announced that she and Allen were going to Alabama Christmas Eve day, so we exchanged gifts at her apartment in the afternoon, then made it to Sue's door before her 6 p.m. deadline.

On New Year's Eve, I threw a big party at Doo-wagger, had it catered, and invited practically everyone I knew to come help me usher in 1978. It was an unusual mix, with country music establishment people like Curly and Bernice Putman, Sparky's hard-drinking brother Ott, most of my pot-smoking friends, and the totally abstemious Mike Kosser. Dixie Gamble came with her new boyfriend, Jimmy Bowen. This Bowen, not to be confused with "Indian Jim" Bowen, had produced hits on the West Coast a few years before with people like Frank Sinatra and Dean Martin, and, perhaps during a little lull in his career decided to give Nashville a shot. Within two years he would be the most powerful person on Music Row, as a producer revolutionizing the way Nashville records were made, and as a record executive heading up, at one time or another, almost every major record label in town.

After the party I went to Sparky's apartment to spend the night. I wrote in my journal "We've never been closer." We talked about how the new year would be even better than the old one. I had been writing a lot, and Sparky had been singing the demos of my female songs, getting a lot of nice comments on her voice. She had also been doing some writing with both me and Deborah Allen. She seemed to be very happy in Nashville and very happy with me. Our plans were to get married as soon as my divorce became final.

We went to Florida, where I introduced her to my mother. I think Mom suspected that Sparky was a little on the wild side, but she never said as much to me. I'm not sure how much Sparky liked my mom, but she was kind to her and spoke kindly of her, and after almost fourteen years of Sue tearing my mother down, this was a welcome change.

There was an energy present in those days that I don't quite understand today. Looking back from another century, where there doesn't seem to be enough time to do anything, it's amazing that in those days I was able to take vacations, write about ten songs a month, party—it was almost as though my life with Sparky then was one big party—and there was still time for us to see movies and watch TV, and I was still constantly reading, often aloud to Sparky. I somehow found time to be a family man, and my life always seemed better when Jeep was around. There were many late afternoons when Sparky and I drove up and down Murfreesboro Road, where Sparky's apartment was, with Jeep and Allen and Gail's little boy, Tommy, the kids arguing with each other over whether to eat pizza or burgers or fried chicken. We home-filmed a lot of little comedy skits featuring the kids.

We were very close to Rafe and Deborah and always had great fun with them, as well as standing in awe of their talent. Don Cook's outrageous stories about relatives back in Texas always had us splitting our sides—and I could today blackmail him over some of the nasty songs he co-wrote back then, if not for the fact that I was the other writer.

One especially unforgettable memory is of the night that Rafe, Cook, and I were sitting at my spinet, all three of us pounding out some rocking song on the keys, while Sparky, Deborah, and Charmaine danced on top of the piano. "How did we get so lucky?" Rafe mumbled. "Three of the most beautiful women in Nashville; we don't deserve this," I said in a whisper. "Well, don't tell *them*," Cook chuckled gleefully, looking very much like the cowardly lion.

Sometimes we hung out with Terry Choate, who worked at Tree, and his wife, Wanda. Terry was friends with country star Del Reeves ("The Girl on the Billboard"), so one night we went to see Del perform at a local night club. From the stage he announced, "Well, we have with us tonight Terry Choate and his wife, Wanda, and Bobby Braddock and his girlfriend, *Porky*." It was an honest mistake, and a good thing that Sparky was slender.

Don Gant was the center of our universe and the one we all looked to for everything—the one I looked to for getting my songs recorded; the one Sparky looked to for putting her in the spotlight. He told us he was going to record an album on both of us when Tree's new state-of-the-art, twenty-four-track studio was completed in the summer.

As I look through old journals, May of 1978 evokes a special nostalgia. There was the time Sparky and I were riding around with a big jug of wine while the radio played my Johnny Paycheck record, "Georgia in a Jug." There was Sparky's twenty-seventh birthday party at Doo-wagger that led to a cake fight, and I recall an old home movie of Rafe, Gant, Sparky, and Deborah rubbing cake into each other's faces, as Don Cook's demonic chuckle plays on and on like a soundtrack. There was a blissfully loving night with Sparky that moved me to write in my journal, "God, if you're doing this, thanks." There was a trip to Choate Mountain, a beautiful peak in western North Carolina owned by Terry Choate's family; about twenty of us camping out beneath the stars, telling funny stories around the campfire, and Sparky and I trying to keep warm in our tent as the cold mountain wind blew without end.

Hugh Prestwood told the truth when he wrote "The Song Remembers When." I don't advocate marijuana use, and think I would possess considerably more brain cells if I had never smoked it, but whenever I hear the marvelous sax solo on the 1978 hit "Baker Street," I feel stoned all over again, though I haven't smoked pot in years. It takes me back to the party at Don Cook's house when that record played over and over as I got higher and higher. Memories are like biopics; they probably make life seem more interesting than it actually was.

My divorce proceedings continued to drag on, and Sparky and I decided not to wait any longer to move in together. We started looking for a house, against the advice of my attorney. However, I did take his advice to rent rather than buy a house while I still had a wife. We found a large house that we loved, 832 Forrest Hills Drive, in a neighborhood just north of the Williamson County line and the upscale town of Brentwood. It was the only rental house on the street (a horsey-set neighbor girl would very snootily inform Jeep). When I told my mom that we were moving in together, she waved the Bible at me from across the miles, even though I assured her that we would have separate bedrooms for the kids' sake (which was true). I wrote about the house in my journal: "We love it. We love each other."

Sparky and I lay in her bed on the upstairs floor. It had been a wonderful night together. I was reading to her—she loved that—and she was starting to drift off. We were high on a hill, and higher up the hill behind the house, the wind was whispering through the trees. When she was finally sound asleep, before going downstairs to my own bedroom, I decided to stare at her pretty face for a while as she lay there. For the first time in my life I was in a thoroughly happy relationship. I didn't doubt her happiness any more than I doubted mine, which I didn't doubt at all. Hal David and I had written a song three years before, on the day that I was late for my writing appointment with him, the day I showed him Sparky's pictures, and he was amazed at her beauty but said it was no excuse for me being late. The song title was his (after all he was a famous lyricist): "Nothing Lasts Forever, Not Even Forever." That doesn't apply here, I thought; this will last forever.

8

PARTY TIME

Belle Meade is Nashville's ritzy little city within a city. Chet Atkins, the world's most famous guitarist and one of the chief architects of the cosmopolitan "Nashville Sound" of the 1950s and '60s, became a member of the exclusive Belle Meade Country Club, and every year he and his extended family ate their Christmas dinner there. Many of the high-hats in that dining room must have been remembering the time when country *clubs* and country *music* didn't go together.

The club epitomized Nashville's old money—the investment bankers, the insurance moguls, the manufacturers—the aristocrats who had been embarrassed that this Southern capital of commerce and education was thought of by many around the world as "the home of the Grand Ole Opry."

Then in the latter half of the twentieth century, country artists started crossing over into the pop charts. Non-country acts started coming to Nashville to record—pop singers like Perry Como and Bobby Vinton, folkies like Joan Baez and Bob Dylan, and rockers like Roy Orbison and Paul McCartney. Elvis recorded many of his hits on Music Row. In the early 1970s, the Opryland theme park opened for business. By the late 1970s, the local music biz was not as much of an embarrassment to the bluebloods. They had discovered that there was gold in those hillbillies, and there was a genuine ecumenical outreach. (Many of the country stars lived north of Nashville in Hendersonville, sometimes called "the hillbilly Belle Meade.")

There is a now-legendary story about Eddy Arnold—the most chart-topping country singer of all time—who had a very large farm south of the city, which he subdivided into what became the upper middle-class Nashville suburbs around the town of Brentwood. Mr. Arnold was attending a party at a Belle Meade mansion when he was approached by a grande dame. "And what is *your* name, suh?" she asked in the Old South accent of that generation's Nashville gentry.

He answered slowly in his deep mellifluous voice, "My name . . . is . . . Eddy Arnold."

"And just what do *yew* do, Mistuh Arnold?" she further inquired.

"Ohhh," he drawled, "mostly . . . just stand around . . . being . . . Eddy Arnold."

Of course, not just *any* hillbilly could be integrated into local high society. The "best families'" doors were rarely open to songwriters. But at the time, it was something I never even thought about. I was having a great year with my music, and I was involved with a sweet, beautiful girl. What more could a "hillbilly" have asked for?

Ooo ooo ooo, don't they sound lonely
Ooo ooo ooo, don't they play sad
Oooo ooo ooo, three quarter only
Watch how he holds her while the band plays The Last Cheater's Waltz

The chardonnay-drinking, pot-smoking crowd practically swooned—female and male alike—as the emotion-packed, high tenor voice of Sonny Throckmorton blared through the big speakers in Don Gant's office on the second floor of Tree International. Gant smiled lazily and slowly nodded his head from behind his big desk as he looked around the room at the twenty to thirty people—on the couch, in chairs, on the floor; Tree writers, many of them with their girlfriends or wives (most of the company's hundred-plus writers were male). Sonny was in the process of recording an album for Warner Bros. We were there to hear the same songs we had heard two or three nights before, before the fiddles had been overdubbed, and we would be back two or three nights later, after the vocal harmonies had been added. Take away the marijuana fog, and it was a nice camaraderie—all of us pulling for each other—and on these nights, all of us pulling for Sonny. The songs wouldn't make Sonny the superstar recording artist we were so sure he would become, but some of them had already been hits for other artists, and some, like "The Last Cheater's Waltz," would be hits for more artists in the next few years, in one of the hottest songwriting hot streaks in country music history.

"Son, son," muttered a contented-looking Gant.

"Sonny," said Don Cook, the hilarious substance-abusing English major who resembled the cowardly lion, and whose own songwriting career was taking off big, "that's the best song ever written about an old drunk breaking up with a whore."

"*Haaaaaaaaaaaaaaaaaaaaaaaaaaaaa!*" Sonny's hyena laugh penetrated the room, and possibly all of Music Row. "*Ol' drunk breakin' up with a whore!*" he screamed in his high-pitched, country voice, then after inhaling a donkey-bray laugh, he let loose with one more shrill one. "That's pretty funny, puddin.'" Sonny called practically everybody "puddin.'" A silly, stoned grin dominated his round-featured, ruggedly handsome face, and there was a twinkle in his glossy blue eyes. He bent over a coffee cup and released a long stream of tobacco juice.

Part of the Tree crowd. (*Front*) Charmaine Denney, Sparky Lawrence, Sonny Throckmorton, me; (*rear*) Rafe Van Hoy, Don Cook, 1978

Sparky announced, "I think Bob's gonna have a #1 song in a week or two." She was referring to Tammy Wynette's "Womanhood," a song about a girl having a tearful talk with God about losing her virginity. I had thrown it in the garbage can, but fished it out when Sparky kept urging me to take it in to Tree. It was a good thing that I listened to her, because it was sitting at #3 in the *Billboard* country charts. (In the very early 1950s the *Billboard* country Top Fifteen essentially consisted of fourteen men and Kitty Wells, but by 1978, fully 42 percent of the #1 country songs were sung by women.)

Jack Stapp and Buddy Killen had no idea that all this pot-smoking was going on inside their building after they left at closing time. It's not that the Tree second floor was just some kind of private bar or dope den; we had Scrabble games, serious poker, and even wrestling matches—Deborah Allen and Sparky, both tomboys, wrestled with Gant one night and accidentally cracked his rib. Every once in a while, everyone gathered around while I made one of my crank/prank calls to the information operator, which went on until someone in our group could no longer stifle his or her laughter. If someone had stepped off the second floor elevator at night, they would have seen a large group of adults at play, or heard loud music coming from Gant's of-

Sparky and me, 1978

fice—sometimes both. One night Gant told us, "Enjoy this, because there will never be times like these again."

If I had to pick one thing to thank Sparky for, it might be for taking my hat away from me. By the time we moved in together, Sparky was used to my bald head and perfectly okay with it, so I quit wearing a hairpiece. But whenever I left the house, especially when going to Music Row, I wore a black leather cap. I was happy that Sparky approved of my barren pate, but I had no intentions of letting anyone else see it. One day there was business at Tree that had to be attended to, and as I climbed out of the car, I told Sparky that I would be right back. With lightning speed she snatched my cap and slammed the door and locked it. I begged her to give me the hat, but she assured me that everyone would like me just as much without it. I went inside, angry at Sparky and agonizing over my appearance, but very few said anything about my naked dome, and those who did commented favorably ("Hey, lookin' good!"). At last I was free to be me, and never again felt the need to hide my follicly challenged head.

We were a happy family at 832 Forrest Hills Drive. In the summer of 1978, twelve-year-old Jeep saw *Grease* for the first of what would eventually be fifty-plus times. Ten-year-old Allen was so into the group Kiss that I nick-named him "Ace" after lead guitarist Ace Frehley. We had what I liked to call a complete democracy at our house, which wasn't entirely true because the kids didn't get to vote on everything. But I tried to make sure that Allen was treated the same as Jeep.

With school out for the summer, Jeep was spending about as much time with me as with her mother. Sometimes, when Sue was particularly angry at me, she tried to keep Jeep from being around Sparky. At other times, when she needed something, and I let her have extra money, she was more cooperative.

I felt that Jeep was old enough to be at the house with Allen if we were away for short periods in the daytime, but when we went out at night, as we often did, they went to a sitter. One night we went with Rafe Van Hoy and Deborah Allen to the Putman's mansion near Lebanon. After several drinks, we went out to their pool. Rafe and I jumped in naked, and when we urged Deborah and Sparky to do the same, they stripped down to their lingerie and joined us. Later when we were saying goodnight, I loudly announced to Curly and Bernice, "I sure had fun," to which Bernice replied with half-smile, half-frown, "Well, Bobby, I believe you *did*."

I thought poolside nudity had found its way to Music Row one warm afternoon as I stood on the second-floor balcony outside Gant's office, looking down on the swimming pool at Spence Manor. I motioned Gant and Rafe out to see the topless woman with long gray hair, whose back was to us. The bather finally turned around and it wasn't a woman at all—it was Willie Nelson!

Late summer brought me heartbreak when Sue, who knew how much Jeep loved the Gulf beaches of northwest Florida, rented a condo at Panama City Beach and enticed Jeep to move down there and go to school. I firmly believed that it all had to do with how much child-support money she could get in the final divorce settlement. On the day that Jeep left, Sparky and Allen, very sad themselves, did all they could to try to bring me out of a deep funk that came from the prospect of being so geographically separated from my baby. I knew I would be taking a lot of weekend trips down to the Florida Panhandle.

This was about the time that the state-of-the-art, twenty-four-track Tree International Studio opened on the ground floor of the affectionately called Taco Bell Building. When Jack Stapp told me that legendary producer Owen Bradley had urged him *not* to allow people to smoke in it, because it would ruin the recording console and stink up the place, I said, "Jack, most musicians smoke, and if you don't allow them to light up whenever they want a cigarette, I don't think they'll play as well." He lifted the smoking ban before it was a day old.

At the first session I saw there, Rafe was cutting a demo on a song he had written about Deborah (and her ambitions), "Prisoner of the Sky." She was singing harmony on it, and they were soaring powerfully and magnificently.

Gant fulfilled his promise to produce an album on me, through Tree's production company. The objective, of course, was to get me a recording deal. On my MGM recordings, ten to twelve years before, I had been singing with a vibrato that sounded like I was sitting naked on a block of ice and shivering all over. On the Mercury sessions that Buddy had produced, my singing style was more unaffected—I think I was being myself, and I should have stuck with that. But for this album project with Gant, I, the musical chameleon, for some reason decided to sing with a prolonged eh-eh-eh-eh vibrato on my soft notes—it sounded good when Barry Gibb of the Bee Gees or Lee Greenwood did it, but mine sounded like a lamb bleating at slow speed. On the high notes, I elected to be big and bombastic, like Neil Diamond, and the overall effect was way too melodramatic. Gant was a first-rate music man who had produced some wonderful recordings, but I think my overkill influenced him similarly to push the envelope too much, and I found myself surrounded by an ocean of strings and horns, and a gigantic soul-chick choir. Listening back from another century, many of the tracks are cringe-inducing. There are maybe three that I like. "Charley's Gone" is one I wrote about the death of a husband and father, and the accompaniment is Ron Oates playing killer piano, plus a string section playing Gershwin-like lines that I composed. "Blow Us Away" is a song I wrote after reading *The Book of Lists*, which named (incorrectly) all the nations of the world having—or about to get—nuclear capability. Probably the strongest song was a dark ballad that Sparky wrote with me, one that mortified my mother, "Between the Lines."

The story isn't new, a lonely girl, a crowded bar
Another drink or two and he looks like a movie star
He whispers soft and low, she's heard these words so many times
But never seems to know how to read between the lines

When he says
I don't mean a word I say
LOVE is just a game I play
YOU are not the first one I've said it to
I will try to act sincere
LOVE is what you want to hear
YOU will get just what you want
I LOVE YOU

So he slips off his ring, her dress is on the bedroom floor
He's thinking of one thing, while she's hoping for much more
There's not much time for proof, so any evidence will do
He's whispering the truth, but all she hears is "I love you"

I don't give I only take
LOVE is something that I make
YOU are just someone to make love to
I will leave you in the night
LOVE will vanish in the light
YOU think this will make it right
I LOVE YOU
I could never LOVE someone like YOU

Despite what I now hear as pretentiousness and self-indulgence, recording the album had been fun. I played piano on most of the tracks, joined by close friends such as Rafe on guitar, Cook on bass, and Eddy Anderson on drums. Just as all of the Tree crowd had gathered night after night in Gant's office, following Sonny Throckmorton's album from conception to delivery room, now it was my turn. After long days of tracking, overdubbing, then mixing, at night Gant was holding court, sitting behind his desk, wearing a lazy smile and scanning the room with his glassy gaze, as everyone closed their eyes and took in every single sound of my songs. It goes to show you that a bunch of people smoking dope will like just about anything.

My old friend Dixie Gamble had married Jimmy Bowen, who was now the head of MCA in Nashville. Dixie had heard some of what we were recording, and she became a strong advocate for me, urging Bowen to give a serious listen to the album. When Gant played him "Between the Lines," his response was, "How can I pass *this* up?" and he expressed interest in signing not only me, but also Sparky. We were ecstatic.

One afternoon, Gant and I went to Bowen's office for a conference. Dixie was there too. Bowen received much of his inspiration from the dried leaves and flowering tops of the pistillate hemp plant that yielded THC, as did so many music people in those days. Cannabis gave me the "munchies," and its use often sent me to Kroger supermarket to purchase cookies and cakes. So, as I walked into our meeting, I noticed a giant economy-size bag of Famous Amos chocolate chip cookies sitting on Bowen's desk. After Gant and I shook hands with Bowen and exchanged hugs with Dixie, we all sat down to talk about the album, as the hot little substance from Central America made its way around the table. Though Bowen's voice was low and lazy, his words typically came fast, in kind of a mumble, but in the smoky haze they seemed to become slower and slower. Later, when we broke up, I thought it had been a productive meeting.

As we left the building and headed for the parking lot, Gant put his hand on my shoulder and said, "Goddam, son, after you'd had a few tokes, you grabbed that giant bag of chocolate chips, put it in your lap, and kept it there."

"How many cookies did I eat?" I asked in sort of a buzzed embarrassment.

"Every damned one of 'em," he said.

Within a few days, the word was out that Bowen, who just a few months before had steamrolled into MCA and fired practically everybody, was just as suddenly on *his* way out. Dixie called us and told us to hang on, something was in the works. It was. Within a couple of days, Bowen had found a new home; Elektra/Asylum, a division of Warner Bros. Instead of being on MCA, I would be on Elektra.

Christmas was wonderful because Jeep was in town with her tiny toy poodle—her Panama City dog, Breezy—and I had my family together. Jeep and Allen were like long lost brother and sister. Sparky and I were closer than ever. She loved for me to read to her, and our nightly ritual was me reading from my favorite book, Thomas Wolfe's *Look Homeward Angel*. A few weeks before, I had gotten her roses for our third "falling in love" anniversary, with a card that read: "Maybe we didn't know it then, but it was true."

It had been a good year for me as a songwriter. "Womanhood" was Tammy Wynette's biggest record in two years. I had received BMI Awards for Bill Anderson's "Head to Toe" and also for the lickety-split "Something to Brag About," as recorded by Willie Nelson and Mary Kay Place. Tommy Overstreet's record of "Fadin' In, Fadin' Out," which I wrote with Sonny Throckmorton, was currently in the Top Ten, and I had a new one coming out by Tammy: hit-bound "They Call It Making Love," with me singing an "answering" part with her ("I don't know why," producer Billy Sherrill had told me on the phone, "but Tammy wants you to come down here and put your voice on it").

My album was finished, all mixed and mastered, and Bowen wanted me to do a showcase on February 1, 1979, performing every cut on the album. He told me all the top people from Elektra on the West Coast would be there. A choreographer was assigned to me, to help me develop a little more stage presence, which would have been fine if you could actually teach someone that sort of thing, but this guy saw me as a "dancing Beethoven." I told Gant if I had to be a dancing Beethoven, I didn't want a recording career, so he talked to Bowen and got me off the hook. I wouldn't have to dance.

The showcase event was at Nashville's legendary Exit/In, and it was packed. Practically everyone from Tree was there, and there were forty Elektra people who had flown in from all over the country. I had a large back-up band, made up mostly of talented friends. Sparky and Charmaine (Don Cook's girlfriend) were my back-up singers. The show was broadcast live on a local radio station. Everyone did well, but the show just didn't seem to come together, and before it was over, I had lost my enthusiasm. Maybe a dancing Beethoven wouldn't have been such a bad idea. The finale was pathetic. We were closing with my nuclear holocaust song, "Blow Us Away," and at the end of the song the synthesizer was supposed to sound like a hydrogen bomb ripping up the planet as the stage was engulfed in smoke. Instead, a tiny wisp of smoke went up as the synthesizer made a little fart sound.

The album was titled *Between the Lines*, all of us oblivious to the fact that there had been a Janis Ian #1 pop album with that title three years before. My cover was very artsy. There was a picture of me adorned in black, with my arms folded, and to my right was a ghostly looking standing half-profile of Sparky, sort of a blur. On the back was a head shot of me with my fairly long beard, looking all dreamy-eyed. Sparky thought it was sexy; my mom thought it looked evil. The album would sell about 18,000 copies, and only one single, the title song, would chart, when Beethoven danced up to #58, then quickly boogied back down the charts.

Far more important to me was the fact that I was able to convince Sue that she would not do nearly as well in the divorce settlement if she continued to keep Jeep out of the state, so Daddy's little girl—not such a little girl anymore—was moving back to Nashville. Hallelujah! She would stay with her mother on schooldays and with us on weekends.

These were the glory days at Tree for our little crowd. Sonny Throckmorton had his blazing hot streak going. Rafe and Cook had become the new hot writing team in town, and they also collaborated in other combinations, Rafe often writing with Deborah Allen and by himself. Late one afternoon as I walked into the Taco Bell Building, there was Rafe, carrying his guitar case, about to get on the elevator. To country music fans thirty-plus years later, Rafe then looked a little like a combination of Dierks Bentley and Billy Currington. As we got off on the second floor, we could hear music coming from Don Gant's office. Rafe said, "I just wrote a song that I like pretty well, but I don't know whether I should go into Gant's office and sing it or not."

"Why don't you let me hear it first?" I asked. So we went into an unoccupied room where he opened up his case, whipped out his guitar and tuned it, then proceeded to sing me a song that was inspired by a "solid" couple, friends of his, whose breakup had shocked everyone who knew them.

"Holy shit, you d-d-definitely n-need to go into Gant's office and sing it for everybody," I said enthusiastically after he finished. "What's Forever For" would be recorded by ten different acts before becoming a monster pop and country hit for Michael Martin Murphey in 1982.

Rafe and Deborah were in the process of moving in together. Rafe had an album out on ABC, and Deborah happened across an opportunity that paved the way for a successful recording career.

There was a "guitar pull"—that is, a guitar was passed around to various songwriters who would each sing one of their songs—at a party at the home of Tree songplugger Dan Wilson, near Lebanon, Tennessee. Deborah's singing so impressed Bud Logan, producer of country star John Conlee, that he asked her to do some recording. Bud had been the bass player for pop/country legend Jim Reeves, whose records had continued to do well in the fifteen years since his tragic death. RCA wanted Bud to put the voice of an unknown but powerful female singer with Jim Reeves's vocals and tracks; he thought Deborah would be perfect. Some people would refer to this as the "dead man duet." Deborah's haunting harmony was a perfect match for Jim Reeves's rich baritone voice and gave a sense of earthiness to the recordings. Three of the duet singles, "Don't Let Me Cross Over," "Oh How I Miss You Tonight," and "Take Me in Your Arms and Hold Me," would make *Billboard*'s country Top Ten and lead to Deborah signing with Capitol Records.

Sparky and Deborah were doing a considerable amount of co-writing and had the new single by Stella Parton, Dolly's sister, with a song titled "(Go On and Leave Me) The Rest of the Way." Sparky was also co-writer of three of the songs on my *Between the Lines* album, so she was already having more songwriter action than some people who had been on Music Row for years and years.

I had gotten so close to Sparky that one night when she was in Alabama visiting her family, I had a nightmare and fell out of bed onto the floor, screaming, "SPARKY!" Life with Sparky was like a vacation. Sometimes on a vacation you might have a flat tire or run into a little bad weather, and we had our little run-ins, but even then she was funny and never crazy. The closest we had come to a real fight was a dispute over who would get the one remaining little carrot cake at a convenience store in Panama City, Florida, when we made the mistake of taking a beach trip when we were both trying to quit smoking. With few exceptions, every day and night was a blast. We both loved games: poker and other card games, Battleship, even Monopoly; but we were almost fanatical about Scrabble. It was beginning to be a nightly ritual. One day I came home and found her reading the Scrabble dictionary. I was keeping an aggregate total of our scores over the months, then the years. Whenever I played all seven of my letters, earning me a fifty-point bonus, she would glare at me and whisper, "*Bastard.*" When she did the same, I would glare at her and whisper, "*Bitch dog.*" Those were our Scrabble combat names for each other, all in fun, and we always hugged at the end of the game. Whenever I was away from her for even a little while, I missed her. When she was visiting in Alabama, she would call me and say, "I wanna come home."

Sparky and I were like a team. One night we had finished a big dinner at a country cookin' restaurant called Couzer's. I was ready to leave, but Sparky said, "Why don't we stay another few minutes and relax and talk?" It sounded like a good idea to me, so I said okay. After a couple of minutes she suddenly blurted out that the man in the booth behind me was choking and couldn't breathe, and she suggested that I do "that thing I've heard you talk about." I jumped up, grabbed the old man under the armpits and pulled him to a standing position as I situated myself right behind him, but rather than doing the correct Heimlich maneuver—arms around the waist, fist above the navel, then pressing hard into the abdomen with quick, upward thrusts—I took the tops of both fists and started banging the bottom of his rib cage, and banging *hard*. The obstructive piece of chicken-fried steak whizzed across the room like a flying squirrel, and as soon as he could get his breath he reprimanded me for nearly breaking his ribs. I sat back down with Sparky and soon felt a tap on my shoulder. It was the old man, saying, "Uh, I think yuh saved m' *life.*"

Sometimes we were a *comedy* team. We were lying across a bed, and I made a complimentary remark about some woman with long hair, and Sparky told me in mock disgust that I would be attracted to a *dumpster* if it had long hair. At that moment, the lit end of my cigarette fell off onto my T-shirt, burning a hole through the material and causing me to jump up off the bed, frantically slapping my chest. "See," she bellowed, "just the *mention* of a dumpster with long hair gets you excited!"

Sparky was a party girl, and I wanted her twenty-eighth birthday party to top the one she had thrown for me on my thirty-eighth, several months before. There were twenty-seven people invited to her party, and thirty-two showed up. I got her a bald-headed cake man who looked very much like me, with a dill pickle between its legs. Our party room was our large rec room, with people sitting on bean bags or on the floor. Kieran Kane, who would be half of the successful "O'Kanes" duo with our friend Jamie O'Hara in the 1980s, sang something he wrote called "Surrender to Your Heart," while all the girls danced around in a circle, pounding on their hearts in time with the music whenever the title line came around. We filmed a "Herman" contest, the objective being to see who could come up with the funniest way of saying "Herman." Then we showed a movie we had made the week before of Deborah and Rafe lip-syncing her duet with Jim Reeves, with Rafe wearing a tux and playing the part of Gentleman Jim, as Reeves was called. As usual, the leader of the pack was Don Gant, lying on his back, all glassy-eyed, smiling peacefully as his loquacious wife, Lynda, talked on and on. There was Don Cook's demonic chuckle and Sonny Throckmorton's hyena laugh, Sparky saying something cute and loud as her ocean-green eyes twinkled in the smoky haze, where time took its time and the wine flowed like wine.

The house sat on a hillside in a nice suburban neighborhood a few miles south of downtown, and if this had been chronicled by a movie crew, as the camera backed out you would hear the music and laughter mixed in with the sound of the wind in the tall trees higher up the hill. On nearby Franklin Pike there may have been a car full of teenagers listening to the Bee Gees singing "Tragedy" or the Blondie hit "Heart of Glass." Parallel with Franklin Pike, on I-65, there might have been a truck driver on his way from Birmingham to Cincinnati, listening to Charley Pride sing "Where Do I Put Her Memory" or Conway Twitty belting out "Don't Take It Away." A few miles to the northeast, Allen was spending the night with Sparky's friend Gail and her little boy, Tommy. A few miles to the northwest, Jeep was at her mother's latest Nashville residence.

Just a few days before, during Lauren's weekend time with me, I had been on the phone with Sue who was at the home of her friend Bobbie Komisar, a well-to-do older lady who had been charmed into befriending Sue. "Please, don't keep me away from my baby," she suddenly began crying loudly, obviously for Ms. Komisar's benefit because I certainly had not been keeping her away from Jeep; this was my little weekend with my daughter. Sue was putting on an act, and when I asked her to put Bobbie on the phone, she just kept on "begging" me. After two years of telling Jeep "you've got to love your mother," she had finally started getting closer to her, and now I was afraid that my trying to do the right thing was going to bite me in the butt. So I signaled Jeep to pick up the extension so she could hear what deceitfulness her mother was employing.

After school was out for the summer, Sue pulled a similar stunt from her attorney's office, apparently attempting to elicit some sympathy from him as well. "I haven't seen my baby in two weeks and don't know if she's alive or dead," she wailed. Jeep and I had in fact been trying for two weeks to get in touch with her; I had insisted that Jeep call her every day.

My attorney was Jack Norman Jr., one of the most honest and decent men ever to grace Nashville's courthouse square. One day he called and told me that Sue was demanding, through her lawyer, that I make up a list of every single time and place that Sparky and I had had sex. I wrote in my journal, "When will Sue get out of our otherwise happy lives?"

Late one afternoon, when I met up with Sue to leave Jeep with her for a few days, she gloatingly told me that the judge who would hear our case was an old drinking buddy of hers. When I told Jack Norman, he said I needed to wear a small recording device, and see if I could get her to repeat her claim. I did and she did, and the judge quickly recused himself.

At the deposition, I was questioned for three hours and asked to produce all of my journals. Though I didn't say so, I was prepared to burn them, bury them, or even go to jail before having my privacy invaded. I was proud of the way Sparky handled herself while being interrogated. After asking her some horribly personal questions, Sue's attorney, who smoked cigarettes in a holder and spoke in the accent of Nashville's upper class, went off the record to drop back into his chair and say, not really very convincingly, "This probably hurts me more than it does you," to which Sparky replied, "I doubt that."

One day I went by Sue's apartment and there was a moving van, hauling away her belongings. The manager said she had skipped out, owing them nearly two thousand dollars. She owed her attorney considerably more than that. Eventually she called me from Bobbie Komisar's house and told me if I would give her all her money in a lump sum, she would be willing to take half as much. She was desperate and didn't even resist when I insisted that although we would have joint custody, I wanted Jeep to be in my domicile. Buddy Killen told me, "Valentine, I'll loan you the money. You can't miss this opportunity." So we had finally come to an agreement.

In the midst of all this turmoil, I proposed to Sparky, in front of the kids. We talked of getting married at Tree, and writing our wedding vows in a song that we would sing to each other.

On the day of our divorce, in the hall outside the courtroom at the Davidson County courthouse, came Sue with outstretched hands. She had gained considerable weight. When she smiled and said, "Well, Daddy," I told her I thought she had played pretty dirty, to which she said, "Divorces are dirty." I reminded her that she had a daughter, and she snarled, "Yes, and I'll be spending some time with her. I'll call her tonight and keep her for a week."

"Well th-that may not work," I told her. "Jeep hasn't heard from you in weeks and weeks."

"I'm sure her *new* mother will take care of her," she hissed hatefully.

Jack Norman pulled me aside and pleaded, "For God's sake, Bobby, please don't say anything else to her."

That night I wrote in my journal:

Marriage of Bobby and Sue Braddock
b. July 20, 1964
d. Sept. 6, 1979

There was a big bachelor party for me at Tree. One guy had gotten a lovely twenty-one-year-old hooker as a wedding gift for me, and for whomever, but I was about to get married and had no interest in having sex with anyone but my wife-to-be. Deborah, Charmaine, and Sparky had gone shopping while we had our party but got through early and came by Tree. Although Rafe, Cook, and I were having nothing to do with the girl, the arrival of the trio threw the place into a panic, and the babe was being whisked away or hidden; I wasn't quite sure which.

I was in high spirits. Unlike fifteen years before when I had gotten married reluctantly, there were no cold feet this time around! October was my favorite month anyway, with a slight chill in the air, the Easter-egg blue skies, and leaves ablaze in every shade of yellow, orange, and red.

I went to Billy Sherrill's office to pitch him some songs. He had gotten a Japanese cut on the Tammy Wynette hit that he had co-written and produced, "Your Good Girl's Gonna Go Bad." He handed me a printout of what he thought it sounded like the Japanese singer was saying, and it was hilarious to read as the song played, with phrases like "Lutheran assholes, I shit comedy."

At the BMI Awards a few nights later, I received recognition for "Womanhood."

Then, on the day before I was to marry, Sue told Jeep on the phone, "Wish your daddy and Sparky good luck." The gesture was uncharacteristic and much appreciated. I sat down and wrote a song, not for my new wife but my old one. It was called "Hey Pee Wee," and the conclusion went:

Tomorrow is my wedding day
If you still love me like you say
Then be a pal and go away
And when the smoke has cleared away
If we can be friends, then okay
But now for God's sake go away

On Thursday, October 18, 1979, at 3:30 p.m., Sparky and I were united in marriage at the Williamson County Courthouse in Franklin, Tennessee, by County Judge Wilburn Kelly. Jeep and Allen were present as witnesses and somehow managed to evade us long enough to practically ruin my Mercury by writing "Just Married" all over it with lipstick. After running by the residence of photographer Hope Powell for pictures, we headed for the car wash. That night Sparky and I went to dinner at the Cork 'n' Cleaver for old-time's sake, dropped by the Gants' house and told them we had gotten married, then after a couple of drinks, headed for Rafe and Deborah's. In amazement, I kept saying to Sparky, over and over that night, "You're my wife. You're my *wife*!"

Many years before becoming a Music Row mogul, Jimmy Bowen enjoyed a brief career as a recording artist and had one hit, "I'm Sticking with You." He was definitely sticking with *me* as a recording artist, because despite the fact that my first album hadn't sold enough to pay for the recording sessions—and no matter that several deejays had responded that they didn't like my voice—Bowen was perfectly willing for me to make another album. "We're gonna stay with you 'til you have a hit," he mumbled. The next album would be called *Love Bomb*.

I told Don Gant that I would like to do this album without the accompaniment of strings and horns. He agreed. I also reminded him that I typically came up with many of the instrumental licks and grooves and requested that the album notes credit me underneath his name, with something like "Arranged by Bobby Braddock." He agreed to that as well.

This was a collection of songs that were up close and personal. "I Love You Whoever You Are" was written a couple of years earlier about a fickle Sparky. As I began to back away a little from substance abuse, I started worrying about a couple of friends who were getting in deeper, and that inspired "Burning Down." Some of the songs reflected my liberal drift of the 1970s, and I'll say this for Don Gant: his politics were way over to the right, but not once did he criticize any of my songs for what they said politically—with Gant, it was always about the music. And some of the songs were on the silly side. When I was a small child, "grunt-grunt place" was the name for little Braddock buttocks, and my mother thought it was scandalous that I wrote "Everybody's Got a Grunt-Grunt Place" and included it on this album.

For the *Love Bomb* album photo shoot, I donned songwriter Red Lane's leather flight jacket, flying helmet, and goggles, and climbed into a World War II fighter plane. (I who had a hard time flying even in a modern passenger jet.) The helmet was a bit small for my head and scrunched up my face, making it look older and more wrinkly than it actually was. The photographer's assistant was a young New Yorker who had never been in the South. I kept giving her my Charles Manson imitation, and it was sorta freaking her out. The camera caught me wearing that expression, and Jimmy Bowen told me a few days later, "That's the one we're using, or the album won't come out"—he finally agreed to use it on the back, rather than the front.

I liked *Love Bomb* better than the first album, *Between the Lines*, and initially had high hopes for it. Songwriting legend Mickey Newbury listened to it and said, "They're all gems." The single, "Nag Nag Nag" (featuring Sparky doing the nagging) jumped into the charts, and the album got some great reviews. *Billboard* said I was "Nashville's intellectual songwriter" (I had to laugh), and another trade magazine called me "Nashville's Art Buchwald," (referring to the political humorist, sort of the Al Franken of his day). When critic Laura Eipper wrote in the *Tennessean*, "There's only one clunker, 'Everybody's Got a Grunt-Grunt Place,' which slides over the edge of humor into tastelessness," Gant mailed her a copy of a very dirty song Don Cook and I had written "to show you what tastelessness really is." But the truth is "Nag Nag Nag" did very little, and the next single didn't even chart. The album was self-indulgent. Who was I to be chronicling my life in song and pushing my opinions off on the public? I wasn't Bob Dylan. In a review of both my albums side-by-side, *Rolling Stone* critic David Marsh wrote, "With his all-too-obvious social conscience and high school assembly melodies, Bobby Braddock could be called the Harry Chapin of country music. Unfortunately, Braddock *also* writes love songs." It definitely wasn't meant as a compliment to Harry Chapin ("The Cat's in the Cradle") *or* Bobby Braddock. I was pretty insulted at the time, but looking back from another century, I think maybe he was right.

A chilly draft of arctic air found its way across the Southland that January, but at 832 Forrest Hills Drive, all was warm and well. Jeep was thrilled to be part of a happy family at last. Sparky never played the role of mother in my daughter's life; rather she was more like a big sister. She didn't discipline Jeep, and I didn't discipline Allen, so there were never any step-problems. In the spirit of democracy, I did clothing inventories, to make sure that everyone in the household was treated as an equal, and Jeep was understanding when Allen came up short and got a lot of new clothes.

Sparky, who had dropped out of school to get married when she was barely sixteen, passed her general educational development test, known somewhat pejoratively as a GED. She was pretty hard to embarrass, but I managed to do it whenever we were out in public, and I would tell some total stranger, in my best hillbilly accent, "Hey, mah wife's a high school GRADGY-ate!"

The Northern-like winter continued, and Curly and I spent much of February 5, 1980, running back and forth in the snow between Tree and Billy Sherrill's office. Billy had requested that we write an additional verse for "He Stopped Loving Her Today" (which George Jones was set to record the next day)—a recitation verse about the deceased song character's unrequited love interest coming back for his funeral. We had initially written such a verse, so we dug it up and presented it to Billy, but it wasn't quite what he had in mind. Legend has it that we wrote so many versions that the stack of papers was as thick as a magazine. Curly and I recall that we came up with three or four versions at the very most, the last of which Billy Sherrill deemed "perfect."

Frankly, I didn't understand all the hullabaloo about this song. I thought it was good, but not great. I was more excited about a left-field religious song of mine, "Would They Love Him Down in Shreveport," which several artists had already recorded, and which George was also planning to do. I was even more excited about a "retroactive cheating song" that I had just written, "I'd Rather Have What We Had."

Billy firmly believes that they started recording "He Stopped Loving Her Today" in early 1979, and that it took until February of 1980 for George to get his vocals on. I think they attempted to record it in 1979 and canned it. Our new verse—written in 1980—made the song longer, so how could they have tracked the song *a year before* to accommodate a verse that hadn't even been written yet? Imagine Billy Sherrill saying to the musicians, "Play an entire extra verse before the last chorus. It'll be blank for now, but *in a year* Curly and Bobby may write a recitation that we can put there." We wrote the recitation verse on February 5, 1980, the day before the session, and it's in my journal that George went in and recorded it the next day, on the 6th.

Several days later, I went to Billy's office with Curly, Rafe Van Hoy, and Dan Wilson—the man who had pitched the song to Billy two years before—to hear what had taken place at Columbia Studio B on February 6 and in the following days of overdubbing at Studio A. There was no intro; George hit it cold:

He said I'll love you 'til I die
She told him you'll forget in time
But as the years went slowly by
She still preyed upon his mind
He kept her picture on his wall
And went half-crazy now and then
But he still loved her through it all
Hoping she'd come back again

We found some letters by his bed
Dated nineteen-sixty-two
He had underlined in red
Every single "I love you"
I went to see him just today
Oh, but I didn't see no tears
All dressed up to go away
First time I'd seen him smile in years

He stopped loving her today
They placed a wreath upon his door
Soon they'll carry him away
He stopped loving her today

[recitation]

You know, she came to see him one last time
Aw, we all wondered if she would
And it kept running through my mind
This time he's over her for good

He stopped loving her today
They placed a wreath upon his door
Soon they'll carry him away
He stopped loving her today

I was awestruck and speechless. I think there was a power in the song that Curly and I had never realized, and it took this great performance and great production to bring it out.

One critic would say the lyrics were maudlin, and in the hands of anyone but George Jones, they would have been overly sentimental and corny. That may be true; I can't say, because I'm too close to it to be objective. There are certainly a lot of people who wouldn't agree with that critic because in 1999 a poll of music business people would name it the country song of the century, and polls conducted by the BBC and both *Country Weekly* and *Country America* magazines around that time would name it the greatest country song of all time. Ten years later it was still topping polls; in 2009 the viewers of ABC's *Good Morning America* would name it their favorite country song. While it doesn't top my song list, I certainly don't mind other people telling me that it tops theirs. I do think this was and is the greatest performance by a country singer. And having given the great George Jones his due, I don't think any of this would have happened if not for Billy Sherrill's vision and his unflinching faith in this song. I think Billy is an American original who made his mark on country music like no other producer, with the possible exception of Owen Bradley.

When George's stark and haunting voice kicks off this sad song, there is the low, dark, foreboding sound that many people thought was the great Pete Drake playing steel, but it was Phil Baugh on electric guitar using a custom pedal pull-string contraption. On the second verse, Charlie McCoy plays perhaps the most lonesome-sounding harmonica ever recorded. The critics of the era often castigated Billy for using too much orchestration, calling his records "slick," but when George belts out "He stopped loving her today" on the chorus, and a room full of cascading violins, violas, and cellos paints a vivid mind-picture of a tortured soul's ascent to Heaven, I think it's pretty stunning. And the icing on the cake is during George's sad, sad recitation, when Millie Kirkham sings her "ooo" notes, sounding like the angel of death hovering over the casket of the pitiful departed soul. No, I don't believe it was the greatest country song ever written, but I do think it was possibly the greatest country *record* ever made.

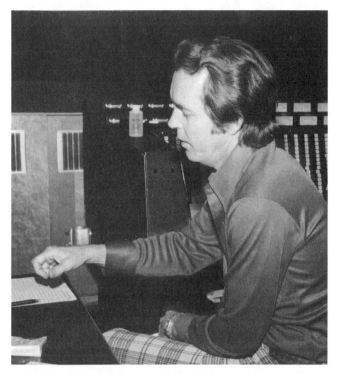

Genius record producer Billy Sherrill

Jimmy Bowen, Music Row's most powerful man
of the 1980s

In the spring of that year, after being notified of a sharp increase in our rent, we decided to buy a house. We found a cute, affordable little home in a new subdivision in a semi-rural area southeast of the city, near the working-class suburb of Antioch. Despite the hit songs, my history of money mismanagement and IRS delinquency relegated us to modest habitation. The sizable profit from the sale of the house on Newsom Station Road automatically went to the IRS as my liability grew more and more intimidating, with fines and penalties multiplying like rabbits. None of this looked good on my credit record, and we were able to get a bank loan for the down payment only through Buddy Killen's influence at First American Bank, where he sat on the board of directors.

The pastel yellow frame house looked small on the outside but had a roomy interior, with a large carpeted above-ground basement that would make a perfect music room for me. We loved the huge stone fireplace in the living room.

Jeep wasn't very happy about the move because she wanted to continue going to school with her friends, some of whom snobbishly kidded her about having to attend Apollo Junior High, which they referred to as "Appalling Junior High."

I recall Sparky and me driving from nursery to nursery, buying trees (hemlock, for some reason) for our new yard while the radio played "He Stopped Loving Her Today," which hit the #1 slot in *Billboard* the first week in July. There were several songs in 1980 that stayed at #1 for two or three weeks, but this was not one of them. At the time it seemed like a hit, but not a monster hit, and certainly not a standard. Apparently, the public took to it more than radio, because the single would sell over half a million copies. It would have a momentum that would just keep building over time. The echo would be much louder than the first shout.

In the very early summer, I took Jeep down to Florida with me for a short visit at my mom's. We had driven straight through without staying over at a motel, and in the late night as we approached Polk City, a little rural community several miles north of my hometown, I started talking about Gloria, my long-ago girlfriend, and the terrible family tragedy that had happened at her house eighteen years before, in 1962. I told her about Gloria's brother Rodney, who, in his early twenties, had fallen in love with a thirty-six-year-old married woman named Madeline, and about the woman's sudden decision to stop the affair, and how it drove Rodney over the deep end. I recounted the story of Rodney kidnapping Madeline and her mother at gun point near downtown Lakeland and forcing Madeline to drive the three of them to his parent's house near Polk City. I went on about how Rodney's beloved older brother David tried to take Rodney's gun away from him and got a bullet through the heart. Jeep was spellbound as I told about Madeline running from the house down the clay road, and Rodney catching up with her and shooting her in the head before turning the gun on himself.

"Here's the clay road down here," I said. "Do you want to drive by the scene of the tragedy?"

"Uhhh, I *guess* so," she said tentatively, nervously, her eyes wide open and hands to her mouth. I turned onto the rural road and drove past orange groves on the right and little Lake Helene on the left.

"There's the Gelders's house," I said as I pointed to the little white frame structure flanked by groves on both sides. "And here's where Rodney chased after Madeline," I whispered as I drove slowly down the country road then stopped. A big bloody moon was rising over the swampy little lake. "Right there's where he shot her."

"E-YIIIIIIIIIIIIII!" went the loud, shrill scream, echoing across the water. It was the sound of a woman screaming in horror. Then Jeep was screaming as I started the car and hit the accelerator hard. I sped along the clay road and rural blacktops to Highway 559 and kept the pedal to the metal all the way to Auburndale, as though we were trying to outrun a ghost. I didn't really slow down until we got to my mom's house.

Florida panthers, nearly extinct that far north but then reputed still to be living in the area, have a shrill cry. Foxes also have a high-pitched scream, and I had seen foxes before around the swamps and woods and groves on those back roads. But at the moment all we could think about was this poor soul reliving her moment of terror and giving us ours.

After we got back to Nashville, I drove home one afternoon, and there was a lady in our driveway standing next to a minivan, talking to Jeep. It was Sue. She had gained so much weight that I honestly didn't recognize her. She was there to take Jeep to Panama City Beach, where she was renting a nice condo—she was spending her "lump sum" as fast as she could. The van belonged to Sue's friend, Bobbie Komisar. When mother and daughter were together, I was often called to referee over the phone, with either Jeep telling me that her mother was being mean to her, or Sue telling me that Jeep wouldn't mind; in which case I would scold, "You've got to mind your mother." Actually, I had been having a problem with Jeep minding *me*. Fourteen is a difficult age anyway, and even worse if those years have been spent in a dysfunctional environment. But this time was different. When I met them halfway between Nashville and the beach to pick up Jeep, somewhere in Central Alabama, both of them were telling me how well they had gotten along this time. Now that the money issues had been settled and the tug o' war was over, I was happy to hear it. I wanted them to have a good relationship.

In late August Sue was to pick Jeep up again for a long Labor Day weekend in Florida. She didn't show. The next day Jeep got a telegram from her stating that there was a delay because she was in the hospital. Two, three, four days went by. I called her family in Alabama, and they had seen her a few days be-

Jeep and stepbrother, Allen
Lawrence, Opryland theme
park, 1979

fore but not since then. I found out that her condo in Panama City Beach was
empty and that she was way behind on the rent.

I had a long talk with her friend Bobbie Komisar, who said she was ready
to call the police because Sue had disappeared with her van and her credit
card (and most of Sue's Nashville roommate's clothes). She talked about Sue
throwing money away when she had it, and about her chronic lying, heavy
drinking, and her being obese while thinking she was still a size three. I told
her, "Sue needs help bad."

Two days later Bobbie's van turned up, parked around the hangars at the
Birmingham airport. There was a bag filled with groceries and men's magazines; workman's gloves were in the van. If I had been a good detective, I
would have realized that it looked very staged, to appear as if she were at the
airport with some man and that they had been whisked away. Maybe I was
influenced by the Nashville detective I had talked to when she was first missing, who told me Sue had been hanging out with cocaine dealers. Though we
didn't actually say it to each other, Jeep and I were both speculating that her
mother had been kidnapped or murdered. This would be the beginning of a
frightful head trip for Jeep.

Then there came more darkness, as surely as if a large slow-moving gloom
system had moved into the area. I called it "the days of the daily death." One
day my half-sister Lucille's daughter Diane, six years older than me, died of
a heart attack in Tifton, Georgia, just after getting home from a trip to Las
Vegas. The next day Pam Hudson, a sweet and pretty Tree employee who
had undergone surgery for a brain aneurism, died in the intensive care unit
at Baptist Hospital as about thirty of us held hands in the parking lot and
silently prayed. The next day Jeep's maternal grandmother, Sue's mother

Louise, died in Alabama from a blood clot that developed after her she broke her leg. Then the next day, also in Alabama, Sparky's Uncle Dan and Aunt Deanie were killed in a car wreck. We were beginning to panic, wondering if we would continue to lose someone we knew every day for the rest of our lives.

On the night of Monday, October 13, 1980, country-pop star Anne Murray faced the CBS television cameras, opened the envelope, and announced the Country Music Association Song of the Year. "He Stopped Loving Her Today," she said, "Bobby Braddock and Curly Putman." Curly and I walked past the cheering throngs and made our little acceptance speeches. It was a solid win all the way around as George Jones won, for the first time in his historic career, the CMA Male Vocalist award; and "He Stopped . . ." was awarded Single of the Year. After an hour of interviews and a party at Gant's house, gorgeous Sparky and happy Bobby went home to "Congratulations Daddy" signs that Jeep had put up all over the house. This was just the dawning of the age of answering machines and several years before the use of cell phones; I got a long succession of calls, and Mom called to say that a lot of people had called her as well. There were many times in my youth when I didn't make my mother very proud of me, so I was glad to be doing it at last. The next night I won two BMI Awards, so it had been a glorious week and a grand year.

A few nights later Sparky and I went to Buddy Killen's popular nightclub, The Stock-Yard. George Jones hugged and kissed me, and a drunk Faron Young, who had been a twenty-year-old country superstar in the early 1950s, told me, "Braddock, you're a good songwriter, but you can't sing worth a shit." Waylon Jennings would do one better than that on the *Austin City Limits* TV show when he said about me, "He's a *crazy* sonofabitch."

It's hard to discuss country music's Outlaw Movement without thinking of Waylon Jennings. Any list of "outlaws" invariably includes or is headed by Waylon, the subgenre itself being named for his 1972 album *Ladies Love Outlaws*. Whether the movement came about as a protest against record labels for not giving the artists enough creative freedom, or as a revolt against the Nashville Sound (that country-pop style that was born in the 1950s and continued into the 1980s), the music itself has always been difficult to define. I think if there's an "outlaw" rule, it is that the song has to be badass or the singer scruffy. Waylon Jennings fit both criteria.

Waylon struck me as a guy who didn't have a phony bone in his body. He was a handsome but ornery-lookin' cuss who sang with a menacing, testosterone-filled delivery. Someone once asked Don Davis, who ran Harlan Howard's publishing company, why so many women liked Waylon Jennings. Davis held out his hands far apart, as though he was describing the biggest fish he'd ever caught, and said, "Because he sings like he's got a dick *this long*."

The music kept coming. My "Hard Times" sung by Lacy J. Dalton hit the country Top Five, and I learned that Sonny Throckmorton and I had the next

T. G. Sheppard single, "I Feel Like Loving You Again." Thanks to the song-plugging efforts of Buddy Killen, Don Gant, and Dan Wilson—and I was pitching a lot of my songs myself—I was getting more major song cuts than ever before.

Don Gant was such a keen visionary that he attempted to do something that could have made me a billionaire. A couple of years before, I had bought a movie projector that had some nice bells and whistles such as film editing and sound overdubbing (not unlike our VCR). I eventually started putting together what would later be called music videos. My first effort starred Jeep, and I directed her through various typical household scenes to a song I had written about her, "Baby Blue Eyes." The editing—and, for that matter, the camera work (and the camera itself)—were amateurish, but Gant loved it, and thought the ideas were great. Then I started videotaping my little stories to popular songs, such as the Kiss classic "Rock and Roll All Nite," with Nashville's night life as a light-show backdrop, concluding with my stepson in Kiss makeup, wiggling his tongue a la Gene Simmons.

"Damn, son," said Gant, "you need to be making these little movies with country records—you writing and directing them, but using a professional film crew—making 'em for the record labels to sell to the public." We weren't thinking of a video channel; there was no such thing in existence at the time. He took his idea to the Tree hierarchy, but they didn't get it. He talked to some people outside the company but nobody was willing to fund it. Don Gant was ahead of his time. This was a year before the debut of MTV and three years before CMT.

Not long after this, Gant pulled me aside and told me he was going to leave Tree and start his own publishing company. I was in shock. I wanted to go with him right then, but we agreed that in a couple of years he might be in a better position to afford to pay me what I needed.

One thing that was usually able to pull my attention away from music was politics, but I didn't have a lot of enthusiasm about the 1980 presidential race. After watching a debate between President Jimmy Carter and former California Governor Ronald Reagan, I wrote in my journal:

> Guess who's got the biggest boobs in the world. WE do—Carter and Reagan. Personally I think Carter OUTBOOBED Reagan. Hope it doesn't give Reagan the presidency, he scares me.

Looking back from another century, I don't think that either man was a boob. Jimmy Carter is widely regarded as America's greatest ex-president, and whether you agree with the change or not, Ronald Reagan seriously changed the political landscape of America like few other presidents. I was tempted to vote for an independent candidate, moderate Republican congressman John Anderson of Illinois, but I pulled the Carter lever on election day.

Winnin CMA "Song of the Year" award with Curly
Putman in 1980

Music City News award for best song, 1981: Curly, Tanya Tucker, George
Jones, Jim Stafford, and me

The election was not the most jarring news event of 1980, at least not to the Nashville Braddocks. Jeep was into the John Lennon hit "(Just Like) Starting Over," and had just bought the new John & Yoko album, *Double Fantasy*. I had been a Beatles fan from the beginning. So the assassination of John Lennon resonated with both of us. Jeep then wanted to hear every Beatles record I owned—and we eventually got *all* the Beatles albums—and I discovered Beatles gems that I had missed. We also got most of the post-breakup music by the individual former Beatles. I went from being a fan to a devotee. Had there been cable news when John Lennon died (or when Elvis died), I believe there would have been the same oversaturation that the media would exhibit following Michael Jackson's death in 2009. But the media can run things in the ground only if there is a receptive audience. The truth is, music and those who make it are a huge part of our lives. Despite the twenty-five-years' difference in our age, my daughter and I were equally impacted by the Beatles. From the time the group broke up in 1970, there was a hope among all Beatles fans that they would someday get back together, a hope that was shot down for all time on the night of December 8, 1980.

Several days later, Jack Stapp died. The founder and Chairman of the Board of Tree International was sixty-nine, but his bout with encephalitis a couple of years before had left him feeble, and he seemed more like a man well into his eighties. In my journal I wrote, "Always a kind word, always telling me how proud he was of me." We had planned a trip to Florida but delayed it long enough to attend Jack's funeral.

Sparky, Jeep, Allen, and I spent Christmas in Auburndale, on our way to Key West. It was almost as though my mom was on a mission to drive everyone's blood sugar levels through the roof. In the two days and three nights we spent with her, she made key lime pie, apple pie, eggnog pie, mincemeat pie, rum cake, poppyseed cake, and chocolate chip cookies.

We got back to Nashville in time for the "Congratulations Buddy" party at Tree—that's what the giant banner read—to celebrate Buddy exercising his option to buy out Jack Stapp's part of the company from his young widow, thereby becoming the sole owner. With Don Gant gone (he had already opened up an office three blocks away), Donna Hilley was the only vice president at the company, and in a more powerful position than ever.

"Do you think it looks bad, having a party so soon?" Donna whispered, giving me the impression that the festivities were Buddy's idea.

"Well," I answered frankly, "I think it looks kinda like having a 'Congratulations LBJ' party nine days after JFK was assassinated."

I remember reading an account of the historic 1959 plane crash that took the lives of rock & roll legends Buddy Holly, Richie Valens, and the Big Bopper. As they flew away into the snowy Iowa night, the people at the little airport watched the blinking light of the plane growing more and more distant in the sky, but also descending slowly as though some giant finger were pushing

With my brother, Paul, in Auburndale, circa 1981

down on the top of the aircraft. The young pilot, not instrument rated and encountering unexpectedly bad weather, probably thought they were ascending when the opposite was true. In retrospect, that's sort of how I see myself in 1981. Sparky and I were walking hand-in-hand down an embankment; I thought we were going up, too blind to see that we were going down.

I knew there were several things that Sparky was disappointed about. I was, too, but that didn't make me melancholy. I had Sparky in my life and that made me happy. Only in retrospect, sometime later, did I realize that she had been significantly depressed.

When Gant left Tree, the old gang seemed to break up, and we didn't go out as much. That was fine with me; I *loved* staying home and having Sparky all to myself. It never crossed my mind that she might be the woman in the Steve Wariner song who was "planning her nights by the *TV Guide*." Sparky and Deborah had had a falling out, so except for one time when Rafe dropped by with Dan Seals and played Scrabble with us, neither Rafe nor Deborah came to see us anymore. And Sparky's dream of being a recording artist, once seemingly on the verge of coming true, disappeared when she realized that Gant wasn't going to produce her and Bowen wasn't going to sign her—

offers that most likely had been contingent on fulfillment of my own success as an artist, which didn't happen. So for Sparky, it wasn't party time anymore. In just a matter of months, there had been a sea change in her life. The partying, close friends, a potential career—all seemed to have disappeared.

Someone once asked me, "She was a prize, so once you won her over, did you lose some of that loving feeling?" I took her for granted, no doubt, but I hadn't lost the loving feeling. Though I wasn't blind to other women, I never considered running around on Sparky. She was the one that I wanted. I wasn't a fan of male jewelry, but I proudly wore the gold chain and lion's head that she had given me for my fortieth birthday. I did have moments of enlightenment, such as when I wrote in my journal:

> *Sparky needs to get out more and be around people. She lives her days*
> *for me and the kids, and needs more than that. Her value is much higher*
> *than that.*

However, for the most part I was living at the corner of Oblivious and Denial. I strongly felt that Sparky loved me very much (I was right; she did) and that I could never lose her (I was wrong; I could).

Indeed, there was a sadness in the air. One day I went to Jeep's room, and she was crying. She had found an old letter from her mother, in which she had written that she loved and missed her. Jeep was feeling guilty because she had always taken my side and rejected her mom. My heart ached for her; though fourteen, she was still Daddy's little girl. She had been having bad headaches, but no doctors had been able to find anything wrong. A neurologist concluded that it was related to her mother's disappearance.

Amidst all the sadness, the saddest of songs kept winning the biggest of accolades. "He Stopped Loving Her Today" was voted best song of the year by the membership of the Nashville Songwriters Association. BMI gave a special party for Curly and me, and Sparky and I were happy to see Rafe there. Afterward several of us stood in the Tree parking lot inhaling helium, which made us talk in little Munchkin voices. At the televised *Music City News Awards*, "He Stopped . . ." was named Song of the Year, on a show emceed by my old friend Jim Stafford, with George Jones on stage addressing Curly and me with "If it wasn't for you, *I* wouldn't be up here."

There was a little bit of excitement for a few weeks when Sparky sang the demo of a rockin' song I had written called "A Married Man." She sang it great, and it sounded like a hit record. Producer Bud Logan, who had become affiliated with Tree, liked it so much that he went in the studio with me and we re-cut it—co-produced it, as a master record. He pitched it around to various record labels—we played it for Chet Atkins at RCA—but nobody signed her up. The excitement faded away, as did her uplifted mood.

There were still a lot of great times, times when I heard the laugh that

I loved, and saw the sparkle in those ocean green eyes. One night we ate at a Hibachi restaurant with Sonny Throckmorton and his unlikely new girlfriend, Hillary Kanter, a rich, gorgeous young Jewish woman who seemed more amused than embarrassed when Sonny threw in five dollars with my tip and said, loud enough for all (including the *Japanese* server) to hear, "Pore ol' Chinaman prob'ly needs the money."

Another time, Roger Miller invited me to a party at his suite at Spence Manor. Sparky and I both had our pretend heartthrobs. Mine was Crystal Gayle, and my brains turned to jelly whenever I was around her. Hers was Kris Kristofferson, but she had never met him—not until this night at Roger's party. I said, "Here, honey, let me introduce you to Kris." Kris gave me a big wave from across the room, and I told him I had someone I wanted him to meet, and introduced them. Sparky awkwardly moved forward to shake his hand and tripped over Tanya Tucker, who was sitting on the floor, and fell flat on her face.

I bought a nice camera with various lenses and attachments and decided to do a picture shoot on Sparky. I told her, "We're going to sell you as an artist. I think I can take some really good pictures of you." Her friend Gail came along as her makeup artist, and we spent a couple of hours in Nashville's Centennial Park. The shots turned out good enough that she was excited about them. I thought she looked like a movie star, and several years younger than twenty-nine. The pictures were made with love, and I think it showed.

One day Sparky and Allen were in Alabama visiting her folks. I was writing with Sonny James, of "Young Love" fame, who wanted a song that would get him back on the radio. After Sonny left, Jeep came out of her bedroom and said, "I just got the strangest phone call." (Jeep and Allen had their own private numbers.) A lady in Tampa, Florida, had called and asked for a "Sue Williams." Jeep quickly told her that her missing mother was named Sue. The caller's name was Linda England, and she said that someone named Sue Williams had been staying with her, and after she vanished, she looked at her phone bill and discovered several brief unexplainable phone calls to Jeep's number. Most likely, these were (in the days before caller ID) the mysterious hang-up calls Jeep had been getting.

Linda operated a home for battered women in Tampa. Sue had showed up one day and told her she was Sue Williams, wife of a piano player named Bobby Williams who was abusive of her. She had sent me back in time to my old job, changed my last name to Williams, and made me the abuser instead of the abused. Linda said she had taken a liking to Sue, and that her parents "fell in love with her." Sue: always the charmer. She told them, with accuracy, about the baby boy, Brian, and how he had died suddenly at eight weeks old. But she made no mention of having a daughter.

Many years later, based on new information about her bad childhood, I would start to feel compassion for Sue. Both Jeep and I would eventually forgive this poor lost soul who seemed to have disappeared off the face of the earth. But in April of 1981, I had very hostile feelings toward her for putting Jeep through months of agony and guilt.

Jeep, at fifteen, was being allowed to ride around occasionally with friends, all of whom called her Lauren. She also went on her first double date. Her mother was missing that, as she would all of the future important events in her daughter's life.

I think Sparky and I knew we had a problem and began to discuss getting another house, as though we could move out of the one we were in and leave our cares behind. We talked about getting something closer to downtown Nashville and Music Row. While riding around near the upper-middle–class Green Hills area, we saw a FOR SALE sign and turned onto Shy's Hill Road. The place was on the side of a hill, down from the street. For some reason, I immediately fell in love with this white brick house. We knocked on the door. It was for sale by the owner, an attorney who was moving to Memphis. He invited us to come inside and take a look around. I liked the inside even better than the exterior. I don't know how much Sparky liked it, but she said, "Baby, if you love it that much, I think we should live here." It was on Shy's Hill, scene of one of the bloodiest encounters of the Battle of Nashville, and the thought of soldiers charging up the hillside titillated the Civil War buff in me. I was excited about the house, and when we took the kids to see it, they were, too. Jeep loved the idea of attending Hillsboro High School in the fall, rather than Antioch High. It was as though we all wanted to get out of the other house as quickly as we could, and move into this one. It never occurred to me that a house in the middle of a battlefield where hundreds had died might hold some spiritual turbulence. And it never occurred to me that my marriage might be in serious trouble, and that moving to a different house probably wouldn't save it.

9

THE BEST OF TIMES,
THE WORST OF TIMES

One day in the late spring of 1981, Sparky asked, almost casually, "Bob, what would you say if I told you I couldn't handle marriage anymore?" Within minutes, she was saying that she only wanted to see how much I cared. Within days, she was saying she was only being silly. Within weeks it was completely forgotten, until decades later when an old songwriter sat reading his old journals, and heard a jolting voice from the distant past.

I find it amazing that over these many years I had forgotten such significant and pivotal events in my life—apparently they were disturbing memories that I chose to block out. But here it is, jotted down in my own handwriting, Sparky saying to me, "Maybe you should put me through some hell, have an affair, or make me think I'm losing you." And here it is, written down in code, me walking in the park with a beautiful young woman whom I had dated before Sparky, discussing the possibility of an affair, but not going through with it because of guilt.

Our street dead-ended at a large undeveloped area known as the Burton Farm. It looked like the perfect place for my family to take walks, with a pathway that passed through deep woods, grown-over fields, and an old abandoned schoolhouse. About the time that we moved into the area, Lillie Burton, great-grandmother of Christian pop star Amy Grant, died in her nineties, and the Church of Christ college to which she bequeathed the Burton Farm would sell it off to developers. But in 1981 the property set a peaceful, rural tone for the neighborhood.

Country star Dottie West lived down the street from us. Her house, like ours, was in the middle of a major Civil War battlefield. A few years later she would have to auction off almost everything she owned, but in 1981 she was at the top of her game. Like Dottie and her husband, Byron, I too was drawn to this neighborhood—drawn like a smitten fool to some beautiful angel-faced, devil-hearted temptress. And from the moment we moved to this hill, everything fell apart.

Sparky started going out at night fairly often, looking for a band that she could sing with. She was usually accompanied by her best friend, Gail. One night she told me she was taking a tape to a singer, sort of a preliminary audition, someone who was looking for a female back-up vocalist. He was an Elvis-Tom Jones type, a nightclub singer who lived in Phoenix with his wife and kids, but often came to Nashville because he had signed with a local independent record label. His professional name was Joe Vegas. When Sparky went with her folks to Florida to visit an aunt, she managed to catch a show that Joe was doing down there. Then she started rehearsing with him whenever he was in town, always at night—*late* at night. During this period I had quit smoking and was determined not to start back, so my patience had probably worn pretty thin. We began to argue a lot about her coming home so late, but I wrote in my journal, "it's not as sordid as it sounds," perhaps trying to convince myself. When Gail moved in with us for a couple of weeks, in between apartments, the two of them were out more often than in. Gail's new boyfriend was Joe's best friend. After one particularly bad argument, Sparky shouted, "I want a *divorce!*" Within a few hours she was saying that she didn't mean it. It was about this time that we traded in my Mercury Marquis on a new silver Trans Am that Sparky called her dream car. I started driving her Cougar.

Sparky and Gail went off in the Trans Am on a three-day trip, to get away from it all and to help Sparky through *her* no-smoking crisis. In my journal I wrote, "Apparently Gail has a calming effect on her." There were a couple of days when she never called. "I love her, but resent her breaking-away attitude," I wrote. That the two of them might be off with Joe and his friend crossed my mind, but I kept telling myself that Sparky wouldn't do that.

When she returned home, she said she wanted us to separate so she could feel free to pursue her career without a hassle from me. I promised to quit giving her a hard time about being away. I was scared to death at the prospect of losing her.

Sparky firmly contended that there was nothing but singing going on between her and Joe Vegas, and thought the best way to dispel any notion otherwise was to have him over for dinner. The oven didn't work, so Sparky got drunk. When Joe, Gail, and her boyfriend, Dick, arrived, I suggested that we go to Ciraco's, a wonderful restaurant near Music Row. Joe was a big, good-looking guy with jet black hair, about a year younger than me. I thought he was a bit stuck on himself, but liked him okay. Incredibly, I wrote in my journal, "I put to rest any jealousies I had."

Two nights later Sparky suddenly said she wanted to go out alone, for a drink. She went to Gail's apartment for three hours, then came home, and we talked for the rest of the night. "I'm not happy in our marriage, and for several months I've wanted to separate, not to screw around but to have freedom," she said. "I want to split for a couple of weeks, move in with Gail, and see if I miss you." The next day I took off for Florida with Jeep and Allen. On the phone Sparky told me she already missed me and thought everything would be all right.

So we continued to live together, with Sparky gone much of the time. I had resigned myself to keeping my mouth shut. I thought if I didn't give her a hard time, she wouldn't go through with leaving. I don't think Jeep and Allen had any idea what was going on. One night I wrote, "Everybody I know in the music industry conducts business in the daytime or early night. But Sparky and Joe's rehearsals take place in the wee hours, in Joe's motel room. I'm not saying there's anything going on—I don't think there is—but I don't like it."

And that's the way September of 1981 went. I was generally pretty miserable, but keeping quiet as much as I could, smoking again; Sparky was doing whatever she wanted to do. Looking back from another century, I can view it all with a certain detachment, but in reading what I wrote down long ago at the end of each sad day, I can still recall the pain that went into it.

Sparky and I agreed to take a major step—she staying sometimes with me and sometimes with Gail until she got her own apartment—during what would be the biggest week of my career so far. It would be the most wonderful and the most heartbreaking time of my life.

On Sunday, October 11, Sparky and I sat the kids down and told them we were going to separate. They took it okay; Jeep better than I expected. "We'll probably get back together before long," I said. "Maybe a month, maybe two or three months," said Sparky. Then we put on our nice clothes and went downtown to the luxurious old Hermitage Hotel, recently renovated, where the Putmans had rented a suite for a pre-Hall of Fame party. Why would they be doing such a thing if one of us were not being inducted into the Nashville Songwriters Hall of Fame that night? In those days, writers were not supposed to know in advance that they were being inducted. I had gotten a few hints here and there, but I played dumb.

The song that was probably getting me in, "He Stopped Loving Her Today," had been introduced to the public only a year before. In fact, it was nominated for CMA Song of the Year for a second time. It had been only thirteen years since my first big hit, and by today's rules—there must be at least twenty years from first hit to induction—I would have been ineligible.

Curly was the natural choice to induct me, but Curly *hated* getting up in front of people. I think he thought it would be funny (and make the situation less tense) if, instead of mentioning some of my hits, he were to reel off the titles of some of my silly songs, songs nobody had ever heard of. I think he did this because of my "other" reputation as a songwriter ("other" than my serious side)—the guy who wrote the novelty songs, the crazy stuff. He asked Mike Kosser to gather up some of my goofier titles. When Kosser went nosing around the tape room at Tree, he discovered a box that he didn't realize was a dummy that I had placed in my tape bin a couple of years before as a practical joke on Don Gant. The box contained a blank tape, and the titles written on the box were the worst ones I could fabricate—there were no actual songs

Michael Kosser

with those names. Kosser jotted some of them down and passed the list along to Curly.

Later, after dinner in the large hotel ballroom, Curly stepped up to the mic, his voice quivering with stage fright, and said, "I'm here to induct a good friend of mine into the Hall of Fame. He's written such great songs as 'The Pentecostal Boogie,' 'The Dingleberry Waltz,' and 'Hosing Down the Embers of a Red Hot Love Affair.'"

There were titters of laughter, and people looked at each other in puzzlement. Then when he announced my name, a majority smiled and stood up applauding. Curly had been told that the speakers would blare out some of my hits as I walked up to the stage. The only problem was the record player; it wasn't working. Nobody heard the names of any of my real songs. Curly handed me my "Manny" (for "manuscript"), and Maggie Cavender, the dear lady who was fulltime director of NSAI (Nashville Songwriters Association International), unveiled a portrait of me onstage. Then cowboy songwriter Ray Whitley was inducted posthumously. After that, a special "songwriters' friend" award was presented to Darrell Royal, the popular country-music-loving head coach at the University of Texas, who was known for having writers participate in "guitar pulls" in his home.

When the festivities were over, Dan Wilson told me he understood they were going to have a celebration in my honor at Tree. I invited several people to come along.

Buddy Killen was at Tree's front door, letting everyone in. The crowd followed him upstairs to the second floor. He was not in his usual jovial mood, and it was obvious that he didn't want to be there. Not one word was said about me. Coach Royal took a seat in the middle of the room as Buddy held up a guitar and said in a Bullwinkle monotone, "Okay, who's first?" And then it hit me. This wasn't a celebration in my honor; it was a damned guitar pull for Coach Darrell Royal!

"Come on, Sparky," I said, "Let's g-get out of here." I stormed out of the room, bypassing the elevator and bounding down the stairs, Sparky a few steps behind me.

Behind her were Dan Wilson and Terry Choate.

"Braddock, *come back!*" Dan shouted, as the Braddocks left the building.

"*Fuck Tree!*" I yelled at the top of my voice. (In Buddy's defense, a couple of days later a billboard appeared on Music Row screaming "CONGRATULATIONS BOBBY BRADDOCK!")

I was losing my wife, the love of my life, so having the Songwriters Hall of Fame honor bestowed upon me—and it was indeed a great honor—meant very little. And the way everything had come down, especially what happened at Tree, had left me with a sense of worthlessness on this night when I should have been holding my head high.

In the cool wee hours of this October morning, I sat in my car behind the Newspaper Printing Corporation building at 1100 Broadway watching all the trucks and carriers coming in to load up with copies of the *Tennessean*, soon to be tossed into front yards and delivered to convenience stores and restaurants all over Middle Tennessee. I walked up to the little office in the back. What would the headline in the "Living" section of the paper say? NSAI INDUCTS BRADDOCK? Would they tell that I was the youngest living member of the Songwriters Hall of Fame? I handed the man some change and grabbed a paper, my hands shaking a little. I took it out to the car, turned on the interior light, and quickly went for Section D. The headline read: SONG-WRITERS HONOR DARRELL ROYAL. There was a picture of the coach's smiling face and a long feature story about him. At the very end of the article it read, "Songwriters inducted into the Hall of Fame were Bobby Braddock and the late Ray Whitley." End of story.

That next night, on the nationally televised CMA Awards, the Gatlin Brothers opened the envelope that would reveal the winner of the Song of the Year honor. Curly and I were there because our song was nominated, but I didn't think we had a chance of winning it a *second* year in a row. Larry Gatlin sang, "He stopped lovin' *herrr* todayyyyyy." Cheers went up from the crowd. "*Bobby Braddock* and *Curly Putman*!" Those at home would see me stand up, wearing an ugly brown tux, as pretty Sparky with the corn-row hairdo applauded wildly. From the stage I said something about not expecting the song to win a second time, and when I got back to my seat I leaned over and apologized to a couple of the other nominated writers—*apologized for winning*.

The next night while I was getting dressed for the BMI Awards banquet, Sparky called from Gail's and begged off at the last minute, saying she needed to rehearse with Joe Vegas. I went to the banquet alone. I was miserable. I won heavy-airplay awards for "He Stopped Loving Her Today," "I Feel Like Loving You Again," and "Hard Times." I was miserable. Joe Bonsall, of the Oak Ridge Boys, told me they were going to do "Would They Love Him Down in Shreveport," joining the list of others who recorded it: George Jones, B. J. Thomas, Roy Clark, and the Mercy River Boys. I was miserable. Afterward I went to a party at Tree. I spent about an hour-and-a-half riding around, smoking pot with Merle Haggard and songwriting genius Dean Dillon, Haggard not saying more than a dozen words the entire time. I was miserable. On the way home I went by my post office box to check the mail and found a nice long letter of congratulations from Nashville Mayor Richard Fulton. I was miserable.

A couple of nights later, after having a couple of drinks at a popular watering hole, Close Quarters (sometimes known as the "rock & roll hotel"), with

Kieran Kane and early sixties rock & roll star Bruce Channel ("Hey Baby"), I went to Capitol Gardens to see Sparky sing back-up with Joe Vegas and solo on a couple of songs herself. I wrote later that night, "Most of the Tree guys there didn't dig Joe Vegas. He's a huncher."

Sparky's friend Gail came up and hugged me and said, "I'm caught in the middle between you and Sparky. I love you both, no matter what happens."

Sparky's sister Fay told me, "I'm sad about you and Sue (Sparky's old name). Just from talkin' to her, I think it's gonna work out."

An old friend of Sparky's from Alabama, Jurleen Wallace, said "I think you're the only man Sparky really ever loved."

Sunday, October 18, was our second anniversary, and we had an anniversary "date." We went to the Cork 'n' Cleaver for old times' sake, had an argument, and ended up at my house, where I pried it out of her. She was in love with Joe Vegas. She swore she had remained faithful to me while we were together. I assumed that was the reason for our separation: Joe Vegas.

A few days later we went into the Tree studio for a demo session. A song called "Dead" was one of my favorite things I ever demoed. It had no chance of getting cut, especially in Nashville; it was too personal and autobiographical. This is what happens when you write a song while in shock, half-crazed. A sad country song wouldn't do—it had to be a hard rockin' primal scream. In fact I had a fever of 101 when I sang it. And the perpetrator, Sparky, was singing harmony with me. Though the lyrics were humorous on paper, when you hear it you know it was dead serious (no pun intended). With my electric piano and Brent Rowan's guitar, we were reading each other's musical and emotional minds.

> *I need a woman but I can't get up*
> *I wanna boogie but I can't get down*
> *Bring me some strychnine in a coffee cup*
> *And tell my loved ones they can gather 'round*
>
> *Cause I'm dead (dead, dead, dead, dead, dead, dead, dead)*
> *Dead (dead, dead, dead, dead, dead, dead, dead)*
> *Since you walked out of my life*
> *I'm just as good as dead (dead, dead, dead, dead, dead, dead, dead)*
>
> *My heart is beat-beat-beatin' outta my chest*
> *My brain is think-think-thinkin' outta my head*
> *My blood is pump-pump—pumpin'*
> *My body's jump-jump-jumpin'*
> *I'm gettin' seasick in my water bed*
>
> *But I'm dead (dead, dead, dead, dead, dead, dead, dead)*
> *Dead (dead, dead, dead, dead, dead, dead, dead)*

Since you walked out of my life
I'm just as good as dead (dead, dead, dead, dead, dead, dead, dead)

And there was one I had written from what I thought was Sparky's perspective of what went wrong in our marriage and had her sing it. That in itself is a little crazy. It was called "You Weren't Listening to Me." The verses were almost like an early rap, followed by a shoutin' chorus. Sparky's sarcasm made the happy, old-time rock & roll arrangement seem like a farce, a false front to a dark situation, and I loved it in a sad, painful way. Both these songs would be holes in my heart for a long time.

The one thing that didn't stop, through all this turmoil, was the music. One day I dropped by Tree and went to lunch with Harlan Howard, Curly Putman, and laid-back tobacco-chewing country star Bobby Bare. On the way back to Tree after lunch, Harlan was seated in the back next to me. The craggy-faced, gray-haired legend started telling me about this song idea he had and said that he was excited about it. It was a story of a guy so hurt by the loss of his woman that he had completely blocked her out of his mind, not even recognizing her when she visited him at the mental hospital. "I call it 'I Don't Remember Loving You,'" he said.

"Harlan, I *love* that idea," I told him. "I wish *I'd* thought of that."

"Well, gyod dimmit, Double-B, why the hell do you think I'm *tellin'* ya about it? I want you to *write* it with me. You're really good at these kinds of songs."

Hanging out with Cowboy Jack Clement and the king of country songwriters, Harlan Howard

So Harlan came over to my house, and we knocked out a mid-tempo dark comedy song. I was amazed that this man in his mid-fifties could think and write so quickly, but looking back from many years later, I now realize he wasn't really all that old (if this were an e-mail, the smiley face would go here). But there was one line that we didn't agree on. He tried hard to convince me that his line was better, and I was just as stubborn about mine. The morning of the demo session, I was seated at the grand piano in the Tree International Recording Studio, and Harlan was walking circles around me and the instrument, around and around, again and again. We were still at an impasse on how to write the line (and I have no recollection of which line it was). Finally, when the musicians started to arrive, Harlan said, "Oh, hell, go ahead and do it your way." The song would go on to be a hit for John Conlee.

Harlan and I wrote several songs together, almost all of them his titles. He once complained that he was more generous with his titles than I was with mine. (The truth is if I came up with a good title, most likely I wrote it right then, and usually happened to be alone.) One Harlan co-write that I particularly liked was "God May Forgive You but I Won't." Lyle Lovett wrote and recorded a very similar song, "God Will"—one of those crazy musical coincidences—and only an idiot would think that we stole a song from Lyle Lovett or that Lyle stole one from us. But when he came out with his, that was pretty much the death knell for ours, although we were fortunate enough to get a cut on it by a young lady named Rosie Flores.

One day Norro Wilson, who had co-produced some of my MGM records, came to Tree searching for songs with the legendary Eddy Arnold—a decade having passed since his last hit but still, after all, Eddy Arnold. I saw up close why he had such a reputation as a raconteur. I don't think I've ever encountered a better storyteller. He told an unforgettable tale of the great jazz violinist and practical joker, Joe Venuti, who stroked the appendage of Roy Rogers's horse, Trigger, with his fiddle bow, right before Roy mounted him and rode onto a theater stage in front of a thousand kids. The kids went wild, laughing and pointing, as Trigger did his usual stunt, standing on his hind legs and rearing up, only this time displaying a gigantic erection. The "King of the Cowboys" thought all the excitement was about *him*.

I figured that I needed to try to move on with my life. I finally went out on a date, but when I went to the girl's apartment and saw the pictures of two singers on her refrigerator, I decided that her taste in music was a big turnoff. There was basically one thing wrong with her: she wasn't Sparky.

I had a rendezvous with my old lover, Charlotte, who had moved from Florida to Central Kentucky. We lay in a Holiday Inn bed smoking dope. I wasn't attracted; she wasn't Sparky. I pretended to be asleep until it was time for me to leave.

In late December, Joe was with his family in Phoenix, so I asked Sparky if she would like to go with Jeep and me to my hometown for "Bobby Braddock Day," and she said yes. Somewhere between Atlanta and Auburndale, Jeep—

for the first time—opened up with her feelings about Sparky and Joe Vegas. It was a heated discussion, Sparky on the defensive, both of them making their points. I stayed out of it, my stomach churning. Then there was a time of long silence.

"Jeep," Sparky asked, "how would you feel if your dad and I had an open marriage?"

"Fine," Jeep answered, "if you didn't fight about it. I would be happy to have the family back together. I was so happy because I thought I finally had a family."

Sparky began sobbing, and reached over the seat and put her arms around Jeep. "Please never stop loving me," she pleaded.

After my "Bobby Braddock Day," Jeep stayed with my mom in Auburndale while Sparky and I went to Daytona Beach for a couple of days. It was sexy, romantic, like old times.

I could tell that there was something bothering Mom. A few weeks before, my friend Michael Erickson, a reporter for the Nashville *Banner*, did a feature story on me, and in the interview I had unwisely told all about the split with Sparky and how I was determined to get her back. This became the theme of the article, which told about me being on the phone with the electric company to make sure the electricity was turned on in the apartment I was renting for her. Sparky even came over to my house to pose with me for pictures. We were putting our laundry on public display. Someone in Auburndale who had Tennessee ties read the piece and showed it to my mother. Mom told me about it while Sparky was in the shower and out of earshot. "When I read it, I was mortified," she whispered.

For the next several weeks, after we got back to Nashville, my mood was affected by Sparky's mood, which was affected by Joe Vegas. Sometimes she would be angry at him and would head straight for my house to be with me. Sometimes she would be madly in love with him, walking like Joe, talking like Joe, and when I saw her she would have a hickey on her neck ("I've stolen Bobby Braddock's woman," the hickeys seemed to say). Sometimes she would break up with him, then start missing him and resenting me. It was all taking its toll on me. I started having panic attacks when driving to her apartment. *Was I not listening to my instincts?* Once, while upset, I took my blood pressure at a Kroger supermarket, and when it was a little elevated, it scared me. I developed a blood pressure phobia, tensing up whenever I took it, my normally normal blood pressure becoming abnormally abnormal. I saw a psychiatrist whom I didn't like and refused to take his advice and go on an antidepressant. I was blaming *him* for my depression because I felt that he had planted the seed when he told me that my panic attacks were a part of depression.

I finally met a girl I really liked: Angela Thornton—a beautiful honey-blonde, intelligent, eccentric, manic-depressive video editor. A twenty-year-old who told me she was twenty-five, Angela was involved with a prominent

Nashville attorney who was even older than I was. My interest in her was a diversion, but nothing was able to remove me from the scary roller coaster ride I was on with my estranged wife and her new boyfriend.

Then suddenly the wild ride seemed to come to a slamming halt. WHAM! Sparky was through with Joe Vegas. She had set a trap for him regarding another woman, and he walked right into it. She told him on the phone that she was lucky to have me to go back to. My journal page was emblazoned with two words in gigantic letters:

AT LAST!

Sparky seemed so happy and loving. The future was looking bright. I wrote, "Beautiful girl sleeps peacefully at my side."

Two days later: we fell in love with a house on Granny White Pike and made a deposit of $7,000 earnest money.

Two nights after that: Sparky drove across Nashville on treacherous ice to see Joe Vegas "one more time, because he wants that and I want that."

Two days after that: Sparky and I decided to split. She started crying, "I don't want to grow old without you." We made up.

Two days after that: we really split. She went back to Joe. I lost the $7,000 earnest money.

So I started having the blood pressure phobia again, the panic attacks, depression, and a new one that I named, "Krogerphobia," the fear of walking into a supermarket. I started pursuing Angela, hoping and praying she would split up with her lover. My shrink told me Sparky was a flake, and that Angela sounded even flakier. I told my shrink that I didn't like him or his advice.

One night I met up with a new friend, Ron Hellard, one of the funniest people I would ever know. He co-authored a cartoon that appeared regularly in the Sunday *Tennessean* called "Music Row Joe." He and his song collaborators had been having considerable success and were coming to be known as "those three guys at Tree." "I want some songs written by those three guys at Tree," producers would say. Those three guys at Tree were actually five guys who wrote interchangeably in a group of three. Besides Ron Hellard, the group included Michael Garvin, Bucky Jones, Tom Shapiro, and Chris Waters. Ron told me that our mutual friend Jamie O'Hara was drunk at Close Quarters and had been asking for me, so I dropped by there to see him. And that's where I met a cute twenty-seven-year-old redhead. Her name was Molly O'Neal, and she would become my girlfriend.

At times it felt like Molly and I were in a real relationship, then Joe Vegas would leave town and I'd stop dead in my tracks, drop poor Molly, run to Sparky's side, and stay there until Joe Vegas was back in town. On top of that, I went out with other girls a couple of times and continued to hang out with maniacal Angela, wishing she would break up with her lover and thinking she was the one who could cure my addiction to Sparky. Molly O'Neal was loving and nurturing when I needed her, needy and clinging when I didn't.

I was crazy and not getting any saner, so Molly and I were a sad, short-lived pair. She was a sweet girl, and I always felt badly about her getting caught up in my craziness. Twenty years later I ran into her at a funeral and apologized effusively.

In my journals I was often writing that I needed to focus more on Jeep and give her the attention she deserved, but I was too selfishly self-absorbed to be the father I had once been (and would be again one day). I loved her as much as ever, but I wasn't there for her like I should have been, especially considering the absentee mother (and stepmother). Indeed, there were times when *she* seemed to be the parent, more than once talking me out of depression or a panic attack.

Jeep (really preferring to be called Lauren) was enrolled at Barbizon Modeling School. At Hillsboro High she was interested in music and drama. At fifteen she'd had a telephone boyfriend, but now at sixteen she was going out with a guy who had been her grade-school dreamboat. Lisa Gauld and Margaret Beasley were her new best friends—and partners in crime—and would remain so throughout high school.

When I wasn't starring in my own private soap opera, I still managed to write songs and take them in to Tree International, where those who knew me were sympathetic to my sad set of circumstances. Buddy Killen urged me to put my unhappy energy into my music. Buddy had finally filled the old Don Gant position of Creative Director at Tree with Roger Sovine, son of country legend Red Sovine. Roger was experienced in the world of music publishing and had also worked for BMI. He was a likable, capable guy, but there would be no sounds of late-night music and laughter coming from his office, as there had been with Gant.

In the summer of 1982, I had a Top-Five record that wasn't placed by Tree's songpluggers, but by Bob Doyle, who a few years later would be the manager of a dynamic young singer named Garth Brooks. Bob worked for ASCAP, the rival of my performance organization, BMI. In other words, he had no official interest in or connection to the song in any way, but simply liked it and decided to play it for my fellow Floridian, John Anderson. The song, inspired by a lovable but washed-up country singer who had been dating a friend of Sparky's, was called "Would You Catch a Falling Star."

On July 1, there was a group of young people in Dan Wilson's office at Tree. Dan's connection to the entourage was the daughter of a friend of his. His friend was backup singer Icee Berg, and her daughter was future Hall of Fame songwriter Matraca Berg, a beautiful young woman whose penetrating eyes were so dark that they were almost black. Matraca was only eighteen, but the original songs she was singing that afternoon impressed me greatly; I particularly liked one called "Omnibus." Within a few days Matraca and I had written several songs, one of them a rhythmic ballad titled "Faking Love." When we demoed the song, Creative Director Roger Sovine told me, "I wish

Me, Mac Davis, Frances Preston, Willie Nelson, Jimmy Buffett,
Johnny Rodriguez, and Gail Davies, at the BMI Awards

you'd write more traditional country songs; pop-sounding things like 'Faking Love' are having a hard time getting cut lately." It would be the #1 country record in just a few months. Working with this fresh young talent restored a modicum of sanity and began a lifelong friendship. Matraca would always refer to me as her mentor, but I don't think I ever taught her a thing that she didn't already know.

On August 6, 1982, the day after my forty-second birthday, I wrote in my journal:

> SPARKY CALLED ME EARLY THIS MORNING AND ASKED ME "CAN I COME HOME?" *meaning permanently. She said the one thing that made her finally go through with it was not anything in particular that Joe did, rather it was the pep talk I had given her the night before, telling her she was too good and too special to be treated the way Joe treats her.*

Simply put, Sparky, Allen, Jeep, Jeep's friend Lisa, and I went to Daytona Beach, Florida. We got one oceanfront cottage for all the kids, and one for Sparky and me. It was wonderful, like a second honeymoon. The Frank Zappa record "Valley Girl" was a current hit, and Jeep and Lisa spent the entire vacation doing "valley talk." It was surely one of the best weeks of my life. The minute we got back to Nashville, Sparky went immediately to a pay phone and called Joe Vegas. That night they were back together. Simply put.

The next day I didn't have time to enjoy the news that Ray Charles had recorded my song "The Happy Hour" because that's the day that the IRS took every penny I had in the bank, a complete mine sweep. I ditched my accoun-

Buck Owens's guest on *Hee Haw*. In the background are Karen Blumberg, Lisa Gauld, and Jeep.

tant for not seeing this coming. Buddy and Tree bailed me out, and set me up with their accountant who arranged meetings with the IRS that would get me on a payment plan and lead to an eventual Offer in Compromise.

On August 25, I filed for divorce. The next day I met Sparky near the office of my attorney, Jack Norman Jr., in downtown Nashville. Sparky was getting cold feet about signing the papers, but had nothing to offer me other than us getting together whenever Joe Vegas wasn't in town. I said, "Let's g-get it over with." She wanted to get a drink first, so we went to Printers Alley, a wide alleyway lined with nightclubs, popular with tourists in those days. We went into a little place and had three rounds of wine, then went into my lawyer's office giggling. After beginning the end of our short marriage, we had a very sad farewell.

I went to a restaurant called Dalt's to meet a beautiful singer-writer in her late twenties whom I had been out with a couple of times, but had never been to bed with. On this melancholy night she could see that I was despondent and invited me to her apartment. I would later kick myself for telling her I was too sad and just wanted to go home.

I was determined to move beyond Sparky and get on with my life, and for a while I was feeling pretty good for a change. In September I started dating Karen Blumberg. Karen, who had just turned thirty-four, was a tall, slender, dark-haired woman who proudly called herself an old hippie. She was intelligent, easygoing, spiritual rather than traditionally religious, and I loved the lovely, lazy accent of her native Savannah, Georgia. And she was a psychiatric nurse! Rather than being turned off by my psychological problems, she seemed eager to help me. She was just what the doctor ordered.

Jeep and Karen became buddies, and one night Jeep, her friend Lisa, and I piled into Karen's hippie bus "Freida" and away we all went to Birmingham to see The Who in concert. Karen, Jeep, and Lisa sort of became my family unit. I have a clear memory of all of us hanging out backstage at the *Hee Haw* show where I was about to do a guest appearance. Buck Owens puffed on his pipe and looked over a note that Jeep had gotten from a lady in a salad bar line a little earlier. The lady wrote that she had come there for one last meal before committing suicide, but Jeep and Lisa's silly antics had cheered her up so much that she changed her mind and decided she wanted to live.

I called Sparky to tell her that the divorce was close to becoming final. She told me she was depressed about the whole thing, was thinking about "us" a lot, and wondering what she was doing with Joe Vegas. Allen stayed with Lauren and me more than he did with his mom, and she said she missed us all being a family. She begged me to ask my lawyer to put our divorce on hold. So I did. I was back to seeing Sparky whenever Joe Vegas left town. Karen didn't like it, but she was a strong woman with a healthy self-respect; she did whatever she wanted to, including dating others.

I was having panic attacks in spades, suffering from deep depression, and imagining that I had some kind of hideous physical malady. I wrote in my journal that I suspected "infection, heart leakage, blocked arteries, internal bleeding, and cancer."

But Sparky continued to be with Joe, and I continued to be with her when he was out of town, and my mental health continued to deteriorate. I would have been better if Sparky had come back to me *or* if I had gotten completely out of her life, but this in-between stuff was killing me.

My journals indicate that I was constantly trying to figure out what had happened to my marriage. You could say that it changed radically the moment Sparky and I set foot in that white brick house on Shy's Hill Road. Before we moved there, the marriage needed some work, but soon afterward it immediately went on the rocks. Every couple that entered those doors had either split up or was having problems. Guests had commented on seeing "soldiers" marching through our backyard. Cigarettes popped out of ashtrays. A seemingly healthy half-grown cat that Allen had adopted fell over and died one day without warning. Sometimes one specific room would suddenly get very hot. Jeep had become obsessed with magic and didn't want to leave her room. I had a friend who was raised in New Orleans who seemed to know a lot about ghosts, and when I showed her around she said, "There's something really wrong around here." Jim Stafford was about to emcee a TV special about haunted houses, and he told me he thought our place was under an evil influence, and that Jeep and I were at "the threshold of possession." It all seemed very real to me, but looking back I can't help but wonder how much of it was coming from a haunted house and how much from a tortured mind?

Then one day I was listening to Bruce Springsteen's *Nebraska* album and got it in my head that something horrible was going to happen to Jeep. All kinds of incoherent thoughts seemed to be consuming me. In an awful panic, I called up Sparky and told her I was losing my mind.

"It's that damned *house*, Bob, you know it's haunted. You need to *get out of there!*"

So I did. It's almost as if I got Jeep by the hand and we ran away from there as fast as we could. For several months we had been leasing the place, with that money going toward a purchase in January. That was two months away. I knew that I not only did not want to buy the house, but I was determined to leave and never come back. I checked into a Holiday Inn off West End Avenue, and Lauren would stay with Karen Blumberg, who had been filling the role of surrogate mother. Within a couple of days, I wrote, "Jeep is like a new kid." Right away we found a house we loved, 2301 Sterling Road, in a beautiful neighborhood between upscale Green Hills and artsy Hillsboro Village. It was a lovely two-story frame house. I put down some earnest money, and a date was set for closing. I took Sparky by to see it, and she said she loved it and talked about the possibility of us getting back together and living there someday. So I had the addiction and Sparky had the fix: little shots of hope that kept me hanging on.

One night at Close Quarters I ran into country star Tanya Tucker who seemed to be in full party mode. We had hung out a few times before, but had never actually gone out together, so we made a date. I think she was still recuperating from a romance with Glen Campbell. Her father, Bo Tucker, called me at Tree and said he was hopeful that I would be a good influence on Tanya. She was staying in town with a girlfriend, so I went by there to pick her up. It was like high school date night. I waited in the living room for a couple of minutes, and she came down the stairs, looking really nice.

We went out to dinner, then ended up at Close Quarters. I told her about the haunted house—the rent was paid up for a few more days, and I still had some boxes there—and she insisted that we go there, stay the rest of the night, and try to write a song. I was feeling sane enough to do it because she seemed so into checking out the ghosts. While we were sitting out on the Close Quarters patio on this mild-for-November night, with several people seated at our table, a beautiful young woman whom I had lusted after for some time came and sat down beside me. She whispered in my ear, "If you'll leave her and take me away from here, I'll go to bed with you."

"Oh, my God. Please let me have a rain check," I pleaded. "I can't just g-get up and leave Tanya. She's my d-d-date."

"Well, if you want to go to bed with me, that's the only way it'll happen." As much as I wanted to, I wasn't about to do it.

Tanya has talked publicly about doing cocaine, and I can honestly say I was never fond of being around anyone doing coke. Often, I would be talking to somebody who was being an aggressive jerk, thinking, "What's wrong with this person?" then it would dawn on me: of course, cocaine (I've heard it called "instant asshole"). Tanya could be pretty obnoxious when she was on the stuff—not mean, but motor-mouthing. On this night, though, she wasn't snorting and was a pleasure to be around, and I loved talking to her. On our way to Shy's Hill Road, she laughed, recalling the time she was lounging on the floor at Roger Miller's party when Sparky tripped over her.

Tanya and I lit candles in my old music room and wrote a song we never finished called "Gone with the Wind" (pretty original). It was good to go back and have closure and spend some sane time at the place that may have housed the restless spirits of Southern men shot down on that lonely hillside, nearly a hundred-and-twenty years before.

On the way back to her friend's house, we drove up Belmont Boulevard, and Tanya asked me, "What percentage of people in these houses do you think have heard of Tanya Tucker?"

"Oh," I said, "maybe sixty percent?"

"Is that all?" she asked, looking disappointed.

"Wellll," I backpedaled, "maybe seventy-five percent." That seemed to make her feel better.

I was glad that Jeep and I could put Shy's Hill Road behind us and be living in the house on Sterling Road. We already had two pets, but Jeep talked me into getting her an old English sheep dog that she named Martha, after Paul McCartney's dog of the same breed that inspired the song "Martha My Dear." Unfortunately, Martha turned out to be too big and too much maintenance, so I sold her. This was about the time that Jeep's British sweetheart left Nashville (he was the only guy she ever dated whom I thoroughly disliked), so she was in tears over the loss of her new English boyfriend and her old English sheep dog.

One night I went to some event at Buddy Killen's popular night spot, The Stock-Yard, a gigantic old warehouse along the Cumberland River that had been converted into Nashville's biggest dance floor, plus two popular restaurants. I remember seeing a couple all wrapped up in each other, and what a pang I felt, missing the days when Sparky and I had been like that. I was up front in the club, watching the floor show, seated next to an up-and-coming singer-writer-pianist, Lee Greenwood, whose "God Bless the USA" would seem to become America's second national anthem. We had a good talk, discussing how we were both influenced by the piano playing of Ray Charles, Jerry Lee Lewis, and Floyd Cramer. There were good feelings until I was called up on the stage and sang "He Stopped Loving Her Today." This was when I was still using the ech-ech-ech vibrato, the very same kind of vibrato Greenwood was known for, except he was a much better singer. He must have thought I was making fun of him because when I returned to my seat, he would barely speak to me.

December of 1982 was the month of me making myself crazier and crazier. It was as though Sparky had revolving doors—Joe out, Bobby in, Joe in, Bobby out. She and Joe were in a seemingly perpetual state of breaking up and making up, with me as Sparky's backup plan. Initially Karen Blumberg was interested in having a relationship with me, but I was wondering how much longer she would put up with my running back and forth to Sparky.

There were times I was so depressed that it felt like a giant hand was pushing me down to the ground. One day I got my psychiatrist on the phone while I was having a terrible panic attack; it was around the time that Marty Robbins died of a heart attack, and the shrink told me, with a sarcastic tone, "You *don't* have Marty Robbins Disease." I hung up on him. Karen had told me about a young psychiatrist with a great reputation, Robert Jamieson, so I made an appointment with him. He had hippie hair and hadn't been practicing medicine very long, but I immediately liked and trusted him. He said I had a chemical imbalance, aggravated by my marital breakup, resulting in depression, anxiety attacks, and agoraphobia, which *Merriam-Webster* defines as "abnormal fear of being helpless in an embarrassing or inescapable situation that is characterized especially by the avoidance of open or public places." He convinced me that I should start taking an antidepressant, Tofranil.

It takes a couple of weeks for an antidepressant to kick in, so the side effects were freaking me out, causing even more panic. I went to see my primary care doctor, Carter Willams Jr., who had been my physician since I was in my mid-twenties. Dr. Williams was nine years older than I; his father, Carter Williams, had been head of the Vanderbilt University School of Medicine, and his grandfather, Robert Taylor, had been governor of Tennessee. I felt fortunate to have a doctor who was held in high esteem by Nashville's medical community, yet who was down-to-earth and easy to communicate with. I was so upset over my side effects that Dr. Williams put me in the hospital for a couple of days, and urged that I stick with the Tofranil.

I remember thinking that 1983 couldn't possibly be as bad as 1982 had been. The hits had kept coming—Jerry Reed's "The Bird," which was part mine because it included a parody of "He Stopped Loving Her Today," had just hit #1 in *Cash Box*—but even if I had held the #1 slot every week for the past year, my life would still have been painfully sad. The side effects from the antidepressant didn't go away, and I started freaking out once again, convinced that I was dying. Dr. Williams put me in the hospital again. He said my blood pressure was really high—from anxiety and my *fear* of it being high, he felt—but nevertheless thought I should go on the beta blocker Lopressor. After several days in the hospital I went home. I loved our new residence (mine and Jeep's) on Sterling Road, but I was feeling just as crazy in that house as I did in the haunted one. When I woke up the next day I called my shrink, Dr. Jamieson, and told him that my limbs were numb. He insisted that I be admitted to Parthenon Pavilion, a psychiatric hospital, where he would switch me to another antidepressant, nortryptiline. Karen came over and drove me there.

This was not the first time in my life that I had wandered off into Crazy-land, where one day you're jerking around like your finger's in a light socket, and the next day you're feeling lower than whale poop. When I was nineteen, I took way too much speed one night and that triggered two-and-a-half years of insanity, and here I was in my early forties, going through it again, only this time the drug that precipitated anxiety and depression was love instead of speed. In those dark periods, it's not as though I had moved 180 degrees on the mental health scale, because, after all, I was already a little bit nuts to begin with. It would have been nice if I had been diagnosed with Tourette's syndrome when I was young, rather than thinking I just didn't have the discipline to keep from blinking my eyes, contorting my face, and stammering. And if some health care provider could have told me that I had classic obsessive compulsive disorder (OCD), maybe I wouldn't have gone through life thinking it was perfectly normal, that compulsion to accurately predict the number of steps from one point to another or the belief that my clothes always had to be color coordinated, right down to my underwear.

I was at Parthenon Pavilion of my own volition and would be allowed to walk in Centennial Park, across the street from the hospital, or leave for short periods with family or friends. It would be the next day before they had room for me in the "saner" part of the building, so I encountered some pretty scary people that first night. "I'm psychic," one young man said, "and your problems are being caused by a brain tumor." Just what I needed to hear.

The next day they played music for all the patients on our floor. Apparently they thought it would be therapeutic for us to hear a song about a man in a mental institution. I wasn't about to tell them that the song was mine, the one I wrote with Harlan Howard which had recently hit the country Top Ten, "I Don't Remember Loving You."

I don't remember loving you
And I don't recall the things you say you put me through
You tell me that you've had a guilty conscience for so long
You say that you walked out on me, you say you did me wrong
Well I just don't see how that could be true
Cause I don't remember loving you

I don't remember loving you
You might talk to my doctor, he drops by each day at two
I get a funny feeling when I look into your eyes
There's something in your smile that gives my stomach butterflies
You must look like someone I once knew
No, I don't remember loving you

I don't remember loving you
I heard you mention children, did you say there's one or two
You say I quit my job and then I drank myself insane
You say that I ran down the highway screaming out your name
Now that's not the sort of thing that I would do
No, I don't remember loving you

I don't remember loving you
I absolutely positively know that can't be true
But everyone I know here in this place is very strange
If you'll hand me my crayons, I'll be glad to take your name
In case I run across the guy you knew
But I don't remember loving you

The patients included a couple of teenage girls who had records of attempted suicide, a charismatic Kentucky coal miner, an old man with dementia, and the manic-depressive—now commonly called bipolar—wife of a country music star (the husband asked me not to say who).

The most memorable inmate was a Church of Christ minister. His wife had committed adultery, which went against everything he had been taught and everything he ever believed—preachers' wives just didn't *do* that—and it absolutely drove him nuts. He was one paranoid little man. In the dining room he told me, "You can't sit with that group one day and with our group the next. You have to be with either one group or the other." He had carried the old Church of Christ "us against them" mindset from the sanctuary right into the nut house.

Actually, I did start to get a little better; not all at once, but over time. Dr. Jamieson's bedside manner and constant attention were a godsend. So were visits from Jeep, and from Karen (though she was thoroughly drained from having to deal with our relationship issues and my mental problems). Sweet, lovely, crazy Angela Thornton came a couple of times and played Scrabble with me. Sparky called and said, "This morning I cried for an hour-and-a-half. I wanted to come get you and bring you home and take care of you."

I had been having runaway heart rates, but the Lopressor had slowed my pulse down to normal. When nurses took my blood pressure it was still high, but when Dr. Jamieson took it, it was perfect. I was like the Beatles song, "I've got to admit it's getting better, a little better all the time."

The first thing I did after Karen drove me home from several days in Parthenon Pavilion was to visit Tree. I ran across Harlan Howard and told him about them playing our song in the hospital. When I told him about my problems, he said, "Gyod dimmit, Double-B, you don't have anything to be depressed about." Well, yes, actually I did, but you don't even *have to* have anything to be depressed about to be depressed.

It's easy to feel sympathy for or empathy with someone who has a broken leg or the flu, but a lot of people are like Harlan; they think depression or anxiety are conditions that you can just "snap out of." Believe me, people who live in that dark place don't want to be there. Whether this hideous disease, depression, has manifested itself in the form of melancholia, panic, or alcoholism—whether it's congenital, hereditary, reactive, or bipolar—the anguish is just as real and just as hard to bear as physical pain. So whenever your heart goes out to the sick, include the emotionally sick as well.

Despite the improvement, there were still some problems. The "Kroger-phobia" was especially hard to kick. Don Cook had a similar phobia, and writer Jamie O'Hara had a fear of running into someone he knew in a public place. One night the three of us showed up at the Green Hills Kroger supermarket at the same time. Jamie and I saw each other in one of the aisles and he got wide-eyed and started running away from me, as if he were in a marathon. I then encountered Cook who laughed hysterically with me as we watched our friend disappear down the aisle.

While I was AWOL, Lauren had been staying out late, skipping school, and her grades were beginning to suffer. I said, "Okay Jeep, I'm in charge now." I told her I had been too focused on myself and Sparky, and not enough on her. I vowed that I would try to do better.

My depression, like a fog, started to lift—not all at once, but I was getting there. The gray clouds were breaking up, and I could see the sun. I was getting an early spring; the cold, icy wind had become a cool breeze. The fog was lifting, and I wanted to walk in the sunshine.

It was time for me to enjoy the fruits of my labor. "Faking Love," which I wrote with Matraca Berg, went to #1 as a duet by T. G. Sheppard and Karen Brooks. Tree's creative director, Roger Sovine, was able to land me my fifth recording deal, this time with RCA. Label head Joe Galante wanted "It Took Ernest Angley To Get Me Over You," another Matraca co-write, to be my first single. Because Ray Stevens had recorded the song, I told him I would like to do it for my project and offered to repay him his session costs, but Ray told me not to worry about it and wished me luck with my record. Jim Stafford wanted to sing it on Johnny Carson's *Tonight Show*, and told me if I would give him permission, he would say my name on national television, which he did—three or four times—but unfortunately I failed to tell him to mention Matraca's name too.

Karen Blumberg and I had mutually agreed that we would do better as friends than sweethearts, and she was now working as my personal assistant. She was a big fan of folk icon John Prine and told me that he said he wanted to write with me (he never said it) and told Prine that I said I wanted to write with him (I never said it). This was positive manipulation that worked out very well. The croaky-voiced, sweet-natured genius showed up at my door, with his guitar and two great ideas, "Unwed Fathers" and "Children Having Children." I suggested that we incorporate the two ideas into one song. We couldn't agree on a couple of the lines, or even the melody, but it was a friendly disagreement, and we ended up with two slightly different versions, one that pleased him and one that pleased me. Several people recorded it, including Tammy Wynette, Gail Davies, Johnny Cash, and the great John Prine himself. Some cut it Prine's way, some cut it my way, and some cut it in between. This is highly unusual and a bit chaotic, having more than one written version of the same song; John and I were bending the rules. This is the version of "Unwed Fathers" that I like best.

> *In an Appalachian Greyhound station*
> *She sits there waiting, in a family way*
> *"Goodbye brother, Tell Mom I love her*
> *Tell all the others, I'll write someday"*

> Chorus:
> *From teenage lover, to unwed mother*
> *Kept undercover, like some bad dream*
> *But unwed fathers, they can't be bothered*
> *They run like water, through a mountain stream*

> *In a cold and gray town, a nurse says "lay down*
> *This ain't no playground, and this ain't home"*
> *Someone's children having children*
> *In a gray stone building, all alone*

> Repeat Chorus

> *On a somewhere-else bound nighttime Greyhound*
> *She bows her head down, hummin' lullabies*
> *Scared and crazy, she holds her baby*
> *Says "I think maybe you got your daddy's eyes"*

> Repeat Chorus

One day when Karen came by to get checks from me to pay my bills, she said there was something she had been wanting to talk to me about. A few weeks back, before we quit dating, Karen and I had fixed Ron Hellard up with Karen's roommate. Hellard and his blind date didn't really hit it off, but Karen thought Ron was good looking, and loved his great sense of humor.

"Would it bother you if I went out with Ron Hellard?" she asked.

"No, n-not at all," I said. "I think it would be great." They would fall in love, get married, and become one of the best couples I've ever known. Jeep,

Ron Hellard

who bonded with Karen while we were dating, would always remain close to "Aunt Karen and Uncle Ronnie."

At age forty-two, I was dating like a high school boy. If I thought constant female companionship was going to get me over Sparky, I was mistaken, because that would take a very long time. It's hard to get over someone you're still seeing and occasionally spending the night with. She asked me to continue holding off on the divorce, and I did. She was renting a small house in the Green Hills area. When I dropped by and played her a George Jones recording of a song that she and I had written together, she cried. Ironically, it was a song we had written about her: "She Hung the Moon" ("but she hung it upside down").

One day I went to Billy Sherrill's office, and George Jones was there. I told them I had a new song, "Who Was the First," but hadn't demoed it yet. Billy invited me to go into a room that had a piano and sing it for them. I sat down at the piano and sang my heart out, then turned around to discover that Billy and George were gone. That was Billy's Don Rickles sense of humor at work, but I figured if they had been loving the song, they wouldn't have left the room.

Supposedly, anti-depressants normalize your brain, rather than make you feel good by drugging you. Some will tell you it's the placebo effect that makes you feel better. Whatever it was, I thought of this medication as a really good crutch, but now I was ready to throw away the crutch and walk. I had been reading a book called *Feeling Good*, written by Dr. David D. Burns, that outlined the techniques of cognitive therapy. It explained what causes mood swings and how to nip negative feelings in the bud. Overall, my depression was gone and my anxiety attacks were much less frequent. I was determined to be emotionally healthy on my own. I quit cigarettes cold turkey and cut the antidepressant and blood pressure medicine in half. My theory was that if I quit several of my hang-ups at the same time, each one would take my mind off the others.

The first couple of days I felt really out there, and it was pretty scary. But by the third day I felt great. Dr. Jamieson said, "I can't believe that you haven't totally lost your mind!" There was little or no depression and my blood pressure was no higher than before I cut back. Within a few days I would completely quit both the antidepressant and beta blocker. Not only was I well, but I had quit cigarettes, and something told me that this time it was for good. Soon I would even quit caffeine. I did meet a new friend who helped me through all of this, introduced to me by Dr. Jamieson: a little lady named Xanax. (But beware; she can be habit forming.)

Indeed, just like the title of the book, I was *feeling good*. I felt that I had once again gotten really close to Jeep (who was now insisting that all the new people in her life call her Lauren, though her high-school girlfriends had started calling her "Beep"). I got a kick out of her being so into new wave and punk rock. We took daily walks around our pleasant neighborhood with her tiny toy poodle, Breezy, at our heels, and the Siamese cat, Bangkok—that she had bought "for me" the year before—running along beside us, yowling all the way.

From the time I first rolled into Nashville, the songs always came. They came at the feast and in the famine; they came in the sunshine and during the storm. In the early part of 1983 I wrote sort of a geriatric waltz, "Arthur and Alice," that would be recorded twice. I was self-producing my new RCA album, *Hardpore Cornography*, and the cartoon cover would show me (looking a lot like comedic pop-country star Ray Stevens) and a tall bimbo climbing out of a single-engine plane as two federal agents flashed their badges, while multiple ears of corn were falling out of my briefcase. Ironically, my mental health was on the upswing, but my career as a songwriter was about to hibernate.

Sparky kept wanting me to delay the divorce, and I complied. Then one day Karen, who had become pretty good friends with Sparky, told me that she had been by her place while Joe Vegas was there. "They're so into each other," Karen said. I called Jack Norman and told him to go ahead with the divorce.

It would be easy to look upon Sparky as the self-indulgent woman who wanted to have it both ways, being catered to by both her lover and her husband. But in the almost two years of matrimonial upheaval, we had found plenty of time to look back over our marriage, and I had come to see a lot of it from her point of view. I had taken her for granted—being faithful, yes, but with an eye for other women. Often she saw me as the guy with the *TV Guide* in his hand. After the assassination of John Lennon, I had become obsessed with all things Beatles, and she was subjected to hearing every album the group had ever made, over and over and over again—even when she didn't want to. I was no prize. She had been a joy to me, and we had spent a couple of very happy years together. She was a big-hearted girl with a gentle nature who throughout her affair (which she referred to as her "craziness") was never mean-spirited—indeed hardly a day went by when she did not express remorse or guilt over what she was putting me through. Instead of fighting so hard to get her back, why didn't I try to be more like the guy she first fell in love with, and give her more reason to *want* to come back? So it was, as we moved toward the end of that commitment we had so lovingly made less than four years before. *Two* divorces in less than four years. I didn't think I was very good marriage material, and I would never think so again.

On the night before our D-I-V-O-R-C-E became final, I wrote in my journal, "Sparky called, asking me to delay tomorrow's divorce. Said she's scared. It was hard but I resisted." The next morning, we went to the Metropolitan Nashville–Davidson County Courthouse where we were granted a divorce. I went home, called the florist, and sent Sparky a dozen roses. She called me up, crying like a baby. The roles we played in each other's lives would not come to an abrupt end. Our relationship with each other wasn't over, but it would never be the way it used to be, and would gradually fade away like the stars in the sky on the dawning of a new day.

10

COLD WIND BLOWING

The day my second divorce became final, George Strait was working his brand new record, which would become his second #1; ten-year-old Brad Paisley was probably riding his bicycle through the hilly streets of Glen Dale, West Virginia; and Carrie Underwood was wearing diapers. The biggest album in America was Michael Jackson's *Thriller*, and the top country album was Alabama's *The Closer You Get*. The hot new movie was *Return of the Jedi*. The best-selling toy in America was the Cabbage Patch Doll. That morning's newspaper headlines told of the spacecraft Pioneer 10—the first man-made object to leave the solar system. In just four days, and closer to home, Sally Ride of Murfreesboro, Tennessee, would become the youngest American (and first woman) to enter outer space. Still closer to home, my own immediate journey would not be nearly as auspicious.

I was ready to focus on my music—or so I thought. I had been a full-time professional songwriter for seventeen years, and except for a two-year glitch, my songwriting skills had never let me down. In fact, I had just recently enjoyed another #1 single. Little did I know that I would not write another hit for eight years.

RCA was promoting the new single from my album *Hardpore Cornography*—a song titled "Dolly Parton's Hits." I wrote it as a tip-of-the-hat to the song's namesake, who got her start on country star Porter Wagoner's TV show (on Music Row, Porter was as famous for being well-endowed as he was for his singing). Dolly eventually became one of the most famous females not only in country music but also in pop music and on the movie screen. Though only in her mid-thirties, she was already a true legend. But in my song, "hits" obviously was a euphemism for "tits," so the record was probably too risqué for 1983 country radio. The label thought it might be helpful if I called the stations myself, so I went to the office of independent promotion man Stan Byrd. I had been on five major labels, and I had certainly had my share of opportunities to become a successful recording artist. At forty-two I figured this might be my *last* shot. I could write hits for other people but apparently not for myself, and this record looked like it wasn't going to do any better than all the others I had put out. Though my heart wasn't in it, I made nice conversation with program directors and music directors around the country; a few said they were playing my record, while others said they would consider it. And then I found myself talking to a very pious program director in Utah.

"You know, you're a really good songwriter," he said.

"Oh, th-thank you," I replied.

"That's why I can't understand why you would associate yourself with something like this. I think it's in very bad taste. I mean, Dolly Parton's *hits*, it's obvious what you're talking about."

"Well, you're right. Sorry you don't like it."

"This is a family station," he went on. "Little children listen to us."

"Well sir, m-m-maybe you'll like my next single," I offered.

"What's it called?" he asked.

"*Porter Wagoner's Dick!*" I said, slamming down the phone.

Of course, my focus wasn't entirely on writing songs and making music, as long as there were women around. A sane thing, at this juncture, would have been for me to take a breather and just stay away from women altogether, until I had recovered from my long, tumultuous roller coaster ride. A *sane* thing. But no . . .

I had started dating a woman named Jewel who had nice, long dark hair, deeply tanned skin; and high cheekbones. She reminded me of an Indian princess, and I thought she was quite attractive. I showed Sparky a picture of her. "She looks like one of the Hager Twins," she said, referring to the singing comedians on the *Hee Haw* TV show. They weren't bad looking *guys*, but no *woman* would want to look like that. The next time I was with Jewel, whenever I looked at her, all I could see was a Hager Twin. Thanks, Sparky.

To commemorate the approaching sixty-fifth anniversary of a well-known Nashville tragedy—the worst train wreck in American history—I wanted to persuade Joe Galante to release one more Bobby Braddock record on RCA. Rafe Van Hoy and I had written a song titled "The Great Nashville Railroad Disaster," and took it upon ourselves to go into the studio and record it. As a finishing touch, we decided to seek out people who had been in the wreck, so we could interview them and put their voices on the recording. The accident had occurred when the engineer of a westbound train from Nashville mistakenly thought that the eastbound train from Memphis had already arrived at the station. He followed a single track westward into the early morning mist. The two iron beasts, both doing about sixty, collided head-on at a sharp curve a few minutes out of town. The impact could be heard for miles around. The official death toll was 121, a figure widely thought to have been low-balled by the image-conscious Nashville, Chattanooga & St. Louis Railway. We ran newspaper ads seeking survivors, and our best prospects were one eyewitness well into his seventies, and three surviving passengers, all in their eighties.

The record never came out, but the tape of these conversations is a price-less document not only because of the never-before-published vivid accounts of this historic disaster (one of the survivors sobbed as he relived the night-mare), but because of the permanent record of how people used to talk. These are the accents of four white Tennesseans, but none are alike. They were born and raised when people had distinctive dialects that were characteristic not only of their region, but of their class and their part of the county, town, or neighborhood. They had learned to talk in an era when people were not much affected by outside influences, before the days of radio and talking movies. Today people sound more and more alike. These old people took their old way of speaking with them to their graves. Not many people talk that way anymore. These ancient voices echo now like whispers in the wind, akin to the ghostly strains of old train whistles.

In 1983, I think the best song I turned in to my publisher was my love story about an elderly couple, "Arthur and Alice." It would be recorded by the great John Conlee, whom I had known since his days as a DJ on station WLAC-FM, and by T. G. Sheppard, a Joe Vegas on the surface but a hell of a heartfelt singer on the inside. My track record had been good with both of them—there had been two #1's by T. G. Over the years I've had mediocre songs that became hits and really good songs that were never released as singles, and unfortunately "Arthur and Alice" was in the latter category. I wrote it while I was in my early forties, and wondered then if I would have an Alice by my side when I got old.

Arthur and Alice played shuffleboard
Down in the park yesterday
Then they packed the best picnic they could afford
And drove down by old Tampa Bay
Forty-nine years on assembly lines
Way back up Michigan way
Now they're in a trailer 'neath Florida pines
Arthur and Alice are doing okay

Arthur and Alice make love every night
But in their own special way
Sometimes by just holding each other tight
Or in dreams of yesterday
But then sometimes they still love up a storm
Just like on their wedding day
Way down where even the winters are warm
Arthur and Alice are doing okay

Arthur and Alice have great grandkids
In Ann Arbor and in LA
They'll come to visit, last winter they did
A Busch Gardens-Disney World Day (poor Arthur . . .)
He's got a bad heart and she's nearly blind
At least that's what doctors say
But his heart's full of love and she reads his mind
Arthur and Alice
Arthur and Alice
Arthur and Alice are doing okay

Of course, to grow old together, a couple has to be close to the same age. After two months of dating a beautiful model (who then reconciled with her ex-fiancé and got married), I started going out with a Belmont College student who insisted that I meet her parents. I met them one Sunday afternoon at the school commissary. Her dad, a man about my age who looked thirty, stood behind the soda fountain fixing drinks for his wife and daughter, then asked me, "How about you, Bobby, *prune juice*?"

The annual awards handed out by performance rights organizations, like BMI, are a pretty good measure of how songwriters were doing about a year before. In 1983, I was tied with the writing team of Kye Fleming and Dennis Morgan for the most BMI Awards (four), and mine were for "Would You Catch a Falling Star," "Faking Love" (with Matraca Berg), "I Don't Remember Loving You" (with Harlan Howard), and a song called "The Bird." Jerry Reed actually wrote and recorded "The Bird," which was about a singing parrot, but since the parrot sang "On the Road Again" and "He Stopped Loving Her Today," Reed had to share his song with Willie Nelson and also Curly and me.

Songwriters were finally getting a lot of attention around town. Hal Leonard Publishing Corporation put out a series of books spotlighting songwriters and their songs—there was the *Bobby Braddock Songbook* and other editions featuring Curly Putman, Harlan Howard, Hank Cochran, and Sonny Throckmorton. Writers' nights were becoming so popular that several venues, such as the Bluebird Cafe, were exclusively booking songwriters to sing their own compositions.

One chilly night in early March, I went to the Nashville Songwriters Association awards banquet (in those days, a separate event from the Songwriters Hall of Fame inductions) with Rafe Van Hoy and Deborah Allen. The three of us hung out together so much that we dubbed ourselves the Three Musketeers. Rafe and Deborah had been together for about five years, married about a year-and-a-half. Most people had no idea when they married because there had been no real wedding ceremony, and they had been together from the beginning—soon after they met, Deborah moved in with Rafe. Music was their life—writing songs alone, together, and with other collaborators (they had just gotten a John Conlee cut on future #1 "I'm Only in It for the Love," which they wrote with Don Gant's new writer, Kix Brooks), but most of the focus at this time was on Deborah. She had finally gotten her big hit as an artist. "Baby I Lied" was a pop-country monster.

The "Ten Songs I Wish I Had Written" awards ceremony was underway, and just as we entered the large banquet room, the speakers began blaring out "Baby I Lied." As Rafe and Deborah walked to the stage to accept the award with their co-writer, Rory Bourke, the crowd came to their feet for Deborah. Possibly the best looking woman in country music, she looked beyond gorgeous in her sexy black dress, and I was immensely proud of her.

Though Deborah didn't know it at the time, this was the end of an era. "Baby I Lied," Kenny Rogers and Dolly Parton's "Islands in the Stream," and Julio Iglesias and Willie Nelson's "To All the Girls I've Loved Before" would be among the last of the country records in this era that crossed over, also to become big pop hits. The days of *Urban Cowboy* were over. George Strait was burning up the country highway, and Ricky Skaggs, Randy Travis, and Keith Whitley were just down the road a piece. They would all be part of a new subdivision in Music City called new traditional or neotraditional.

Several people from my native Polk County, Florida, had found success in the music world. There had been World War II big-band singer Frances Langford, Southern gospel bass-singing icon J. D. Sumner, and Ted Harris, a reporter for the Lakeland *Ledger* who wrote several country hit songs. Among my contemporaries were Jim Stafford, the late Gram Parsons, songwriter Carl Chambers (Alabama's "Close Enough to Perfect"), and 1970s pop-folk singer Lobo ("Me and You and a Dog Named Boo").

One day when Lobo—real name Kent Lavoie—was in Nashville, I hooked up with him. He had an idea for a country song that would play on the name of popular glam rocker Boy George: it would be about George *Jones* and the title was "*Our* Boy George."

I loved the idea, and we wrote it quickly. I took it to Billy Sherrill that very day and sang it for him live, and he wanted to do it on Jones, which I didn't (and still don't) get—the song was supposed to be *about* George, not *by* him. Deborah Allen was to do a duet with George that next day, a song she and I had written called "Our Love Was Ahead of Its Time," so Billy said, "Come on by tomorrow and sing it for Jones. If he likes it, we'll cut it then." So the next day George said, "Yeahhhhh, you sing it with the band and I'll put my voice on it later." I sang it in George's key, and thought "I'm gettin' to be George Jones for a few minutes." Later George started to realize that he couldn't do a song about himself in the third person, so he never bothered to sing it. No one else did either.

Lobo wasn't the only early classic rocker with whom I got together to co-

Nancy Jones, George Jones, Deborah Allen, and me, lunching at Nashville's legendary meat-and-three, Hap Townes Restaurant, 1984

write in the summer of 1984. I also got with Del Shannon, whose "Runaway" had been one of the biggest records of the early 1960s. Instead of actually writing anything, though, we spent the afternoon sitting around my music room with me probing him relentlessly for stories of his days on the road and for character sketches of the various stars he had toured with. He was a great storyteller and a sweet man who would take his own life a few years later.

My music room usually looked pretty much the same, no matter which house I was living in. It could be a converted garage, a side room, or a basement. There would be various awards on the walls (sometimes aptly referred to as "ego walls"). In the house on Sterling Road, the music room was housed in an addition to the original structure. My music room served as both a writer's room and home recording studio. There I had all my equipment—eight-track recorder and mixing board, effects, synthesizer, drum machine, and also my old faithful spinet piano. When I had a song I wanted someone at my publishing company to hear, I spent hours playing and replaying the instrumental parts and "stacking" the tracks until I had what I thought sounded like a fairly tight amateur band. Then I would sing until I got an acceptable vocal, and finally, I would mix it to an audio cassette and take it in to Tree to play for Dan Wilson or the new guy, an honorable man named Walter Campbell who would become the company's longest-employed song-plugger. Unless they disliked what I had written and talked me into disliking it too, I would then wait until I had four songs and we would hire a complete band and do a full demo session. As I mentioned earlier, the demos were what we pitched to the producers or record label representatives. I tried to make my demos sound as much like records as possible, and when I got a song recorded, sometimes the record would sound quite similar to my demo.

In late summer I played some of my demos for John Schneider. He was a major TV star, playing Bo Duke on the popular *Dukes of Hazzard* show. He was also sitting at the top of the country music charts. John was a nice enough guy, sort of a "golly gee-whiz" type of fellow from upstate New York. Of the five songs I played him, he held on to three, but suggested lyric changes on each one of them, a request that I rarely got from recording artists.

In September Lauren went off to college, but not very far. Middle Tennessee State University (MTSU) in Murfreesboro was only thirty-five miles away, but she wanted to live on campus. It gave me more room and her more space. She was home every weekend anyway, and sometimes during the week. At last working as hard on required subjects as elective ones, she would be making the dean's list.

Having turned eighteen, Lauren voted for the first time—in a presidential primary. I told her who I planned to vote for, so that was good enough for her; she would follow suit. But when I got in the booth I decided to vote for someone else instead. Jeep was not very happy that Daddy had sent her down one path and then taken another.

As the 1984 presidential election drew closer, political conversation became more common. Roger Sovine and I dropped by a downtown hotel to pick up Phil Walden for drinks late one afternoon. Walden had put Macon, Georgia, on the musical map by discovering Otis Redding and founding Capricorn Records. He had much to do with the creation of the Southern rock genre with artists like the Allman Brothers, the Marshall Tucker Band, Elvin Bishop, and Wet Willie. It has been written that Walden struggled with alcohol and drug addiction in the 1980s, and I bore witness to some of it that night. He was close to Jimmy Carter and had put together a campaign entourage for his fellow Georgian's 1976 presidential bid. We talked politics, and I wrote in my journal:

> *He is now a Reagan fan. I asked him if Carter knows that. He said he hadn't been able to confess that to him. Knows Jesse Jackson and Walter Mondale; says that he likes Jackson though Jackson is a bit of an anti-Semite, says Mondale is a nerd and a pompous ass.*

I doubted that Phil's strong support for Reagan was so much about his distaste for Reagan's Democratic opponent, Mondale, but was more about Phil himself: like many white Southerners, he had left his ancestral Democratic Party for the more and more conservative Republican Party.

The first order of business for me in the new year was in the role of producer. Marty Raybon was a great singer at a nightclub in Printers Alley. I had used

him on a demo a couple of months earlier. On the strength of that vocal performance, I talked Tree into financing a master session on him (an attempt to
get him a record deal). We went into the studio with the best bluegrass play-
ers in town. We did, among other things, a bluegrass version of the Beatles' "I
Want to Hold Your Hand." Many of the people I used on this recording date
would eventually become well known in their own right: singer Dan Seals,
Kieran Kane of the future O'Kanes, fiddle virtuoso Mark O'Connor, and Jerry
Douglas, who would define how the dobro was to be played in future years.
Marty himself would be lead vocalist for Shenandoah, the hit group that Don
Cook produced in the 1990s. Buddy Killen did not usually encourage those
around him to produce, but when he heard the "Beatlegrass" number, he said
"Valentine, this is pure genius." But we were unable to get anyone to pick it
up. One label person said, "The guy sounds too much like Keith Whitley."
Another said, "We put out a Beatles song one time and nothing happened."
Nevertheless, I was proud of what we had done. If I had seriously pursued
a career as a producer in the mid-1980s, I think in those days I would have
made a lot more money than I did as a songwriter.

Sparky had entered and exited three relationships since our divorce and her
eventual breakup with Joe Vegas ("I'm still changing men like baby diapers,"
she said). We still hung out, with and without our children. Sometimes we
watched a video or went to a movie, sometimes we spent a night of game-
playing with a delightful Minnesota-born couple, pianist-arranger Tom
White and his wife, Barb.

My lingering closeness to Sparky was relegated to the back burner when
I met a girl I'll call Wendy Parker. She was a local singer—I'd seen her on TV
a few times. Wendy looked about twenty, but I knew she was several years
older. Short, with closely cropped auburn hair, big blue eyes, and a knockout
figure, she excited me when we spoke in the hallway on Tree International's
first floor. It was instant mutual attraction, and an almost-instant affair—like
blueberries, sweet and wild. It was like someone had given us this crazy drug,
and we couldn't help ourselves. There was one little kicker: she was married.
My convenient poor-excuse mantra had always been "I've never been unfaithful to anyone I was committed to, but if someone is unfaithful to be with
me, well, that's *her* decision." (This adultery thing, I don't wear it as a badge
of honor.) But after the first stage of craziness wore off, the affair started getting to her. She had often told me that not only had she never been unfaithful
to her husband until I came along, but that she had never even dated anyone
since they became sweethearts back in high school. One evening she came
by my house and told me, "I love two men, and I have to choose." She chose
him. As I walked her out to her car, she cried and said, "If I had chosen you,
I would have married you." I was heartbroken as she drove off into the night,
and I knew that I would miss this magical, mystical girl who sang love songs
on my answering machine and dropped by my house and planted tulips and

sunflowers in my front yard when I was away. But I also knew that Wendy had made the right decision.

As the summer heat receded and the cool September breeze blew in, I was spending a lot of time with my friends Deborah and Rafe. After writing hits for other people and then enjoying the celebrity of Deborah's crossover hit "Baby I Lied" and a couple of Top Ten follow-up singles, they wrote the songs for her next album, and what an album it was! *Let Me Be the First* was more pop than country, but in the twilight of that particular crossover era, RCA felt that the album "fell in a crack" between pop and country. The music Rafe and Deborah were working on at this point was pure pop and dance and rock, recorded in their own home studio. They were living in a nice old home on Estes Avenue, in an upper-middle-class part of town. They had been spending a lot of time in LA and had become friends with pop-funk star Prince. They banged on my window early one morning, wanting me to meet their actor friend David Keith, the guy who hung himself in the movie *An Officer and a Gentleman*. David was in Nashville trying to get himself a country music career. He and Rafe eventually had a falling out over some disrespect that Rafe felt David had shown Deborah.

Every day that went by, I was one day deeper in debt to both Tree and the IRS. Tree was Buddy's company, but Donna Hilley was a powerful figure there. An attractive woman, approximately my age, Donna was born and raised in the steel mill suburbs of Birmingham and had been a classmate of my first wife's older sister. Donna's strength was in the business end of music, and she would be the first to admit that she was not a song person.

If one were to view Tree's second floor as filmed in time-lapse cinematography, in which all the images are sped up, faces would quickly appear and

Donna Hilley, vice-president of Tree International and future president/CEO of Sony Music Publishing (succeeding Buddy Killen)

Don Henry

disappear as people zoomed by in a publishing company and an industry in a constant state of flux. Don Henry would be whizzing around the tape copy room for the first half of the 1980s, then, in 1985, this little genius would be zipping in and out of the songpluggers' offices, in his first year as a full-time songwriter. Just as my favorite Tree singer-writer in the 1970s was someone not in the mainstream—John Hadley, an art professor who commuted from Oklahoma—my favorite Tree singer-writer of the 1980s, Don Henry, would always dance to the rhythm of his own guitar. Like Randy Newman, he would write songs that were ingeniously funny yet startlingly profound. In time he would become a local favorite, Grammy winner, and close family friend— Lauren's "big brother" and frequent collaborator.

Lauren's main interest was musical theater, something she had pursued in both high school and her freshman year at MTSU. She wanted very badly to attend the American Music and Dramatic Academy—widely known as AMDA—in New York. She submitted an audition tape: two powerful monologues and a great performance of "Look at Me, I'm Sandra Dee," from *Grease.* She and I kept our fingers crossed and were very excited when she was accepted. Excited but sad, too. It was scary for both of us, knowing she would be so far from home, for so long. Her boyfriend, Kirby, was taking it so hard that I took him to dinner (how could I not like someone who was so crazy about my daughter?) and told him the best way to hold on to Lauren in the long run was to be supportive and let her go. I had a big going-away party for her at my house. We drove up to New York, arriving there Sunday, September 29. She would be living at what was once called a theatrical hotel, the Beacon, on the twenty-third floor! I liked her two roommates, both AMDA students, of course, and I liked the excitement that was in the air. I wrote in my journal: "Sad parting . . . will miss my baby, but I get the best feeling about her future in New York."

On my drive back to Nashville I heard the new single by the Whites, a song I had written with Deborah and Rafe titled "I Don't Want to Get Over You," produced by Sharon White's husband, neotraditional bluegrass guru Ricky Skaggs. Ricky was a sweet and sincere guy who I once observed calling up his wife, just prior to his own recording session, to have her join him in a prayer over the phone. "I Don't Want To Get Over You" was a beautiful record, but it topped out at only #29 in *Cash Box*.

I bought a house—my intent being for investment purposes—on Highcrest Drive, in a neighborhood that was developed in the 1950s in the southeast part of town, not far from Whispering Hills Drive where Jeep spent her first seven years. I rented it to Ric Cassity, Sparky's new boyfriend, so in a sense Sparky was once again living in my house. The IRS quickly slapped a lien on it, just as they had on the house I was living in on Sterling Road. When the lease was up on my Trans Am, I leased a more conventional Pontiac product, a Sunbird—a black Sunbird. So, as the financial thunderheads piled up on the horizon, here I was buying houses and cars, oblivious to the severe storm that would soon come blustering in.

In my quest for good health, I had been trying to eat "better" since the early 1980s, and no longer ate beef or pork, but a little fish or occasional chicken, and a whole lot of nonfat protein from non-animal sources. I was almost but not quite a vegetarian. More recently, I had learned to savor the taste of a glass or two of good wine with dinner, rather than guzzling an entire bottle. I was well on my way to completely giving up the brain-cell-killing, paranoia-inducing pleasures of pot smoking.

One day at Tree, I ran into someone I had met once briefly but didn't know very well, Sue Powell. She had been in to meet with Buddy Killen, and told me, "Whenever I listen to songs from here, your songs are always the ones I like best." She was twenty-eight but looked much younger. Several years earlier—in 1977—she had gotten a dream job. The group Dave & Sugar—Dave Rowland plus two girls—had already had a #1 hit ("The Door Is Always Open") when one of the Sugars, Jackie Frantz, quit the group to have a baby. The trio members were equal partners, so there were dozens of girls auditioning for a slot in a hit group, guaranteeing instant stardom. Twenty-year-old Sue got the job and sang with them on a long list of hits, such as "I'm Knee Deep in Loving You," "Tear Time," and "Golden Tears." It was a smooth, mellow pop sound, with voices stacked on top of voices. In 1980, the girls signed a contract with Rowland that, without their knowledge, actually gave him complete ownership of the group, leaving them mere salaried employees. He cut his own throat as well as theirs. RCA let Rowland go but kept Sue as a solo act. She had a couple of records that charted but, unfortunately, no big hits. She went on to co-host a syndicated TV show with Jim Stafford, *Nashville on the Road*.

From the beginning, Sue Powell reminded me of Wendy Parker. Sue's hair was longer and blonder, and she seemed more foo-foo frilly than Wendy, but like Wendy she was very short with an extraordinarily great figure and had those same big blue eyes. Like Wendy she was married, and she started writing songs with me. But unlike Wendy, she wasn't going to be having an extramarital affair with me.

The songs we were writing together were unlike anything I had ever done, sort of bubble-gum pop, but stuff she sounded great on. I don't think the people around Tree really got it, but when I played it for hit producer Paul Worley, an old friend, he got excited about it and was agreeable to us co-producing Sue and trying to get her a major label deal. This never went anywhere, but it made Sue and me determined to work together until we brought the project to fruition.

On New Year's Eve, Lauren (home for the holidays) and I met Sparky at a night club called Cajun's Wharf, on the Cumberland River. Sparky's boyfriend, Ric Cassity, was the sound engineer there. He bought Sparky a red rose for love and me a yellow rose for friendship. As the new year got closer and Sparky got drunker, she started crying, "I really love Ric, but it makes me sad, thinking about what you and I had." She got even sadder later when it was announced from the stage that singer Ricky Nelson had died in a plane crash.

In my journal, I wrote, "God be with us all in this year ahead, 1986. I think it's going to be a wonderful year." If I had listened very carefully, I might have heard a deep majestic voice from the sky saying, "Yeah, right."

I started off the New Year writing songs with a couple of Florida boys. David Bellamy was the younger brother and primary songwriter of the famed Bellamy Brothers duo. I think their hits—like the Statler Brothers' hits of previous decades—represented the hopes and dreams and lifestyles of country fans of their generation and would have been the perfect time-capsule artifact to share with future generations. When not on the road, the brothers lived on the family ranch near Darby, Florida, about fifty miles northwest of my hometown of Auburndale. Not as laid back as older brother Howard, David was nevertheless a good guy and fun to write with.

The other one was honky-tonk star John Anderson. John had sleepy eyes and a lazy drawl. He came from Apopka, Florida, a citrus town like Auburndale (though Orlando suburbia today). One of the new traditionalists, his singing style mixed a whole lot of Lefty Frizzell with a little touch of rock & roll. You might say that John liked to *weed* through our song ideas before deciding which one to write.

It was bound to catch up with me, and it did. I was in debt to Tree for $400,000 and owed the IRS almost that much. My songs were not earning as much as Tree was paying me. I knew we couldn't keep on like that; something had to give. Willie Nelson went on a concert tour to pay his way out of debt, but of course, I couldn't do that. Getting a hit record was essential to survival, but that wasn't happening. Donna Hilley suggested that I might be better off at another publishing company. Buddy Killen said, "I'll close my doors as a publisher before I let Bobby Braddock go somewhere else. That's not even an option." Those were comforting words, but famous last ones.

Buddy had me meet with Joe Huffman, a partner in Tree's Christian music subsidiary, Meadowgreen Music. Buddy thought Joe was a financial wizard. Maybe it was my fault more than Joe's, but those meetings with him made me feel like a forty-five-year-old child wearing a dunce cap. The humiliation got worse. A Tree employee, Lindsay McCorvey, started paying my monthly bills, and I was given a weekly allowance. An arrangement was made with First National Bank, where Buddy was on the board of directors, for a loan that I had to pass along to the IRS posthaste. When I went by the bank to get my check, the loan officer, a man named Will Vance, handed it to me and said "Here you go, cowboy." Basically, what he was saying was, "Here you go, irresponsible redneck songwriter."

A personal vote of confidence at Tree came from the new creative director, curly gray-haired, gray-bearded Bob Montgomery, who was filling the old Don Gant and Roger Sovine position. I wasn't happy when I first heard that Bob was coming to Tree because from my experience he seemed grouchy and unfriendly, but as we got better acquainted I found that despite the gruff demeanor he had a really good heart. Bob was known for being a lot of things: Buddy Holly's closest boyhood friend, hit songwriter, hit record producer, successful music publisher, and label head. I felt that with Bob and the Tree songpluggers and me working my songs, I was bound to get a hit again.

One day I went to pitch some songs to Billy Sherrill. As I was walking across the parking lot, I saw Johnny Cash coming out of the building, dressed in black, long cloak and all. I had been around him occasionally when I was a new kid in town playing on the road with Marty Robbins, but never really knew him. I introduced myself.

"Well, Bobby Braddock," said Johnny Cash in that big booming voice with the little quiver. "We were just talkin' about you in Billy Sherrill's office. We were talkin' 'bout some of your songs."

I went inside and played Billy a few songs. Somehow the conversation turned to food, and I told him I had quit eat eating red meat two years before. Billy said, "Yeah, and that's when you quit writing hits."

Soon after that, there was another Johnny Cash encounter, though not a face-to-face one. At Tavern on the Row, one of Cash's daughters got pretty intoxicated (Kathy Cash told me years later that it might very well have been her). Apparently, someone had called her father. He suddenly appeared at the door, again in black, looking like the hero in some old cowboy movie, coming to rescue a damsel in distress. He came bounding through the door, stopping briefly as he surveyed the room, then headed for the bar where he took his daughter by the hand and led her away. It was one powerful scene.

I loved living in a neighborhood that was nice and quiet, yet less than ten minutes from the bars, stars, and guitars. That was about to change. My financial situation dictated that I sell the house I loved on Sterling Road and move into the house that I had been renting out to Sparky's boyfriend, Ric. I never liked the house at 527 Highcrest Drive and never would. My distance from Tree jumped from three miles to nine miles. I wrote a song line "the jumbo jets fly low on my side of town." It was an okay ranch-style, and the neighborhood was nice—for the area. Most of the people were older couples who had lived there since the 1950s. While rummaging around the attic, I discovered that previous occupants had left behind a box full of photos, letters, and cards that told a very sad story. It was the story of the young mother who lived there in 1954. She was an attractive lady who went to the hospital for what was supposed to be routine surgery. There were the cheery get-well cards. But something had gone terribly wrong, because then there was the laminated obituary and all the sad sympathy cards. I often thought of the boy, just a few years younger than I, left behind by this unfortunate woman, thirty-two years before I moved in.

In a concerted effort to come up with some recordable songs, I wrote a song called "Alien" and one titled "Now and Then" (I only think about her now and then / but I think about her now more than I did then). When it came time to do a demo session, I threw in one I had written earlier about Wendy Parker, "I'd Rather Be Crazy" (than crazy and lonely), and got a great singer, Dana McVicker, to do the vocals on these songs. "I'd Rather Be Crazy" was a driving mid-tempo, with a beat similar to the Police's "Every Breath You Take." The next day I took the demo session into Bob Montgomery's office to play for the pluggers. The reaction was the biggest I had gotten over any of my songs in years. Bob played "I'd Rather Be Crazy" three times. He got up and shook my hand and said, "This is absolutely great." I was told that nobody had ever seen him react that way. He said, "If we can't get these cut, we'll all resign." Dana, who demoed "I'd Rather Be Crazy" would cut it for her first single on Capitol. The record, sounding quite similar to the demo, would chart for a few weeks but not be a big hit. Tanya Tucker would record "Alien," but it would be only an album cut and never a single. "Now and Then" would never be recorded by anyone.

Perhaps it's not surprising that a man who wrote songs about craziness and aliens and now-and-then would undergo a *hypnotic regression*. Ever since my teens I had experienced occasional déjà vu feelings, but these feelings weren't random; they always had something to do with the military and war, and always seemed very real to me. The hypnotist took me back to what he said was a time before my childhood. He taped what I said under hypnosis. I told of being a proud twenty-year-old German soldier named Herman. I said I had a fiancée waiting for my return from the war and that I'd had no intentions of dying. On the tape, I was noticeably upset as I told of a horrible explosion that took my life in 1940. I said that I came back the same year, as Bobby Braddock. I had to ask myself if that explained the horrible nightmare that I had endured over and over as a toddler: someone counting higher and higher and higher until there was a violent explosion that jolted me awake and made me sit up in bed screaming hysterically. I also thought it might explain a phenomenon that my two wives knew all about—me speaking German in my sleep.

Lauren had attended AMDA for the full 1985–86 term; then she went there that summer, which meant she would be able to graduate from the two-year school the following January. In early October of 1986, I drove her back up to New York.

She was having a good time in acting school and was forging friendships that would last for many years to come. The hot play on Broadway was *Big River*, a musical based on Mark Twain's *Adventures of Huckleberry Finn*. The songs were written by Roger Miller. Roger and his wife Mary were more than kind to Lauren while she was living in New York. One day, one of Jeep's classmates ran up to her screaming, "Lauren, you have a call from *Roger Miller!*" To the girl, Roger was a hot writer of musicals who was perhaps going to give her friend a big break, but to Jeep he was a country singer-writer friend of her dad's, checking in on her to see if she was okay.

I took an Amtrak train to New York in January to see Lauren perform in a couple of AMDA productions and then get her diploma. Mom flew up from Florida, and on our first night in town I took her to see *Big River*, accompanied by one of my Georgia cousins, Janice Vinson, who was then living in the city. An extremely embarrassing moment occurred when Ron Richardson, playing Jim, belted out "Free at Last" and Mom said to me in a voice loud enough to be heard several rows away, "The *nigra* is a really good singer!" Cousin Janice and I wanted to crawl under our seats.

A couple of nights later, I got on a southbound train and left my loved ones behind in the big city—Lauren to try to get a break in show business, and Mom to wait for the weather to improve so she could fly back to Florida. In my journal I wrote of my mother, "My heart aches at the beginnings of her senility." There was heavy snow along the eastern seaboard as far south as Georgia. As I lay in my bunk in the sleeping compartment, I looked out at the little cities of north Jersey. The streets were deep in white and the cars were slow in motion, but my train was rolling on through, as I peacefully drifted off to sleep.

February of 1987 felt like love. There were a lot of spring-like days. The radio was playing songs of lost, longing love—"At This Moment" by Billy Vera and the Beaters on Top Forty, "You Still Move Me" by Dan Seals on country radio, and "Have You Ever Loved Somebody" by Freddie Jackson on soul stations. There was a lot of dirty dancing across the big screens, and there were crime stories and dynasties on the small ones. I bought my first CD player. I was still unsuccessfully writing songs with Sue Powell and unsuccessfully writing them by myself. I wrote a song about the AIDS scare called "Be Careful" that nobody at Tree liked, but the Bellamy Brothers loved it and put it on hold (but never recorded it).

Sparky and I were hanging out on a nice almost-balmy day and started talking about Don Gant, so we decided to pay him a visit. He was at the new location of his publishing company, Old Friends, which had moved about four miles away from Music Row to the Berry Hill section of Nashville, sometimes referred to as Little Music Row.

Gant seemed very glad to see both of us. We went outside and sat in some lawn chairs and enjoyed the nice clean breeze. He was happy with the success of his company and was enjoying his resurgence as a record producer, with several hits by Eddy Raven. When I was around Gant, I sometimes felt that it was my job to crack him up. He had a quick but gentle laugh, and he looked you straight in the eye while he was laughing. I don't remember what we talked about, but I can still see that laugh.

A couple of weeks later, in the first week of March, he went to Florida on a deep-sea fishing trip with a couple of friends and broke his leg in a boating accident. After seeing a doctor, they drove straight through to Nashville where he checked into a hospital for surgery. The next day he suffered a major stroke, probably from a blood clot in his broken leg.

I went to the hospital that night. They were allowing only immediate family in to see him, and his wife and brother reported that his entire right side was paralyzed and he was unable to speak. The next day he suffered another stroke, a massive one. Sparky and I spent the day at the hospital, then picked up Jeep, who was in town for a few days, and went to Red Lobster and made ourselves feel a little better with some wine. Sparky and I were remembering what Gant once said about Lynda when he married her: "I want a wife who'll wipe my ass when I have my stroke."

We got back to the hospital just before Gant drew his last breath. He was forty-four years old. The visiting room was so packed that there was little room to move around. Everyone was in tears—grown men hugged each other crying hard. I wrote in my journal:

> *He probably had more close friends than anybody in town. Always a brother. Sometimes the mischievous bad boy, sometimes the sweet soft-spoken gently-laughing friend. . . . Gant, if he loved you, would look you in the eye with that lazy little smile on his face, and tell you so. "I love you, son." Well, Gant, I love you wherever you are.*

Kix Brooks, one of Gant's star songwriters in those pre-Brooks & Dunn days, said, "Now we'll all have to kick ass a little bit harder."

Johnny Cash's "The Night Hank Williams Came to Town," which I wrote with Charlie Williams, entered the charts, but would not go very high or stay very long. This would be my biggest song of 1987. I knew time was running out. I wrote in my journal, "How much longer can they (Tree) keep holding me up?"

One afternoon, after seeing that my support from Buddy Killen was beginning to evaporate, I walked out the front door feeling about as mentally unstable as I ever felt in my life. Ron Hellard asked me if I would drop him off at Close Quarters. We rode the three or four blocks in silence. As I pulled up in front, he asked me, "Cocktails, Bobby?"

"Ronnie," I said, "the way I feel right now, if I started drinking I might go out and shoot up Music Row."

Ronnie looked at me through his sun shades, with a hint of a grin on his face, and said, "I dig that about you." I laughed so hard that all my blues went away, at least for a little while. At least until the next day when Donna Hilley told me that one option Tree had was to drop me.

I had to laugh to keep from crying. On April Fool's Day, I told Sue Powell, who knew she was accused of having "blonde moments," that a parrot had cut one of our songs and she believed it ("I thought, shoot, great to get a cut," she said, "even if it's by a bird"). And on Bob Montgomery's fiftieth birthday he was wondering why he had received so many calls from Lakeside Nursing Home, soon learning that I had given them his number and told them he was a ninety-year-old multimillionaire who wanted to move into their facility and give them a huge donation. Then there was the time that I got a phone call and wrote in my journal, "It was a hang-up call, surely someone so mad about me that she fainted at the sound of my voice."

One nice diversion, one that didn't make me a penny, was a project that I did with Rafe Van Hoy. I got a tape of President Reagan's speeches, and we wrote a rap song, tailored to the digital samples that Rafe made of Reagan's voice. The hilarious result was a song that sounded like the president was rapping. I went to the local Republican headquarters and got a life-sized cutout of the Gipper. In the picture we had made, it looked like Rafe and I—wearing Blues Brothers suits, thin ties, fedoras, and sunglasses—had our arms around the president. We called ourselves the Plain White Rappers and the song was called "Yo Ronnie." We had a thousand 45-rpm records pressed up for radio stations, with a picture on the record sleeve of us and our new friend.

Donna Hilley told me one day that things were looking grim, that she and Buddy didn't know what they were going to do with me. Then a few days later she said she loved me and she had some kind of a plan. One day I overheard a half-soused Curly fussing at someone in the executive offices about Tree letting good writers go, and saying he was glad they hadn't done it to him yet. He was told, *"But you didn't get in debt like those other asshole writers!"* I noted in my journal that in just a few short years, I had gone from being a hero at Tree to just another asshole writer.

Rafe Van Hoy and me as The Plain White Rappers, with
a cardboard-cutout President Reagan, 1987

Knowing Curly, his loyalty came as no surprise. When times get rough,
real friends come to the surface, and they are your most valuable assets when
material resources have dwindled. I could always count on Rafe and Deborah's friendship, and Michael Kosser's as well. Bob Montgomery at Tree was
super-supportive, as was his assistant (and future wife) Cathy Moore. Other
really good Tree friends were Ron Hellard, Don Cook, and Chris Waters.
Chris was having a good run producing his sister, Holly Dunn (who one day
came upon me while I was cussing a blue streak, and from that moment on
referred to me affectionately as "Mister Nasty").

I wrote in my journal that "Buddy and Donna are easing me out the door."
I had bargained with the IRS to accept a little less than $45,000, their price
for me not losing my house right then. Though Buddy had agreed to help me
with that amount, he changed his mind and I had to talk him back into it. He
seemed about ready to shut off all money to me.

All of this made me feel desperate. Bob Montgomery had urged me not
to write "out of desperation," but that's exactly what I was doing. I knew that
George Strait was looking for material, so one day I got a cassette of his most
recent album and headed south on Nolensville Road into rural Middle Tennessee. I drove for two hours listening to everything on the album over and
over. When I got home, I tried all night to write something like the songs I
had heard on the cassette.

During one of my desperate visits to Tree to try to save my ass, I dropped by Curly's office to visit for a while. After a few minutes, Harlan Howard came bounding through the door ranting about *Sunshine and Shadow*, the new memoir written by his ex-wife, singing star Jan Howard. "Gyod dimmit," he fumed, "Jan's gone and written all this shit about me."

"Is it not true?" I asked.

"Gyod dimmit, I didn't say it wasn't *true*," he groused.

I thought compared to my problems, Harlan's didn't seem so bad.

Potential relief came shortly when my mother cashed in a bond and sent me a substantial sum. I got out my legal pad and started figuring out the wisest place to put every penny of this, right? Wrong. I did research on which drug companies might be most likely to come up with a cure for AIDS. I had read about people getting rich when penicillin was invented in the 1940s. I invested most of the money in "biotech" stocks, and used the rest as down payment on land in Dickson County, two counties west of Nashville. A few weeks later, on "Black Monday," the stock market crashed, and my biotech stocks came tumbling down like bowling pins in the path of a big black ball. I might as well have flushed many thousands of dollars down the toilet.

In the last month of the year, there were a lot of things on my mind and in my journal. I longed for the days of Gant, and wrote "Gant made me feel like a first-rate writer, which probably *made* me a first-rate writer." I thought about the consistent over-the-years sweetness of beautiful, flaky Angela, no longer a Nashvillian but a video editor for CBS in LA. Angela was asking me if I would marry her if she divorced her husband of a few months. I wrote about it being Ronald Reagan's finest hour, because he signed a treaty with the Soviet premier eliminating intermediate missiles in Europe ("The whole world should be proud of both Reagan and Gorbachev today"). I wrote "Buddy's agonizing, wants to work something out but Donna thinks I should go." I noted that I really liked Lauren's boyfriend, Jonathan Weseley, son of two prominent New York doctors but looking every bit like the rock musician that he was.

In January I wrote that I "saw the New Year come in with Rafe and Deborah at the Bluebird Cafe where the Kingsnakes played," and reported that my two friends' raves about the group were not exaggerated. I printed in large letters atop the journal page RADIATE IN EIGHTY-EIGHT, a little phrase from Rafe and Deborah, and then began what would become a daily ritual for the next twelve months, printing—with different types of lettering and design on each journal page—YEAR OF THE COMEBACK. I told of Dixie Gamble and me seeing the film *Broadcast News* with Rodney Crowell and Rosanne Cash, and Rodney saying, "Bobby, you're a pretty good date." I chronicled my mother falling and hitting her head at the Tampa airport and then the ensuing surgery on her eye.

Then one cold, gloomy evening the awful reality of what was about to happen caught up with me. I lay around my house with my psyche so brutally wounded that I wanted to die. Sparky knew how bad I was and came over and refused to leave, stayed with me all night.

A few days later at Tree, Donna asked me, "Have you looked into getting a deal somewhere? Buddy can't go on." Bob Montgomery commented, "You're in too deep." My response was, "Hell, yes, I'll find me somewhere else to write songs," as I left in a huff and slammed the door.

Bob Montgomery followed me out and apologized, saying, "I love you as a friend." Dan Wilson commented, "It may not do any good, but I'm going to the wall for you." I later heard that Donna cried for two hours that day. But Buddy had reversed himself and was planning to cut everything off, so it looked like this was it. Rock bottom.

The next day I went back. I talked to Donna, then Buddy. They wanted to know if there was some way I could really cut down expenses. Not appreciably. Buddy was very kind—hardest decision of his career, etc. My actual income from songs had fallen to the lowest point since 1975, considerably less than what Tree had continued to pay me to keep my income pumped up to what I said I needed. Lindsay McCorvey, the girl in the accounting department who had been paying my bills, offered to continue doing that on her own time for nothing. Curly, a saint of a man, offered to loan me money. I thanked him and said, "Curly, I've never borrowed money from friends and don't want to start now." In my journal I declared, "I hate the sympathetic smiles. I think I know now how terminally ill people are treated."

That night I went to Deborah and Rafe's house. They had company, bass player Tom Robb. I went upstairs and plopped down on a bed. Deborah came up and rubbed my feet for a couple of minutes, then went downstairs and announced, "Bobby needs us." Tom left. They took me to dinner and made me laugh. I wrote in my journal, "Life savers."

I started setting up appointments with the heads of different publishing companies. I hadn't had a hit in five years and would be asking for advances on a writing career that was starting over from scratch. I would be asking potential publishers to take a gamble on a forty-seven-year-old songwriter who was as cold as the proverbial "well-digger's ass in January." I had developed a taste for living on $150,000 a year at the very least (which would be equal to way over twice that much in 2015 dollars) but I knew that would be too high for a three-year deal, so I decided to ask for that much in advances the first year, half that much the second year, and *zero* the third year. I was willing to gamble on my belief that I would have a hit or two within the next year—I'd certainly done it before—and generate enough money for the new publisher to recoup and fill up my own bank account as well. Of course if I had no hits by that third year, well, I would have no choice but to file bankruptcy, get out of the music business, and get a day job.

I met with several publishers, but seemed to have the most rapport with an old acquaintance, Pat Higdon of Warner-Chappell Music. He didn't refuse my proposal, and he said he thought we could do great things together but a lot depended on what the corporate people said, "Just keep bringing me songs, and we'll see where we are in a couple of months."

Sparky was working as a waitress at the Quality Inn's restaurant and club, just across the river in East Nashville. She and Ric had broken up. Since she was in between boyfriends, she asked how I would feel about her moving in with me for a while. I told her I would love her company. She said we could sleep together if I liked. I told her as much as I would love that, I knew it would lead once again to me developing a big "thing" for her. As I look back, I can see that it was one of the sanest decisions I ever made—letting her move in *and* abstaining from sex—both were good decisions. She was one of the few people with whom I felt sufficiently comfortable to be under the same roof. We had a wonderful time watching movies and playing games. It turned out to be a really nice time for us both.

I was trying fruitlessly to get Buddy to let me receive my money from BMI, the money that performance organizations collect from radio and TV stations and pay directly to the writers. I had signed my BMI earnings over to Tree a couple of years before, so they (Tree) would continue advancing me money. With Tree no longer advancing me money, they would be continuously recouping my debt whenever they received "mechanicals"—that is, the royalties that publishers receive from music labels. Why couldn't he let me have back my performance money to live on? He wouldn't do it. But he suggested that Tree could buy the writer's share of my songs and subtract the amount I owe them from that. I was incredulous. Why would I want to give up my right to ever receive money on my past songs just so we could do a quick debt payoff to Tree; I mean, after subtracting $400,000, what would be left for me? Not a lot. Why would I do such a thing? But his offer did plant a seed in my mind.

I asked Buddy Killen if he personally wanted to buy the writer's share of my catalog. He quickly told me that he did. "This is something I really want to do. I wouldn't be doing it to make a profit, but to help *you*, Valentine. Someday I'd like for you to get your songs back." My name would remain on the songs as the writer, and I would always get credit for writing them, but they wouldn't belong to me anymore. In other words, I would no longer receive royalties on them. The only songs I would own were the ones I would write from that day forward. He offered $420,000, I asked for $500,000, then we agreed to $450,000—though I didn't really think that was enough for that huge catalog of 1,200 songs from over twenty years, including several #1 hits. Then he subtracted $13,000 from the total sale price for a reason so complicated that I would rather not confuse things further by attempting to explain. I sold my rights to all my songs for $437,000. I received $150,000 immediately, and the remainder would be paid to me over the next two years. I was giving up a lot, but felt it would pull me out of potential bankruptcy and poverty, and give me a second chance.

As it turned out, I would never be able to get my catalog back, as Buddy had said he wanted me to do, and I knew with his passing in 2006 that there was absolutely no chance of it ever happening. In 2010, I consulted with the royalty department at Tree's descendent, Sony Music Publishing, to see how much money the songs had made for Buddy and his estate up to that point in time. I was just curious: how much would I have made if I had held on to the catalog? It would have made me $2,200,000 over a twenty-two year period. That's $100,000 a year, which would have been nice pocket change to supplement a much larger regular income from recent songs. But for the moment, with my financial situation resolved for at least the next three years, all pressure was removed, and both heart and mind were feeling sweet relief. Buddy Killen had saved my life, but he would get a very nice return on his investment.

On July 22, 1988, I wrote in my journal: "Played songs for Bob Doyle, for singer he manages (now signed to Capitol)." The singer's name was Garth Brooks. I met with Garth a couple of weeks later and played him several songs, some of which he put on hold. When I met with him again the next week, he said what he would really like to do was write with me. He talked about the kinds of songs he had in mind, and paced the floor as he explained his ideas to me. My impression of him was "very serious young man." Over time my opinion would expand to "very special young man" and eventually "very extraordinary young man." Garth wasn't afraid to speak his mind to the big shots. One story goes that when a label executive urged him to drop his producer, Allen Reynolds, Garth responded with two choice words. But he treated everyday people with dignity, remembering the names of receptionists, drivers, and servers many months after their brief encounters with him. His acts of charity would be without boundaries and without fanfare. Despite his megastardom, his demeanor would remain courteous and his attitude humble. One night I would introduce him to my date at a BMI Awards dinner, and he would remove his hat, as he always did in the presence of a lady, and go on to lavish me with praise (obviously for her benefit), praise so high that I would be embarrassed to repeat it. That warm day in 1988, I had no idea that this very serious young man would someday become the biggest-selling country singer of all time, or that he would handle success better than any entertainer I had ever known.

One of Garth's early co-writers was a man in early middle age named Kim Williams. Kim had been severely burned in an industrial accident, and ten years and two hundred surgical procedures later he was well enough to come to Nashville to pursue an early, unfulfilled dream to make it as a songwriter. Kim was so outgoing and charismatic that after getting to know him, you soon forgot about his injuries. He would have the good fortune to get in on the ground floor with Garth Brooks, and when Garth exploded across America, so would some of the songs that Kim wrote with him. Then there would be other hits with other artists. Kim Williams had the best work ethic of any songwriter I've ever known, often scheduling co-writing sessions with four different people in a single day. He got his first cut at age forty and was so successful that he would be able to semi-retire in his fifties, moving back to the mountains of his beloved East Tennessee (but still writing an occasional hit).

I was thankful that I was finally in a position to help Lauren with some of her expenses. She was thinking that she might like to take a shot at LA. I told her to come on home to Nashville for a while, that I would take her out to California and we'd check it out. I thought a road trip across the American West would be fun. As it turned out, Sparky and her boyfriend, J. R., (I called him "Junior," and he called me "Pa") were getting serious and about to move into a place together, so Sparky moved out of my house right before Lauren moved in. On her first day home, I played Jeep a Conway Twitty record, the great Gary Burr song about love between parent and child, "That's My Job," and she burst into tears.

With Lauren back in Nashville, my mom decided to fly up to visit for a few days. She wanted to go to church on Sunday, so we took her up to Madison (once a separate community to the north, before all of Davidson County became a consolidated government in 1963). The Madison Church of Christ, with several thousand members, was known as the largest Church of Christ congregation in the world. When I was a kid, drifting off to sleep at church would prompt a big *pinch* from my mom. Some things never change; it was no different in 1988 than in 1948. I dozed off, and my mother reached down and pinched me on my leg.

Shortly after my mom's visit, Lauren and I headed out for the left coast on I-40, passing through the lovely mountains of northern New Mexico and Arizona. This was my first time ever in LA. I especially loved the Hollywood Hills, where we checked into the Hyatt-on-Sunset. Lauren's boyfriend, Jon Weseley, had flown out from New York, so they were glad to see each other. A family friend, Diana Haig, who worked at Warner Bros., gave us a tour of the movie lot and said she would help find Jeep an apartment. Then there was beautiful, flaky Angela (the CBS video editor): she and I, romantic and sexy on the phone, sort of freaked out in person but had a good time. Jeep did some interviews. She wanted to move out there. She *thought*.

We began our return trip far to the south, on I-10, through the California deserts, which I thought resembled the surface of the moon, and the much more beautiful painted desert of Arizona. In El Paso we hired a taxi man to drive our car down into Mexico, taking a little tour of Juarez, back then a relatively safe city. Leaving El Paso, we drove parallel with the border, seeing Mexican mountain peaks on our right, and listening to Linda Ronstadt's wonderful new album, *Canciones de mi Padre* (Songs of My Father), with Lauren reading the English translation of each song as I listened to the voice I had been in love with for years. It was a great trip and a great time together.

When we got back to Nashville, I told Jeep I would buy her a new car—with one stipulation: it had to be one with an air bag (a majority of new cars still didn't have them). Her LA car would be a white Ford Tempo. *If* she moved out there. My daughter never met a decision that she liked.

In late September, Sparky's boyfriend, J. R., drove Jeep and her rescued Siamese kitten to LA. Within three days after leaving Nashville, she already had an apartment, near North Hollywood in the San Fernando Valley. Diana Haig let her have some furniture, and my friend Angela helped her decorate. The word was that Jon would soon migrate westward. For the moment, all was well in Southern California.

I always liked the first days of fall. In Tennessee, I especially liked the scent of burning leaves in the cool afternoon air. I enjoyed watching the school kids get off their buses, making new friends and new memories, some that would last a lifetime. And though I didn't know it at the time, in the fall of '88 I was heading into a new season of my own life.

Now that the financial bear had loosened its grip on me, with the sale of my writer's rights, I knew that the smartest thing for me to do was sell 527 Highcrest Drive. The sale of my house would satisfy a big part of my IRS debt, and writing a hit or two would help get me out of debt with Tree. I started looking around for a place to rent, a "getting-out-of-debt house." When I saw the only rental house on Autumn Trail, all it took was half a minute inside the place to know that I wanted to live there. The nice little 2,000 square-foot brick home was built in 1945, had a separate garage and nice yard, and was on the very edge of the ritzy Oak Hill area (I would tell people that I lived in "the slums of Oak Hill"). The yard and the lush neighborhood were definitely very autumn-looking on this early November day, with leaves ablaze, piles of them blowing through the yard in the fall breeze as the squirrels and chipmunks scampered about.

Sue Powell and her husband, Dave Bowling (not her former singing partner Dave Rowland in Dave & Sugar), had separated and she moved into an apartment. When Sue saw 4402 Autumn Trail, she loved it. She offered to help me figure out how to furnish and decorate the house. We went from place to place, getting wicker furniture, an antique office desk, curtains, and Levelor blinds. I asked her if she would be interested in working as my assistant, paying my bills, etc.—my motive probably just wanting to be around her more. But she gladly took me up on it, took it very seriously, and did a great job.

Sue and I had become very close friends, so when she became single it just seemed natural that we start dating. She had big blue eyes and long hair that looked like spun gold. She was short, sweet, cute, glamorous, shapely, and talented. The dresses that she made from tie-dyed T-shirts were always in demand from people who knew her. She was a bit on the naïve side but always quick to laugh at herself, often giggling with her hand over her mouth like a child.

With Sue Powell, 1989

We went in with a few musicians to try to fuse her bubble gum sound with late 1980s country. One of the musicians we used was an old friend of mine, Byrd Burton. In the 1970s, Byrd had been a part of the Amazing Rhythm Aces, producing their records and playing the well-known guitar licks on the big hit "Third Rate Romance." Hot producer Paul Worley, who had replaced Bob Montgomery as chief creative officer at Tree, was very supportive of Sue's session, though he was unable to place it with a record label.

It was about this time that Tree ceased to be Tree. Buddy Killen, the biggest publisher in town, sold his company for $42 million to CBS—who would soon sell it to Sony. Looking back from another century—and so many Sony acquisitions later—that figure looks small, but it was a pretty big deal back then. A country boy at heart, Buddy had his banker make some calls to Las Vegas and establish him a line of credit, then he hopped on a plane and went out there for several days of gambling. Buddy would stay on as CEO of "Sony/Tree," (as it would be called before long) but he would not be comfortable working for someone else, so within a year, he would pass the torch to Donna Hilley, who had negotiated the sale and was actually running the place anyway.

Sue Powell and I got serious pretty quickly, and it worked out beautifully for a while. But after the reality of her divorce set in—her marriage was the only relationship she had ever been in, in her life, before me—she started having bouts of depression. We drove up to Indiana to visit her mom, and from there we went to Chicago where we took an Amtrak to Los Angeles to see Jeep. I had always had a thing for trains, and Sue was loving her first railroad trip. Sue and I and Lauren and her boyfriend, Jon, drove from LA up to San Francisco and had a wonderful time.

When we got back to Nashville, we agreed it had been great fun, but I also knew that Sue was unhappy and sometimes wondering if she should never have left Dave. One day she was on a movie set—she had a part in a Jim Varney film playing a *filing cabinet*! Dave called me, moaning and groaning in agony with an abscessed tooth, saying he needed Sue. I felt sorry for Dave and told Sue he needed her. She took him to the dentist, then called to ask me what I thought she should do. I said I thought she should take care of him. "If I go back to Dave, I'll probably regret it and be sitting around missing you," she said. They did indeed get back together, but it didn't work out. There would come a time when I really wanted her back, but she was dating someone, and after that she would be available but I was involved with someone. The gods of love may have been on our side, but the gods of timing were not. She would eventually marry Rod Scott, a young attorney from nearby Murfreesboro.

I wrote a song about some of the most special females in my life, filed away under eye color. The green eyes belonged to Sparky. The gorgeous brown eyes belonged to a sweet girl whom I have chosen not to write about because I don't want to embarrass her (even though the relationship was never sexual). I guess you could say that one of the blue eyes belonged to Wendy Parker and the other one to Sue Powell. "Eyes" would be recorded by a group called Asleep at the Wheel. The song concluded with:

> *They say the night has a thousand eyes*
> *But all that I can see*
> *Are green eyes . . . brown eyes . . . and blue eyes*

Keith Whitley was one of the brightest lights in the country-starry sky. He was a Sony/Tree writer and always had a sunny smile and a great sense of humor. One day he wanted me to hear a song he had written about Buck Owens. He grabbed a guitar and sang "Bring Back Buck," sounding just like the head Buckaroo. He had the talent to become one of the greatest country singers of all time, and we can only imagine how huge he would have been, had he lived on. I never even knew that he had a drinking problem; most people didn't, because he wasn't a social drinker and he never got just a little drunk. He was a binge drinker and would drink until he passed out. He and Don Cook were very close friends. One day Keith's wife, country singer Lorrie Morgan, was worried because she had been unable to get in touch with him, so Cook drove her to an apartment where Keith was staying at the time, off West End Avenue. There was no response at the door, so Cook boosted Lorrie to climb up over the rail of the balcony. She found Keith unconscious, and Don carried him to the car. It was a two-seater, so Keith was in Lorrie's lap. On the way to the hospital, she started screaming, "He's stopped breathing!" Don slammed Keith's chest with his fist and he started breathing again. The ER physician said his blood alcohol level was the highest he had ever seen in a living person. But his friends couldn't be there for him every moment of his life, and on May 9, 1989, he went on a binge that he wouldn't come back from. At the time of Keith Whitley's death at age 33, his biggest and most recent single was "I'm No Stranger to the Rain," written by my friends Ron Hellard and Sonny Curtis. It was a sad week in Music City, and the offices and light poles on Music Row were draped in black.

As December chilled the Tennessee hills, I continued to stay in close touch with Angela in sunny California. We talked a lot, and it seemed that we were always on the verge of really starting something. One night, she called me up, slurring her words so badly that I could hardly understand her. When she told me she was making out her last will and testament and leaving me her art, I called the Los Angeles County Sheriff's Department and told them they needed to get to her as soon as possible. Thankfully, they did, in time.

Lauren and I headed for Auburndale to see my mom for Christmas, but North Florida was having its first major snow in thirty years, and the roads were impassible, so we had to stop in Macon, Georgia, where we spent the next two days, including Christmas Eve.

Back home in Nashville, in one of the coldest Decembers on record, I not only looked back at the 1980s that were coming to an end, but at the past twenty-five years that I had lived in Nashville, and all the changes I had seen. When I first came to town, music was being recorded on three tracks, with vocals going to one track and instruments on the other two; in 1989 the songs were being recorded on as many as forty-eight tracks. Of the top fifty charting country artists of the 1960s, only four were still among the top fifty of the 1980s, four so famous that only their last names need be told: Jones, Haggard, Jennings, and Williams Jr. When I first arrived, Nashville's biggest tourist draw was the Grand Old Opry; twenty-five years later it was the Opryland USA theme park, attracting 2.5 million visitors in 1989 and owned by Gaylord Entertainment, which by this time also owned the Opry—which would, ironically, outlast the theme park.

On New Year's Eve, I was with Deborah and Rafe at their new 10,000-square-foot mansion atop a hill so high that the wind was blowing all the time (and you could see the lights of both Nashville and Brentwood). Deborah had designed it, and they named it "the Pink Palace." We opened up a bottle of champagne and started writing a song (actually Deborah wrote most of it) called "Hurt Me." In a couple of years, she would record it herself, and eventually LeAnn Rimes would, too. The 1980s had started off wonderfully for me, but it had been downhill for most of the decade. I figured if life was a roller coaster, then it was about time for me to start going *up* again. So when I heard 1990 knocking on the Pink Palace door, I must have felt like shouting out an old song title, "Come On In!"

11
COMING BACK

The bright winter sun shone through the opened blinds as I sat down at the dining table, at home on Autumn Trail in Nashville. I began eating my late-morning breakfast of oatmeal and raisins while poring over the morning *Tennessean* to see what was going on at home and abroad, a little ritual that I carried out every morning. It was January 1, the first day of the 1990s.

The local weather forecast called for a mostly clear day with a high in the 40s. Nashville mayor Bill Boner declared that his New Year's resolution was to figure out how to solve the problem of disposal of solid waste. Country music's Kathy Mattea said she felt she was finally coming into her own as a singer, after being compared for so long to Canadian songbird Anne Murray. The Nashville ACLU was filing a lawsuit against the city of Pulaski, Tennessee, birthplace of the Ku Klux Klan, demanding that they allow the Klan to march in the Martin Luther King Day parade there. Five thousand University of Tennessee football fans had shown up at a Dallas pep rally in support of the Vols in their matchup against Arkansas in the Cotton Bowl. President George H. W. Bush had also shown up in Texas, visiting troops who had been injured in the recent invasion of Panama. And across the sea, over five thousand miles away, the Romanian Communist Party was being characterized as "dead."

Certainly no one could say that *country music* was dead. The New Traditionalists had already been changing country, and then came the *new* New Traditionalists. George Strait had been around for several years, Randy Travis for a few less, Clint Black and Garth Brooks had arrived on the scene the year before, and Alan Jackson was brand new. Country music was hot, but it was about to get a lot hotter.

I had been away from the top of the charts for much too long, and I desperately wanted to find my way back. The hot writers on Music Row were Paul Overstreet, Dean Dillon, Aaron Barker, and the genius who wrote "The Gambler," Don Schlitz—but no longer Bobby Braddock. At Sony/Tree, some of the older writers like Hank Cochran and Max D. Barnes were still doing well—but not I.

Dammit, I was trying! I wrote a song that everyone around Sony/Tree seemed to be excited about. "Look Away" was about the changing face of the

South (Dixie's had a facelift, I guess she's lookin' better / But I kinda liked the old one, I never will forget her). It would be recorded by John Anderson and included on his best-selling album *Seminole Wind*, but it would not be a single and become the hit I was hoping for.

Just as there was historic change going on around the world—East Germany followed Romania to freedom after the Berlin Wall came tumbling down—I saw a major era of my own life come to an end when Sparky got married. She and her sister Fay came by my house one afternoon, and I sang them a song I had just written called "She's Getting Married," and they both cried. But it had been a long time since I had harbored any hope for reconciliation. I genuinely liked J. R. Reed and sincerely wished them the best.

Far from the echoes of days gone by, I was sitting in the lobby at Sony/Tree when Garth Brooks, wearing a baseball cap, stepped off the elevator on his way to a meeting with the Tree songpluggers. "Hey Bobby," he said cheerfully.

"You've sure come a long way since the last time I saw you," I told him.

"We're just havin' fun," he modestly replied. Then he said, "I heard a song you wrote. What a great idea! 'The Day Before You Stopped Loving Me.'" I realized that he liked the idea better than the song, so I invited him to rewrite it.

"I wouldn't take any of the writer's share," he said.

"Go ahead and make it a Garth song," I told him. "It would be an honor to be on a song with you." He told me he was flattered. However, that was the last I heard about it.

From time to time I would hear that Garth had said he wanted to cut a Bobby Braddock song, but it never happened.

Somebody needed to cut a hit with one of my songs, or I was going to be in trouble. The last installment from Buddy Killen on my catalog was dwindling. Sony/Tree had been recouping on my indebtedness for three years, and the time was coming when I would need to ask them for an advance. Donna Hilley was president and CEO of Sony/Tree in Nashville, but answered to Marvin Cohn at Sony in New York. To re-sign me, Cohn wanted to offer me an annual advance that would have meant a 60 percent drop in income. My financial world would have collapsed. It made Donna nervous, acting as my go-between with New York. One day I had to sit and wait hours for a meeting with her, and on another day, she saw me coming down the hallway and turned around and ran. Paul Worley, Sony/Tree's senior vice-president of creative, told me he believed in me and was going to stick his neck out for me. Paul was an excellent guitarist, a great record producer, and normally a lovable, congenial guy. But he didn't strike me as really comfortable in a corporate position, and he definitely was not enjoying the experience of sticking his neck out. One day he snapped at me, "Bobby, if we keep on buggin' Marvin about this, he's gonna get pissed off!"

I meditated about what might be the perfect letter to write to Marvin Cohn and got one off to him the next morning. I reminded him of my major track record, told him how much I was writing, and the reaction I was getting on my new songs." He wrote back, "Your message did not fall on deaf ears" and said he wanted to think about it. It worked. He agreed on an amount closer to what I had asked than what he had offered. But I knew this was only a temporary fix and that I needed to start writing hits again. I had to generate enough income to pay off my deep indebtedness to Tree and the IRS, and then make a good living for myself.

One night I was hanging out at Deborah and Rafe's house, The Pink Palace. I expressed a desire to write a song in the vein of the George Strait hit "All My Exes Live in Texas." Rafe said, "Maybe we could write one about a guy who leaves town for a few months, and when he comes back, all his ex-girlfriends have gotten married. They all have new names."

"All my old flames have new names?" I asked.

"Yeah, *exactly*," he said.

The next day I got up and started working on it. I called Rafe, and we wrote it over the phone. Because the title "All My Old Flames Have New Names" was a bit long, we decided to call it "Old Flames With New Names." It was western swing, and we were living in an era in which you could still write that kind of song. The lyrics were sorta comical.

> *I left town two years ago and moved on up to Idaho*
> *But swore that I'd be back again, pick up where I left off, oh man*
> *I left behind some lovely ladies, grown-up sexy Texas babies*
> *I got back in town tonight anticipating much delight*
>
> *I pulled out my black book and called up my old lovers*
> *I got five newlyweds and two expectant mothers*
>
> *All my old flames have new names*
> *There's a lot of girls in town*
> *Who tied the knot and settled down*
> *I thought I'd start a fire with one of my old flames*
> *But they've all got new names*
>
> *My sexy little dirt-road sport is now called Mrs. Davenport*
> *My pretty little black-eyed Susie's now Ms. Susan Van Der Hoosie*
> *Rosie who could blow my mind is sister Rose on channel nine*
> *The wildest lover of my life is now a federal judge's wife*
>
> *They don't want to recognize this old familiar face*
> *I'm just a bad reminder of their wild and woolly days*
>
> *All my old flames have new names* etc.

I made a home tape of the song and took it in to play for my songplugger "point person" at Sony/Tree, Dan Wilson. Dan wasn't overly enthusiastic about the song, but thought it was pretty good and didn't object when I told him that I wanted to include it on my next demo session.

The purpose of a demo session, of course, was to get the songs recorded and make money. A demo was made to sell the song. Hopefully, a demo would sound like a hit record, and the artist would envision it being his or her hit. I had a reputation for making good demos and saw it as an opportunity to hone my skills as an arranger and producer.

Sony/Tree paid for demo sessions up to a certain amount. I used one or two more musicians than many writers did (which ran up the cost) so the overage was charged against my account like an advance.

Somewhere along the way I came to the conclusion that both my singing and playing were too stylized, so I started hiring a piano player and a demo vocalist. I usually got on a mic and sang along with the band so they could hear the song in their headphones while they were recording, then after the tracking session the demo singer put on the permanent or "keeper" vocal.

In 1991, when I demoed "Old Flames With New Names," my piano player of choice was Dennis Burnside, a descendent of Ambrose Burnside, the Union general in the Civil War whose facial hair inspired the word "sideburns." I often added my own keyboard parts (organ, synthesizer strings, etc.) on my sessions after the musicians left.

There was a large roster of great players to choose from (having a lot of respect for musicians, I always called them "players" rather than the Nashville-cute "pickers"). I typically gave Sony/Tree's studio coordinator, Debbie Tenpenney, my list of first and second choices of musicians to call and book. The group might vary from time to time, with one exception: the electric lead guitar, which I always considered to be the superglue on a country recording. I had used Rafe Van Hoy followed by Paul Worley on "lead" until they started making so much money in other endeavors—Rafe writing songs and Paul producing records—that they quit playing sessions. Then in 1981 I started using a twenty-four-year-old Texan, Brent Rowan, on lead guitar. Brent was so good that I started checking with him first to see if he was available before putting together a session and booking other musicians. Generally, for electric guitar there was no one else I wanted to use but Brent, the one exception being Chris Leuzinger who played on all the Garth Brooks records. I typically went into the studio with an arrangement in my head for each song and told the players what I wanted them to play, but I often left a blank space for electric guitar because I knew that Brent would come up with something on his own that would blow me away. He and I worked so well together that we practically read each other's minds. I always made Brent the leader of the session (the union required that every session have a leader, and that the leader be paid twice as much as the other musicians). But the day I demoed "Old Flames With New Names" was an exception to the exception—Brent and

Chris were both booked every day for a month playing master sessions (making real records with recording artists rather than demos). I didn't want to wait a month, so I used a highly recommended guy named Bill Hullett, with whom I was very happy.

"Old Flames . . ." was demoed along with three other songs of mine at the twenty-four-track studio at Sony/Tree on January 30, 1991. This was a three-hour session beginning at 10:00 a.m. After the tracking session, demo singer John Wesley Ryles sang the "keeper" vocals. This process took longer back then than it does now because today's technology enables vocals to be tuned whenever someone hits a sour note. But before the days of vocal tuning, the sound engineer had to "punch in" on the vocal track while the singer replaced an out-of-tune word, phrase, or line. If it wasn't right, we had to do it over and over until it was.

After John sang my songs, it was time for Dennis Wilson (not the Beach Boy of the same name) to sing harmony. I considered Dennis as indispensable as Brent Rowan.

Though he just sang a simple harmony part on "Old Flames . . ." on some songs I had him sing various parts, often doing three parts two times each, creating a six-voice group—and sometimes creating an even larger group. I could ask him to sound like the Jordanaires, the Eagles, the Beach Boys, or 10cc, and he always knew exactly what to do. He wasn't the only singer on Music Row to work sessions as a one-man group, but I thought he was the absolute best. I nicknamed him "The Wizard of Oooohs and Ahhhhs." Everyone sat in awe when they watched Dennis work. I saw one good-looking young female singer develop an instant crush on long, lanky, slow-moving, middle-aged Dennis Wilson because she was so mind-blown with his talent.

John Wesley Ryles and Dennis Wilson would become the premier harmony singers in town in the 1990s, and John eventually would not have time to work demo sessions, only masters (which paid much more money). Dennis, who was a good friend, would continue to work for me on into the twenty-first century when he developed problems with his vocal cords.

The most important part of putting together a session was—and is—the mix, so you might say that the engineer has the most important job. You can have some of the best players in the world, the best singer, and the best song, but if the mix is bad the whole thing will sound like crap (and of course the mix won't matter much if the song is weak or the performance is bad). The first-rate engineer on this date was Ernie Winfrey, an old friend who engineered the Paul McCartney Nashville sessions in 1974. Today everything is recorded digitally on a computer, and a recording can have a thousand different parts if you want to spend that much time on it. But at Sony/Tree in 1991 everything was recorded on large reels of tape with a maximum of twenty-four tracks. Ernie's job was to commit everything to tape, then later see that each track—the vocal track, the drum track, the piano track, etc.—had the right effect on it (such as reverb or delay), the right kind of equalization or EQ (low-end, high-end—think bass and treble), and that the volume level of each voice and instrument be just right, to strike a good balance. After Ernie spent a good deal of time with each song, I came in and *closed* (or *closed down*) the mix with him; I would ask him to make so-and-so louder, or such-and-such dryer (less reverb), or any number of changes. After we did all that, we had the *final mix*. By the wee hours of the next morning, we had mixes on all four songs. The difference between cutting a demo and a master was time; much more time was and is spent on a master. (Looking back from 2015, full demo sessions are quite similar to the early 1990s one I have described here, but more and more the full demo session is being replaced by a tech-sharp song-writer stacking drum loops and a few instrumental tracks in a home studio—or even on a computer in an office or bedroom—resulting in what serves as a demo and, in some cases, part of a master recording that finds its way to radio.) Two days later I took the demo to the second floor at Sony/Tree—the creative department—where it was well received by the professional staff (songpluggers) and where I signed a contract on each song.

A couple of weeks after that, Dan Wilson and Walter Campbell had a *pitch meeting* with producer Mark Wright who was looking for songs for his hot new artist, Mark Chesnutt. Both pluggers had taken along a few songs, and Walter included one that he was particularly fond of: "Old Flames with New Names." Mark Wright put the song *on hold*, which meant he was go-ing to play it for Chesnutt, until which time Sony/Tree would not play it for anyone else. Within a few days Wright played it for Chesnutt who liked it and wanted to record it. The song then had an *artist hold,* so we wouldn't further pitch it unless Mark and Mark backed out and didn't record it.

Several weeks later Donna Hilley told me that Mark Wright had asked if we would be willing to change the title from "Old Flames with New Names" to "Old Flames Have New Names." I told her I liked our way better, and that I would need to check with Rafe. Donna said she had already told them it was okay to change it. I wasn't very happy with that but I needed the cut.

That next week they cut the song! Rafe and I went out and had drinks with the two Marks after the session. Chesnutt, a genuine country boy from East Texas, asked, "Where'd you come up with that name Van Der Hoosie?" The song was officially recorded, meaning Sony/Tree would issue a license giving MCA Records the exclusive right to release the song before anyone else.

I was excited in the summer when I heard the song would be a single, probably the first single from Chesnutt's forthcoming album. In the fall I would have a hissy fit when I heard that it wouldn't be the first single after all. In January of 1992 word came down that they had changed their minds still again, and it would soon be released as the album's debut song.

MCA would be paying the new royalty rate, 6.25 cents per unit sold (as compared to 9.1 cents twenty years later), the writers' share being half of that, 3.125 cents a unit. Since there were two writers, the rate came down to 1.5625, or a little over a penny-and-a-half, that I would receive for each album sold.

So even if it were a million-selling album, I would earn only $15,000 from *sales*. By 1991 sales (called "mechanicals") were no longer the primary source of income for songwriters, because of the decline of vinyl record sales (and more recently audio cassette sales). CDs were the new thing, and CD singles were not practical, so singles sales had practically disappeared. By the 1990s, a hit song wouldn't make much more income from sales than any other song on the same album. The *real* money from a hit single came from radio air-play, the *performance* royalty that writers received from ASCAP, SESAC, or, in my case, from BMI. If "Old Flames . . ." was a hit, the money from sales would be a drop in the bucket compared to my BMI checks.

Most writers with my history got to share in the publishing; in other words, instead of getting fifty cents on every dollar that the publisher re-ceived on the song, the writer would get seventy-five cents. I didn't share in the publishing because every time I negotiated a new contract my financial neediness dictated that I opt for money up front instead. It would be sev-eral more years before I had a "co-pub deal," which amounts to a 50 percent increase in income above that which a writer would otherwise receive. Of course, some writers had their own little publishing companies and received everything, but then they had the responsibility of doing all their own pitch-ing and record-keeping, plus they had the burden of hiring someone to do the administration of foreign royalties.

In late February, "Old Flames Have New Names" would debut in the country charts and peak in April at #5 in *Billboard*, #4 in *Radio & Records*, and #1 in *Cash Box*. Though *Billboard* was considered the "bible" of music industry trade publications, Donna Hilley would give us a #1 party based on the *Cash Box* position. She would say, "We'll throw a party if it went to #1 *at the bus station*!" About that time I would be one of those working the phones at the Cerebral Palsy telethon, sitting next to Mark Chesnutt and laughing myself silly as the TV producer kept asking Mark what song he was going to sing and Mark kept telling him "I'll Think of Something"—the producer not knowing that was the title of Mark's next single, and Mark not understand-ing that the producer didn't know that.

"Old Flames Have New Names." Not a monster but a hit. It wouldn't come close to getting me out of my tremendous debt, but it would end a nine-year cold spell and remove what was beginning to feel like a jinx.

But in the late summer of 1991, a few months before the release of the Chesnutt record, despite the high hopes, I had no absolute assurance of a forthcoming hit single. My crystal ball didn't work very often, and my rare glimpses into the future seemed to pertain to other people's lives, not my own. I was doing quite a bit of writing, always hopeful that something good was going to happen. My publishing company was banking on me, and I didn't want to let them down. More than that, I couldn't *afford* to let them down.

I was, as always, doing some of my own songplugging. Steve Buckingham, a well-known executive and producer, had made much out of the fact that he ran songs by his dog, and if the dog got excited he considered that a very good sign. So one day while mixing a song I had demoed, engineer Mike Bradley and I added a dog whistle, a sound so high that only canine ears could hear it. I left the song for Buckingham who called and told me that he really liked the song and was putting it on hold. Nobody ever recorded it, so I figured Steve's dog must have changed its mind.

One warm afternoon, I had an appointment to play a song for Tammy Wynette at her house. Her husband, George Richey, met me at the door and said, "Come on in, Bobby, Tammy'll be right back. She's on a tour bus." He then explained to me that occasionally when the Gray Line bus stopped in front of their mansion, Tammy would run out and hop on, giving the tourists a thrill as she rode around the block with them.

At summer's end, I decided I was going to take a September road trip to visit my daughter in Los Angeles and then swing down to San Diego where my friend Angela, the video editor, lived.

Lauren (Jeep) and her musician boyfriend, Jonathan Weseley, were living in North Hollywood in "the valley" with Maura Hanlon, Lauren's best friend from her AMDA days in New York. In the nearly three years that Lauren had lived in LA, she had worked at various jobs including nanny work for celebrities (a couple of times for the Spielbergs) and had been pursuing her music and acting careers. I always said that she was so multitalented that it split her focus; she could write, sing, act, dance, draw, you name it. She had gotten a few acting jobs, the biggest break happening the year before when she got a speaking role as Lindsay Wagner's kid sister in the made-for-TV movie, *Shattered Dreams*.

I have a video of a memorable night: Jeep singing a great rockin' song she had written called "Don't Turn Away" as Jon, the good-looking sleepy-eyed boy with long black hair, backs her up on guitar, a little grin on his face; Maura lending her wonderful voice to "Send in the Clowns" as I make goofy faces every time I hit a wrong chord on the keyboard; and Jeep's big Siamese cat Wicky doing his little stunt of pushing the water cooler lever with his paw and catching the water in his mouth.

I was looking forward to seeing Angela in San Diego. It had been several years since her lawyer ex-boyfriend had found her a job at CBS in LA (to get her out of Nashville and away from his new fiancée). Over the years Angela and I had come close to starting something, though I always felt that she would definitely be a headache and maybe a heartache. Earlier in the year she turned up in Nashville for a few days, going through a divorce, and pregnant. Angela was beautiful, brainy, funny, and affectionate. She was also unpredictable, tactless, alcoholic, and probably bipolar. And now she was a mother! I went shopping in Beverly Hills, looking for something special for her thirtieth birthday. Angela was a Frank Sinatra fan (unusual for someone that young). I found her the perfect gift at an antique store: a very nice silver and silk comb, brush, and mirror set from the 1940s that included an attractive frame holding a picture of a young Sinatra. I also got a little bear for her three-week-old baby girl, Kaella.

Angela's stepfather had been a career Navy man, so she was raised in San Diego. She also had an aunt and uncle living there, and moved back there to be close to them when it came time for the baby to be born. She was actually living in El Cajon, a few miles inland from San Diego, in a run-down apartment complex; but typical of Angela, the interior of her living quarters looked immaculate. Kaella was a beautiful little baby with wise old eyes. Angela was obsessively attentive to the baby, but she got unrelenting lectures from me about smoking around the child and continuing to drink, though she was nursing. After all, I was supposed to be Kaella's godfather.

We talked about finally having a relationship more serious than friendship. As we discussed it, I knew I was crazy to be doing so. We had a wonderful couple of days together, and her Aunt Judy and Uncle Jim were very nice. Angela told me she was sad that I was leaving and asked me to please stay another day. I told her I needed to get back, but let her have some money to help out with her move to Nashville.

I thought a lot about Angela on my trip back across the continent. I referred to her in my journal as a "cuckoo bird" but she was a cuckoo bird that I was very fond of. When it was time for her to arrive three weeks later, I was ready for her.

I picked up Angela and Kaella at the airport on a pleasant evening in early October. I thought the baby had grown amazingly in three weeks, and thought Angela looked ultra pretty. She rented a car and I followed them to the home of Bob and Sherry Skillen. Sherry was her best girlfriend. They lived in a ranch-style house in a middle-class neighborhood not far from the mighty Cumberland River in East Nashville. We left Kaella with Bob and Sherry and went out for sushi.

A couple of days later we hooked up for a little while. Then two days after that, on a Saturday, I went to Bob and Sherry's to pick up Angela. She had gone to the store. When she returned, she said something to Bob and Sherry but didn't even look at me or acknowledge my presence. When she went in to see about the baby, I told them what they could tell Angela to do, then left in a huff. When I got home (I owned no cell phone yet), she was on my answering machine twice. When I called her back, she was crying: "I got my hair all fixed up for you." We both apologized and I went back. Because Kaella had a cold, Angela wanted to take her to the ER at Vanderbilt Children's Hospital. She was drinking vodka miniatures on the way there. She started freaking out every time the baby cried, and she got very upset at the hospital because waiting for a doctor was taking so long. She finally grabbed up the baby and said, "Let's go." She insisted that I stop at a little shopping center, where she went into a liquor store and got a not-so-miniature bottle of vodka, then ran into a supermarket to buy some shrimp, which she said she was going to fix for dinner.

In East Nashville, we got on the wrong road, a street named Hemlock, which dead-ended into the river and became a boat landing. The Cumberland River is deep and dark and wide, with swift currents. "Hey," she joked, "this would be a great place to commit suicide."

Back at Bob and Sherry's house, Angela continued to drink as she cooked shrimp for everybody. After her hosts went to bed, she and I tried to write a song but she was too drunk, so we just hung out. When the baby woke up crying, Angela got terribly upset but calmed down after Kaella went back to sleep.

"I'm afraid I might hurt my baby," she said, sending chills down my spine. "But I love her too much to give her away." This girl was in no condition to be mothering; she badly needed help.

I asked her, "How would you feel about taking Kaella down to Alabama this next week and letting your sister take care of her for a few days? Just temporarily, while we see what we can do to make you feel better."

"Oh, I'd love that, Brat," she said, calling me the goofy name she'd always called me. She seemed relieved and happy, and fell sound asleep.

The next day, late Sunday afternoon, I took her to a nearby Western Sizzler for dinner. We made plans for the following Wednesday night; she was going to come to my house. We also talked about driving Kaella down to northern Alabama on Thursday morning, to stay with Angela's mom or sister.

As we sat across the table from each other, Angela seemed calm and sane and looked beautiful. She was a tall girl, with big blue eyes and honey-blonde hair. When she wasn't freaked out she was very funny. And I had played enough Scrabble and brain-teaser games with her over the years to know how scary smart she was. Though she was a first-rate video editor by profession, her biggest aspiration was to be a validated songwriter. She had once given a song idea to a couple of successful Nashville writers. They wrote the song, and part of Angela's premise became the title. The most important part of a song is the title line—the idea—so she should have received one-third on a three-way song, but they gave her only 10 percent. She was very excited when a popular country-pop group recorded the song, but it was a major disappointment when she learned that only the other two writers were credited on the album. That album—actually a cassette—was her proudest possession, even though the song that she initiated didn't even have her name on it.

After I paid the Western Sizzler's cashier, I turned and looked at Angela. My eyes locked on hers, and her big blue eyes locked on mine. We stood there staring at each other in freeze-frame for what seemed like a very long time, but it may have been only ten seconds. Her eyes were wide and unblinking, giving her expression a hint of amazement; her mouth was slightly open, making just a little bit of a smile. It was a look I would never forget. I didn't know it then and I don't think she did either, but we were probably saying goodbye.

On the way to Bob and Sherry's, she was vowing to lay off the vodka. I was telling her what a pleasure she was to be around when she was sober. "I'm not going to let you down, honey" she said as she squeezed my hand. "There I go calling you honey again." She was laughing at herself for coming up with a new word, "reluthless," which she said was a combination of relentless and ruthless. When we got to their house, we kissed and I said, "I'll see you Wednesday."

The next night, Monday, October 14, I heard Angela on my answering machine: "Hey Brat, it's me, Angela." I picked up, and she told me she had a dynamite song idea. She also told me she'd had a great interview that afternoon at the very popular (but now defunct) Nashville Network, where she was applying for a video editor position. She asked what I was doing, and I told her I was waiting to hear from Deborah and Rafe about possibly meeting up with them.

"Can we get together and write tomorrow?" she asked.

"I'm in the studio tomorrow with Joy White and Ernie Winfrey."

"Could I come by? I'd love to say hi to Ernie." I could tell by the slight slur that she had started drinking.

"Sure, if it's okay with Joy. I'll ask her . . ." My voice was cut off by the beep of another call coming through. Angela said, "Well, there's Deborah and Rafe," and hung up. Later I called back and Sherry said Angela had of course gotten drunker, called someone, dressed, handed her twenty dollars and said, "I'm leaving." Bob had gone out to her rental car to try to talk her out of it, but she took off.

About 10:10 p.m., Deborah came by with our mutual friend Chari Pirtle. While they were at the house, I got a call. It was Angela's Aunt Judy in San Diego, and she was hysterical. *"Something's happened to Angela!* She's in Memorial Hospital and I think she has the baby with her." I was in shock, but I managed to tell her that she had left Bob and Sherry's house without Kaella, that the baby must be okay. Apparently Aunt Judy's number was the first contact information that had been found. Probably the rental car agency had Bob and Sherry's number and got in touch with them, because when I called the Skillen residence Bob said, "You'd better go to Memorial Hospital right now. Angela drove her car into the river. She's hurt real bad. They're keeping her alive with CPR." She had driven to Hemlock Street, the dead-end road to the river that we had accidentally come upon two nights before. A man and his wife had seen her sitting in her car, and pulled up alongside her and asked if she needed help. She said "Remember my name, it's Angela Arkle," then took off, rounded the curve, gunned the accelerator, and headed for the river. The car went out 150 feet before sinking into the deep waters.

I told Deborah and Chari they didn't need to go with me but they insisted. I was glad they did. I was shaking all over, so Chari drove Rafe and Deborah's SUV. We went to Memorial Hospital in Madison, just north of East Nashville. When I told the lady at the front desk why I was there, she motioned to a man who introduced himself to me as a Metro Police chaplain. I asked if Angela was gone, and he nodded yes. He asked me if I would identify the body. I followed him to a room where they unzipped a blue plastic bag. I thought why did they zip her up like that? What if she were still alive? That would suffocate her. It was difficult to talk, but I whispered that it was her. I knew beyond a shadow of a doubt that she had changed her mind and wanted to live once she hit the water, because her face was frozen in an expression of sheer terror.

The rest of the night was a blur: police officers were questioning us all at Bob and Sherry's house; I went to Deborah and Rafe's; I made a lot of phone calls. That night I wrote in my journal: "Angela Carolyn Thornton Arkle died young tonight."

For the next two days I went through the motions of keeping Music Row commitments, moving around in slow motion in that weary, dreary land of dull, unyielding pain that only the grieving know. Paul Worley was in his van, in a hurry to go somewhere, when I told him; he turned off the ignition and slumped in his seat, saying "She was a sweet girl." When I told Paul's estranged wife Jessica, she started bawling, "She was a good kid." When I told Mike Kosser, he said he used to call her "Sunshine." Those not close enough to her to have seen her fighting off demons remembered her that way: sweet girl, good kid, "Sunshine."

Angela was emotionally ill to start with. More recently she was suffering from postpartum depression. And she was an alcoholic. One night she got drunk and killed herself, plain and simple. And profoundly sad.

On Thursday, the day I was going to take Angela and Kaella down to Alabama, her friend Sherry and I were driving down there for her funeral. Sherry said she had gotten a call from someone at the Nashville Network that morning; they were trying to get in touch with Angela to tell her she got the job.

I don't know what the cynical Angela would have thought of the traditional Christian funeral. I know she once told me that she didn't want to be buried in Alabama. The girl in the casket wasn't as beautiful as Angela. It was crossing my mind that the people who prepared her didn't know her. Athens, Alabama, was her stepfather's hometown where he retired with his wife after his military career, but Angela was a California girl. Sherry opened up her purse and pulled out the cassette that included the song Angela co-wrote but got no credit for, and placed it in the coffin with her. Long after the splitting up of the singing group, long after the coming and going of many things, this little tape would remain enshrined deep beneath the ground in Limestone County, Alabama.

Sparky, who had liked Angela very much, was at the funeral with her husband J. R. They lived just down the road a piece. J. R. had to go to work after the funeral, so Sparky rode to the cemetery with Sherry and me.

Would Angela and I have sustained a great romantic relationship? It's very

Angela Thornton Arkle, still missed

doubtful, but I loved her nevertheless. I grieved for a long time and miss the lovable cuckoo bird to this day.

I would not actually see Kaella again until the summer of 2009 soon after her graduation from high school when she made the decision to connect with me, her godfather. However, in the mid-1990s I would see a picture of her when she was a little girl. It was mailed to me by the lady who was raising her—her grandmother, Angela's mom. The eerily close resemblance of Kaella and Angela would inspire a song that Sammy Kershaw recorded: "I Saw You Today."

> *Despite all the distance and time*
> *And the changes that I have gone through*
> *You never strayed far from my mind*
> *And I never stopped hoping once more I'd see you*
>
> *Then I saw you today*
> *In the backyard at play*
> *Baby-blue eyes, blonde hair in the wind*
> *She's you all over again*
> *Although you went away*
> *I saw you today*

I used to wish on a star
And I used to send up a prayer
To Heaven where I know you are
That someday I'd see you up there or somewhere

Then I saw you today
In the backyard at play
Baby-blue eyes, blonde hair in the wind
She's you all over again
Although you went away
I saw you
I saw you today

When I went down to Auburndale over the Christmas holidays, my brother and I found ourselves at that dreaded juncture where we had to acknowledge that our mother, at eighty-four years old, was no longer able to take care of herself without assistance. The first step was home care, hiring people to stay with her. And fortunately, she lived just down the street from my brother and his wife, Jo Ann.

I realized that her driving days were numbered when she told me on the phone a couple of weeks before: "I went into Dr. Tanner's office this morning to get a shot, and when I went back out to the parking lot, there was a man lying down on the pavement underneath a motorcycle, and he said that I'd run over him. Have you ever heard of anything so silly?"

Lauren and boyfriend Jonathan had flown in to Nashville from LA and driven down with me on this visit. One night poor Jon had to sit through two hours of my mom's videos of her ballroom dancing. We were all relieved when she finally drifted off to sleep.

When we got back to Nashville, I gave myself a Christmas present: the Bearcat Scanner. I had owned a police-band radio years before and enjoyed hearing the real-life cops and robbers, as well as people talking on ship-to-shore phones on houseboats. But I discovered that the Bearcat picked up cell phone conversations at both ends, including land lines as long as there was one cellular phone involved. Never dawning on me that it might be illegal, I found myself sometimes tuning in to this little window on the world, mesmerized by the conversations I was hearing.

One time I heard a man tell his wife, "Have you listened to our answering machine today? You can't hardly understand a word anybody says. It's all gullible." When one lady told her boyfriend there would be no more sex unless he started using condoms, he whined, "But baby, when I wear a rubber it makes my dick go down!" When I heard some guys planning a robbery, I felt helpless because I didn't know the location. Most cops sounded honest and brave, but one night I heard two police officers planning to viciously beat up some guy they didn't like. I heard a couple of African American policemen discussing Michael Jackson: "His nostrils are so small," one said. "How does the man *breathe*?" I got the impression that blacks had more phone sex than whites. I realized that a gay man talking to his best friend about his relationship problems was no different from a heterosexual man doing the same thing. I heard a wife's "what-can-I-get-you-from-Kroger" call turn into a discussion about her lack of affection, a depressing hour-long going-nowhere discourse in a grocery store parking lot that finally concluded with her asking again what he would like from the store and him saying "maybe Apple Newtons." Even worse than that was the girl who told her boyfriend "I was really tempted to crash into a telephone pole on my way home." A conversation that truly touched me was between a man (perhaps forty) and his mother (maybe late sixties) in which the son opened up about sexual problems he was having with his wife, and I envied the sprinkling of profanities and the mother's invitation to "come over to the house, son, and let's open up a bottle of whiskey and talk about it," wishing I had that kind of easy and open communication with my mom—then learning that the guy's mother was terminally ill with cancer.

I swore I would turn off the scanner if I ever heard someone I knew. I never heard any profitable information such as a song idea or an insider stock market tip; I never happened upon a crime that I could have prevented; and I never obtained any information that would have led to the arrest of a criminal or a traitor (which I would have promptly reported to the proper authorities). When I was told that it might be illegal to even listen to cell phone conversations, I quit doing it. It only worked on analog phones, so within a few years, when most cell phones were digital, cellular eavesdropping would become a thing of the past. This was as it should be because no one needs to be listening to someone else's private conversation. I'm sure the Nashville woman whose husband overheard her talking to her lover felt that way. But damn, it was entertaining!

As a side note: a close friend urged me not to tell the story of the Bearcat Scanner for fear that my reputation might be besmirched if people knew that I had listened to other people's phone conversations. But if I display only my beauty moles and hide all my ugly warts, then I'm not being true to telling the truth. I'd rather have a good book than a good reputation.

In 1992 I met several young women who had an impact on my life in varying degrees. One was Chely Wright, an attractive twenty-one-year-old singer from Kansas who came to my house with Grand Ole Opry star Porter Wagoner on a song search. Porter was acting in the role of mentor-manager-producer. As I got to know Chely pretty well, she told me she was freaking out because Porter, whom she considered grandfatherly, seemed to have a big thing for her. So I called her up and did my best Porter Wagoner country accent, saying "Chely, it's Porter, honey, and I'm in your neighborhood and comin' by your place." She gasped. When I told her it was me, she screamed,

"You scared me to death!" Little did I know back in those days that Chely was probably turned off by Porter's gender as much as his age.

I met Lana Beaudet in Dan Wilson's office at Sony/Tree. I was there with Billy Burnette to play Dan a song we had just finished writing. Billy was a member of Fleetwood Mac and the son of rockabilly singer Dorsey Burnette. He was dark and strikingly handsome, and I was used to seeing girls go crazy over him, so I was shocked when I later got word that good-looking twenty-three-year-old Lana (two years younger than my daughter) was interested in *me*. When we went out, she seemed to really like me at first, but was taken aback when I told her that she reminded me of a friend of mine who had committed suicide a few months before. Taking her home, I ran a red light and she asked me to let her drive. End of crush. She told a friend of hers, "He said I reminded him of a dead girl, then he almost killed me!"

And then there was Tami Jones. I first met her in December of 1991, at Mark Wright's office where she was temporarily employed. A couple of months later she called me at Sony/Tree and asked if she could interview me about "Old Flames Have New Names" for a local magazine. The interview led to lunch, which led to me catching her karaoke gig at Gilley's near Music Row (she sang great!), which led to my inviting her to write with me. I might have looked in the mirror and said, "You're deceiving yourself in thinking that this beautiful twenty-seven-year-old blonde is interested in you," but that *is* what I was thinking.

Tami came to my house where we attempted to write a song. We decided that we had a lot in common—for instance, we both doodled tornado funnels. She called me a few days later and told me there was a possibility that she had cancer of the cervix. She was awaiting test results. While on the phone with me she got the call from her doctor, and three minutes later clicked back in softly crying—the test had come back positive. Her mother, who was a nurse, wanted her to come back home to Oklahoma for surgery. Before she left, I took her several books on positive affirmations and holistic and spiritual healing..

Tami's surgery proved successful. During her convalescence we had long phone conversations every day. She told me that her marriage had been in serious trouble before she got sick, and she had since made up her mind that she wanted it to end.

When Tami came back to Nashville in the warm days of late spring, she told me she couldn't and wouldn't date me until she and her husband separated. He soon moved out and I was both excited and scared half to death about my first date with Tami Lou Jones. I had just gotten my first cell phone (when I'd recently told Tanya Tucker that I didn't have a cell, she said "Well, you ain't shit!") and talked to Tami all the way from my house to her apartment. I saw her pretty face looking out her window for me as I drove up. Her cute and lovable little boy, Saxon, was the oldest two-year-old I'd ever met. I quickly hit it off with Saxon and their tiny toy poodle, Prissy.

Surprising Tammy Wynette at the Harlan Howard Birthday
Bash, September 1990

With "Texas Tornado" Tami Jones, October 1993

Tami had a great plaintive singing voice and an unusual style, a unique way of trailing off at the end of certain notes. I tailor-made some songs for her and did a demo session. Paul Worley thought she was a wonderful country singer, and took a copy of the demo to MCA executive (and great producer) Tony Brown, who was likewise excited about what he heard. He said he wanted to hear her sing live.

I booked some of the best players in town, the ones I used on demo sessions. Tami's showcase would be at 12th & Porter, a popular night spot named after its street address. Lauren had moved back to Nashville because Paul Worley liked her writing and signed her to a deal at Sony/Tree, so she worked with Tami on choreography for the show. Even though Tony Brown was coming with MCA label head Bruce Hinton, I thought I'd try to get all the birds with one stone by inviting every label head in Nashville. In fact, I sent out invitations to every human being I knew who lived within driving distance.

We did a sound check and rehearsal at 12th & Porter the night before, a Sunday. Everything sounded marvelous, just perfect. I had hired the best sound engineer in town for the show, but everything sounded so great at rehearsal that I decided to use the *sound-check* guy, the club's regular engineer.

On November 14, the night of the showcase, when they opened up the doors to the huge performance room of the club, people came teeming in like an army of giant ants. The place was packed. In came Tony Brown and Bruce Hinton clad in expensive-looking overcoats, looking every bit the power brokers that they were. Practically everyone I invited showed up, including the music label people.

Although the music had sounded great the night before, the dynamic had changed from an empty room to one that was packed like a sardine can. The previous day's sound levels would not work on this crowded night. Tami couldn't hear her voice in the sound monitor, and the band guys were basically hearing a blaring cacophony. No seasoned superstar could have dealt with it any better than Tami did. She handled it professionally and sang with confidence, and despite the terrible circumstances she sounded good, but it wasn't the stunning performance that Tony and Bruce had heard on her demos. I blamed myself. I should have stuck with the first-rate engineer. And it was stupid of me to invite every label head in town. It was like having the president, vice president, speaker of the house, and everyone in the line of presidential succession all traveling on the same plane—what if it crashes? You lose them all. Our plane, filled with all the gods of Music Row, went down at 12th & Porter.

Tami was a bit discouraged about her career setback, but we forged ahead. I wrote a song, "Strangers," and she sang it so phenomenally on the demo that I felt certain we could get her a deal with it. But the ill-fated showcase seemed to be working against us for the time being. No deal was forthcoming for Tami so Paul Worley recorded the song on a new female singer he was producing named Martina McBride.

I was getting high marks from my publisher. Sony/Tree had some newer pluggers—Jim Scherer, Greg Dorschell, and Tracy Gershon—but most of my dealings were with old standbys Dan Wilson and Walter Campbell. I also continued to pitch songs myself. One of my most delightful afternoons of 1992 was playing songs for (and drinking whiskey with) Ronnie Milsap, who had thirty-five #1 hits behind him but none ahead of him.

Over the holidays, Lauren and I went to Florida in separate cars and visited my mother in her new home, an assisted-living facility on pretty Lake Howard Drive in Winter Haven, a few miles from Auburndale. Though Mom missed her house, she seemed to realize the wisdom of living in a cute apartment, having nurses if she needed one, eating her meals in a nice big dining room, and participating in planned activities and making new friends. Her lights were definitely dimming, but she seemed to grasp how her money was being handled and invested. Several months before, I had offered to take her to Nashville and find an assisted living facility for her there, but she wanted to stay in Florida. I had also suggested that Paul and I try to find her a roommate, but she didn't seem too keen on that idea either. She asked Lauren and me to take her to her house, and when we went there she cried. It was her little dream home that she had built in 1972, after my father passed away. I flashed back to a previous visit with her there, the two of us sitting on the dock as a beautiful multicolored sunset cast its reflection on the gently rippling waters of Lake Ariana. I asked her why, since she was a robust sixty-four back when Dad died, she never remarried. I will never forget her reply: "Once you've had the best, nothing else is good enough."

Jeep drove back to Nashville, and I drove to the Orlando airport to pick up Tami, who had been visiting her parents in Enid, Oklahoma. I showed off my *hot* young girlfriend to my middle-aged boyhood friends, and I showed off my *sweet* young girlfriend to my mom. We had a wonderful three days, far from Nashville and a couple of issues that seemed to pull us apart.

When we got back to Nashville, I learned that John Anderson had been recording a new album and was doing his final session for the project that very day. I was disappointed because I had wanted to pitch a particular song to him but didn't know he was recording so soon. It had taken me by surprise. The song was "Nashville Tears," which may have been partly inspired by Angela's suicide ("That old Cumberland River, so deep and so wide / Is nothing more and nothing less than Nashville tears"). When I had demoed it a few months before, none of the songpluggers seemed to like it very much, but I so strongly believed in it for John that I called the studio where he was recording and got him on the phone. It was unusual for me to be that aggressive or ballsy. When I told him that I had a song he needed to hear, he said it was probably too late to get it on the album they had been working on—they had already picked out the songs they were going to record that day—but he would be glad to listen to it for the next project. I immediately ran it by the studio anyway and handed it to John's doctor who often hung out with his famous patient. Amazingly, John and his producer, James Stroud, listened to my song that day and recorded it right there on the spot. It was one of the finest cuts I'd ever gotten. Both John and his manager, Bobby Roberts, lobbied hard to make the record a single because of the strong reaction from radio, but BNA label head Ric Pepin would fight it tooth and nail. Years later, I would run into long-haired John and tell him I'd heard that his former label head was chairman of the Lung Cancer Foundation of America. John would drawl, "Well, I hope he knows more about that than he does about runnin' a label, or there's gonna be a bunch of *dead* fuckers out there."

While we were out of town, Sony/Tree took up temporary (and rather cramped) residence in the Greenwood Building on Edgehill Avenue, on the southern end of Music Row, while seriously remodeling the "Taco Bell Building," inside and out.

I kept plugging away at my career and working with Tami on hers. One warm evening in June, she and I went to dinner at Applebee's. When we came out of the restaurant there was a big guy standing by the car—Tami's red Mercury Tracer—complaining about it being over the edge of the parking space. His wife and small child were in the car next to Tami's and his wife was pleading, "Get in the car, Glee-yun." Glen was pretty much in my face, so I told him that his point had been made and asked him to get in his car and move on.

"Don't lecture me like I'm some little kid," he said.

"Well *you're* lecturing *us*. You've made your point, so go on and leave us alone."

Glen, who seemed to have had a little too much to drink, let loose with a stream of expletives.

"You shouldn't be talking like that in front of your child," Tami snapped.

"Shut up, you fuckin' bitch," Glen said.

I was so infuriated that he would say that to her that I forgot about his size, grabbed him around the neck, and pushed him up against the Applebee's building. It was just my luck to have attacked the Karate Kid. His fingers gouged my eyes, causing me to lose my grip on his neck. Then he picked me up and started body-bashing Tami's car with me. The car looked like it had been run into by another car, and I had several broken and dislocated ribs, one of them sticking into my lung. Tami sprayed his face with mace. He started to lunge toward her, but his wife was now out of the car screaming at the top of her voice, *"Glee-yun, get in the car right now!"* I was on the ground, and they may have thought I was dead, because Glen did get in the car and they took off—but not before Tami had written down the license number.

Tami rushed me to the ER at Vanderbilt Hospital. She said I was her hero. I thought *she* had been heroic. I had been stupid! I decided if I had it to do over, I would not have said anything in the first place, just gotten in the car and shut the door. We could have driven away with all my ribs in place.

I was bedridden for days and unable to drive for weeks. Tami was then working as a dental assistant, but took several days off from her job to be my nurse. After she went back to work, Lauren and Jonathan (who was in town from LA visiting Lauren) looked after me and drove me around. Instead of pressing criminal charges, I hired a good lawyer and got a settlement, more or less giving Glen a bill. At that time singer Bobby Bare had been taking me and a couple of other hit songwriters out on the road with him to sing our songs; it was fun, and we were getting paid well. I billed Glen for the several shows that he caused me to miss, for my medical expenses, and for body work on Tami's car. He took out a loan to pay me. On our day in court, he realized that I was in the music business and got it in his head that I was some kind of celebrity. "That there was a bad deal," he said about what he had done to me.

"Are you apologizing to me, Glen?" I asked.

"Well, yeah, that there was a bad deal, I shouldn't uh did it."

Glen never could have coughed up enough bucks to compensate me justly for the misery he had caused. Nor could it ever have been enough to restore me to fiscal health. I was riding in the same rough waters in the same old leaky financial boat. I was once more in the position of having to crawl to my publisher, and I was so humiliated at the thought of it that I did something I had vowed not to do: I went to Curly and asked him for a loan. He never hesitated.

One November day I got an idea for a song that would lead me to the beginning of some very positive changes in my life. Though Tami was raised in Oklahoma, she was born in Texas, and she was fascinated with tornadoes, sometimes wishing she had gone into storm-chasing as a profession. So I got the idea of "Texas Tornado." I was also thinking about the fact that we had a relationship that was sometimes stormy. This slightly mid-tempo ballad wasn't literally about Tami and me, but that was what inspired it.

Typically, I would get a song idea at night, then literally sleep on it and wake up with the song pouring out of me. After breakfast (and sometimes before) I would go down in the basement to my music room and sit down at the piano or electronic keyboard. I would usually work it out pretty quickly, then get stuck for the last line or maybe the entire last verse, then rack my brain trying to come up with something that would work. If I got up and started pacing around the room, that was a sure sign that I was close, that something was on the way.

But "Texas Tornado" wasn't typical. I got the idea one night and sat down and wrote it right then. The next day one thing was bothering me: I had the line "I'm like a tumbleweed in the wild West Texas wind." Were there actually a lot of tumbleweeds in western Texas? I called a couple of agricultural colleges out there and learned that there were indeed. I had a demo session on the books for a couple of days later, so the song was demoed while it was still a baby. Though Dan Wilson liked it, none of the other songpluggers did. I thought it was one of my better melodies. There was much made in those days of Harlan Howard's call for "three chords and the truth." This song was eleven chords and partly true.

After going to see my mom for Christmas, I dropped Jeep off at the Orlando airport and began a very long drive toward Enid, Oklahoma, where Tami had been spending the holidays with her parents, Paul and Betty Spruill. I had a great time with her folks. Then Tami and I headed for the state of Tennessee, and the year of 1994.

We had one major rub between us that would cause me to lose her eventually, and had I been more accommodating I probably wouldn't have. After losing her, *then* I was willing to do anything to get her back, but it was too late. She had made up her mind to move on. She was a beautiful young woman, and there were guys standing in line waiting for her. Despite our differences, I would miss this sweet and funny girl for a long time. The saddest part of all may have been that I had grown so close to her little boy, Saxon. Tami left behind her pretty long-haired cat, Tiger Lily, who had long ago become a sister and companion to my Siamese cat, Bangkok.

Just as Sparky had met and married a great guy a few years before, and Sue Powell had met and married a nice young lawyer the previous year, Tami would meet and marry a wonderful man a few years hence. Sparky would have a loving partner to care for her when she developed health problems. Sue and her husband would have two adorable and talented children. Tami, who was all about family and animals, would be with a man who had two children around Saxon's age, and they would live in a beautiful house in the country with a little lake and plenty of acreage to accommodate a menagerie of creatures ranging from domestic to barnyard to wild. I think all three women ended up better-matched than they would have been with me. All three women would remain close friends of mine for many years to come.

One thing that helped take the sting out of the breakup with Tami was the reemergence of Deborah Allen. She had been in my life for many years, but as a part of a team: Rafe and Deborah, Deborah and Rafe. Now they were divorced, and there was a new man in her life: Raymond Hicks. Raymond was in the process of getting a divorce, and Deborah understood that everyone has to go through that process at his or her own pace, especially when, as in Raymond's case, there was a child involved. They were seeing each other, but they couldn't live together as a couple yet. So while she was "waitin' for Raymond," we renewed our friendship and got closer than ever. We had a lot in common, but the most powerful bond was music. Deborah was a gifted and energized co-writer, and I loved collaborating with her. Her musicianship was as good as her riveting voice: she was a solid acoustic guitar player who had a pounding piano left hand that I envied. But it was understood that she was Raymond's girl. I was glad just to get to hang out with her. Still, I wrote in my journal: "If Deborah didn't have a boyfriend, I think I'd apply for the position (*especially* for the *position*)."

In the summer of 1994, Sony/Tree moved back into their permanent home, which had undergone a radical makeover. They used the skeleton and foundation of the old building upon which they built a structure more in harmony with the neighborhood—and the region. Stucco was replaced with brick. To these eyes, it seemed to be a combination of classic and modern, and it reminded me of a bank. It definitely looked more corporate. The first floor housed a large conference room and a new, improved recording studio and kitchen / break room. Like the old place, the second floor was populated by the creative staff and tape-room guys; executive and administrative offices were on the third floor. There was a second studio and several writer rooms in the former fire hall next door, and Sony was acquiring additional office space a couple of blocks to the south.

Lauren was living in a small garage apartment a few blocks from my house with her two cats and a rescued pit bull mix, Scooby (a very energetic guy who seemed to be sexually attracted to me). Though Jeep was a first-rate songwriter, she had a problem keeping it country. Despite her love and respect for country music, she had been a big fan of punk and new wave in high school and was basically a folk/rock girl. Since Sony/Tree wasn't getting her cuts with country artists, she lost her writing deal. The occasional modeling and acting gigs didn't provide a steady income, so she went to work as a server at a trendy little restaurant called Iguana.

Lauren and Jonathan were dating other people after she moved back to Nashville, but they remained close and often talked on the phone. Jon urged her to come back and visit some weekend, so she flew out to LA, looking forward to seeing him again as well as her best friend, Maura. On her first night in town, Lauren and Maura were one car behind Jon and his band mate who

The new Sony offices, built on the skeleton of the "Taco Bell Building," 1994

were traveling very slowly down an alleyway, in a *Jeep* as irony would have it, on their way from a recording studio to Jon's apartment. When Jon attempted to hop out of the vehicle, he caught his foot in the door and fell to the pavement, hitting his head. His brain stem was seriously injured, and he immediately went into a coma. The next day, just a few minutes after his mother arrived at his bedside, Jonathan passed away. He was thirty-one years old.

Jonathan Weseley was buried at Mt. Sinai Cemetery, overlooking the Hollywood hills that he loved. Jeep came back to Nashville in the deepest of funks. She said she was so depressed that she couldn't even cry. She referred to herself as Forrest Gump because she would start talking about the tragedy to anyone who would listen, even total strangers. She had a small part in a movie being filmed in Nashville starring Ann-Margret, *Following Her Heart*. It didn't take her mind off the tragedy, of course, but it was good that she had the movie to keep her occupied. She was a gloomy girl for a long time.

I thought it would be a good idea to take Lauren to Florida. We went to the beach, where she had lunch with a childhood friend who happened to be living there. Then we went to Auburndale, staying with my brother Paul and his wife Jo Ann. Mom was now living in a nursing home in Winter Haven; Paul had checked out several places and felt this was the nicest one in Polk County. I was forewarned that Mom, eighty-seven and suffering from fairly advanced dementia, probably wouldn't recognize me. But when I walked in she told her nurse, "That's my son."

"So you know who I am?" I asked.

"Yes, you're Bobby Braddock," she replied, but within a few minutes she was telling me, "I sure wish Bobby could be here."

On another day, she was sitting in the hallway in a wheelchair, crying as she said, "Paul's over there cutting the grass and won't talk to me." She pointed to a young African American man who was vacuuming the floor. I later told brother Paul, "The good news is we'll probably live a long time. The bad news is we may not know what's going on."

I have a theory that Alzheimer's and other forms of dementia are like dreaming. In our dreams, we think it perfectly normal to be aboard a plane in the nude, to have a conversation with a great uncle who passed away when we were young, or to receive a visit from the president in our home. Then eventually maybe it's like falling into a deep, deep sleep without dreams—sleep from which we will never awaken.

When I got back to Nashville, I was dealing with the same old financial troubles, only they were worse than ever. Sony had merged with Michael Jackson's ATV (and the entire Beatles catalog), making Sony/ATV a towering giant in the music publishing world. Whoever they were and whatever they were called didn't much matter; I still owed them almost half a million dollars. Paul Worley had left the company to head a major label (where he would produce some sides on Tami Jones), and my old friend Don Cook was appointed senior vice-president and chief creative officer. Cook was determined to get me some help, but only a miracle could help me. And that miracle was a tornado.

I enjoyed playing songs for Al Cooley, the sole A&R person for Atlantic Records' Nashville division. Al was a lifelong bachelor, close to my age, who loved to talk about women and baseball. He was also fascinated with conspiracy theories. A transplanted New Yorker, Al had an Italian name with twice as many syllables as his professional one. When I played him "Texas Tornado" he loved it for Tracy Lawrence. Tracy went for it, too. But it wasn't the first single off his album. It wasn't the second single either. I was about to give up on it when it finally came out. It debuted on the *Billboard* country chart on April 15, 1995, four days before the terrible Oklahoma City bombing. Pam Tillis had a song titled "I Was Blown Away" that was racing up the charts until the bombing—when it came to a screeching halt and died at #15 because of the title. I was scared to death that radio would pull my song because of the line "blowing me away again," but they didn't. The record was big. Right away I had a line of credit once more at "Sony National Bank."

Shortly before "Texas Tornado" hit #1, I was at a Tracy Lawrence performance at 1995's Fan Fair, the annual Nashville fan festival that drew tens of thousands from around the country and around the world (and is now known as the CMA Music Festival). Tracy stepped up to the mic at the Tennessee State Fairgrounds Speedway and said "Here's a special song I would like to dedicate to the man who wrote it. He's here today—Bobby Braddock." I sat sweltering in the bleachers with the girl who had inspired it—my ex-girlfriend—Tami "the tornado" herself.

A *new* girlfriend, sort of, was Lita Lovingood who had been a huge rock star's Nashville girlfriend when she was twenty and had also had a longtime affair with one of the most famous men in country music. In fact, she had dated seven members of the Country Music Hall of Fame. By the mid-1990s, she was in her mid-forties, still very good-looking but more inclined to date songwriters than stars—which I considered to be my good fortune. In 2011, when it was announced that I was being inducted into the Hall of Fame, Lita would leave this message on my phone: "You're *eight*! You make *eight*!"

One of the most memorable songs of the mid-1990s was the whimsical hillbilly anthem, "Gone Country," made famous by Alan Jackson. The song was written by Bob McDill. Bob always struck me as the professor type—sometimes he wore tweed coats with elbow patches—but I never knew of a better country songwriter. His songs were smart and solid and unforgettable, many of them written without a collaborator. A small sampling of his huge hit list includes "Amanda," "Baby's Got Her Blue Jeans On," "Don't Close Your Eyes," "The Door Is Always Open," "It Must Be Love," "Rednecks, White Socks and Blue Ribbon Beer," "She Don't Know She's Beautiful," "Song of the South," "Turn Out the Lights and Love Me Tonight," and that wonderful piece of Southern lit set to music, "Good Ole Boys Like Me."

Happy Holidays," sang the piped-in voices at the mall. It was becoming a tradition for Lauren and me to get together every year with Ron and Karen Hellard—Ron, my good friend since the early 1980s, and Karen, who became Jeep's "Aunt Karen" back when we were dating. The annual gathering always fell between Thanksgiving and Christmas, and Karen named it "Thanksmas." The visit invariably ended up with Ron and me playing a Scrabble game or two. Sometimes Lauren or I would bring along a date, sometimes not.

Some of the people I dated in the 1990s (besides Lita Lovingood) included a very nice Tree employee of the 1970s who was now single; a voluptuous girl from Philly whose feisty little Italian-American mama almost never left her side; and a tall beautiful girl who was engaged to someone from out of town but who was glad to be my platonic arm candy.

There was one I never actually dated, but because it's a music business story with a moral, I'll elaborate a little. I met Lori, the twenty-eight-year-old daughter of a successful 1960s New York songwriter, at a Christmas party. She was a petite and good-looking brunette. Even though her dad (my age) was at the party, Lori and I found a corner of the room where we did some serious kissing. When she went back to New York we talked constantly on the phone. She told me she was very interested in dating me and was excited about me coming to the city to do a songwriters show at The Bottom Line, a famous nightclub. She said she couldn't wait to see me and be with me. I thought it was time to be completely honest with her.

"Lori, y-you keep saying you're a material girl. I think it's only fair to tell you that I don't have a lot of m-m-money. I'm not in great financial shape."

"Oh I'm a material girl about myself, but it doesn't matter to me if *a guy* has money. I like you for who you are, not because I thought you had money." I never saw or heard from her again. She wouldn't return my calls.

When I got my royalty statements for "Texas Tornado," I was astonished. I had no idea that country hits were making several hundred thousands of dollars. I'd had a semi-hit four years before, but it had been twelve or thirteen years since a song of this magnitude had come along. There were many more country radio stations, and the writers were being paid at a much higher rate, so big country singles were far more lucrative than they had been a dozen years before. And there was an even bigger hit—making much more money—just around the bend. Had I known all that, I wouldn't have found it necessary to go poor-mouthing to Lori. But I was glad that I got to see the real Lori before I spent a lot of money on her!

When I wrote "Time Marches On," I was thinking about a lot of things. I was thinking about how I had noticed on a recent trip down to Florida that my childhood friends were well into middle age, and that the middle-aged people I knew as a kid were elderly or dead. I was also thinking about people in the South moving north to make more money, and people from the North moving south to retire. I was even thinking about a former in-law in Alabama who had a "sexy grandma" bumper sticker on her car. The song was full of subject matter that you didn't typically find in a country song: Bob Dylan, marijuana, depression, dementia. When I finished writing it, I jotted this in my journal: "Good song, sad though."

> *Sister cries out from her baby bed*
> *Brother runs in, feathers on his head*
> *Momma's in her room learning how to sew*
> *Daddy's drinking beer listening to the radio*
> *Hank Williams sings "Kaw-Liga" and "Dear John"*
> *And time marches on, time marches on*
>
> *Sister's using rouge and clear complexion soap*
> *Brother's wearing beads and he smokes a lot of dope*
> *Momma's so depressed, she barely makes a sound*
> *Daddy's got a girlfriend in another town*
> *Bob Dylan sings "Like a Rolling Stone"*
> *And time marches on, time marches on*
>
> *The South moves North, the North moves South*
> *A star is born, a star burns out*
> *The only thing that stays the same*
> *Is everything changes, everything changes*
>
> *Sister calls herself sexy grandma*
> *Brother's on a diet for high cholesterol*
> *Momma's out of touch with reality*
> *Daddy's in the ground underneath a maple tree*
> *As the angels sing an old Hank Williams song*
> *Time marches on, time marches on*

The song was set to the tick-tock rhythm of a clock. On the demo session, Brent Rowan came up with a signature lick that elevated the song a couple of notches, and from that point on it was impossible to think of "Time Marches On" without thinking of the electric guitar. I knew if this song got recorded, they needed to make sure it sounded like that.

I thought it would be good for Tracy Lawrence. I pitched it to Al Cooley at Atlantic and to Don Cook, who was going to produce Tracy's next project. They both loved it and so did Tracy.

I urged Cook to use Brent Rowan on guitar so he could get the same sound that was on my demo. "I like to use Brent Mason," he said, "He can play anything." The two Brents were both great guitar players, and I had the sense that there was a strong rivalry between them. I didn't know how Brent Mason would feel about playing Brent Rowan's licks. But he did, and he did it masterfully. Deborah Allen went with me to the studio after they had finished recording. Cook and Tracy were saying "Wait'll you hear this!" I wasn't disappointed. I thought it sounded like a big hit.

"Time Marches On" entered the *Billboard* charts in late March of 1996. It went to #1 in June and stayed there for three weeks, becoming—and remaining—the biggest single of Tracy Lawrence's career. His album sales jumped dramatically. "Time Marches On" was nominated for CMA Song of the Year, a songwriter award.

I got a call from a young woman named Shannon McCombs. "I love your song, and I want to interview you on my TV show," she said cheerfully and enthusiastically. Her show was *Saturday AM* on Nashville's NBC affiliate, WSMV, channel 4. In the 1980s, when she was in her early twenties, Shannon had been Nashville's top drive-time DJ, known simply as "Shannon" on rock station WKDF. Her resumé as a DJ, interviewer, and television producer was impressive and would grow more so over the years. I had seen her on TV, but she was even more strikingly beautiful in person, with a sunny but sincere personality that put one at ease, on camera and off. We instantly became friends. I could say I was glad we didn't get involved because it might have affected our friendship, but I would be a liar. I was but one of many men intrigued with this special woman. Years later, someone who had often seen us together would ask if we were in a relationship. I would reply, "Well, we've *talked* about dating. In fact we once took a vote on it, and it was close: one to one." I nicknamed her Daisy; she liked it, and the name stuck.

Deborah Allen and I hung out so much that people not only thought we were an item, many thought we were married. She was my date at the annual Nashville Songwriters Association banquet, and coincidentally we were seated next to Shannon, just a few days after she had done the interview with me. My new friend and I chatted continuously though the big meal and long show. Deborah later said, "No wonder people think I'm your wife, you ignored me and talked to Shannon all night."

My date for the Country Music Association awards show was Jeep. So many people had told me they were voting for my song that I really thought it might win. Backstage, Vince Gill told me if his song didn't win, he hoped mine would. I told him I felt the same way about his song, "Go Rest High On That Mountain." I wasn't just being polite.

Vince started writing this riveting funeral dirge when Keith Whitley died, then finished it years later after he had lost his own brother. I loved it not only as a song, but (with the possible exception of "He Stopped Loving Her Today") thought a better country record had never been made. When they announced that Vince was the winner, I was fine with it—not only because of his powerful song and gracious attitude, but also because I felt that "Go Rest High . . ." meant more to him than "Time Marches On" did to me.

There was special significance in Jeep being with me on this night. A few months before, she had found the original manuscript for my nominated

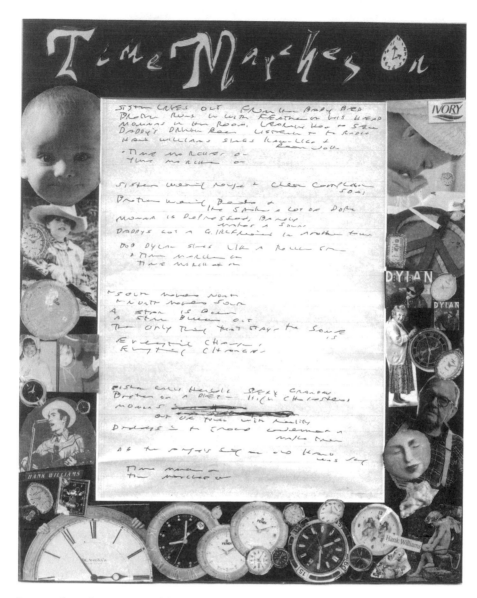

Lauren found my original handwritten lyric of "Time Marches On"
and made it into a collage for a Father's Day gift to me. This hung
in the Country Music Hall of Fame and Museum.

song in a legal pad. She then constructed a montage around the lyrics with
cutouts of pictures related to the story: clocks and watches, Hank Williams,
Bob Dylan, a girl applying makeup, a little boy in a cowboy suit, an old man,
an angel, a marijuana joint. Across the top of the gold-framed picture is emblazoned "Time Marches On." On the back is a little cutout strip from another legal-pad page with a line I'd jotted down before writing the song, a
line I later changed: "Sister cries out from her bassinette." Beneath that she
wrote "To Daddy for Father's Day, 1996. I Love You! Lauren 'Beep' Braddock."

"Time Marches On," #1 party, 1996. Donna Hilley, Tracy Lawrence, Don Cook (*partially hidden*), and me

(Years later this beautiful gift would be on display in the Country Music Hall of Fame and Museum.)

We left the televised CMA show and went to the MCA party at Hard Rock Cafe on Nashville's Lower Broad. George Strait was there and told me he was pretty excited about a song of mine he had just recorded, "The Nerve." The idea for that song had come to me after reading a book Walter Campbell recommended: *Einstein's Dreams*. Soon after I demoed it, I played it for Bill Anderson who paid me the highest song compliment I could get, coming from a master songwriter: with tears in his eyes, Bill said, "That's the best song I've ever heard." Don Cook told me we had to play it for Tony Brown. We did and he put it on hold for Strait. When George cut it, Tony called it "Song of the Year" and said it would probably be the first single. As it would turn out, the promotion department thought it was a bit unusual for a first single, better make it the second. Then the third. Then the fourth. It was never a single. MCA's promotion man David Haley would tell me years later he regretted that they lost their nerve over "The Nerve." I never had such great expectations for a song that did so little.

> *I'm glad I had the nerve to talk to you that day*
> *I could just as easily have let you get away*
> *In that crowded airport, far from my hometown*

If I had lost my courage then, you wouldn't be around
I'm glad I had the nerve.

And I'm glad he had the nerve to get down on his knees
And say I bought this ring for you, won't you wear it please?
My daddy sure touched something in my mama's heart somehow
If he hadn't, I sure wouldn't be here with you now
I'm glad he had the nerve.

Or I never would've lived like this
Or learned like this
Or laughed like this
Or loved like this

I'm glad he had the nerve to sail across the sea
My great grand-daddy's great grandpa in 1833
He met an Indian maiden in the Smoky Mountain mist
If they hadn't crossed that line, I would not exist
I'm glad they had the nerve.

And I'm glad He had the nerve, while staring into space
To give this universe a time and a place
With one tiny atom or an Adam and an Eve
However you look at it, whatever you believe
I'm glad He had the nerve.

Or we never would've lived like this
Or learned like this
Or laughed like this
Or loved like this
Thank God He had the nerve.

And I'm glad I had the nerve to talk to you that day

I'm glad I had the nerve to go to Garth Brooks's attorney, Rusty Jones, and tell him I wanted the best contract he could possibly get me at Sony/Tree. He got it! Sony agreed to pay me all my royalties on my writer's share, to give me half the publishing on all future copyrights, and to collect on my indebtedness solely from the publishing royalties; that way I would be receiving an income and paying off my debt at the same time. I had been writing hit songs since the 1960s and now at last, in 1996, I was going to get to share in the publishing.

There was trouble brewing at Nashville's biggest music publishing company. Dan Wilson was dismissed for sexual harassment, and then turned around and successfully sued the company for age discrimination. I told both

Donna Hilley and Dan that I didn't want to be a witness for either side, and both said that they understood.

Dan had been an important part of my career, most notably in taking "He Stopped Loving Her Today" to Billy Sherrill for George Jones. But he'd had nothing to do with my more recent hits, such as "Texas Tornado" and "Time Marches On," both of which I had placed myself. Those two songs had opened my eyes in another way—they were both recorded very much like my demos. If my demos sounded like records, shouldn't I be making records? I was interested in trying to get recording deals for a couple of demo singers I had been using, but they didn't seem to be enthusiastic about working with me, no doubt because I had no track record as a producer.

One day Michael Kosser, who was running Gosnell Publishing Company's Nashville office, played me a song over the phone and asked what I thought. My interest was not in the song but in the guy who was singing on the demo. Kosser told me it was the kid he had been telling me I should produce, a twenty-year-old writer he'd signed named Blake Shelton. I thought he sounded like a young Hank Williams Jr. The three of us got together; I liked Blake and his robust singing style, and he liked the production on my demos. We decided then that we wanted to work together. Because super-producer Byron Gallimore had shown interest in Blake, I knew I couldn't do anything unless it was okay with Byron (it eventually would be). So here began the long process of waiting for the right moment, the right convergence of factors, but I knew it was something I wanted to do. A lot of songwriters were doing well at producing: Keith Stegall, Buddy Cannon, Don Cook. I had seen Cook get rich producing (and writing with) several artists—especially Brooks & Dunn.

Kix Brooks, who was a good friend, invited me to go on a Brooks & Dunn tour, giving Kix and me the opportunity to write a few songs together. Brooks & Dunn were almost at the point of becoming the biggest-selling duo of all time, in any field. When they first started out, before they had recorded anything, Kix and Ronnie Dunn had hung out around Tree looking for material. At that time they had not yet chosen a name for their act, so I came up with a moniker that Ronnie actually liked: The Coyote Brothers. I wonder if the Coyote Brothers would have enjoyed the same success as Brooks & Dunn.

Kix and Ronnie had been very close to each other initially, and they practically lived down the street from each other. After five years on the road, however, I think they were ready for a little less togetherness. In their many-vehicle convoy, each of the two stars had his own private bus. So on this tour there was nobody on Kix's bus but him, his driver, and me. Every night after their fantastic show—with their grand entrances and gigantic rubber girls, it reminded me of a Rolling Stones concert—Kix and I would watch a movie, then he would have a little toddy and hop into his bunk.

The duo actually had their own laws and judicial system, with their own judge, jury, and real lawyers (often old college friends). The previous week one of the musicians had been tried and convicted of defecating in the band-bus restroom (where only "number one" was allowed). I got to see the video of the entire trial.

Jo Dee Messina was part of the tour, and she and the guys constantly played practical jokes on each other. While Ronnie had a dry and acerbic wit, Kix was a sweetheart, a big teddy bear, and after the closing show of the tour, in Hershey, Pennsylvania, he managed to get a huge Hershey bar and said "Take this to Jeep"—I guess thinking she was still a kid. Kix and I wrote three songs one afternoon. Brooks & Dunn never recorded any of the songs, but the tour had been fun. And the ride was much more comfortable than on Marty Robbins's crowded bus over thirty years before.

I had been doing songwriter "in the round" shows for some time, maybe two or three a year. One of my favorites was one I did at the Country Radio Seminar with nice guy Jim Weatherly ("Midnight Train to Georgia"), my buddy Matraca Berg (still basking in the glow of her biggest hit yet, "Strawberry Wine"), and superstar artist-writer Clint Black. Many years later, Clint would get the reputation of being a control freak when he was one of the participants on Donald Trump's TV show *The Apprentice*, but to me Clint just appeared to be a man who knows what he wants. On this particular night, he wanted my keyboard to be perfectly in tune with his harmonica for his song "Put Yourself in My Shoes," and he called three music stores until he found someone who could tell him how to tune the keyboard to another instrument.

Another superstar from this era was Alan Jackson. I had heard it said that he was shy and even aloof, but he struck me as modest. When I met him and told him he was one of my heroes, he replied in his Georgia drawl, "Well, I think it's the other way around." I was thrilled when Alan cut my song "We're All God's Children" which began like this:

Here comes a Baptist, here comes a Jew
There goes a Mormon and a Muslim too
I see a Buddhist and a Hindu
I see a Catholic and I see you

And we're all God's children
We're all God's children
We're all God's children, why can't we be
One big happy family

On a warm Florida April afternoon I walked into the nursing home to see my mother, who was nearing her ninetieth birthday. I had very low expectations. I felt that she had drifted so far out to sea that she would never come back again. To say I was pleasantly surprised would be an understatement. It was as though some faith healer had walked into her room and cured her of her dementia. She not only recognized me without hesitation, but wanted me to bring her up to date on my songwriting and the music business. How was Lauren? (She had always refused to call my daughter "Jeep.") Where was she living? I had plans in other parts of Florida and back in Nashville, but I cancelled everything and was determined to stay in Polk County as long as my mother was her old self—or perhaps I should say, her *young* self. We had dinner together, looked at family pictures, and discussed the sweet days of Paul's and my childhood. The next day she was in the same lucid shape. I was even thinking (and discussing with my brother) the possibility that if this kept up she wouldn't have to *be* in a nursing home. But by late afternoon she had begun to fade, and by nighttime she was once more the smiley old lady who thought she was a little girl in Georgia. But I had my mother back for two days, and I wouldn't have taken anything for the experience. I knew I would be sad when she left us for good, but I would always be thankful that she came back to tell me goodbye.

When I got back to Nashville I got a phone call from Harlan Howard. He said he was tired of being laid up from his back surgery and he was ready to go out and have some fun. Thus, began the period of several months when every once in a while I would drive by his house in the mid-to-late afternoon and pick up a very slow-moving Harlan and take him to Sunset Grill where we would sit on the patio and drink. I ordered orange juice, and he said "Gyod dimmit, Double-B, if you're gonna drink with me, you're gonna have to drink alcohol." So I whispered to the waiter my request to put a few drops of Coke in a glass of water and bring it to me on ice. Harlan thought I was drinking the real thing, so thereafter whenever I came in with Harlan and ordered scotch-on-the-rocks, the server knew to bring me my sissy water. Harlan always drew a crowd; it was like he was holding court. I often said, referring to the stock brokerage commercial, "Harlan's like E. F. Hutton; when he talks, people listen." Once a notorious womanizer, the oft-married Harlan had finally become domesticated in his marriage to Melanie, who was thirty-four years younger than the sixty-nine-year-old legend. Harlan looked several years older than his actual age, and I think he thoroughly enjoyed every one of those years. One day he told Renee Bell, an A&R star if there ever was one, "Bobby's a great seducer. You'll think he's your friend, then before you know it your brains will be on his pillow." Oh, how I wished that were true—it wasn't even *close* to the truth—but it was brilliantly funny. No wonder Harlan was considered the greatest country songwriter of all time.

One guy who liked to sit with Harlan and me was Larry Henley, a pretty witty fellow himself, a short but nice-looking man a couple of years my senior. I mentioned earlier that Larry was the famous falsetto voice in the Newbeats who sang "I like bread and butter" in the early 1960s; he was also the master song craftsman who co-wrote "'Til I Get It Right" and "Wind Beneath My Wings." Larry told a hilarious story about something that had happened to him many years before when he had a severe crush on a beautiful happily-married singing star, and mistakenly thought the romantic attraction was mutual. One night a drunk Larry Henley encountered her at a gala music business function and told her, "I'd love to fuck your eyes out." Her mouth flew open and she abruptly turned and walked away. From that time on, whenever she saw Larry coming, she would go in the other direction.

Jeep had fallen in love and was packing her bags and preparing to follow her heart. The year before, she and a girlfriend had gone to the bar at Nashville's grand old Union Station Hotel. She met a guy who was a guest there, a publicist from New York named Jim Havey—the son of a prominent New Jersey judge. Jim was in town for the opening of the local Planet Hollywood theme restaurant, a movie-star-owned chain that his sister Lisa represented as vice-president of worldwide marketing. Lauren was easily won over by Jim's mix of Irish charm, Italian good looks, and Jersey music roots. I had just gotten my first computer, and it became a daily ritual, my daughter running by my place to have an instant-message conversation with her new boyfriend. After a year of long-distance dating, the time had come for her to make the move to New York. I knew I would miss her a lot, but they were crazy about each other, and I wanted her to be happy.

In the fall, I got word that Mom was doing very badly. I went to Florida for what turned out to be a bedside vigil. Though "Time Marches On" was nominated for CMA Song of the Year for the second year in a row, I would miss the annual awards show. However, I watched it on TV from Florida and saw Matraca Berg sing a song about her mother-in-law, "Back When We Were Beautiful." I got word from Matraca that she would be thinking of my mom while singing the song.

Apparently having suffered a stroke, Mom seemed to be trapped in her body, unable to move anything but her mouth—speaking gibberish—though sometimes she seemed to be mouthing "Hi" and "Bye." After several days I said what I knew was a final goodbye. I told her what a wonderful mother she had been and how much I loved her. I thought I saw a smile. I kissed her goodbye on the mouth.

Soon after I returned to Nashville, my brother called me at Sony/Tree's recording studio and told me that Mom was gone. I closed down mixes for the rest of the night, and when I walked to my car in the cool autumn dawn, I felt my mother's presence in the parking lot. Two days later I picked up Lauren at the Orlando airport and we drove to Auburndale for the memorial service. I had been grieving over her for years, especially the past two or three years after our regular phone conversations had ended. I was feeling some relief that she finally had her dignity back, but I was also feeling very sad. I kept thinking, "I don't have parents anymore."

When I was a child, Mom went to funeral after funeral, saying, "I'd sure hate to think I wouldn't have many people at *my* funeral." The bulk of her friends had been older ladies in the Woman's Club and the Garden Club. She had outlived them all. Most of her contemporaries were gone or bedridden.

In my journal I wrote, "There was a time when there would have been several hundred people at her funeral." About sixty showed up.

Over the Christmas holidays I visited Jeep and her sweetie, Jim, in New York. His Christmas present to her was an engagement ring. We went to the Jersey shore to celebrate Christmas with Jim's family. His father, known by most as "The Judge," was a dashing man with a powerful presence and a keen intellect. I wrote in my journal: "The judge drank a toast to Jeep and Jimmy, so elegantly put that I could only add 'amen.'" Jim's father, mother, sisters, stepmother, and stepbrother all seemed to be very happy to have Lauren joining the Havey family.

I started off 1998 in a good frame of mind. I was getting out of debt, and for the first time in nearly ten years I owned a house, buying the one I had been renting since 1988, on Autumn Trail. I was getting ready to record some sides on Blake Shelton, the Oklahoma boy I met through Michael Kosser. Blake was tall, funny, irreverent, mullet-headed, and talented. If I had it to do over I would have bankrolled the sessions myself, as I was by then able to afford it. But I ran it through Tree Productions, which was headed up by my friend, writer-producer Chris Waters. Chris believed in me as a producer, and he was sold on Blake as a singer. Sony/Tree would fund the sessions, and in turn get a nice little piece of the action, should there be any.

In February I put Blake Shelton's voice on a song of mine that was originally cut as a demo, "Good Old Boy, Bad Old Boyfriend." A couple of days later we went into the MCA Publishing studio on Music Square East and recorded three sides, including "Ol' Red."

Though the great story-song about a prison dog had been recorded by other artists, including George Jones and Kenny Rogers, it had been taught to Blake by Hoyt Axton who sang it to him a cappella. Blake worked up "Ol' Red" with his solid rhythm guitar, and when he introduced the song to me, it blew me away, and I began to imagine this swampy arrangement. I told Blake, "We've got to cut that one!" We did it with the unlikely combination of harmonica, Jew's harp, and cello.

We spent two days with Blake doing vocals on the three songs, another day recording background vocals (and Rachel Proctor's haunting harmony on "Ol' Red"), then two days on mixing. The engineer was excellent at his craft, but he didn't like my idea of pulling Blake's voice way up (loud) in the mix. I thought Blake's resonant baritone ought to be in everybody's face. The engineer said, "Then please don't put my name on it." He would later change his mind about that.

I took what we had to Tim DuBois at Arista Records, the label of Alan Jackson and Brooks & Dunn. Tim liked it, and said he wanted to see Blake perform live, which is a prerequisite to getting a record deal for any artist. Tim and his entire A&R staff arrived at a club called Douglas Corner for Blake's showcase. They learned something that I already knew: Blake not only sounded great in a recording studio, but he was an outstanding live act. And he was playing to a full house. Tim sounded enthusiastic and said I'd be hearing from them. I thought we had ourselves a deal. But Tim's A&R staff was like a jury—everyone had a vote, and it had to be unanimous. If it wasn't unanimous, the dissenting voice had to be the one to deliver the bad news. Joe Simmons, formerly a Sony/Tree songplugger and a very nice, mild-mannered guy, called me up and told me he was the one who voted "no," and that he just didn't think Blake was ready. Joe was himself producing a young man whom he *did* think was ready who would soon have his first release on Arista. I don't recall the young man's name.

Arista was the first of my dozen stops up and down Music Row, as I tried to land Blake Shelton with a major label. When I played the session for my friend Renee Bell, the head of A&R for the RCA group, we were sidetracked by a serious tornado. After standing outside the RCA building and looking up into the howling, hissing vortex of the storm passing over, I drove Renee to the western part of town where we parked my car, then climbed over fallen trees and walked around downed telephone poles and power lines to get her little dog, Gizmo, from a veterinarian's office where he had been boarded for the day. Renee loved Blake's singing but the label head, Joe Galante, later passed on him.

After hitting every other label in town with no luck, there was but one place left to go: Giant Records. For the past few years, Giant had pretty much been a one-act label, the act being Clay Walker. The company was a partnership between Warner Bros. and Irving Azoff, a manager of successful pop acts. I met with label head Doug Johnson, a straight-talking songwriter-producer from South Georgia. After listening to everything, Doug looked me in the eye and said firmly, "I like it." When I commented that I had Blake's voice mixed louder than most singers, he said, "I know. I like it." Blake and I had breakfast a few days later with Doug's A&R head, Debbie Zavitson. She told us that Giant wanted to sign Blake. We were getting a deal at the last place we went. My reluctance to go there earlier had been because of the rumors that Giant was about to fold, but Doug assured me that the rumors weren't true.

Giant had just signed a family act, the Wilkinsons, who recorded "26¢," a song that would become a hit. This would begin the long, long wait for Blake to have his turn. Many days Blake and I would amble into the one-story Giant Records building on South Street, the little bald-headed guy well into his fifties and the big kid with long hair hanging down beneath his cowboy hat. I told Blake, "We're Elvis and Colonel Tom," and he laughed so loud that you could hear him a block away. Blake was funny; he loved to shock people and invade their space, but always with a big grin. Sometimes in conversation with Giant's head of sales—a middle-aged mustached man named John Burns—Blake would stick his finger in John's ear. That was just Blake. He put in a lot of time on the couch in Giant Records' lobby. Often sitting alongside him would be another long-haired country boy awaiting *his* turn: Joe Nichols.

Sad news usually flies in like a big unwelcome vulture, from out of nowhere and with no forewarning. So it was when Tammy Wynette died at the age of fifty-five. Though media people were calling me for comment, I wasn't a Tammy insider. I daresay she was very important to my career, recording nineteen of my songs, more than any other artist except her ex-husband George Jones. Her husband, George Richey, told me "She really loved you," and I think it was true. She loved a lot of people, and we all loved her. When she did a local TV special in which she sat around and talked informally about her career, I was one of a handful of guests that she included on the show. She was always very kind to me—and practically everyone—but despite mutual love and respect, I wouldn't say we were really close socially. I had only been to her house twice; I would usually see her at music business functions or occasional songplugging meetings or shopping-mall encounters. Sometimes she would call and ask what I thought about her recording of one of my songs ("I *love* it, Tammy"), and once she called to ask if I would help her daughter's boyfriend with his songwriting. Matraca Berg, a big fan of Tammy's, who regarded the women of country music with reverence, asked if she could go with me to the memorial service at the historic Ryman Auditorium. Afterward, singer Emmylou Harris, publicist Holly Gleason, Matraca, and I went to a bar and drank toasts to The First Lady of Country Music.

A few weeks later I drove down to Florida for the Auburndale High School forty-year class reunion. At the gathering, I yelled out from the back of the room, "You know you're getting old when you cut your ear shaving." When one dear soul gave a talk about how happy she was that we grew up in the Bible Belt, I called out that the people at the ten-year reunion down the hall sounded like they were having more fun than we were. One of my female classmates told me afterward that it was like being back in high school, me sitting in the back of the room shouting out wisecracks and making people laugh.

The next day I drove from Auburndale over to Satellite Beach, on the Space Coast, to reunite with Carmen Beecher, a friend from my teens. The year before, when I was learning how to use a computer, she became the first person outside my family whom I regularly corresponded with via e-mail. I called her my "cyberpal" and she has remained so until this day. Though Carmen's "raising" had been in a sleepy Southern town like mine in Central Florida, her maternal grandparents were from Spain and Italy. I soon became good friends with her daughter Stephanie, a successful modeling agent who had inherited her mother's Mediterranean good looks.

Lauren and Jim decided to get married in the place where they met, the beautifully ornate Union Station Hotel, Nashville's converted train terminal. The high-ceilinged lobby area was a popular wedding site, and off the lobby was a large dining room suitable for a party. There were people who would say it was the best wedding and wedding party they had ever attended. Blake Shelton sang "The Nerve," Deborah Allen and Don Henry sang "Chapel of

Lauren Braddock becomes Lauren Braddock Havey—Daddy, Jeep, and Jim, 1998

Love," and a violinist and pianist played Bach's "Air on the G String." I walked Jeep down the stairs from the mezzanine. The bride and groom looked like a couple of movie stars. The dinner was grand, with more toasts from Judge Havey and me. The band was excellent, and after a little wine and a lot of dancing, I sat in and sang and played the blues. Jeep and Jim went to Aruba on their honeymoon, then back to New York to nothing different than before: a condo on the Upper West Side overlooking Central Park, he working for a public relations firm, and she working in a law office, occasionally doing acting gigs, photo shoots, and commercials.

Since the exit of Dan Wilson, I had been working with all the songpluggers at Sony/Tree, but my point person was a guy named John Van Meter. The company made another acquisition, buying a large independent company:

Little Big Town, whose owner, Woody Bomar, became a high-ranking official at Sony/Tree. Woody brought along a first-rate hard-working songplugger, Terry Wakefield, and several successful writers.

My Sony contract allowed me to get half the publishing on any songs I brought in that they liked, and the staff was receptive to the songs of a very talented and unique songwriter named Kathy Locke. Kathy made occasional trips to Nashville from her home in Richmond, Virginia. I first met her at a writers' night in 1995. A strikingly good-looking lady in her late thirties, she was married with children. We would develop a special friendship, like one of those close but innocent friendships that ten-year-old boys and girls sometimes have. Or maybe Kathy was the kid sister I never had. She became not only my writer and co-writer, but a trusted and valued friend to me and my family.

It had been almost a year since I recorded the first sides with Blake, and several months after our first meeting with Giant he was ready to record some more. His interest in music was only slightly stronger than his interest in deer hunting. And that's saying a lot. His little rented house was well outside the city, in the country, and he lived there with his girlfriend, Kaynette Williams, who shared Blake's passion for archery. Kaynette was a very good-looking blonde grade-school teacher, and a few years older than Blake. The first time he asked her for a date, back in their hometown of Ada, Oklahoma, she turned him down because she thought he was too young. He was fifteen. In January of 1999, he was halfway between twenty-two and twenty-three and ready to set the world on fire. And I was ready for him to do it.

Blunt-talking Doug Johnson had two requests and one edict. His first request was that I consider letting Brent Rowan co-produce Blake with me. He told me he had full confidence in me as Blake's producer, but he thought Brent and I would make a great team, and he wanted me to consider it. I didn't think on it very long. I told Doug I wanted to do this alone and didn't think I could do it any other way. (I had co-produced a project for a major label a few years before and knew that I didn't want to do another production collaboration.) Besides, I wanted Brent to be the lead guitarist on these sessions. Doug said, "That's fine, man, I'm behind you one hundred percent."

His second request was that I consider pianist John Hobbs for music director. I didn't even think on that one at all. I told Doug that my greatest strength as a producer was as an arranger. Though Hobbs was an excellent musician, I didn't feel that I needed a music director. "Music director" was not a title or position that you typically heard about on Nashville recording sessions. There was a session *leader* who received twice as much pay, for writing out chord charts and taking care of the union cards and contracts. I always made Brent leader on demo sessions, and wanted to continue that practice on master sessions. So my answer, for the second time, was sorry, but I'd rather not.

"That's fine," Doug said, "but there's one thing I'm going to have to insist on. I want you to use Ed Seay as engineer." I had no choice but to say yes, but I wasn't very happy about it. I knew Ed was one of the best recording engineers in town, but he also had a solid track record as a producer. He produced all the Paul Davis pop hits in his hometown of Atlanta in the 1970s, and more recently, he had co-produced several hit acts with Paul Worley, such as Highway 101 and Martina McBride. My problem with Ed Seay (pronounced "see") was that I would feel weird telling him what to do. Who was I to do that? He was a veteran producer, and I was a novice. But it would turn out that Ed didn't look at it that way; he was being hired to engineer, not produce. He would soon find out that I knew what I was doing. I would marvel at his skill—he was one of the first engineers in town to record 100 percent digital, using ProTools. Ed was ten years younger than me, and bald like me (his remaining hair was curly while mine was straight). He was a bespectacled, mild-mannered man who was just enough of a smartass to make the long hours in the studio a lot more fun. There would be immediate mutual respect, and Ed would become one of my very best friends.

On January 18, we tracked four sides at Ocean Way Studio in Nashville with the great Brent Rowan on electric guitar; John Willis (the class clown) on acoustic guitar; hot young drummer Shannon Forrest; Allison Prestwood (one of Music Row's few female session musicians) on electric bass; Wynonna Judd's keyboard player Tim Lauer; Rob Hajacos (who played on the Garth Brooks hits) on fiddle; and Dan Dugmore (who played on Linda Ronstadt's records) on steel. These were basically the same people I used on demos, and the same ones who played on the 1998 "Ol' Red" session that secured Blake his deal. Tracking was done in the morning; then in the afternoon and night I had the musicians scheduled to come in and fix parts and replay when necessary.

Very crucial to our team were the harmony singers. Though we sometimes used other singers and combinations (whom I will mention from time to time), throughout my tenure with Blake, the core group was Dennis Wilson and Wes Hightower, whose voices were tracked several times to make them sound like a large group. When a female voice was needed we often added Melodie Crittenden. For a single singer to harmonize with Blake's voice, we used Blue Miller, who had developed a hoarse, gritty style singing on the road with Bob Seger for years. Pulled back in the mix, Blue's harmony gave Blake a little more edginess.

Before we put on vocal harmonies and spent several days mixing, we did the most grueling part of recording: vocal "comps" (as in compilations). Blake would sing each song several times; then we would decide, line-by-line, where the best singing was—using a line from one performance, then the next line from another. Unlike many recording artists in Nashville, Blake wasn't having his vocal performances "tuned."

Blake had done a song called "I Love Laughing with You," on which he was supposed to laugh at the end of the recording. He had sung it just fine the night before, but his laugh hadn't been too convincing. The next night I asked him to try to get a better laugh. I came prepared. Over the talkback, I asked him to hold on a minute while an adjustment was made, then I ran to the back of the control room and made a quick change. I put on a "Mimi" mask—Mimi being the redheaded, round-faced, garishly made-up character on the *Drew Carey* TV sitcom—then slipped out of my clothes and put on an ultra-skimpy bikini swimsuit. When we started recording, I stood at the control room window doing an obnoxious bump and grind just when it was time for Blake to deliver his laugh. When he saw me, he laughed huge, even for Blake. It was a great spontaneous bellow. Unfortunately, the song wouldn't make the album.

"I Thought There Was Time" called for the word "time" to be held out for about eight seconds, in a strong clear-as-a-bell voice. It was something most people wouldn't be able to sing. Blake, who was sailing through everything else, was having trouble with this one. I finally told him I was going to run to the market to get him a beer, and to just relax until I got back. As I walked out the door, I said, "Or who knows, you might be able to get it while I'm gone." I thought that without the pressure of my sitting in the control room, he might be able to do it. That's exactly what happened; he nailed it while I was away. I had thought of Blake as a really commercial singer, but when I started working with him, I found out that he was a truly *great* singer, one of the best in Nashville.

The most and least fun of producing was the song search—looking for songs and listening to them. The great songs were inspiring, and the terrible songs were funny, but the in-between songs could be just plain boring. I remember riding around with Blake one day, listening to songs, and everything he didn't like (practically everything we listened to) he would sail out the window, littering the countryside with cassettes. Debbie Zavitson at Giant sent out word to all the major publishing companies that we needed songs. New, unknown artists don't get a lot of prime songs presented to them. That's why, on this first album project, we had to rely more on songs written by Blake and me. One publisher who sent us good material was Sony/Tree, possibly because Tree Productions owned a piece of the action.

I listened to every single thing that came my way, no matter who wrote it or where it came from. Not only that, I got back in touch with whoever pitched it to me, and let them know I had listened. This gesture was greatly appreciated by the publishers and writers accustomed to producers getting back in touch only if they wanted to hold on to a song. Whenever I put a song on hold, I tried to let publishers and writers know as quickly as possible if Blake and Giant wanted to keep the song on hold, because I knew if I didn't tie songs up for too long they would be more apt to send us more. Of course in those days it was much easier to get a quick response from Blake, because he was not yet working the road; he was still spending a lot of time hanging out at Giant, touching people's noses and sticking his finger in their ears, and laughing his boisterous laugh which could be heard a block away.

In June we went in to cut some more sides, this time at Sound Stage Studio. Just as I had always done with demos, I would spend a lot of advance time coming up with arrangements for the songs. Blake would come by my house the day before the session, and I would show him my blueprint for each song, to make sure he was on board with it. The time for Blake and me to disagree was in private, not in front of the musicians.

The relationship that the artist and producer have with the musicians is a key element of success. Blake was funny and cut up a lot, so the musicians enjoyed working with him.

I always went out of my way to treat the musicians with great respect, and although I had arrangements worked out, I was always open to any ideas that the players had; I would have been a fool not to be. And as was the case in cutting demos, I rarely had a solid note-for-note plan for Brent Rowan, because he always seemed to come up with something I loved.

I felt that these were magic sessions. If I were a super-religious person, I would have suspected divine guidance, but I think God has more important things to do than oversee recording sessions in Nashville. We recorded several songs over two days, and the three that would end up on the album were all Blake co-writes, including future single "All Over Me" (which he wrote with Earl Thomas Conley and Mike Pyle).

The personnel were the same as in the February sessions except for the addition of Mike Rojas playing piano on "All Over Me" and Deborah Allen and Curtis Young singing on a song called "Problems at Home," doing Patty Loveless-Ricky Skaggs-type harmonies (that I clearly borrowed from Tony Brown's production genius on Vince Gill's "Go Rest High on That Mountain"). Some of this work involved additional recording at the Sony/Tree studio with Jim Dineen, who had become my regular demo engineer.

This was back in the days when it was fairly typical for record labels to allow a catered lunch (taking place between the morning and afternoon sessions) to be worked into the recording budget. I didn't want the musicians to be slow or sluggish after lunch, so I made sure that the meals were heavy on protein and fruits and veggies, and as carb-free as possible.

After the tracking session came the long days and nights of instrumental fixes, vocal comps, background harmonies, followed by a string session for "All Over Me" and "Problems at Home." String arrangements involved my collaborating with keyboard player Tim Lauer. I sat down with Tim at a keyboard with string samples (with a sample, you get the recorded sound of another instrument when you press the key). I would play my orchestration ideas, then Tim would write them down, sometimes expanding on my ideas with his own arrangement. Then he would conduct the orchestra on the session. The string section consisted of four violins, four violas, and two cellos, doubled to create a string section of twenty.

I had Ed Seay booked for a couple of weeks to mix what we had recorded. Doug Johnson was on vacation in another state and wanted to hear Blake's vocals to make sure they were okay before the songs were mixed, so he made the decision to shut down everything we were doing until he got back in town. I knew that Ed Seay was a very in-demand engineer, and it might be a few months before we could reschedule the mixes. That would delay the release of Blake's album. And what if Giant folded? Then the album would *never* come out. I tried to talk Doug out of shutting down the mixes, but he was adamant. A resounding *no*!

I felt there was only one way that I might be able to change Doug's mind. Long ago I learned that if I wanted to find a lost billfold or set of keys, the best thing to do was write down an affirmation in small, neatly printed letters: "I will now find my keys," for example. My subconscious mind knew where I had laid them; the image of me putting the keys, say, on top of my piano was stored in my mental hard drive. Often, I would write down the affirmation, then go about my business and find myself eventually gravitating to where the keys were and putting my hand on them. It worked! So I decided if affirmations helped me find lost items, perhaps they would direct me to say or do the right thing to get my way about something. Obviously, an affirmation was not going to put a movie star in bed with me or make me the king of the world, but for a goal within reason, it did sometimes work. Everything I knew about Doug Johnson, human nature, and how to influence people was stored in my brain, and I just needed to open it up. So before I went to bed that night, I wrote down on a piece of paper, "I will know what to say to Doug Johnson tomorrow to change his mind about shutting down the mixes." The next morning, I got Doug on his cell phone. Before I said much he cut me off and told me he had made up his mind.

"Doug, all I ask is that you hear me out. I promise I won't take long." He said okay. I don't recall everything I said, but I do remember telling him that shutting down the mixes would mean that his friend Ed Seay would lose thousands of dollars in income, and the short notice wouldn't give him enough time to get other engineering work to make up for it. And I reminded Doug that my judgment about the vocals had been right in the past. There was a long pause. He said, "Okay. Go ahead and mix."

Ed typically spent at least a full day mixing a song. Then I would spend anywhere from two to six hours closing down the mix with him. We rarely butted heads, but Ed didn't mince words when he felt strongly about something. Even though we sometimes disagreed, when it came down to a final decision Ed knew I would be the one whose butt was on the line with the record label when the session was turned in. In the future when people would tell me how good everything sounded, I would know how fortunate I had been to work with a great singer, some of the world's best musicians, and a brilliant engineer.

On July 30, Doug Johnson, a manly man in every sense of the word, said with tears in his eyes, "I've never heard a better country album. I wish we could put it out right now."

The plan was for Blake to do a radio tour in January, then kick off his first single at the Country Radio Seminar in February. Ah, the best laid plans of mice and men! As Doug spoke those words, Blake's album release was almost two years away, and the big monster hit that would kick off the album hadn't been recorded yet. In fact, I don't think it had even been written.

Jeep and Jim came to Nashville for the holidays. On the night of December 31, we went out on the town and ended up at a party at F. Scott's restaurant. The new century had already clicked into place in other time zones, and we were relieved to learn that all the computers on the planet had not crashed, as many had predicted. I was fifty-nine years old, but instead of fretting about the biggest part of my career being behind me in the twentieth century, I was hopeful that maybe the best was yet to come.

12

BRAND NEW CENTURY

I woke up at 4402 Autumn Trail on the first day of the brand new century, glad that I had lived to see this milestone. Many people never get to see the beginning of a new century, let alone a new *millennium*.

The twenty-first century! What kind of wonderful and horrible things lay in store? What miraculous discoveries? What unthinkable disasters? It was highly unlikely that I would see half of the new century, and impossible that I would see all of it. With constantly advancing medical technology, Jeep might. Her children could live indefinitely. Unless the *world* ceased to exist! It all boggled the mind.

At the dawning of this new century, I was obsessed with my computer, visiting the AOL message boards every night—anonymously and safely sounding off on subjects that I wouldn't discuss with friends and associates unless I knew they were like-minded. I was also addicted to the treadmill that I had set up in front of a TV screen in my basement studio. And as always, I was hooked on a book, playing catch-up with two first-rate "Southern" works that had been around for a year or so: Tom Wolfe's *A Man in Full* and Rick Bragg's *All Over but the Shoutin'*.

This new century—the media hadn't yet told us if we should say "two-thousand-and-whatever" or "twenty-whatever"—was looking good for country music. Tim McGraw was still hot, his wife Faith Hill was having the hit of her career, Lonestar was big, Brad Paisley had just enjoyed his first #1, and the Dixie Chicks' sales were through the roof. But this was about as good as it was going to get. Music business people were already worried about the effect that Napster and peer-to-peer file-swapping would have on CD sales. In the first decade of the new century, those sales would begin their downhill slide; and after legal downloading became the next big thing, CD sales would continue to decline—and at an even faster rate. The days of Garth and Shania selling twenty million albums would disappear before our eyes like a bouquet of helium-filled balloons sailing away into the sky.

But the music business was looking quite healthy at the moment—like a seemingly robust man not too long before his heart attack. I was convinced that Blake Shelton would be a superstar of Garth-like magnitude. In fact, I may have had bigger ambitions for Blake than he had for himself. There was a song of mine that he liked titled "Same Old Song," a belligerent country rocker about the monotonous and sanitized side of contemporary country music. The chorus went:

I'm tired of the same old guy with the same old song
About the same old love that goes on and on
The same old guitar with the same old strum
I may be country but I'm not dumb

I was and would remain very cautious about Blake recording songs that I had written. The last thing I wanted was for my record producing to be seen as a vehicle to get my songs cut. Some producers had that reputation, and I didn't want it. I wanted to shine as a producer. And there was already one song of mine that would make the album: "I Thought There Was Time." But since we had no product out there and, therefore, no track record, there weren't many people knocking on our doors with songs for us. Blake had heard a lot of material that I had demoed and "Same Old Song" was a particular favorite. Doug Johnson liked the demo so much—with its twangy electric guitar and mournful steel—that he wanted me to upgrade it instead of cutting it over, and replace the demo singer's vocal with Blake's. Oddly, a few months before, a guy in Giant's sales department had heard the demo and said, "Wow, that's maybe the best I've ever heard Blake sing," not realizing that he wasn't hearing Blake but demo singer Ron Wallace.

I sang that one and several others at one of my favorite writers nights, on April 4. Tin Pan South had become a popular annual music event, sponsored by the NSAI (Nashville Songwriters Association International). For an entire week there would be writers-in-the-round shows at venues all over town, each one featuring well-known songwriters. There were several clubs and shows each night to choose from. I was featured on the "legends show" at the Ryman Auditorium, along with the renowned Loretta Lynn, the 1970s and '80s pop and country star Mac Davis, and the celebrated Broadway writing team of Betty Comden and Adolph Green. The big hall was packed. There were a lot of celebrities in the audience, and most of the Tennessee state legislature was present.

In the past several years, I had come to know and like Mac Davis, finding him down-to-earth and very funny. Like me, he took a Valium before the show to calm down. When I said "I can't believe that a man who used to work three-hundred dates a year and had his own top-rated TV show would need a Valium," he laughed and said, "Back then I was drinking a quart of whiskey every day."

Instead of "in-the-round," this event was like a regular stage show, each writer doing his or her set alone. I ended my set with "He Stopped Loving Her Today." There was a thunderous standing ovation, not for my perfor-

Kathy Locke—
like family

mance, I'm sure, but for the song. As I left the stage, Loretta Lynn (standing behind the curtain, holding her guitar and ready to go on) said, "You booger, you booger, makin' me foller that." Of course, Loretta Lynn was Loretta Lynn and could easily have followed ten of me put together.

This was about the time that I was beginning to write a memoir. This slow-as-a-snail authoring would definitely be on-the-job training, with much help and encouragement from my friend and mentor, the great Southern writer John Egerton. Little did I know that what I was writing would encompass only my childhood and very young adulthood and would not be in bookstores for another seven years.

In the latter part of April, I was on the phone with my friend Kathy Locke in Virginia. I had something I wanted to tell her but never got the opportunity. Normally, a good two-way conversationalist, Kathy was having a hard time at work because her assistant had been dismissed, which caused her workload to double. She talked about that for a long time—a *very* long time—and I barely got to say a word. It inspired what would become the first #1 country rap song. When I made a home demo, I called up Kathy and played it for her. This is what she heard:

Yeah, Yeah
That's right

We talk about your work, how your boss is a jerk
We talk about your church and your head when it hurts
We talk about the troubles you've been having with your brother

About your daddy and your mother and your crazy ex-lover
We talk about your friends and the places that you've been
We talk about your skin and the dimples on your chin
The polish on your toes and the run in your hose
And God knows we're gonna talk about your clothes
You know talking about you makes me smile
But every once in awhile

I wanna talk about me
Wanna talk about I
Wanna talk about number one
Oh my me my
What I think, what I like, what I know, what I want, what I see
I like talking about you you you you, usually, but occasionally
I wanna talk about me (me, me, me, me)
I wanna talk about me-e-ee (me, me)

We talk about your dreams and we talk about your schemes
Your high school team and your moisturizing cream
We talk about your nanna up in Muncie, Indiana
We talk about your gran'ma down in Alabama
We talk about your guys of every shape and size
The ones that you despise and the ones you idolize
We talk about your heart, 'bout your brains and your smarts
And your medical charts and when you start
You know talking about you makes me grin
But every now and then

I wanna talk about me
Wanna talk about I
Wanna talk about number one
Oh my me my
What I think, what I like, what I know, what I want, what I see
Now I like talking about you you you you, usually, but occasionally
I wanna talk about me (me, me, me, me)
I wanna talk about me-e-ee (me, me)

(I wanna talk about me) mmmm me me me me
(I wanna talk about me) mmmm me me me me
You you you you you you you you you you you you you
I wanna talk about ME!

I wanna talk about me etc.

Kathy had very little to say about the song, but called me the next day and asked if I had written it about her. I said, "Thaaaaaas right." That summer I demoed "I Wanna Talk About Me," with Blake singing. He had been the other inspiration for the song—going around doing a funny little rap which, in his Ada, Oklahoma, white boy drawl, I thought sounded hilarious. I wrote in my journal, "We might have cut a Blake master." Brent Rowan came up with a killer guitar intro that elevated the song a couple of notches.

The people at Giant were pretty excited about the song for Blake, but then the label "tested" it and "research" showed that nobody liked it, so not only would it not be a single, it wouldn't even make the album. But I thought their research was wrong ("Texas Tornado" had tested poorly), and I was determined to find a home for "I Wanna Talk About Me" somewhere.

Then we learned that Blake's release date had been moved still further back, until January of the next year. It had been two years since Blake signed with the label, and he still didn't have anything out and they were putting it off again—*way* off. Partly this was because other artists were being given priority over Blake, and partly it had to do with finance and budgeting. Because we knew and liked Doug Johnson, we had a tendency to put the blame on the man we didn't know: label-owner Irving Azoff in LA. I told Blake that the label should be named *Midget* instead of Giant. He thought that was pretty funny, so we started calling it Midget.

When I returned to Nashville after spending a few days in the beautiful state of Colorado—doing some shows with Matraca Berg and her husband,

Matraca Berg—
longtime friend

Jeff Hanna of Nitty Gritty Dirt Band fame—I went by Giant with Blake to listen to some songs that had been put on hold by A&R head Debbie Zavitson (or Debbie Z as we all called her). She played one called "If This Is Austin." About a third of the way through the song, I was thinking, "This is pretty corny." About two thirds of the way through, I thought, "This is kinda like one of those Tom Hanks-Meg Ryan love stories." By the end of the song, I had a lump in my throat. Blake, not the real "sensitive guy," found it a little mushy for his taste, but I asked him to listen again, and he warmed up to it a bit. By now I was in love with this story about the guy who, just in case his former girlfriend ever calls, ends his outgoing phone greeting with "And PS, if this is Austin I still love you." We asked Debbie to keep that one on hold.

In early September we recorded three sides at Tree International studio including "If This Is Austin." I thought it came off beautifully. I credit Doug Johnson with making the Austin song sound even better—he felt that the intro wasn't "signature" enough, so we got Brent Rowan to come back in and overdub an acoustic guitar part.

After we mixed the new cuts, I took "If This Is Austin" to play for the writers, David Kent and Kirsti Manna, neither of whom had ever had a hit. I don't think they were expecting anything extraordinary from this country boy named Blake who was being produced by an old songwriter, because they were clearly surprised and blown away by what they heard. I told them I couldn't see "If This Is Austin" sitting at the top of the charts, but I *could* see "Austin" sitting there, and asked their permission to shorten the title to "Austin." Now very excited by their Blake Shelton cut, they readily agreed.

A few days later there was a "pick the single" meeting at Giant. The producer might not always be included in such a get-together. But Blake's original manager rarely said much at label meetings, so Doug Johnson considered me to be actually filling the manager role and, therefore, wanted me to participate. I voted for "Austin" as did sales manager John Burns. Blake and Debbie Z voted for a song Blake co-wrote, "All Over Me." Doug Johnson voted for our version of the Police song "Every Breath You Take" (which Blake was strongly opposed to as a first single). The next day we voted again. I cast my vote with Blake and Debbie Z for "All Over Me" so there would be a majority. We all agreed to make it unanimous. "All Over Me" was to be Blake's debut single.

This was on a Thursday. On Friday I made copies of all the songs we had been considering and overnighted them to Jeep in New York, my friend Kathy Locke in Virginia, and my "cyberpal" Carmen Beecher in Florida. I was just curious about what the feedback would be. On Saturday I heard from all three within the same hour, and all of them were having fits over "Austin." On Sunday night I had dinner with my friend Chari Pirtle, and later played her the songs too, and her reaction to "Austin" was the same as that of the three other women. On Monday I had lunch with a newer friend, Sylvia, the beautiful songbird who had been one of the hottest stars of the 1980s. When I played her the music, she got teary-eyed over "Austin." She made a good point when she said, "'All Over Me' is probably also a hit, and Blake really shines with his falsetto, but that's not a good way to introduce him; that's like an added attraction that should come later."

Holy cow, I thought, it's been decided that "All Over Me" will be Blake's first single, and I've just had five females react enthusiastically to "Austin." Debbie Z had left me a message saying since we had made our decision on "All Over Me," there was no longer any need for us to have our 3:00 p.m. meeting. I called her back and urged that she get everyone to meet at three as planned. "I have important new information," I told her.

I knew I had an almost impossible task. I somehow had to get all four of them to change their minds. I had just enough time to go home and meditate for a few minutes. I wrote down "I will know what to say in order to convince all concerned that Blake's first single should be 'Austin.'" I can recall me standing before them at the meeting, like a lawyer in front of a jury, making an impassioned plea. There was strong resistance at first, but one by one they came around. Debbie Z said that what Sylvia told me really resonated with her. Anyway, that settled it; the single would be "Austin." Blake, the big, tall, long-haired boy in the cowboy hat, put his hand on my shoulder and said, "Well, buddy, you'll get the credit or the blame, dependin.'" I didn't mind that responsibility because I had never felt more certain of anything in my life.

On a pleasant October morning, Sylvia accompanied me to Don Cook's house for a fundraiser and the opportunity to meet the wives of the Democratic presidential and vice-presidential nominees. As we approached Don's large colonial home (where President Harry Truman had once slept), Sylvia said "Good morning" to one of the robotic Secret Service agents who continued to stare straight ahead behind his shades and answered, staccato-like, "Good morning, ma'am." When I was introduced to Joe Leiberman's wife, Hadassah, I told her that I smelled Democratic victory in the air, and she replied, "From your mouth to God's ears." When I told Tipper Gore that I thought her husband was the most qualified person to run for president in my lifetime, she responded enthusiastically, "Oh, he IS, he IS!"

Back in 1976 when Al Gore was elected to a Tennessee seat in Congress at the age of twenty-eight, I watched his victory speech on TV with Sparky, who was hanging out at my bachelor house. I told her, "That man will be president someday" and I thereafter believed that to be his destiny. So I was telling Tipper Gore the truth when I lauded her husband's qualifications for the office, but I hadn't been too keen about some of his campaign moves that year. Still, I thought he was smart enough and forceful enough to be a great president. But when Gore lost, I was never one of those who thought George W. Bush's presidency wasn't legitimate. Just because a candidate barely wins doesn't mean that person should barely govern. It's like the old adage: "Close only counts in horseshoes and hand grenades." Although Gore won the popular vote, the rules are that it's the candidate with the most *electoral* votes who wins—such a scenario had played out three times before: John Quincy Adams in 1824 (when Tennessee's Andrew Jackson won the popular vote), Rutherford Hayes in 1876, and Benjamin Harrison in 1888. When people told me they believed that Florida was stolen from Gore, I reminded them that some folks believed Texas and Illinois were stolen from Richard Nixon in 1960, giving the presidency to JFK. The democratic process can't please all of the people all of the time; ideally, it pleases a majority of the people a majority of the time.

I thought "I Wanna Talk About Me" would be a natural for Toby Keith. Toby had written and recorded a talking blues song, "Getcha Some," a couple of years before. I thought maybe he would then be open to doing a "country rap" song. So Terry Wakefield from Sony played "I Wanna Talk About Me" for Allison Jones, Toby Keith's A&R person at DreamWorks records. Allison was a very capable and highly regarded young woman. It's foolish for a songwriter to resent anyone for *passing* on a song, even if that person really dislikes the song. And dislike it Allison did! She told Terry, "Not only am I passing on this song; I *hate* this song!" So I knew that the only way I could pitch it would be to get a meeting with Toby's producer, James Stroud (who headed DreamWorks in Nashville). James did not typically take song meetings. He produced so many artists, I think he felt it would be impossible for him to find the time to listen to songs, too. That's what A&R people are for. By luck, I ran into him at a convenience store one day not long after Terry's meeting with Allison. I said, "James, I have one song for Toby. If you'll just give me four minutes, I think there's a good chance you'll think it was worth your time." I had him in a corner. He flipped open his cell phone, called his assistant, and said "Find me five minutes to listen to a Bobby Braddock song." I went by DreamWorks a couple of days later. Almost from the beginning of the song, James Stroud's face lit up. A gregarious, bearded, bear of a man, he ran out from behind his desk and grabbed me. "This is a damn hit!" he bellowed. He called up Toby Keith and played it for him over the phone. Toby, who rarely recorded songs that he didn't write himself, said he wanted to do it. James loved the demo, thought it sounded like a record.

The year 2001 started off great for me with Toby Keith cutting "I Wanna Talk About Me." James produced the record very much like my demo, only better. Brent Rowan played his same demo licks, only better. It would go on to be what was probably the hottest song I ever wrote, and at the #1 party, Allison Jones would pull Terry Wakefield aside and whisper, "I still *hate* it!"

Several years later, in 2010, I was offered a pretty lucrative sum for the use of "I Wanna Talk About Me" in TV ads for Houston Democratic mayor Bill White's race for governor of Texas against Republican incumbent Rick Perry. The money would have been nice, and Mayor White's politics were in line with my own, but I passed because I didn't want to politicize the song. I felt that it belonged not only to me, but to Toby Keith and his fans as well.

With Clint Black

Celebrating "I Wanna Talk About Me" with Toby Keith

With Tim McGraw

I drove down to Florida for what someone referred to as "the world's biggest middle-aged sock hop" at a venue on the grounds of Cypress Gardens. Before Disney World, Cypress Gardens rivaled Silver Springs as Florida's leading theme-park tourist attraction. The occasion for the sock hop was a concert featuring the PolKats, a name I coined for people from Polk County, Florida, who had gone on to pursue successful careers in commercial music. This included Winter Haven's Jim Stafford and Kent Lavoy (Lobo), both of whom had recorded national hits in the world of pop during the 1970s, and Auburndale's two country songwriters, Carl Chambers and me. Also there, in spirit but not in the flesh, was Gram Parsons, the so-called "father of country rock," who had OD'd on drugs in California twenty-seven years before.

While in Polk County, I got word that my half-sister Louise was dying in a hospital in the southwestern part of the state. She told her children that she wanted to see me before she left, so I drove on down to bid her farewell. I sat in a chair next to the bed and pulled up close to talk. When I told her how much I appreciated her having been so kind to my mother—who became Louise's stepmother when they were both twenty-six—she replied in a barely audible whisper, "I loved your mother." As a merry widow in her seventies, Louise had fallen madly in love, perhaps for the first time in her life, with a man her age. They went on to have about twenty lovely years together. A few months before, when he had passed away, ninety-four year-old Louise told me on the phone, "Honey, I don't want to live without Wes." Despite the sad ending, Louise and Wes's love story was truly a great one.

Speaking of love stories, there have been twenty-first century women in my life, of course, but I choose not to write much about them (as I did about women in earlier decades) because it's too recent. I don't want to cause any embarrassment including my own. But there is one little story that I can't resist telling. In the early 2000s, when there were a lot of open-faced cell phones with exposed keys or buttons, "pocket dialing" (or "butt dialing" or "purse dialing") was pretty common. For instance, a woman might lean her pocketed phone against something or poke the phone with some object in her purse, and inadvertently call someone at the beginning of her contact list or redial the last person she had a conversation with—like *you*. You might answer and hear her talking up a storm—about *you*. There was a lady going through a divorce who adamantly told me that I was the only man she was seeing, which I believed until one day when she butt-dialed me, and I heard her telling a girlfriend, "I feel like a whore. I'm fucking two men." Another lady accidentally called me, and I heard her and her sister making fun of my stammer.

B lake and I were deeply disturbed—but not shocked—when we were told that the release date for "Austin" would not be in January but in April "*if Giant doesn't fold*." AOL had bought Time/Warner. We were hoping that Irving Azoff would either sign a five-year deal with the new Warner organization

(Warner and Azoff co-owned Giant) or go it alone with Giant—we had heard both scenarios—but we also had heard that Giant was really about to shut down. Fortunately, a Giant promotion man named Fritz Kuhlman committed mutiny: he took it on himself to have "Austin" sent to radio stations several weeks before he was supposed to. Radio jumped on it—they didn't care what was going on in Nashville, they had something to play that their listeners were excited about. *Thank you*, Fritz Kuhlman! On the day that "Austin" was the most requested song in Kansas City, Giant announced that they were shutting down operations. If not for Fritz, Blake might not have made it to radio (at least not then).

Warner Bros. had the option to sign some of the Giant artists if they so chose. Jim Ed Norman, the tall, courtly preacher's son who ran the Warner Nashville office, told me they were taking a look at Blake. A couple of days later he called to say he was going to see if radio could hold on to their excitement if Warner waited and re-released "Austin" in a couple of months—I thought this was a very bad idea, but at least he was now talking about Warner signing Blake. Then "Austin," without a record label, jumped into the national charts, #58 in *Billboard* and #47 in *R&R* (*Radio & Records*). Jim Ed called again and said "Austin" was unstoppable. I wrote in my journal:

> *He expressed his enthusiasm for Blake and having him*
> *as a Warner artist, and said it would be an honor working*
> *with me, that I'm one of his heroes.*

As the record galloped up the charts, there was a frantic effort to get things done. Debbie Z became Blake's manager, something they had planned to do even if Giant hadn't gone out of business. A video had to be shot. Blake was getting a band together, and I helped him rehearse the musicians.

We needed to record two more songs to complete the forthcoming album. One was "Every Time I Look at You," which Blake wrote with Doug Johnson. The other was "If I Was Your Man," which Lauren wrote with Don Henry. I had nothing to do with Blake hearing that one. Debbie Z, who had known Don when they were growing up back in California, loved the song, but thought Don was the sole writer, having no idea that my daughter had anything to do with it. She called Don to tell him she had played it for Blake and that he wanted to record it. Coincidentally, Jeep and I were at Don's apartment when he got the call. When Lauren told songwriter Mark D. Sanders, formerly her high school substitute teacher, that Blake Shelton was recording a song of hers, Mark said, "Well *of course* he is." I'm certain many people suspected nepotism when they knew that Blake had cut my daughter's song. The truth is, I wouldn't have dreamed of pitching him this hard-rocking, New-Age, old-hippy song.

We went to Georgetown Mastering to have the songs mastered ("master" can be a verb in the music business). Mastering is the final fine-tuning of recorded music to prepare it for radio play and retail sale. The tracks already having been mixed, mastering can't remove anything that's already there, but it can change the way it sounds with further equalization, or perhaps increased or decreased compression. The mastering process can also give the songs on an album some commonality—to make sure, for example, that they are all at the same volume level. Georgetown was owned by mastering engineer Denny Purcell, a funny little guy who spent at least a half-hour with each song before hitting a hotel desk bell that summoned us into the mastering room to give it a listen. Blake and I often deferred to the opinion of Ed Seay, our engineer extraordinaire. The only reason Blake was there was that he was a brand new artist and not yet working the road a lot.

One day, about the time that "Austin" entered the Top Ten, Blake and I went to the Longhorn, a popular eatery/drinkery near Music Row, and we had several people coming over to our table. A couple of weeks later when we went back to the Longhorn, Blake was mobbed. All of this sudden success was getting to him and making him a little crazy.

One memorable night, Blake and his girlfriend, Kaynette, Jeep and Jim (in town from New York), an old family friend of ours named Diane Dickerson, and I were driving down lower Broadway in downtown Nashville. The radio was turned up loud as the DJ said, "Here it is, number one all over America this week: Blake Shelton singing 'Austin.'"

On August 29, the song had been at #1 in *Billboard*'s country chart for five weeks—the biggest debut single since "Achy Breaky Heart" ten years before—and it was #18 in *Billboard*'s "pop" chart. The #1 party at Warner Bros. was a very big deal, with three hundred people in attendance, all of whom seemed jubilant except Kaynette, crying over the prospect of losing Blake, who was telling her that he wanted more freedom. From the stage, Blake said wonderful things about me. Warner Bros. presented huge stuffed Bugs Bunnies to the tall young singer, the songwriters, and me. Ed Seay was recognized for engineering the first all-digital #1 in Nashville. I had never felt so much personal power and glory. Chari Pirtle, my movie buddy who had never shown any kind of boy-girl interest in me, was constantly at my side holding my hand.

Later on, as the roar and excitement faded away, I lay in my bed feeling magnificently happy. I had taken this kid, gotten him a record deal, and his first record was a mega hit. I had started off my sixties with a brand new career.

And the *old* career was doing well, too. Super producer Tony Brown had told me that he'd heard Toby Keith's record of "I Wanna Talk About Me" played at some meeting in LA—"What a monster hit that's gonna be," Tony said. Chuck Cannon, who had co-written some of Toby's biggest hits with him, e-mailed me, "Screw in your cleats! Bobby, you're going to have a huge hit on this one." I had just seen Toby's video and thought it was maybe the best I'd ever seen. It would be the only big country rap hit until Jason Aldean's recording of "Dirt Road Anthem" almost ten years later.

Not only were things going gangbusters for *me*; everything around me seemed to be doing well. Bill Clinton had left office with the economy in great shape, and it didn't appear that George W. Bush was going to do anything to change it. America was at peace, and there seemed to be no wars on the horizon. I think I probably went to sleep with a big smile on my face and slept like a baby.

When I woke up on September 11 at about 11:00 a.m., I looked at my caller ID as usual. By this time of day, I normally would have received a few calls; two or three or four or five. I did a double take when I saw that I had received *thirty*! Although my ringer was off, I knew I was getting still another call because a number popped up in the little window. It was my former stepson, Sparky's son Allen Lawrence. "Is Jeep okay?" he asked.

"What do you mean?" I asked, raising my voice.

"Have you been watching TV?"

While Allen was telling me that New York City had been attacked, I was scanning through the calls, frightened half out of my wits. I felt slightly better when I saw that several of the calls were from Lauren, first from her home number, then later from her cell phone. When I wasn't able to get through to her on the phone, rather than searching for her calls on my voice mail I ran to my office and sat down at the computer. I signed on to AOL and found an e-mail that read, *"You must be sleeping, we are safe, you may not be able to get through to us on the phone because all circuits are busy . . . just know that we are safe—I love you very much—Beep."*

She had been five miles from Ground Zero in their Upper West Side condo. Jim had called her from his office in midtown Manhattan, about two miles from Ground Zero, and he was very upset. He told her to turn on the TV. Together on the phone, they watched the first tower collapse, then felt the aftershock.

Jeep forwarded me several e-mails that captured the high drama of America under attack. From Jim's stepmother in Bayville, New Jersey: *Where are you children? PLEASE check in with me by e-mail, can't get thru on phones. We love you.*

From Jim's sister Aly who worked for AP in London: *I CANNOT GET THRU TO ANY OF YOU. NEVER IN MY NEWSGATHERING LIFE HAVE I SEEN SUCH DESTRUCTION AND TERROR. I AM SHOCKED AND SOBBING AND TRYING TO WORK!!*

From Lauren's "Aunt Karen" in Nashville: *Just got up. Am freaking. Are you okay? Couldn't reach you by phone. Ron's not home. As soon as possible let me know you & Jim are okay. Foggy about what's happening. This is so scary. Are we at war or what?*

Another message from Aly in London: *It was bin Laden.*

From Jeep's friend Shane Tarleton: *we're still missing 2 of our friends that worked in the trade cntr . . . i've done nothing but cry all day.*

Jim's other sister, Lisa, wrote from California: *Dylan's school just opened. Do you think he will be safe? He wants to go.*

And again from Jim's stepmom, Joy: *I would like to know how in God's Name four planes were hijacked on one given morning. We better start taking lessons from Israeli Security and damn fast.*

Within a few weeks it was bombs away over Afghanistan. I supported the invasion because we were told that was where al Qaida was. I wrote: "The people around Bush—Cheney, Rumsfeld—if there's one thing these guys can do well, it's wage a war."

Back in the late summer, Karen Hellard and I had been scouting houses for Lauren and Jim, who had decided that they wanted to move to Nashville. I shot videos of the homes and sent them to the kids. They fell in love with a Cape Cod-type house in a development called Tanglewood in Pegram, a small town twenty miles west of Nashville. They loved what they saw of both the exterior and interior and made a deposit on the house based solely on the video. A house like that in Nashville proper would have cost almost twice as much. They had found buyers for their Manhattan condo shortly before 9/11. Remarkably, the buyers didn't renege after the tragedy and went through with the closing, although real estate values in Manhattan would soon plummet. Jeep and Jim rolled into Tennessee in early October. After working for a PR firm for several years, Jim was ready to go into business for himself. His first job in Nashville was the star-studded "Rock the Barn" charity event at Ronnie Dunn's place. He did such a good job getting publicity, that Donna Hilley put him on salary to represent Sony Publishing.

Blake's self-titled album—we couldn't agree on a better name for it—was selling well. We also were having trouble agreeing on the follow-up single to "Austin." For several weeks, the big contender was the one that Lauren and Don Henry wrote, "If I Was Your Man." Blake leaned toward it and so did Warner label head Jim Ed Norman. If I had jumped on the bandwagon, it would have looked like a conflict of interest, but if I had opposed it I would have felt disloyal to Jeep, so I just kept my mouth shut. When they started to cool on that one, I strongly urged them to put out "Ol' Red," because not only did Warner Bros.' research show it to be the strongest contender, but my own "rate from one to ten" survey of about thirty people showed it to be way ahead of everything else. Yet the label decided that the single should be a song Blake co-wrote with his singing hero, Earl Thomas Conley, "All Over Me," the one that had almost become the first single instead of "Austin." Good thing it hadn't been first: even following up a monster multi-week single, "All Over Me" tanked at #18. Had it been Blake's debut single, it's hard to imagine that it would have done anything at all. Only an undeniable monster like "Austin" could have gotten into the charts without a label.

I have always been amused at how little the general public knows about songwriters and songwriting. Unless acquainted with or standing face-to-face with a songwriter, a majority of people seem to think that singers all write their own songs. A rather extreme example of this was the rural store clerk who misunderstood what songwriting was, and asked Sonny Curtis's wife if her husband was a songwriter, and when she replied that he was, the old man said "Well, see if he'll write out the words to 'Mule Train' (a song from the 1940s)." But if I thought that songwriting was an unrecognized and misunderstood profession, then I hadn't seen anything—not until I became a producer. I was referred to as Blake's manager, Blake's agent, Blake's promoter, you name it. So I shouldn't have been surprised at what happened when Jeep, Jim, and I went down to see Blake and his band perform at the County Line Saloon, a country music venue near Melbourne, Florida. There were probably two thousand people at the humongous honky-tonk. From the stage, Blake had introduced me with a big buildup: "The man who gave me a career and a life, *Bobby Braddock*!" After the show there were hundreds waiting to get his autograph, lined up alongside the walls of the club. A lady clad in western wear and a cowboy hat approached me and said she had to get home soon to relieve the babysitter, so would I be so kind as to get her ahead of the line so she could get Blake's autograph. She seemed very nice, so I agreed to do it. As we headed over toward Blake she said, "You might not like me saying this, but he sure sounds a lot better in person than he does on the album." I thought of the weeks I had spent in the studio making sure each little sound was just right, and getting Blake's vocals as perfect as possible. When you see a live show, you get caught up in the excitement, and maybe it seems like everything is sounding great, but if you listen to a record and then hear the live performance (without being there to see it), in most cases there is no comparison—the studio recording is usually going to sound ten times better. "Where are you going?" the lady shouted as I turned around and headed back toward my table. I figured if she thought Blake was so much better without me, I would just sit back and let her get his autograph without me.

Christmas was in the air as I pulled up at Sunset Grill to meet Harlan Howard for lunch. Standing there by his long Cadillac was America's greatest country songwriter: white-haired, craggy-faced, tall and hunched over. I rolled my window down.

"Why don't we eat at the Palm?" he asked. I opened the door of my black Lincoln LS, and Harlan climbed in. He was seventy-four but looked ten years older. We headed for downtown Nashville and the fancy chain restaurant known for its lobster. As the valet guy handed me a ticket, Harlan asked if I would like to sit at the bar, so we went there and ordered drinks and our lunch.

"Well, double-B, you've had you a hell of a year," he said with sort of a pleasant grumble. About the time that Blake's "Austin" had spent five weeks at #1, along came Toby Keith's record of my "I Wanna Talk About Me," which turned out to be just as big as "Austin." Back when I had first started working with Blake, it had gotten back to me that Harlan was wondering aloud why I was producing, saying that songwriters had no business producing. It made me angry at him, and I foolishly let it affect our friendship for about a year. That was just Harlan being Harlan. I loved the man and was glad to be hanging out with him again. Of all the people who had been inducted into the Country Music Hall of Fame at that time, there were only four nonperforming songwriters: the husband-wife team of Boudleaux and Felice Bryant, Cindy Walker, and Harlan Howard.

"I'm gonna write some letters, and start the process to get you in the Country Music Hall of Fame," he said.

"Harlan, that's nice of you, but I don't see that ever happening for me."

"Oh hell yeah, it's gonna happen double-B. It may take a few years, but it's gonna happen."

We chatted and enjoyed our drinks for a few minutes, then suddenly Harlan got very quiet. He told me he was dizzy. When they brought our food he asked if I wanted to eat his lobster bisque, said he didn't feel like eating. After a few minutes he seemed to recover.

After lunch we headed back toward Sunset Grill. I pulled up behind his car, let him out, and bade him farewell. As he waved goodbye and drove off in his long Cadillac, I thought "Someday I'll see Harlan drive away for the last time." Little did I know it, but this was that someday.

Blake's album had gone "gold" and was moving toward "platinum," with sales so far approaching 800,000. Not bad, but despite the monster airplay for "Austin," those were not the Garth-like multimillion sales I had hoped for. Blake was frustrated because sales chief Chris Palmer had told him that a video on "Ol' Red," the third and final single from the self-titled album, was out of the question. I went to label head Jim Ed Norman, a decent man and one of the really good guys in the music business. "Blake came to Warner Bros. with a monster hit," I said. "Warner didn't let him do a video for 'All Over Me' and now he's been told no on a video for 'Ol' Red.' I have to tell you that Blake's pretty disappointed and I am, too."

Jim Ed replied, "If we have to do a video to prove to Blake that we love him, we'll do it, but it won't get played. CMT (Country Music Television) doesn't like Blake, they don't like his image." CMT didn't like Blake's mullet— a hairstyle in which the hair is short on the top and sides and long in the back—and neither did the label. Though Blake did start out with a mullet, by this time I think that wearing long hair under his hat made it look more like a mullet than it actually was. There had been several people who had told me over the past several months that I should advise Blake to get rid of his mullet or cut off his hair. I always told them that I was Blake's producer, not his hair stylist or fashion advisor. A few days after my meeting with Jim Ed, Blake called and told me that he had just met with Chris Palmer, who told him that a video for "Ol' Red" had been approved.

Written by Mark Sherrill, Don Goodman, and James Bohan, "Ol' Red" was not only a great lowdown-funky groove number, but one of the best story songs I'd ever heard. The premise is this: A lifer who is entrusted with taking Ol' Red, the prison bloodhound, on his evening walk. The guy starts routing Red on a daily encounter with a female hound that his cousin has penned up in the woods. Then after keeping Red away from his lover-dog for a few days, the convict escapes from prison knowing that the bloodhound will be far more interested in running to his canine cutie than chasing a human scent. Of all the singles that Blake and I cut together, this one was probably my favorite, and his, too. Over the years it became a bigger crowd pleaser than some of his #1s. It was his signature song. But at the time—perhaps because it was following up a stiff, "All Over Me"—it didn't quite penetrate the Top Ten. However, the video, reminiscent of classic prison films like *Cool Hand Luke* and *The Shawshank Redemption*, would become the top video on CMT. They may not have liked Blake's hair, but the little retro-looking song movie would be irresistible.

The "Ol' Red" video was filmed at the ancient and abandoned Tennessee State Prison on River Road west of Nashville, the locale of a few prison movies including *The Green Mile* with Tom Hanks. The "Ol' Red" director was award-winner Peter Zavadil. It co-starred NASCAR icon Elliott Sadler as the prisoner's cousin, the one who planted the female dog in the woods. Blake asked me to play his cellmate, and he wanted me to use my Charles Manson impersonation. I didn't take lightly Manson's heinous crimes but thought that he was the scariest-looking dude who ever lived, and I could contort my face to look quite a bit like him. Back in the 1970s—when I was thirty-something going on eighteen—I would often, with a carload of friends, pull up alongside another car and, as we waited for the light to change, stare at the driver with my big evil eyes and crazy grin. I recall a lot of squirmy, nervous-looking drivers (and look back in amazement that one of them didn't shoot me).

Early in the video Blake is shown being led to his cell, then rolling his eyes and sighing when he sees his creepy cellmate. What I wouldn't realize until seeing the finished product was that it looked like I was giving Blake the once-over and salivating over my new bunk hunk.

The song search was hot and heavy for Blake's album No. 2. It was a lot different from finding songs for album No. 1. The boy was now a star, and we no longer had to beg for good songs; a lot of first-rate ones were being pitched our way.

My mail bin at Sony/Tree was constantly overflowing with CDs and cassettes (I was requesting the outdated cassettes because the CD player in my car was in the *glove box*). I was taking these Blake submissions home in cardboard boxes and listening to everything, no matter who sent them. Of every forty songs, I probably sent one to Blake. He showed interest in maybe one out of every three or four songs he got from me, and maybe half of those would stick. Blake wasn't an easy sell. What was really frustrating was falling in love with a song that I couldn't sell Blake on. But I didn't expect him to record something he didn't like.

The first song we recorded for album No. 2 was one that Debbie Z had played us several months before. We were both sold on it then, and we stayed sold on it. Whenever people said that "He Stopped Loving Her Today" was the saddest song ever written, I started saying, "No, the saddest song ever written is 'The Baby.'" Blake and I were the babies of our families, so this song had a huge effect on both of us. Written by Harley Allen and Michael White, it was a warm, wonderful story set to a beautiful, plaintive melody, with an ending that was like an icepick through the heart.

On a very cold February 5, 2002, we assembled at the Sony/Tree studio to start tracking the second album. Though I had gone over the arrangements with the musicians the night before (we had started having pre-production rehearsals) it was not until we were in the studio at the session that an intro for "The Baby" hit me. I started singing "Mama's died and gone to Heaven," which wasn't a line in the song, but it well could have been. I sat down at the piano and played my melody, using a different chord change for each syllable, giving it a majestic and churchy sound. Blake liked it. I knew that it would be just the piano by itself at the beginning of the song, and the string section would play the same thing at the end. The pianist was a sweetheart of a guy named Mike Rojas, who played it perfectly. We would record the strings several days later, at a session booked for the orchestra.

I had hired Charlie McCoy to play harmonica on "The Baby." Charlie, whom I had first met forty-four years before when we were teenage musicians in Miami, was renowned for performing the wonderful harmonica part on George Jones's record of "He Stopped Loving Her Today," so I said, "Charlie, just play the same kind of thing that you played on George's record."

We cut two more songs that afternoon, then the next day's sessions included one that both Blake and I loved, a song that Doug Johnson wouldn't let us cut when Blake was on Giant, called "Playboys of the Southwestern World," a very funny uptempo story-song written by Neal Coty and former pop singer Randy VanWarmer. (That night, a group of about fifty people from throughout Music Row would drop by to drink beer and do a group sing-along on "Playboys.")

Several days later, after all the tracking and overdubs, it came down to Blake, engineer Ed Seay, and me in the little mixing studio, Cool Tools, co-owned by Doug Johnson and Ed. Cool Tools was located in the otherwise empty building that a year before had housed the late Giant Records. We were doing Blake's vocals in the middle of what felt like a ghost town. To make the long hours more bearable, we often cut up and pulled pranks on each other. One night Blake got my cell phone while I was preoccupied, and programmed it to operate entirely in Spanish—which I didn't speak so well— and I was unaware of what he had done until I got home. My revenge was leaving him a message telling him that the computer had completely wiped out everything we had recorded in the past month (eventually saying "just kidding" at the end of the message). Later when checking my messages, I heard Blake saying in his country boy drawl, "Thanks for makin' me shit all over my tractor!" Blake brought the kid out in me. Cutting an album is hard work and dealing with a record label is not always pleasant (and it would get worse after Jim Ed Norman left the label) but Blake, Ed, and I had great fun in our isolated little world.

When *comping*—making a composite, using the best version of each line, sometimes using the best version of just one *word*—Blake and I had invented our own way of rating, to try to add a little joviality to the dreary, grueling process. If we heard a line that Blake had performed particularly well, I might say, "Now that's not exactly a hat pin jabbed into the eardrum!" Then upon hearing the next usable performance, Blake might say, "Well, that's not exactly a sledgehammer smashing your balls!"

Back during our first sessions, I had told Blake, "We can save time if we do what most everyone else is doing. If you have a problem with a particular note, rather than you having to sing it over and over, Ed can just tune it."

"If somebody has to have their vocals tuned, then they don't deserve a damn record deal," he had said contemptuously.

One night, after we finally finished all the comping, Blake and Kaynette (whom he had gotten close to again) came by the studio. He was tired from two weeks of touring, but was there to hear the vocal harmonies that Leslie Satcher and Larry Cordle had put on "The Baby." After listening and giving his stamp of approval, the road-weary country boy stood up, looking forward to getting home to a good night's sleep. I reminded him that there was one note that still wasn't quite right; it was just a little flat and he needed to re-sing it so we could start mixing the song.

"Hell," he said, with a dismissive wave of his hand, "*tune* it!"

A few weeks later, Debbie Z and I drove about one hour on the interstate, then up and down little country roads to the five hundred acre spread that Blake had recently purchased (I called it "Blake Acres") in Hickman County, Tennessee. He and Kaynette, whom Blake often called Kat, lived in a small house there. This land was to be Blake's own private deer-hunting paradise. After driving us around the property in his fifteen-horsepower "Gator," we went inside to review some songs. Blake, a first-rate acoustic guitar player, grabbed his instrument and asked us to listen to a song he had written about Kat and himself. She wasn't present, probably visiting her parents in Oklahoma. The song, which he called "Whisper Your Name," was a powerful ballad about a man who had seen his dreams come true, but in the process almost lost the most important thing of all. I played "song doctor"—suggesting changes for a couple of lines—and recommended that he title it "The Dreamer," telling him I thought that would be a great title for the new album. Both the new song and album No. 2 would be called *The Dreamer.*

Jim Ed Norman's A&R assistant of twenty years was a lady I will refer to as Pam Levin. She once told me, "I'm not trying to be a hard-ass." When someone tells you they're not trying to be a hard-ass, they're probably a hard-ass. She gave me grief without end: about my production assistant, about the budget, about how much to pay the musicians, often with curt directives sent via e-mail. I sent a very courteous response to one particularly nasty e-mail, and made certain that hers was tacked onto mine and copied it to Jim Ed so he could see what she had written me. The first thing the next morning I received an effusive apology from Pam.

I pulled myself away from the business of music production long enough to join a group of songwriters for a few days in Washington. The executive director of Nashville Songwriters Association International, Bart Herbison, had been herding writers through the marbled halls of Congress for several years. Bart, a brilliant lobbyist and fearless advocate for songwriters, was former administrative assistant to Rep. Bob Clement (D-TN). The routine was for several of us to meet with a member of Congress, then Bart would masterfully explain what a small piece of the pie songwriters got and how illegal downloads would eventually drive many of us out of the business. Then it was our turn; sometimes it was known in advance what the lawmaker's favorite song was, and the writer of that composition would sing it—and another ally on copyright issues would be won over. The songwriters of America had some support from both Democrats and Republicans. One of the solons, Sen. Orin Hatch (R-UT), was actually a songwriter of sorts himself.

I especially loved walking through the senate office building and seeing the former offices of senators who went on to be president: Kennedy, Johnson, and Nixon. I broke away from the group one day and went to a meeting I had arranged with the congressman from my home county in Florida. A fifth-generation member of a citrus and cattle family, Adam Putnam (R-FL) had first been elected as the youngest member of Congress a couple of years before, at age twenty-six. With his earnest youthfulness and bright red hair, he was often referred to as "Congressman Opie." He was a very likable young man, and I was quickly learning that there was very little difference on the likeability scale between Democrats and Republicans. The most fun I had was when our group visited with Rep. Howard Coble (R-NC), a man about ten years my senior who was chairman of the subcommittee on intellectual property. He was a fan of my song ("We're Not) the Jet Set," and we sang it together.

I learned a lesson, in those nervous post 9/11 days: don't leave a black briefcase sitting in the middle of the lobby in a congressional office building, even if you're only a few feet away tying your shoes. My little attaché was immediately surrounded by more men in black suits and sunglasses than a Blues Brothers audition.

The spring of 2002 was a time of vigilant searching for songs. In my history as a songwriter, I had never liked it when producers asked me to drop songs off to be listened to, rather than letting me play them in person. It didn't take long as a producer for me to see where they were coming from, learning that I much preferred listening to songs in private. Whenever someone was sitting across from me, I found myself concentrating not so much on the song, but on how I was going to respond to it.

In early June, we recorded in a very large studio—way too impractical to have been built in what had become the digital age, but a great luxurious studio that was fun to record in—The Tracking Room, located just off Music Row on a street that dead-ends at the Interstate. We cut several songs, including Blake's title song, "The Dreamer," and one I had written with my friend Kathy Locke, "Someday," an I-wonder-what-happens-when-we-die song (when Blake first heard it he said, "These are things I've wondered about all my life"). One unique thing about "Someday" was that Brent Rowan, my favorite session guitarist in Nashville, played Wurlitzer electric piano.

There was one change in personnel on these sessions: we switched steel guitar players, from Dan Dugmore to Paul Franklin. I suspect it was because Dugmore was unavailable for these dates, and I had always wanted to work with Franklin. I would characterize them this way: Dan Dugmore was arguably the best steel guitar player in the world, and Paul Franklin was arguably the best steel guitar player in the world. You couldn't go wrong with either one.

Mr. Franklin was not the only Paul who happened on the scene in the midsummer of 2002. There was Paul Worley, whose tenure at Sony/Tree has been chronicled here. Jim Ed was now bringing Paul on board, naming him chief creative officer at Warner Nashville. Paul's producer credits were pretty impressive: Martina McBride, Collin Raye, and the Dixie Chicks, to name a few.

Nashville born and raised, Paul was the unpretentious son of a Vanderbilt professor. He made his mark as a Nashville studio guitarist but soon discovered that he had a knack for producing. Looking young for early fifties, Paul reminded me of a big teddy bear. His squinty eyes and crooked smile gave the impression that he was always about to share something humorous. He was warm and charming most of the time, except for those occasional times that he was, well, not so warm and charming. Paul was usually a great guy when you could find him, but he had a reputation for being inaccessible.

"The best thing I can do is probably just stay out of your way," he told me when Blake and I met with him. He kept his word, because after that first meeting, neither Blake nor I could seem to find him or reach him on the phone. It bothered Blake more than me, because I didn't really want someone breathing down my neck anyway, though feedback from Paul would have been welcome because he was such a great producer.

Blake and I finally met again with Paul—and Pam—and they wanted us to record four more songs. Blake, who was not very happy with Warner Bros. by then, balked at doing that much more recording. He was happy with everything we had turned in and wanted to record no more than two additional songs. I was able to work out a compromise of three more songs.

It was a hard business. Debbie Z couldn't take the stress and quit. Blake's new manager was John Dorris, a genial old-school guy of my generation, a stocky, balding man with a twinkle in his eye and a penchant for calling other men "brother man." My friend Chari Pirtle was feeling that she had gotten in over her head as my production assistant, so she quit and was replaced by Doug Johnson's assistant from back in the Giant days, Milly Catignani (pronounced "cat 'n' nanny"), middle-aged daughter of a local coaching icon. Milly was reliably efficient, always on top of things.

We went in and cut three more songs, two of which would make the album. After the album was all mixed, it was mastered by an engineer whose name was Hank Williams, same as the singing legend. We played everything for Paul and Pam who both danced around the room with delight. "There are six or seven singles on this album," Paul declared. So this phase of *The Dreamer*, the recording process, ended on a good note, and "The Baby" would be the first single. It would be a huge hit, almost as big as "Austin." *The Dreamer* would be my favorite album that Blake and I made together.

When *The Dreamer* was released, I was pretty excited until I looked at the CD cover booklet and read what we refer to as "label copy." Pam Levin giving herself equal billing with the producer—same sized letters at the top of the page right under my name—was not the way it was typically done, but I considered it more irritating than problematic and was inclined to let it pass. What really appalled me was the way the musicians were listed. Pam and I had butted heads several months before over the musicians' pay, when she had wanted them to be paid single scale for this project, after they had received double scale on the first album ("Sure," I said sarcastically, "let's tell the musicians that we're showing them our gratitude for cutting a hit album on Blake by slicing their pay in half.") Then a little later, she had said that she wanted to list all the musicians in bulk, rather than listing them song-by-song and showing who played on what. I had explained to her that Blake did not want that, and I assumed that the matter was settled until I took a look at the CD. Although Allison Prestwood had played electric bass on nine songs and a friend of Pam's on only one, the label copy listed Pam's friend first as though he had played on at least as many cuts as Allison. Shannon Forrest, a brilliant young drummer, had played on everything we cut, but because we used a sample of one drum lick originally played by another drummer on the demo, the two drummers were given equal billing as though we had used one as much as the other. I was furious, and Blake agreed to go with me to tell Jim Ed that this was the final straw, and we didn't want to work with Pam anymore. Jim Ed said, "Done." It was that simple. Our A&R person would be Paul Worley instead of Pam. Jim Ed also promised that future printings of the CD booklet would list musicians individually on each song.

Then it came time to pick the follow-up to "The Baby." The promotion department was convinced that "Heavy Liftin'," a hard-rocking testosterone-filled song penned by four writers, was a hit. I told Blake I thought it would be a mistake and wrote in my journal *"Please* don't!" What seemed to be the Shelton-Braddock curse continued: a monster hit followed by a bomb. "Heavy Liftin'" would peak at #32 in *Billboard*, and Warner would abandon it and put out "Playboys of the Southwestern World," which would go to #24. It would have been a much better follow-up to "The Baby" just as "Ol' Red" would have been a much better successor to "Austin." One can assume that any given song will do several chart positions better on the heels of a hit than coming after a flop. I was in charge of what our product sounded like—in interviews Blake would often say "What you hear on my records comes from Bobby's brain"—but once the music was recorded and mixed, it was pretty much out of my hands.

There were two things that I was agonizing over in 2003. One was of a personal nature. I had an almost fanatical obsession about fair play. If someone gave me credit that I did not deserve, I couldn't stand it; it made me feel embarrassed. Once, when someone introduced me in an audience as the writer of the Statler Brothers hit "Flowers on the Wall," I had to run right up to the stage and correct the person and tell him that I didn't write it. By the same token, I didn't want anything wrongfully taken away from me. I had always been proud of the place that "He Stopped Loving Her Today" seemed to have found in country music history, not only for my own legacy but for the legacy of the song's co-writer, Curly Putman, and the man who sang it, George Jones. For years "HSLHT" had consistently been the top vote-getter for country song of the century or all-time favorite country song. So when I watched *Top 100 Songs of Country Music*, a four-hour special on Country Music Television (CMT) that was said to have been based on an on-line poll taken by the Country Music Association, I was surprised that "Stand by Your Man" edged out our song for the top spot. "Stand by Your Man" was certainly a great Tammy Wynette record, but I thought it strange that the winner would be a song that was twelve years older than ours, and one that had generally placed several slots down in previous surveys. Why was it not a song that had come along more recently, or one that had come close before, such as "Crazy" or "Your Cheatin' Heart"? I started getting some answers. Two people behind the scenes at the show told me that "He Stopped Loving Her Today" had won the actual voting, but the show's producer, Kaye Zussman, put "Stand By Your Man" first because she wanted to promote her Tammy Wynette special that was to be shown three weeks later. These sources also told me that when Ms. Zussman saw the poll winners for *Top 100 Singers in Country Music*, she had asked "Who's Marty Robbins?" then proceeded to take Marty off the list simply because she had never heard of him. In Paul Griffith's *Nashville Scene* article about the top song, an unidentified Music Row veteran was quoted as saying, "An injustice has been done to the entire industry, all the artists and writers. The songs have had their place in country music history manipulated." CMT has made a tremendous contribution to country music over the years, and they stated clearly that the list was not based on voting alone. So my gripe was not with the network but with a television producer who had little knowledge about country music and ignored the actual poll results to suit her own purposes. Zussman's superiors at CMT must have shared my skepticism about her because she was dismissed shortly after this. Our song topped all the polls before her special in 2003, and has continued to top polls, so there you go. It will quite likely be booted into second place someday by some other song, possibly something that someone is writing at this very moment. If so, I'll be the first to congratulate the writer or writers of that song. Incidentally, Kaye Zussman ended up at the Weather Channel, where I hope she didn't rank one kind of weather event over another just to promote an upcoming special about dust storms.

The other thing that stuck in my craw did not affect me directly, but did have an impact on the men and women in our armed forces: the war in Iraq. I knew that Saddam Hussein was a very bad man, but I also saw no evidence that he had anything to do with 9/11. The guy responsible for that was *thought* to be living in a cave somewhere, and we couldn't find him. Osama bin Laden was a dangerous religious fanatic who wore a traditional robe and headdress and hated Saddam because he thought the Iraqi dictator a sinner for wearing European suits, smoking cigars, and drinking Mateus rosé. The two were enemies. Most of the people who attacked America were from bin Laden's country, Saudi Arabia; none were from Saddam's country, Iraq. I thought we were making a terrible mistake. To make a mistake about the favorite country song is a very small matter, but this mistake involved the lives of thousands of men and women who were loyally standing by, ready to serve us, trusting our leaders to send them into harm's way only when it was necessary. When I saw all these old guys on TV staunchly advocating the invasion, I thought of the adage "old men start wars that young men die in." This war's casualties would also include young women.

One day at Sony Publishing I defended Paul Worley and writer-musician Wally Wilson when I heard them being castigated for carrying signs at a peace rally. But being afraid that any involvement on my part in an anti-war demonstration might affect the career of Blake Shelton—hence mine—I took the cowardly route and did not participate. The war in Iraq would almost cause a rift in my friendship with Michael Kosser. A few years later, when his position on the war (like that of many Americans) would change, he would tell me that his wife, Gina, had opposed the war all along. "No wonder you were giving me such a hard time," I would say to Kosser. "You knew I couldn't *divorce* you."

Producing Blake Shelton's second album, 2003

Blake had urged me to travel with him on his tour bus and do some co-writing out on the road. Being something of a control freak, I much preferred to have my own transportation, so I met him at the beginning of his tour in a suburb of Buffalo, New York. As I approached his bus, which was parked behind the hotel where they were staying, I could hear Blake's boisterous laugh a good three hundred feet away. I carried my small portable keyboard to his hotel room where we kicked around some ideas. Around noon we broke for lunch and drove to a nearby Subway restaurant. There were several good-looking college-age girls there, and I asked Blake, "So do you think these are some of your fans who will be at the show tonight?"

"No, man," he said, "that's not my demographic."

"Really?" I inquired skeptically. "What *is* your demographic?"

"Definitely older women," he said.

After lunch, as we approached my car, a van pulled up beside us. "Is that who I think it is?" chirped the lady behind the wheel, practically licking her chops.

"Well, are you thinking that it's Blake Shelton?" I answered with a question.

Then three large women in late middle age jumped out of the van and ran up to Blake, squealing like teenagers. With a grin, he looked at me and said, "What'd I tell you?"

Despite the mullet controversy, Blake was a good-looking guy. But this was a few years before the slimmed-down Blake with short hair and a week's growth of beard, the TV star in the trendy clothes who would be on America's short list of sexiest males.

I caught up with Blake again a few weeks later. He was opening for Toby Keith in Memphis, so I took a date with me and we met Jeep and Jim at the Peabody Hotel, then we all went on to the show together. I had always felt pretty short whenever I was around Blake or Toby, but being around both of them at the same time made me feel like a midget in a redwood forest. For a couple of years, Toby's mantra had been that "I Wanna Talk About Me" wasn't really a rap song because it had been written by the guy who wrote "He Stopped Loving Her Today."

Blake had compiled two lists: a list of songs that had greatly influenced him, and a list of songs that he wished he had recorded. I viewed this as Blake's music manifesto and considered his words to be the template for his next album. I knew that we were looking at music that was a little more country than what we had been doing, and that it would include some drinking songs. I came up with an album title that I was only half serious about—*Blake's Barn & Grill*—which he actually liked. So beginning in the fall of 2003 (after Blake and Kaynette ran off to the Smoky Mountains and got married) we would spend several intense months finding and recording songs that would eventually make up album No. 3: *Blake Shelton's Barn & Grill.*

THE BLAKE SESSIONS

Award-winning engineer Ed Seay confides in me, 2003

While recording "The Last Country Song," 2005. (*From left to right*) John Anderson, me, Blake, Ed Seay, George Jones

We returned to the Tracking Room with the same crew and recorded two drinking songs plus "When Somebody Knows You That Well," a ballad written by Jimmy Melton and the co-writer of "The Baby," Harley Allen. The following January we went back in, this time with a new acoustic guitar player, Bryan Sutton, a young bluegrass whiz whose meter was tighter than a metronome. We cut four more songs including a very funny one written by Paul Overstreet and Rory Lee Feek, "Some Beach."

Warner Bros. had worked out a little scheme with the organizers of the Country Radio Seminar. CRS was an annual event that brought radio executives from all over the country to Nashville. The previous year, the talk of the seminar had been about one well-known radio personality who was having sex with himself in his hotel room, with the lights on, sitting by the window in plain view of hundreds of other seminar participants. He had no idea that he was in a fishbowl, and was deeply humiliated and instantly ostracized. This year Blake was featured in a little video made for a CRS audience, showing him in a hotel room, sitting by the window banging away on his guitar, writing a song, but from the street down below it appeared that he was doing the same thing the guy had done the year before. While Blake, Ed, and I were working away in the studio, Blake got a call from Janice Azrak, art director at Warner. Janice told him that the video director was on his way to her office with a copy, and she wanted Blake to watch it with her. Blake asked her to bring it on to Ed's studio so we could all watch it on the TV in the break room. Janice, a true character, wore colorful clothes and spoke (with considerable volume) in a very distinct New York dialect that a Southern boy like me would call a "Brooklyn accent." As we watched Blake's hilarious video, Janice excitedly squealed, "It fuckin' *woiks*! It fuckin' *woiks*!" From that night forward, whenever Ed and I heard anything coming through the studio speakers that sounded good to us—if we thought it was *working*—we would invariably burst forth with "It fuckin' *woiks*! It fuckin' *woiks*!"

Before we were even through recording the new album, *Barn & Grill* needed a lead single. Manager John Dorris and I favored "Some Beach." The song told a very funny story about a guy who managed his anger by blurting out "Some Beach!" for "sonofabitch!" followed by a description of some peaceful, tropical seaside paradise. Blake was on the fence regarding what to release, so the promotion department won out with "When Somebody Knows You That Well." Unlike the first two albums, this one would be launched with a misfire. But that may have been a blessing, because the other option would have been putting out an inferior version of "Some Beach," not nearly as good as the one that would eventually go to radio. It bothered me that we had recorded "Some Beach" with a strong Caribbean flavor—Kenny Chesney and Jimmy Buffett already had a corner on that market. I suggested that we break down what we had and start all over, make it rawer. I took Brent Rowan to Ed Seay's new little studio where we eventually removed everything from the original tracks except the kick drum. I asked Brent to put in twice as many beats against the original tempo, and he came up with a killer intro that reminded me of the country-rock classic "Third Rate Romance." He then put on electric bass which added to the uniqueness—a guitar player will play licks that a bass player wouldn't normally do. We recorded the other musicians one at a time, which is called "stacking." I talked Blake into being our acoustic guitar guy. Then I had Paul Franklin do a series of steel guitar fills, leaving only two that had the flavor of "the islands." Jonathan Yudkin played like Hank Williams's fiddle player from the 1950s, Jerry Rivers. Shannon Forrest contributed new drum parts, Ed Seay programmed cymbal crashes from his computer, and Shawn Simpson shook the shakers. It sounded like a garage band. We ditched Blake's original vocal and he did it over from scratch, an improvement over the first one. Carl Jackson and Leslie Satcher sang bluegrass-type harmony, and—some beach, we had it! Like "Austin" and "The Baby," "Some Beach" would become a multi-week #1 monster hit.

But we didn't know that yet on the morning of March 2 when Blake and I were at a "song meeting" at Warner Bros. All we knew was that the current single was a loser, and if the follow-up didn't do well the new album would be in trouble—and so would Blake's career. Sometimes I complained in my journal that I didn't have a life. I was spending more time at Warner Bros. than I was at Sony Publishing. On this morning, Blake and I were listening to songs with Paul Worley and Pam Levin. No longer our go-to person at the label, Pam was still working with us on the song search. In the middle of our meeting, Jim Ed Norman came to the door. The lanky label head's skin was almost as white as his neatly combed hair. He had opened up a couple of strange-looking letters from the home office in LA and learned that Pam Levin, art director Janice Azrak, and their assistants had been fired. Then he found another letter containing *his own* pink slip—he and his assistant were both being fired. The long-serving head of Nashville's Warner Bros. label didn't even get the courtesy of a phone call. Blake walked over to Jim Ed and gave him a hug. Paul seemed upset that his friend had lost his job. Sales head Chris Palmer was still at Warner Bros., and I was thinking it might not be good for Blake if Palmer moved up, as there had been considerable tension between them. The position would not be filled for several months, and Paul would occupy the vacuum and become Warner Bros.' acting label boss in Nashville.

We recorded four more songs for the album at the Tracking Room, including two songs that would be hit singles. "Nobody But Me" was a medium-tempo love ditty written by Shawn Camp and Phillip White. "Goodbye Time," written by Roger Murrah and James Dean Hicks, had been a Conway Twitty single fifteen years earlier. Blake would give it what I thought was his best singing performance to date. Conway Twitty's widow, Dee, had always had a negative view of other people's covers of Conway hits, but Blake's rendering of "Goodbye Time" would make her cry.

On these sessions, we used two new players (new to Blake's music). As an old piano man, I was blown away by Gordon Mote's playing. Gordon was a jovial young blind guy from Alabama who kept us in stitches with his Porter Wagoner imitation. Jonathan Yudkin (whom we used on "Some Beach") was a great "utility man," meaning he played multiple instruments—he played not only exceptional fiddle, but also mandolin and banjo, and was adept at stacking violin, viola and cello parts to make a quick orchestra. It was hard to resist one musician who could play so many instruments, but I would still from time to time book Rob Hajacos, whom I considered the best hard-country fiddler in town.

When it came time to do a video of "Some Beach," Blake wanted an encore performance from my Charles Manson character, so I was cast as the crazy sadistic dentist. Jeep, carrying my first grandchild but not yet showing, played my dental assistant.

The year 2004 saw one of the most divisive presidential elections in American history. The country was split down the middle on the war in Iraq, and George W. Bush was both a very popular and very unpopular president, depending on who you were talking to. Four Music Row men—Bob Titley, Don Cook, Tim DuBois, and Bill Carter—wanted to dispel the notion that all people in the country music business were Republicans, so they founded an organization called Music Row Democrats. There were about twenty people at the first meeting, 150 at the second, and eventually there were 2,000 members, though many of them were definitely not in the music business. Because I was there from the beginning, the organizers referred to me as one of the Founding Fathers, but I never thought of myself as such. I did write a proclamation stating that country music fans, many of whom were blue-collar and working-class people, were a natural constituency for the Democratic Party. The proclamation was posted on the MRD website. Most of the organization leadership wanted to stay focused on economic issues and turning out the Democratic vote, rather than bringing up hot-button social issues. When a reporter asked how I felt about gay marriage, I quipped "I'm not even sure how I feel about *straight* marriage," which got some laughs but was an evasive, cowardly response because in my heart I felt that a gay man having a male partner was every bit as natural as me having a female partner. So when I gave a speech to a packed house at the Belcourt Theatre, I toed the line and stuck to economic topics, but at the end of the talk I surprised even myself by going into an extemporaneous rant against the Iraq War. I received applause that was loud and long. When I sat down next to my friend Michael Kosser, he grumbled, "I wish you hadn't said that."

My little excursion into organized politics brought me into the company of some interesting people: Democratic presidential nominee John Kerry (stiff the first time, enthusiastic the next), former Vice President Al Gore (I talked him into doing a Hank Williams imitation), former US Attorney General Janet Reno (a couple of breakfasts with this kind and soft-spoken woman), and award-winning documentary filmmaker Michael Moore (surprisingly humble and gracious, and a big fan of country music).

One day the group's founders took me with them for a brown-bag lunch with the governor of Tennessee, Phil Bredesen, at his office. I didn't find him as friendly as his Republican predecessor Don Sundquist, who had had me over to the governor's mansion to sing some of my songs a couple of years before; but Bredesen was courteous and respectful. I sat next to him and noticed two things: he was eating a baloney sandwich, and he shaved his ears (I mean earlier that day, not while we were with him). Though Bredesen was a Democrat, he was a very conservative one. As we left, he said, "You guys talk to Kerry. Tell him he needs to stop acting like a senator and start acting like a president." Afterward, as we walked out to the parking lot, I told the others, "I think he's going to vote for Bush."

My friend Shannon McCombs was hosting a show on XM Satellite Radio's classic country channel, and she had me on one day as her guest. She played several of the older hits I'd written and interviewed me in between songs. I received a lot of phone calls from people around the country, and the audience seemed to be overwhelmingly older male, and the accents, more often than not, sounded Southern and rural. As the listeners expressed their love for my songs and their respect and affection for me, I couldn't help but think: if they knew my politics, many of them probably wouldn't like me so much. I carried that thought with me until after the first Tuesday in November, when it felt like we had experienced a natural disaster rather than an election. I must say that sometimes I was as concerned about the divisiveness and polarization in America as I was the issues in the campaign.

Just before the election came the release of *Blake Shelton's Barn & Grill*. On the same day, Warner Bros. also released an album by Big & Rich, who were produced by Paul Worley. I was an early enthusiastic supporter of Big & Rich—Paul was recording great stuff on them—and I was well-acquainted with John Rich and a fan of his songwriting. But when I went to Tower Records on West End Avenue and saw a thirty-foot poster of Big & Rich in front of the store, but no in-house promotion of Blake whatsoever, I was not happy, and flipped open my cell phone and gave Blake a call. He was already upset because he had heard that some Warner promotion person had asked stations to play Big & Rich's single instead of his. Nevertheless, *Barn & Grill* sold about 50,000 copies that first day.

With the release of the two previous CDs, I had put together album-listening parties in Sony Publishing Company's large conference room, for the Sony staff and also for the album's songwriters. I wanted to do the same thing with the third CD, but it was looking as though Blake wouldn't be able to attend. He was booked for most of the fall, and on his days off he wanted to be in the woods, hunting deer. Blake and I got along great, and about the only problem I had with him during our years together was getting him out of the woods and into the studio to record. When I told him it was really important that he be there for the album spotlight—"That's the only opportunity Ed and I get to shine," I said—he agreed to rearrange his schedule and show up. But he told me something that I totally got: "Those days when I'm not working are *gold*, and I live for getting off to myself, out in the wilderness." I couldn't help but notice the irony of his referring to the days that he *wasn't* making money as "gold."

My close friend Kathy Locke flew in from Richmond, Virginia, for a long weekend. She had been taking off from work one Thursday and Friday every month, and coming to Nashville and staying at her little condo, which was located less than a mile from my house. Woody Bomar had signed her to Sony as a writer, so since I got half of the publishing of any writer I brought to Sony, I was not only Kathy's friend but her publisher. She was a good one to have around in a crisis. Once, when I picked her up at the airport she told me about her horrific flight through turbulence so bad that people were getting knocked around the plane—men were screaming—and how she put her arms around the young woman beside her who was on leave from Iraq, comforting the girl who cried and said she was more frightened at that moment than she had ever been in battle. There were times I had called Kathy when I was upset, in the middle of a crisis, and she would calm me down as she said in her comforting voice, "Now take a deep breath." This would prove to be a good time for her to be in town.

The next night we went to a nearby popular eatery, Pizza Perfect, to get some vegetarian pizza to take to Lauren and Jim's house. Jeep called to tell me we'd better hold off on the food because they were about to leave for the hospital. After years of attempting to become parents, they had gone to Rockville, Maryland, earlier in the year to participate in the in-vitro fertilization process. Her pregnancy had been a rough one, and she had spent much of it on bed rest, as well as dealing with gallstones ("grounded and stoned" she would call it in her wonderful 2009 book *A Journey to the Son*). The baby boy was not due until January of 2005, but apparently he didn't want to wait any longer. After we camped out for a few hours in the hospital waiting room, we learned that the delivery wouldn't happen until the next day.

Shortly after noon on December 11, 2004, we went back to Baptist Hospital, then Nashville's top maternity facility, to await the arrival of my grandson. A little before 2:00 p.m., Jim told us that the young man should make his debut shortly. Kathy and I sat in the big waiting room with Lauren's "Aunt Karen and Uncle Ronnie" and her buddy Leslie Barr, and waited . . . and waited . . . and waited.

I told Kathy I was concerned that it was taking so long, and made my way down the hallway toward the labor and delivery room, with my friend following several steps behind. I spotted Lauren's doula (childbirth advisor and supporter)—her name was actually Beulah, so she was known as "Beulah the Doula"—in the little family waiting room. She looked disconcerted and

Jim was hurrying around. When I asked what was going on, he responded, "There's a little bleeding." My protective father instincts snapped into action, and I insisted that they tell me exactly what was happening. The baby was not breathing when delivered, but was now in the natal ICU, on a respirator and apparently stabilized. However, Jeep was seriously hemorrhaging. When I asked if there was a chance that she would die, Beulah answered tenderly but firmly, "Yes, there is." She held Jim's hand and mine and said a prayer. When a nurse came in and told us that it appeared that Lauren was going to make it, Jim lost it, shedding tears of relief that proved to be premature when we found out that the nurse had misspoken. In my journal I later wrote "The most frightened I've ever been in my life" and "Kathy said the most beautiful, appropriate, and relevant prayer." Finally, Dr. James Growdon, the OB/GYN, came in and gave us a report: hopeful, not out of danger, but hopeful. Kathy later commented that when I peppered the doctor with questions, it was the first time I had spoken a word since we first got the news. Then I asked him if I could see my daughter and he took me to the operating room. She didn't look like she was dying to me; I thought she looked very tired and woozy. The doctor gave us two more briefings, each one more encouraging than the one before. Finally, Lauren was taken to the intensive care unit, and we were told that she was "not out of the woods" but would probably pull through.

She had suffered a rare obstetric emergency called amniotic fluid embolism, or AFE, which has a very high mortality rate (it's usually diagnosed at autopsy, the doctor told us). Her blood pressure had gotten as low as 76/17 and her pulse as high as 197. Often, if the patient survives the assault on the heart and lungs, the platelets are affected, and she will bleed to death. Fortunately, Dr. Growdon's daughter, Robyn (a friend of Lauren's), was regarded as being psychic, and when she called her father that afternoon at his office, he heeded her plea that he go early to the hospital. Also fortunately, Dr. Growdon had practiced obstetrics long enough to have encountered AFE—many doctors had never seen it—so he knew what they were up against. Lauren was being prepped for a hysterectomy when the doctor came to this realization. Thankfully! A hysterectomy could easily have caused an unstoppable fatal flood of blood. Growdon had his team constantly giving her transfusions as he attempted to stitch everything that was bleeding.

Later that night, in the wee hours, the ICU nurse let me talk to my daughter, and I heard the welcome sound of Jeep's gripes about them not letting her have anything to eat (and why in the hell wouldn't they let her see her baby).

Braddock James Havey—who would then and evermore be called "Dock" (from the "dock" in "Braddock")—was tiny and premature and jaundiced, but it was generally thought that he was going to be okay. Kathy and I scrubbed off for our first visit and I sang a song that I had written for him: "What's Up Dock?"

A couple of days later, I was feeling a little better about Jeep but still concerned about disturbing symptoms such as fever, abnormal pulse, and high blood pressure. When I couldn't get her on her room phone and couldn't reach her or Jimmy on their cells, I started to panic and hurried to the hospital. When I walked into her room and saw her, Jim, and friend Leslie all sitting up on her bed talking, the tears of fear that had been on hold all this time came out in one good cry.

Jeep would be in the hospital for several days ("It's like you've been in a car wreck," Dr. Growdon explained), and Dock would be there a bit longer. When they finally brought the baby home, there was a major ice storm, and the power was out, and the Havey family spent a few hours at the home of their neighbors who had a little generator. But mother and child both had bitten the bullet, made it through a major crisis, and would be a great blessing to each other and to the rest of us. I thought of December 11 as having an ominous sound to it, like 9/11, and for some time I would get a very negative feeling whenever I drove by Baptist Hospital. But all of that would disappear as the dark clouds gave way to blue skies and bright sunbeams.

As 2005 clicked into place, Donna Hilley, who had contracted a serious E. coli infection and flatlined at the hospital a few months before, was back on the job running Sony/Tree, though there was some short-term memory loss and her grasp on things seemed to be a bit tenuous. CD sales had not quite begun their drastic downhill slide; that was about a year away. Blake Shelton's "Some Beach" spent its fourth week at the top of the charts—at the #1 party I met the new Warner Bros. label head for Nashville, Bill Bennett.

One day I said, "Blake, I think I'd like for us to do just one more album together. I can't be a songwriter, author, *and* producer. One of them has to go." With these words, I took the first step toward taking a lot of stress out of my life. It was not only an issue of time management, but my frustration with the process itself. I was proud of our accomplishments—I *loved* going in the studio to make the music, and Blake was fun to work with, but I strongly disliked the deadlines and commitments and listening to hundreds upon hundreds of songs. Most of all I hated the conflicts with the label (to quote a classic rock song "you ain't seen nothing yet"). Blake carefully absorbed what I was telling him. I continued, "And it may be good for you. The change may be good for you."

"Well, could you at least stay with me through the *Greatest Hits* album? That way it would be like a whole chapter." Greatest Hits albums were just that, a collection of the biggest singles, plus a couple of new songs that were potential future hits. I figured I could produce this next one, the fourth album, then do a couple of songs for the "best of" album, which I assumed would be album No. 5.

"Yeah, I could do that. And I want to go out looking good. I want this next album to be the best one yet."

"*Hell* yeah," he said. We even discussed the possibility of going to Austin,

Texas, and trying something with an entirely new group of musicians. But what we finally settled on was doing some unique things with basically the same crew that had played on Blake's previous hits. The best thing we'd had going was that we had made some monster—even record-setting—hit singles. On the negative side, it seemed that every huge single had been followed up by a milk dud, and we kept having to gain the momentum all over again. I felt that was because the label—invariably the promotion department—had put out the weakest songs for follow-ups. But that sounds like finger point-ing, and the people who were in promotion could just as easily point their finger at me. Who knows, maybe it was all my fault. "If we record only songs that sound like hits, that might solve our problem," I said. That aspect of it was already looking better, because "Goodbye Time," the follow-up to "Some Beach" looked like it was going to be a big one.

So we spent much of 2005 recording what I felt was a truly eclectic album, yet something new and different for Blake. I threw myself into listening to as many songs as possible. After Debbie Zavitson quit as Blake's manager, he and I hired her to listen to songs, because experience had taught us that she had a great knack for it—this was the woman who had found us "Austin" and "The Baby." The label's A&R staff were also constantly looking for songs. But a lot of the things on *Barn & Grill* had been songs I found, such as "Some Beach," and I wanted to listen to more songs than ever. I had considered it a grueling task before, but now, knowing that this would be the last time to produce a full album on Blake, I threw myself into it and actually enjoyed it.

I started driving on the Natchez Trace Parkway, which followed the ap-proximate original path of the historic Natchez Trace. This was a unique highway because it was a scenic route that went all the way from Nashville to Natchez, Mississippi, through woods and parks and historic sites but no cities or towns—you had to exit to get to those. Traffic was light, commer-cial vehicles were prohibited, and the speed limit was fifty, and even as low as forty in some places. I would pack a picnic lunch, set the cruise control on forty-five, open up the sunroof, roll down the windows, and sail on down the road in the beautiful Tennessee springtime, listening to music, music, music. In the early afternoon, somewhere between Funnel Cloud, Alabama, and Itchicokka, Mississippi, I would pull over to a green picnic table amid the beautiful Deep Southern wilderness and enjoy a fat-free cheese sandwich, with a banana for dessert. I always left home with a big cardboard boxful of CDs. I would empty it out on the passenger seat and place the box in the back seat. That's where I tossed most of the CDs after listening—the rejects. On the floorboard was a medium-sized box where I threw the CDs that I wanted to listen to again on the way home. Those rare ones that blew me away would go into the glove compartment for safekeeping. There was a song called "Six Months and a Winnebago." I don't recall who wrote it, but I will never forget this powerful story about an older couple who, upon discovering that one of them is terminally ill, buy an RV and set out to spend their last days to-gether seeing the country (I begged and begged Blake to record it, but he never would). I look back fondly on these musical journeys to Mississippi and back, eventually listening to a total of 1,900 songs. I was determined that this would be the best album we ever made.

Other than the addition of Glenn Worf on bass, the musicians we used for album No. 4 were the same as those for the previous one. As always, I occasionally overdubbed piano, organ, or synthesizer where needed. We re-corded a Casey Beathard / Dean Dillon ballad, "I Don't Care" that Blake and I had fallen in love with. We did a great kick-ass soulful John Hiatt song, "A Real Fine Love," that elicited a standing ovation from Terry Wakefield and the Sony Publishing staff when I played it for them, even though it wasn't their copyright. Blake turned out a killer performance on a traditional coun-try song of mine that Paul Worley loved, "Over You," which was about a man who bids his love goodbye as his soul ascends heavenward (*I'm just a breeze / In the tall maple trees / Outside your window / Hello*). A popular live number for Blake was the Bellamy Brothers hit "Redneck Girls," which we recorded with his road band and had the Bellamys join in on the last chorus. Blake wanted to do one that he wrote with Michael Kosser and me—"The Last Country Song" used urban sprawl as a metaphor for the changes in country music. So we stacked it one track at a time, like "Some Beach," and got George Jones and John Anderson to sing it with Blake. A voice mail I will never erase is from George Jones, who got lost and couldn't find Ed's studio (relocated in a house across the street from Sony Publishing):

> *Bobby, this is George, and I'm tryin' to get a-hold of you, son. You need to turn your phone on. It's 2:20, and I'm here at the murder market, and I'm comin' right around there but I can't find out what building it is. If you could call me . . .*

We also recorded a Blake / Rachel Proctor / Michael Kosser mid-tempo, "I Have Been Lonely;" two drinking songs, "One" and "Pabst Blue Ribbon;" a Shawn Camp song, "So Not My Baby;" and an R&B flavored cheating song, "She Can't Get That at Home," a real switch for Blake. As always, there were a couple that Blake liked more than I did, but overall I thought it was a power-ful package. So did Blake and everyone else who had heard it so far.

There were a couple of interesting developments during this period. One involved Miranda Lambert. I had seen Blake's relationship with Kaynette go through various stages of dating, marriage, separation, reconciliation, ultra-togetherness—with her traveling with him on concert tours—and her staying home on the "farm." When Blake met Miranda, I was definitely under the impression that Blake and Kat's marriage was already in trouble. I think he met Miranda at a concert at Riverfront Park in Nashville, and they did a duet together.

One night when we were doing overdubs on "Redneck Girls" at the Tracking Room, Miranda came by to visit. She left shortly before we were finished, and Blake asked me to go with him to a bar called the Tin Roof. I asked him why he wanted me to go.

"Because I'm afraid I may leave with Miranda," he said.

"Blake, I'm not your daddy. I'm not going to tell you what you should or shouldn't do," I told him. I went with him, and we had a big time. Miranda was a cute, feisty, funny little blonde, and I could clearly see the chemistry between the two of them. Blake behaved himself that night, but in the near future he and Kaynette split, and after that he started dating Miranda. (No, Miranda didn't break up Blake's marriage.) Kat was a sweet girl, but I think Blake's love for her had turned into a friendship kind of love. After he and Miranda started dating, I saw him falling . . . madly.

The other development was the new A&R appointment at Warner, Tracy Gershon. I had first known Tracy about fifteen years before when she became a songplugger at Tree. She was an LA girl; she and local label head Bill Bennett had LA in common. Tracy was outspoken, but she also had a good sense of humor and, in general, had always been friendly to me. But I'd had a pretty free rein producing Blake, and suddenly here was someone telling me how to produce, and it seemed like it was simply because she thought she had the authority to do so. In our first meeting I played her "The Last Country Song," which had just been mixed. "That hasn't been mixed, has it?" she asked. She was under no obligation to *like* our mix, but a good seasoned ear should be able to tell whether a recording has been mixed, a process that generally takes a couple of days. When I told her it had definitely been mixed, she told me it needed to be "tweaked." When I asked her what she meant by tweaking it—what did she not like about it—she told me, "Ask Paul Worley, he'll be able to explain it to you." When I later mentioned it to Paul, he said he liked the mix just fine.

During the same meeting she started suggesting changes in musicians. "Why don't you start using Dan Dugmore on steel?" she asked. I told her that I loved Dan Dugmore (his playing often gave me chill bumps) and that we had used him in the past, but were presently using Paul Franklin and were very happy with him. Paul Franklin played steel on both "Some Beach" and the current single, "Goodbye Time."

"Well, it's my job to make suggestions. Paul [Worley] said *he* makes suggestions to you."

Worley had in fact made very few suggestions, but the ones he did make I paid very close attention to because he was a first-rate musician and producer. *His* suggestions always made sense.

When someone asked Tracy how it was going with her new job, she replied, "It was going fine until I had my first meeting with Bobby." That pretty much set the tone for my relationship with Tracy Gershon. After the first meeting

My friend Troy
Tomlinson succeeds
Donna Hilley as
Nashville president
and CEO of Sony/
ATV, 2005

she never came down on me as hard, and I went out of my way to treat her with respect. But I think the alliance was a little shaky for both of us.

Discussing money with Donna Hilley always made her nervous and created some tension between us, but after I got my financial house in order in the 1990s, Donna and I became very close. She often told people that I was her favorite at Sony, and sometimes even asked me which writers I thought she should keep and which ones she should let go. I talked her into keeping a couple of writers but could never bring myself to advise her to drop anyone— I would have been lousy at running a big publishing company.

When the great Frances Preston retired from BMI in 2004, most people on Music Row considered Donna the new most powerful woman in the Nashville music business. That made it all the more heartbreaking when Donna went into decline after her near-death experience and became unable to perform her duties. There was much speculation about who would become the new president and CEO at Sony/ATV Nashville. The youngest contender, forty-one-year-old Troy Tomlinson, got the job, in late 2005. He had come on board with Sony more than three years earlier when Sony acquired Gaylord Entertainment's Acuff-Rose Publishing Company, where Troy was vice-president. With his excellent people skills and twenty years of experience as a first-rate song man, Troy was a perfect fit for the top position at Music Row's top publishing company. I would come to think of him not only as my publisher but as my very good friend.

As I headed down the backside of the new century's first decade, my forward-moving time machine seeming to go faster and faster; I was enjoying my grandson, Dock, tremendously. His face always lit up with a big smile when he saw me, and he loved rubbing my beard stubble. From early childhood Jeep had looked forward to being a mommy, so I wasn't surprised that she and Jim were fully devoted, fully engaged, and fully enjoying parenthood.

My life was a combination of minuses and pluses like everyone's life. On the negative side, there was a man passing himself off as Bobby Braddock and conning wannabe songwriters out of their money—the guy actually *looked* like me, and he was damaging my reputation. On a positive note, my literary mentor, John Egerton, liked the memoir I had written about growing up in small town Old Florida and had submitted it to Louisiana State University

Performing at the Poets and Prophets show at the Ford Theater, Country Music Hall of Fame and Museum in Nashville, 2007

Press who wanted to publish it for the spring 2007 season. I was griping to Jeep one day about the stress of dealing with Warner Bros., having to worry about doing a book tour, and some con artist going around saying he was me. She put it all in perspective for me when she said, "Daddy, you're complaining about the stress of being a successful record producer, a published author, and having someone impersonate you. A lot of people would be envious."

Warner Bros. took one of those gripes off my plate, but the result was that I griped more than ever. On the night of January 18, 2006, Blake called me from Owensboro, Kentucky, where he was doing a show, and asked if I'd had any conversations with Warner Bros. that day. I had not. He said Tracy Gershon had driven up to Owensboro to tell him that they wanted a new producer to come in and do five sides on him for the next album. He said he told Tracy that Bill Bennett and Paul Worley were chickenshit for not having the guts to tell him, and she said they knew he was really close to me, and they didn't want him to feel ganged up on. She further told Blake that the music had gotten "too comfortable" and wasn't going anywhere new. She said if he refused, "We won't drop you, but we won't be able to support your music." I found it amazing that they would tell this guy who was racing up the charts with his third consecutive hit ("Nobody but Me") from an album that was getting close to a million in sales that they wouldn't support his music. I thought he should have said, "So let me go, I'll go to RCA, where Joe Galante is chomping at the bit to sign me." Anybody in town would have been excited about signing Blake. For a couple of weeks Blake tried to talk them into letting me at least finish this album with him—after all, it was the last album I was going to do with him anyway. But they got their way. He *was* ganged up on.

I wrote an open letter to *Music Row*, the bible of Nashville's music industry, because I wanted everyone to know that I was being fired by Warner Bros. and not by Blake. Although publishers are at the mercy of the record labels—if the labels don't cut their songs, the publishers go out of business—several of them trusted me enough to e-mail me that they thought Warner Bros. had made a stupid mistake. I wrote Paul Worley in an e-mail, "I produced a monster hit on Blake the first time out of the box. It took you three years before you had a #1 record with Martina McBride, and seven years before you had a multi-week #1 with her. What if RCA had taken Martina away from you, and kept you guys from having that wonderful legacy together? All I want to do is *complete* my legacy with Blake with this one final album. Why can't you let me do that? The hits have been big, he's still having them, and compared to most artists his sales are good. It just doesn't make sense." He called me and told me that I made a valid point, but said he had stood up for me ever since Bennett had come to the label and he just couldn't do it anymore.

Brent Rowan called and said Blake had asked him to produce some sides with him, and that he told Blake that he would have to check with me first and make sure it wouldn't affect our friendship. I told him how much I appreciated his sensitivity, and no, it would not change our friendship. He said the label wouldn't allow him to use any of the same players I had used, except he would use himself on guitar. I understood why Blake approached Brent: he had been an important part of everything we had done together . . . he was familiar . . . he was Blake's comfort zone. I soon learned that Paul Worley was also going to do some sides on Blake.

Blake's first two singles, "Don't Make Me" and "The More I Drink," didn't make the top ten. Granted, CD sales were down with everyone, but his album, *Pure BS*, was selling at a much slower rate than *Barn & Grill* had sold. I loved both Blake and Brent, but if they had gone in the studio and cut the record of the century, I would have looked bad, and I would have felt bad. I wanted them to do well, but not immediately.

In the meantime, Paul Worley had left Warner Bros. because they wouldn't sign a group he was producing, Lady Antebellum, whom he would take to the Capitol label (and the rest is music history). Paul was replaced by Scott Hendricks, a Music Row veteran, as head of Warner A&R. Scott called and asked, "Now just what happened with you here at Warner Bros.?" I was wondering why he didn't just ask his boss, Bill Bennett, but I explained to him as briefly and generically as I could. He said, "Do you think you'd be interested . . . hmm, I may be talking to you." And that was it. It sounded as though he was about to ask me if I wanted to produce Blake again. But why would Bill Bennett, who fired me, approve of that? Then Scott's new A&R associate, Cris Lacy, whom I had known when she was a songplugger at Warner-Chappell Music, called me and said, "We may be begging you to come back and produce Blake." I doubted that Bill Bennett would allow that opportunity to arise, but decided that if he did, I would do it *if* Blake urged me to and *if* I didn't have to listen to songs.

Then I heard that Blake had recorded Michael Buble's song, "Home." I wasn't familiar with it, so I found it online and was blown away. It was so good by Buble that I thought, "How can Blake top *that*?" But he did. I had never heard him sing with such sensitivity, and Miranda's harmony was magic. Brent produced it similar to the original, only better; the changes were subtle but significant; the strings were similar but more melodic; Brent's guitar solo was better than the other guy's; the mix was superior. And it went to #1, for two weeks. I thought, "Well, there's no way they'll let Brent go *now*!" Wrong. That's exactly what they did. I called Brent up and said, "Welcome to the Cut-A-Hit-On-Blake-Shelton-And-Get-Fired Club." Scott Hendricks became Blake's producer. I had cut some huge hits with Blake, but some flops, too; he would have a consistency with Scott that he had never had with me. Scott Hendricks (along with the Blackstock management family) deserves a lot of credit for Blake's transition from star to superstar. For the first three albums Scott Hendricks produced on Blake, he would invite me over to his office whenever he finished a project to get my opinion on how everything sounded. Scott was a great producer and certainly did not need my advice. I think he did this out of respect for me as his predecessor, an amazing display of kindness that I will never forget.

While we were still working together, I talked Blake into hiring Vanessa Davis as his publicist because I knew of her reputation for getting her clients major network TV spots. I always felt that his outrageous sense of humor would make Blake a natural for TV. Then I was fired, which put his career on hold for a while, so Vanessa never got the opportunity to sprinkle her star-dust on Blake, and she wasn't with him for very long. But eventually the network TV camera would discover Blake and fall in love with him, and Blake Shelton would become a household name, even with non-country music fans who were watching him every week on NBC's *The Voice*.

I had no doubt that Blake would do great things without me. In fact, I always said he would have been a star no matter what. *Somebody* would have gotten in on the ground floor with him, but I'm glad it was me.

I've read about the mental health effects of losing a job. When I was fired for allowing ten minutes of silence on a little Florida radio station when I was twenty years old, it was okay. When I was fired for getting strangled by the trumpet-polishing machine at Hewgley's Music Store in Nashville, I didn't care. But I cared very much about this. It wasn't just the money I had hoped to make off the next album. It was a matter of pride. I looked at it as being publicly disgraced, as if I had done something wrong. Several major produc-ers asked me, "What happened? You were making great records with Blake." They were producers: they knew. But what about all those without expert ears? I was afraid they would think of me as a loser. No matter that I had made the decision that it was going to be my last album, I was fired. They screwed with my swan song.

On down the road, I would hear about Tracy Gershon crying when *she* got fired, and would know just how she felt. And Bill Bennett—the guy who said of me: "What's the big deal? People lose their jobs in the music business all the time"—one day I would hear that *he* got fired, and I must say that a little smile crossed my lips.

Paul Simon was and is a brilliant folk/rock/pop artist/writer/guitarist, re-nowned as a part of the Simon & Garfunkel team of the 1960s, and in his own right as a major artist of the 1970s and '80s. He was an old friend of Nashville producer James Stroud, so when James had him down as a house guest in the spring of 2006, a gathering of Nashville music folk was planned, and I was invited.

Paul struck me as cerebral, soft-spoken, and kind. When one of the guests asked him why he had not spoken out publicly against the war in Iraq, he said practically nothing in response. The inquirer was a bit nervy to have brought it up in those surroundings, considering that James Stroud was a known con-servative Republican. However, a bit later, when everyone was taking turns singing, Simon said, "This is a song that I may do on my next album," then performed a very powerful anti-war song.

When James and most of the guys went outside to smoke cigars, I was able to have a long conversation with the guest of honor. We were roughly the same age, so I was interested in who Paul Simon's biggest musical influences were, and he said the Everly Brothers, who were certainly heroes of mine when I was a teenager. I found Simon to be modest and even self-critical about some of his own songs and recordings. I said, "Well, *surely* you thought 'Still Crazy After All These Years' was good, didn't you?" "Yeah," he smiled, "I thought I had written a pretty good song." I was amused that he was more complimentary of my piano-playing than my songwriting. When he asked me how "He Stopped Loving Her Today" came about, I felt that he was like this nice man with all the pretty children asking some country rube, out of courtesy and kindness, about his ass-scratchin,' nose-pickin' hillbilly kid.

The high point of the evening was when we all went out into the chilly spring night and gathered around portable heaters for an unforgettable Paul Simon poolside concert. Some of the gifted singers among us, like Matraca Berg, joined in to sing harmony. I was in my notorious who-is-that? mode as I marveled at this one guy—a dobro player—who seemed to know me pretty well, and I was greatly impressed with his musicianship. "Wow, that guy plays as good as Jerry Douglas," I said, referring to the world's greatest dobro player. Matraca rolled her eyes and said, "That's because he *is* Jerry Douglas."

James Stroud later told me that he once did an album on Simon, and they spent a lot of time and money on it but it just didn't come off. The loss was James's loss—it was his record label—and Paul was under no obligation to do anything, but when he got back to New York he sent Stroud a check for one million dollars.

Buddy Killen would have been very much at home at this party, because Buddy loved celebrity and celebrities. He was a farm boy from Alabama who almost single-handedly built the biggest country music publishing company in the world. After selling Tree International, he started a new publishing company which would do well, but he would never again be a major player on Music Row. Years before, he had married Carolyn Faulk, a beautiful young waitress at his night club and restaurant, the Stock-Yard. Buddy, more than a quarter of a century her senior, worshipped Carolyn. Of course, there were cynics who speculated that the babe was marrying the older guy for his money, but those who knew them well said that she loved Buddy just as much he loved her. Buddy had the energy and the look of a much younger man. Despite the fact that he wouldn't give me back my catalog as he had once said he would, Buddy Killen believed in me from the day we met, and I felt a great fondness for him. Then one day he became suddenly ill and learned that he had pancreatic cancer. He called me up and said he wanted to invite a few people who meant a lot to him and get a private room at a nice restaurant, drink fine wine, and talk about old times. A couple of days later, Carolyn told me Buddy was too sick to do the dinner, but, she said, "He wants you to come out to the house tomorrow, so he can tell you why he thinks you're so fabulous." The next morning, she called to tell me Buddy was too sick to see anyone. Two days later he was gone, as surely as if a quick and mighty sword had come down upon him.

The Ryman Auditorium, former home of the Grand Ole Opry, is a popular place for celebrity memorial services; that's where Tammy Wynette's was held. Buddy had been reluctant to have his service held there because he was afraid the crowd would be embarrassingly small. The hall was packed. A few months later, the "roundabout" that arcs across the northern border of Music Row was named Buddy Killen Circle in his honor. Buddy would have liked that. "Hey, Valentine," I could almost hear him proudly say in his Bullwinkle voice, "they named the roundabout after me." Ironically, for future generations this great man's name may be most closely associated not with music, but with the weird nude statues freeze-frame frolicking around Buddy Killen Circle.

On December 13, 2006, BMI had what their publicist billed as "a gathering of blue ribbon songwriters and artists" to welcome Barry Gibb on his move to town (though he didn't move here for very long). In the reception line, my friend Kathy Locke was on cloud nine when the Bee Gee took her hand and said, "H'lo, love." I met a cute seventeen-year-old girl there named Taylor Swift—in fact it was her seventeenth birthday—and I was impressed that she knew who I was and could name some of my songs. I think she was impressed that I was familiar with her one single that had been on the radio, "Tim McGraw." Over the years she made it her business to know who everyone was and to be nice to them. I never had much sympathy for those who lamented that Taylor Swift's music wasn't very country. Of course it was country—story songs, many of them written about her own life—what could be more country than that?

I was very excited about getting my book published. It was a memoir about growing up in small-town Central Florida and eventually playing in a rock & roll band. The story ends with my bride and me leaving Florida in 1964 for Nashville, the city of country dreams. I enjoyed a wonderful working relationship with John Easterly, the acquisitions editor at Louisiana State University Press, and the only disagreement we had was over what to call my memoir. He was afraid my title *Crackers and Oranges*, suggested by my friend Carmen Beecher, would land it in the food section of bookstores. I thought the title was clever (a "Cracker" being a native backwoods Floridian, and oranges being what my father grew for a living). Mr. Easterly wanted "songwriter" to be in the title, or at least the subtitle, so I finally came up with something that he approved: *Down in Orburndale: A Songwriter's Youth in Old Florida*. "Orburndale" was the local pronunciation of my hometown of Auburndale, though many natives would later tell me that it was actually pronounced "Orbundale," without the "r" in the middle. I loved the colorful citrus-clad cover that the LSU Press art department came up with. It was decided that I would do a twelve-city book tour, kicking off with Nashville, then going to nine cities in Florida, and finally to Atlanta and Birmingham, places that were also settings for the story. Thanks to my publicist son-in-law and the book publisher's PR people, I was kept busy doing interviews at several local TV stations. I was also featured on National Public Radio's *Fresh Air* with Terry Gross, and on the long-running regional TV book show *A Word on Words* with renowned journalist John Seigenthaler.

Polk County, Florida, was more like a state than a county. Almost twice the size of Rhode Island and nearly as large as Delaware, it is several times larger than some Florida counties. When I was growing up there, it was America's leading citrus-producing county, and home of the world's leading phosphate-mining area (Bone Valley). Polk County was a swampy-here, hilly-there expanse with hundreds of lakes, several small and medium-sized towns, and a "city:" Lakeland. Even today, often called "Orlampa" as it becomes more and more encroached on by Orlando and Tampa's urban sprawl, Polk County retains some of the Southern character, culture, and charm that dominated it in my childhood.

There were 250 at my book-signing at the Books-a-Million store in Lakeland, and I estimated that two-thirds of them were from Auburndale, eleven miles away. As I stood speaking from the podium, I looked out into a sea of aging but familiar faces, largely female. I thought, "Wow, I wish these girls had liked me this much back in high school!" Later when I was signing, Susannah Short, who had asked to see my "peter" when we were five, was accusing Charlotte Taylor, my long-distance lover of the 1970s, of jumping line. In Gainesville, a guy whom I characterized in my book as a thief was there with a girlfriend he was trying to impress, and knowing that he would read the book as soon as he got home, I parked my car a half block from my motel room so he couldn't find me and shoot me. In St. Petersburg I ran into another book character, my ex-fiancée Gloria Gelder, who told me she had stayed up the entire night before, reading my book—"I laughed a lot, I cried a lot, and sometimes I wanted to hit you." After finishing the tour, I went back down to Auburndale with my family for "Bobby Braddock Day" and a book-signing at the public library, where my two year-old grandson, Dock, stepped up to podium, grabbed the mic, and started hawking, "Bobby's book! Bobby's book!" *Down in Orburndale* wouldn't make the *New York Times* bestseller list, but I think just about everybody over fifty who was raised in Auburndale would read it.

Actually the book would be read by a lot of people in the music business. Florida rockers Tom Petty and the Heartbreakers would read it. Country singer and fellow Floridian Mel Tillis would call and ask me to meet him at his tour bus and autograph his copy. Bill Anderson would tell me that my book kept him running to the dictionary, to which I replied, "Me, too." Kris

Kristofferson, who along with several other celebrities "blurbed" the back cover, wrote about me: "I hope he's already writing the continuing story that picks up where this one stops."

Back home in Tennessee I wrote another book—actually a little booklet—for family and close friends only. It was titled *Bubba, the Miracle Cat*. I'm an animal lover and have enjoyed the company of many great dogs and cats in my life, but if one had to top the list it would be Bubba. My ex-girlfriend Tami brought this little bandana-wearing black kitten to my house back in 1996, shortly after the demise of a favorite old feline, and I told her "That's very sweet of you, but I don't *want* another cat." But when the little fellow climbed me like a tree until he sat perched on my shoulder licking my face, I said, "Oh hell, I'll keep him." He would ride my shoulder and lick my face for many years to come.

Not only would he learn to recognize and respond to many phrases and suggestions, I counted about fifty distinct vocal sounds that he made. Sometimes I could gauge his mood and make a good guess at which sounds he would be making, enabling me to carry on a "conversation" with him that might have landed us a guest spot on the Letterman show if I had put forth some effort. I showed off his "verbal skills" with some of the following responses (but not all at the same time):

"Hey Bubba, who's your favorite guitar player?"
"Brent Rowan."
"Hey Bubba, are you ready to go to bed?"
"Not now."
"Hey Bubba, I can bench press three hundred pounds."
"Wow!"
"Hey Bubba, where's the war?"
"Iraq."

Unlike many cats, Bubba loved *everybody*, but he especially loved me. His favorite sleeping place was on top of my monitor while I was working at my computer. When I got a big flat-screen monitor, his favorite sleeping place became next to my feet. If I had him closed out of a room, he would sleep just outside the door until I came out. Sometimes he would get in my lap, swivel his head around until he was looking straight up at me, cock his head to the side, and just gaze trancelike; Jeep said "Daddy, that's pure love."

When he was about nine years old, Bubba developed a tumor on his head, and testing for that led to the discovery of inoperable malignant tumors on both kidneys. The prognosis wasn't good: two months max. I had heard that cancer victims often die of starvation, so I started feeding him people food, twice a day. And although there was a screened porch for Bubba and my other cat, Tiger Lily (also a Tami gift cat), I decided to maximize Bubba's fun and pleasure. I started taking him outdoors for the first time in his life, hanging with him to make sure he was in no danger. The goal was to elevate the quality of his life and keep him well-fed, in hopes of having him around longer than the predicted two months. He lived *twenty-eight months.* Our veterinarian David Edwards, and all the specialists who he consulted, started referring to Bubba as "The Miracle Cat."

I knew that Bubba was literally on his last leg when he tried to rub up against me and fell over. That night I made a little sleeping place for him on the bedroom floor and lay down with him for a while. I had to do a demo session the following day, so I went on to bed, knowing it would be all over when I got up the next morning. He was my most amazing animal friend ever, and I knew I would never see the likes of him again.

Of the many who report "near death" experiences that entail crossing over and going to the light, a considerable number report seeing dogs and cats on the other side. And with the capacity to love without qualification, why shouldn't they have souls and the privilege of eternal life? I like that. I can see it all now.

"Hey Bubba, do you wanna try on your new wings?"

"Not now."

"Hey Bubba, here comes God."

"Wow!"

When I went back to Florida in 2008 for a reunion with five of my old high school buddies, I gathered some interesting data. At our first reunion, shortly after the presidential election of 2004, I had taken a little survey, and three of us had voted for the Democrat, John Kerry, and three for George W. Bush. Then in 2008, I polled again, asking "Who do you think you'll vote for?" Of the six, I was the only one who planned to vote Democratic, the other five were for John McCain. That was the demographic I was a part of, America's most conservative voting group: old Southern white men.

Despite my admiration for McCain, I voted for Barack Obama and the change he promised. It was profoundly historic that a black man won the presidency, even carrying the Southern states of Florida, North Carolina, and Virginia. The Obama legacy is still being written, and only time can measure its success or failure. If the verdict is failure, that won't mean the demise of the Democratic Party, any more than Nixon's malfeasance meant the end of the Republicans. And will historians determine that Obama lacked the political skills to work effectively with Congress, or will they conclude that he was constantly met with partisan stubbornness fueled by polarization and prejudice? It may be many years—or decades—before President Obama's place in history can be viewed objectively in this great but divided nation.

A big disappointment for millions of Americans was that we never got universal health care, which they have in practically every other country in the civilized world (where being uninsured is not synonymous with being untreated). You get sick, you get treated—for free! Most progressives wanted that for America, but many congressional Democrats were afraid they would lose their seats voting for "socialized medicine," so what President Obama settled for was a watered-down plan run by the insurance companies. Better than what we had, granted. But guess what! Obama's enemies still called it "socialized medicine." In truth, what's *really* socialized medicine is Medicare, which all the grannies love. I know a lot of elderly Republicans, and I have yet to meet any who are willing to give up their Medicare. Universal health care would be like Medicare for all ages. Many believe it would be as American as the Declaration of Independence, the rationale being that "life, liberty, and the pursuit of happiness" are all dependent on good health.

While most Americans began 2009 hoping that the new administration would pull us out of the economic morass we had sunk into, I was in my own swamp—a mental swamp—running from gators and snakes. I seem to get a little crazy every twenty years, so for the third time in my life I started experiencing major anxiety and depression. I stopped performing at writers' nights. I missed being in my hometown for my induction into the Auburndale High School Hall of Fame. When I, along with my co-writer Troy Jones and singer Billy Currington, was honored at BMI for Billy's huge hit, "People Are Crazy," I was a wreck standing up in front of the crowd. There is a video of me standing there between Troy and Billy, looking very nervous, then frantically digging down in my pocket and popping an anti-anxiety pill into my mouth and calming down enough to give my little speech.

"People Are Crazy" was nominated for CMA Song of the Year, my sixth

Return of the old dogs: Curly, me, Don Cook, and Sonny Throckmorton

"People Are Crazy" #1 party at BMI, 2009, with co-writer Troy Jones and singer Billy Currington

Dueting with CBS News host of *Face the Nation*, Bob Schieffer, at the National Press Club in Washington, 2010

such nomination, and I sat there in the audience praying that I wouldn't win, because I was too freaked out to go up on the stage in front of over 17 million viewers. But that night I met and began a friendship with CBS News icon Bob Schieffer, who was the one to get me back up in front of people singing, when he invited me to come to DC to perform "He Stopped Loving Her Today" (as he did the recitation) on the night that he received the prestigious Fourth Estate Award at the National Press Club.

So I was feeling a little better but not completely cured when the 2010s began, the advent of my sixth decade as a Nashvillian. That didn't mean that I had lived here sixty years, but that I had lived in Nashville for some or all of six decades spanning from the 1960s to the 2010s (forty-six years plus). And I had now resided in Tennessee twice as long as I had lived Florida.

Of all the things I had done in all my years in Nashville, nothing was more exciting than taking a new young talent up and down Music Row, securing him a record deal, playing a major role in his career, and watching his star ascend higher and higher. It was a delight working with Blake Shelton, not only one of country music's most talented people, but also one of the funniest. A few weeks after Warner Bros. let me go, a statement attributed to Blake that was posted on his fan website stated that *he* had decided it was time for a change in producers. Was this because he didn't want it to appear that Warner Bros. was pushing him around, or were these the words from the label's publicity department, which was in charge of his site? I do know that this happened during a time of great change in his life: a time when he was having to search for a new producer (putting his recording career on hold), going through a divorce, and falling in love with someone new. Whatever the reason for that stance, he would change it within a couple of years when he began saying in interviews that it was the label's decision to fire me, telling one interviewer that it had been a stupid decision. I was constantly being told that Blake had said this good thing or that good thing about me. "Blake sure loves you," I heard over and over. When "People Are Crazy" went to #1, Blake sent me a bottle of champagne, and in 2010 when that song won a BMI Award, he walked all the way across the large hall to embrace me. Two nights later, when he won the CMA Male Vocalist award, he told an audience of many millions, "And before I forget a guy I think who got me into this business, Mister Bobby Braddock, I may never get a chance to say this again: Thank you, Bobby, I love you." His new album was released that week, and in his list of "special thanks" he wrote *"And finally Bobby Braddock. I have absolutely no doubt that your dedication to me and our records was the most important part of my career. I love you my brother."* (In 2011, he and Miranda would even cut short their honeymoon to sing at a very special event for me.) At a time when his stardom was rising to an even higher level—at a time when many people forget—Blake remembered the part I had played in his life, and he made sure that the world knew about it.

ME WITH TWO GREAT LEGENDS

Kris Kristofferson

Garth Brooks

Me as "Homer," with grandson Braddock James "Dock" Havey,
Lauren, and Jim Havey

Grandbobby and Dock,
all matched up

The year 2010 had started out as a good year for me because Jeep and Jim
decided to sell their house in the country and move to town. It all fell into
place very quickly. Someone bought their house for cash, and they moved
into their lovely seventy-four-year-old home on a nice quiet street just two
blocks off Hillsboro Road, the main thoroughfare of the popular and dynamic
Green Hills shopping area. The drive to their house had been reduced from
thirty-five minutes to six, making our regular Sunday evening get-togethers
a lot more convenient. Dock was the center of Grandbobby's universe, just as

Jeep had been when she was a child. Dock seemed to think of me as more of a playmate than some ancient grandpa—once he asked his mom, "How come Grandbobby's not old?"

The 2010 US Census showed Nashville's Metropolitan Statistical Area to have a population of nearly 1.6 million, making it the thirty-eighth largest city in America. When I moved to Nashville, the same area had a population of only 630,000.

The year 2010 brought Tennessee's "thousand-year flood," hitting our city particularly hard with the entire downtown area under deep water. A few miles out, the Grand Ole Opry House and the Gaylord Opryland Hotel were seriously flooded and shut down, and the huge Opry Mills Mall was put out of business for nearly two years. Several thousand homes were damaged or destroyed by the overflowing Cumberland and Harpeth Rivers. My family and I were fortunate, we only had water in our basements. Raymond and Linda Oakley, who had been cleaning my house for years, had clients who were among Nashville's ten dead: an elderly couple, married fifty-nine years, who lived a few streets over from me. Their car was swept away—not by an overflowing river but a gentle creek gone wild—as they were driving home from church. Their bodies, stripped of all clothing, were found in the parking lots of two separate supermarkets. Nashvillians helped themselves and their neighbors heroically, and the music community, including some of the biggest stars, put on benefit shows to help rebuild Nashville—one country act raised two million dollars, another five million, another "several million."

In late May, Billy Sherrill invited me to be present for his induction into the Country Music Hall of Fame, and he had good reason to because I had been lobbying and campaigning for years for him to get the honor. When I walked the red carpet, a local TV news anchor asked me on camera to comment on Billy, and I said "This would have happened for him years ago if he hadn't been the Don Rickles of Nashville." When I got inside the building, I told Sherrill what I had said. He asked, "Is Don Rickles the guy who gets no respect?" I said, "No, that's Rodney Dangerfield. People *respect* you, Billy. Don Rickles is the guy who *insults* everybody. That's you!" His wife, Charlene, laughed and said, "Isn't *that* the truth!"

Billy was honored by various recording artists performing not only his own compositions that he produced, like "Stand by Your Man," but also other people's songs that he produced. Country singer Lee Ann Womack ("I Hope You Dance") had the daunting task of singing a song that many thought no one but George Jones should ever attempt, "He Stopped Loving Her Today." She was amazing! When she finished singing, she turned and looked down at the front row where I was seated. The next day I texted her that singing just didn't get any better than that. She responded, "I've never displayed any awards I've ever won at my house, but I may paint what you texted on my wall."

BMI Million Air Awards, 2010, for nine songs receiving over a million air plays each. BMI's Jody Williams and Sony/ATV's Troy Tomlinson

In September, BMI presented me with nine "Million Air" awards, for songs that had each received more than a million airplays; two of them, "Time Marches On" and "I Wanna Talk About Me," had received over three million plays. At the same ceremony, Troy Tomlinson presented me with a plaque for being the only living person in the world to have had #1 country songs in five consecutive decades. I felt lucky, blessed, you name it. What more could I ask for (except youth)?

Then late one cool February night in 2011, I walked into my house on Autumn Trail and checked my voice mail. There was a message from Steve Moore, the CEO of the Country Music Association. Steve had been involved in many aspects of the music business as well as heading up charitable organizations and fund-raising drives, but I didn't know him very well, certainly not well enough to call him that late. The next morning when I returned his call he said, "I have good news and bad news." I drew a blank. What? He said, "The good news is you're being inducted into the Country Music Hall of Fame. The bad news is you can't tell anybody."

13

LOOKING BACK (AND AHEAD)

As I stood at the podium on the stage of the Ford Theater in the Country Music Hall of Fame and Museum, I looked out at my family and friends, and at the music community's leading citizens. I had just heard Billy Currington, Tracy Lawrence, George Jones, Blake Shelton, and Miranda Lambert singing my songs, and museum director Kyle Young and country music legend Bill Anderson both eloquently singing my praises. I told the audience, "This is like going to your own funeral without having to die."

There had been few songwriters inducted into this hallowed hall, and I was the first of the songwriters to be elected every three years in the non-performing category (the two performers inducted on this night were mega-star Reba McEntire and pioneer Jean Shepard). If Hank Cochran had not died just a few months earlier, which disqualified him for consideration in 2011, I think that Hank, not I, would have been the songwriter on the stage that night.

I thought nothing in my career could come close to becoming a member of the Country Music Hall of Fame, but receiving BMI'S Icon Award was also quite special. BMI's worldwide president, Del Bryant, and his Nashville chief, Jody Williams, were adamant about not letting me in on the surprise of who would be performing my songs.

The list included, once again, Blake and Miranda (this time with Pistol Annies), and also Vince Gill, LeAnn Rimes, and John Anderson. Making comments from the big screen were Toby Keith and Bob Schieffer. When I went to the stage to receive my Icon Award—a lovely inscribed silver bucket— I looked at the audience and saw tall, good-natured Luke Bryan; Jason Aldean in his straw Stetson; and beautiful Carrie Underwood. I told the crowd, "It's a long night, so I'm not going to make a speech," then proceeded to make one. I was proud of myself for sprinting to and from the stage like a twenty-year-old, but as I descended the steps and made my exit, in typical Braddock fashion I turned right instead of left and couldn't find my way back to my table (something I would have done at twenty).

The next night my lovely leggy date, Rebecca Magnuson, and I sat on the front row at the CMA Awards, where they turned the camera on me as Reba

McEntire told of my Hall of Fame induction. Two seats down from us sat Glen Campbell and his wife, Kim. He had been diagnosed with Alzheimer's disease and was in the process of doing a farewell tour. A tribute to Glen and his music was to be featured on the show that night. We had met many years before, but we didn't really know each other. I shook hands with him and told him I was looking forward to the tribute.

"I don't even know which songs they're gonna be doing," he said.

"Then you'll be surprised along with the rest of us."

"Well, I guess *you* know about *surprises*," he said, clearly indicating that he was aware that the songs performed at the BMI banquet the night before were a surprise to me. I saw nothing about him that indicated there was anything wrong. I've heard that music is great therapy for Alzheimer's, and on this night Glen Campbell was being infused with great music, including his own. As Vince Gill, Brad Paisley, and Keith Urban sang the songs that Glen made famous, he sat there beaming and giving them a thumbs-up.

The Glen Campbell thing had a big impact on me. It reminded me that no matter how vigorous or virile we may think we are, when we get older we're walking through thicker terrain, encountering more poisonous snakes and wild animals. There's a heart attack here, a stroke there—a broken hip, a broken brain.

Over the next several months I would receive the Poet's Award at a nontelevised ACM event in Nashville, be honored along with several other songwriters at a reception at the Tennessee governor's mansion, and hear a resolution of recognition from both houses of the Tennessee legislature.

It was about this time that I co-authored an unusual song. My friend Alice Randall had a best-selling book about *Gone with the Wind* from the slaves' point of view, which she called *The Wind Done Gone*. Alice had a song concept that she wanted us to write, about the parallel lives of Elvis Presley, a white singer influenced by rhythm & blues, and Chuck Berry, a black singer influenced by country music. The only thing I didn't like was her title: "Niggerbilly." Alice was African American and could maybe get by with a title like that, but I knew I couldn't, so we changed it to "Blackabilly." I thought it was one of the best songs I was ever associated with, but the reception on Music Row was chilly. Country music: definitely white folks' music.

Later in the year, Lauren and I took my seven-year-old grandson, Dock, backstage at the historic Ryman Auditorium—the venue where the Opry still plays in the cooler months and where I had long ago played piano for Marty Robbins. The main reason I arranged this visit was Dock's often-expressed interest in meeting ninety-one-year-old Little Jimmy Dickens. I had been drilling it into his head that despite his belief to the contrary, his "Grandbobby" was *not* famous, and that people generally don't know or care who writes the songs. When Opry General Manager Pete Fisher approached me and said that the announcer, Eddie Stubbs, wanted to introduce me to the audience, I said sure. As Eddie named a couple of my songs and made the introduction, I stepped out on the stage and stood there waving while they applauded. When I returned backstage, Dock said, "Grandbobby, I thought you said you weren't famous." A few minutes later when we left the building, Dock walked ahead of me, announcing, "Bobby Braddock coming through!"

On a nice spring day in 2013 I was at a resort on the "Redneck Riviera" in Florida's Panhandle, anticipating the arrival of a friend who was flying down to join me in a fun-filled weekend. My daughter called to tell me that George Jones had passed away, so my hour-long taxi ride to the airport was spent on my cell phone talking to interviewers about "the greatest country singer of all time." His obituary would make the front page of the *New York Times*, and Nashville's *Tennessean* would devote its *entire* front page to just the *face* of George Jones. Two weeks later, the biggest and best of my twenty-nine George Jones cuts, "He Stopped Loving Her Today," would re-enter in the *Billboard* country chart at #21, thirty-three years after it first appeared there. No matter who was driving the country music train—music labels, corporate country radio, or the young downloaders themselves—I had no mistaken notions that this meant the return of traditional country music. What we were witnessing was a tremendous outpouring of respect for the greatest voice of country music past. I was proud to have been a little part of George's career, and for him to have played an important role in mine.

On August 5, cringing at the Associated Press's ubiquitous birthday list that includes my name every year along with my increasingly awful age, I posted the following on my Facebook page: "I want to share something that I recently found out. When I was four, my parents told me I was fourteen, so they could have me out of the house by the time I was eight. I've gone my whole life thinking I was ten years older than I am! So the thing that goes out on AP every August 5 is wrong. Subtract ten years from that. If I find out that I'm even younger, I'll be sure to let you know."

Then one laid-back, languid late summer Sunday morning, I was perusing the pages of the *New York Times* and saw an article titled "My Mother's Abortion." I was immediately inspired to write "My Mama's Decision," a song delivered in the voice of an aborted baby, sung from "the other side."

Those reading this book would probably conclude that I'm on the progressive end of the political spectrum, and I wouldn't deny it much, but there's one area in which I am pretty conservative, and that's on the issue of abortion. Although I wouldn't want to see *Roe vs. Wade* reversed and have women and girls return to back alleys to get abortions, I do think the procedure should be infrequent and early. When I saw a sonogram of my grandson in 2004, I became even more resolute in my belief. I'm not even sure that mine is a conservative stance. I could never understand this: if it is considered a liberal, compassionate position to be against taking the life of a murderer, then why isn't it considered a liberal, compassionate position to be against taking the life of a fetus?

When Sparky filed for divorce and moved to Nashville to be with me in 1977, she found out that she was pregnant and said she didn't know if the father was her ex, Troy, or me. She thought she should have an abortion. I told her, "Hey, even if the baby looks just like Troy (who was a very good-looking guy), I'll love it just as much as if it were mine." But she had the abortion anyway, and over time she has often told me that about the time of year that the child would have been born, she always gets depressed. I was thinking about Sparky (who urged me to share this story) when I wrote these last two lines of the song, in the words of the aborted one:

Every year when it's close to that anniversary
She cries herself to sleep and dreams of me

They say death is a thief, and the culprit snuck into Nashville early one morning a few weeks before Christmas 2013, and suddenly and unexpectedly made off with a good man, John Egerton. John blessed us with nine highly regarded, often-awarded books about the South—a couple about Southern food and several about Southern race relations. Way back, when most white Southerners were still segregationists, John was crusading for the rights of African Americans, in a place and a time that made it very unusual and even dangerous to do so. He left behind a loving family, but also a very large extended family of aspiring authors like me, whom he had mentored, edited, and cheer-led just for the sheer joy of it. "I wasn't through with him," I told John's wife, Ann. She said. "He wasn't through with you, either."

Years ago Phillip Self interviewed Marijohn Wilkin for his book about hit songwriters, *Guitar Pull*. Marijohn was about to turn eighty, so he asked her how it felt. She said, "I'm the same as I was at forty, but I'm trapped in an eighty-year-old body. . . . If we're twenty, we're remembering and living twenty years. All the time. At the snap of a finger we remember eating watermelon on the back porch when we were six. So think of all *I'm* remembering . . . I'm living eighty years now every minute." When he asked her how that felt, she answered, "It's tiring. God, it's tiring."

Young people actually seem to think that old people ("Oh, aren't they *sweet*?") were born that way, that they've *always* been old. They can't imagine these codgers ever having been young, and they assume that the old folks haven't a clue as to what it's like being young. Every generation thinks theirs is the first to party, to cuss, and to have sex. What they don't realize is that when we more "mature" folks go to sleep we're still young in our dreams, and this business of being a senior citizen is like a *recent* thing that we're not used to—and we don't like it! In his *Journals*, historian Arthur M. Schlesinger Jr. quoted Leon Trotsky as saying, "People are always surprised to find themselves growing old. They expect it in others but not in themselves."

Although many people guess me to be at least fifteen years younger than

I am, when I turned seventy I couldn't help remembering my father turning seventy, and darkly observing, "According to the Bible, man's allotted tiiiiime on earth is threeee score and tennnn years," indicating that he was on borrowed time. Though he ate the typical unhealthy Southern diet and his heaviest exercise was trudging through the deep sand in his orange groves, he would live another nineteen years.

When I was twenty-nine, I thought, "Damn, I'm the age Hank Williams was when he died." About the time I turned thirty-two, I started fretting over these lines I often heard in a current hit song: "You know my heart keeps telling me / You're not a kid at thirty-three." When I was thirty-four, I found out that I had reached Dagwood Bumstead's perennial age. Forty was really hard because *Webster* told me that I was officially middle-aged. Then there was the much-younger girlfriend who had assured me that age made no difference with her, but in our first argument told me angrily, "Bobby, you're *fifty-two* years old!" When "I Wanna Talk About Me" was a big hit, one songwriter asked, "Did you write that a long time ago?" Another asked, "Did you have some help with that?" Still another said "You're an inspiration to us all." What they all really meant was, "It's amazing that you can still string words together at your age." When we were in our early sixties, my friend Michael Kosser told me that while he was jogging through a park, a young woman turned around and hollered, "Good for YOU!" I was trying to keep a young perspective by listening to what young people were listening to—I may have been the only white man in America past sixty who was riding down the highway singing along with the Black Eyed Peas' "My Humps" (and the only father in America trying to get his mid-thirtyish daughter into Eminem). But while on my Florida book tour in 2007, a newspaper reporter said during an interview, "Driving across the state by yourself at sixty-six? Way to *go*, sir!" I was starting to be "sirred" to death. When someone tells you, "Yes sir, it was good talking to you, sir, goodbye sir" it may be intended as showing respect, but to me it sounds like, "I can't talk to you with the same comfort and informality that I feel when addressing my peers."

It was long ago when wife No. 1 and I rolled into town—back in the days of cars without seat belts, TV without color, tornadoes without warning, and communication without keyboards and keypads. It was in those big-haired, cigarette-smoky, old-timey days of so long ago. It doesn't seem like "only yesterday" nor does it seem like "a million years ago"—it seems like fifty years ago and that's a long, long time.

Nashville the municipality is vastly different from the Nashville of a half century ago. The traffic has gone from tolerable to ferocious, the decent restaurants from few to many, and the city's personality from charming to hip. When I moved here, the men and women of the establishment spoke with Southern accents as thick as molasses, but today the accent of the ruling class (especially the younger ones) is turning "valley"—like in every American city:

north, east, south, and west. A member of the Junior League in Nashville may sound no different from her counterpart in Peoria or New York City. Conversely, younger working-class Nashvillians, like those in every American city, still sound a little bit like their parents and grandparents. I'll leave it to the experts to explain why, but my observation is that American speech has been doing the same thing that British speech started doing a few decades earlier: the well-to-do in the UK sound the same in all parts of the kingdom (it's called "the King's English," and sometimes referred to as the "BBC accent"), but the working classes have accents that are indigenous to the city or region that they're from. That's what's happening in America. You can tell what beehive an American worker bee comes from by listening to it buzz, but the queen bees are all starting to sound alike.

When I came to town, Music Row was young, like me. Over the years we've grown old together. None of the people who were running Music Row back then are running anything there now. Of those now in charge most of them were little children—or not even born—when I came to town in 1964. I got to know the executives and the artists of that day, and I know the executives and the artists of this day. I feel as though I'm a living link to the past. I've always felt that way, and I don't mean it as a matter of accomplishment; I mean it as a matter of *age*. My father was approaching senior citizenship when I was born, and *his* father was pushing middle age when *he* was born. That grandfather, Joseph Decatur Braddock, enlisted in the Confederate Army while in his teens, making me one of the youngest people in America to have a grandfather in the Civil War. (In the 1980s I learned that "My grandfather was in the Civil War" was *not* a good line to use in singles bars.) My father learned songs from former slaves, songs like "Massa Had an Old Gray Mule" and "Watermelon Hangin' on the Vine." I once heard my father and my uncle recalling their father running out in the yard to stop them from fighting, shouting, "Part them!" Imagine hearing such biblical-sounding language today. When my father was a child, he knew people born in the *eighteenth* century, and it is entirely possible that my grandson will live to know people born in the *twenty-second*. Hence, my link to the past . . . and future.

This songwriting business has brought me many glorious moments. As thrilling as the big awards and inductions were the personal career milestones: the first time I heard my song on the radio, the first song on the charts, the first Top Ten, the first #1. There was also the thrill of being able to do exceptional things, like writing out the lyrics to my songs and decorating them with little sketches, then seeing them bring several thousand dollars each at charity auctions; or inducting fellow writers into the Nashville Songwriters Hall of Fame: Sonny Curtis in 1991, Wayne Kemp in 1999, Roger Murrah in 2005, and Matraca Berg in 2008.

And fame? Being a little introverted and not very comfortable in a crowd—I've often said that I'm an introvert who does a good impersonation of an extrovert—I enjoy the tiny doses of fame that a songwriter gets; it's just enough to suit me. (I realized the difference between singing stars and songwriters one day when Bill Anderson and I happened to be arriving at doctors' offices at the same time, and he invited me to come sit with him in his private waiting room.) I can walk down the street or go through a supermarket and most people don't know or care who I am, but occasionally someone will and that's nice. Even in talking on the phone with someone out of town, making a payment or a reservation, every once in a while someone will ask, "Are you the songwriter?" When I walked up to the red carpet on Hall of Fame induction night, there were hundreds of fans lined up outside, and, of course, they were there to see Reba. A few knew me, and when my name was announced as I stepped from the limo (very embarrassed) most of them cheered because they had been told that I was being inducted. But I think mine was a new name to a majority of them; most people don't know who writes the songs. On a YouTube site for "He Stopped Loving Her Today," I found hundreds of comments raving about the song, but had to scroll down for a very long time to find my name or Curly Putman's name mentioned by anyone, because most people weren't even thinking about who might have written the song they loved, or they assumed that George wrote it himself ("George Jones is a true poet," one wrote).

So I think fame is like wine; a little bit is nice but too much is intoxicating or even crazy-making. A country star once told me about getting underneath his truck at a filling station to look at the oil pan or something, and he glanced around and saw several people crawling under the truck with him. "It made me crazy," he said. "I just wanted to get behind the wheel and get the hell out of there." Some people might say, 'Well, he should appreciate his fans and be grateful that they're there," but I think people who say that would feel differently if faced with such a situation. The late Dan Miller, the beloved news anchor for Nashville's NBC affiliate, was such a local superstar that he had to go to Atlanta to do his Christmas shopping. Being the man behind the scenes is a pretty good gig.

My father handed me fifty cents and said in his W. C. Fields–meets–Foghorn Leghorn drawl, "Enjoy the showww, dah-lin,' and get you some popcorn and a cooooool *drink*."

Seven years old, I hopped out of the Plymouth coupe with a little notepad in my hand. There were hordes of kids crowded around a man wearing a white hat and a white cowboy suit. Every Saturday afternoon (except during the big polio epidemic) I was at the Park Theater in downtown Auburndale, Florida, along with two hundred other kids and an old country man named Elwood McGrew, to see the weekly cowboy movie, cartoon, and serial. These Saturday afternoons gave me my first ongoing experience with country music. While waiting for the likes of Gene Autry, Roy Rogers, or Hopalong Cassidy to ride across the screen, I was hearing Eddy Arnold's "Molly Darling" and "Can't Win, Can't Place, Can't Show" over the big theater speakers. This particular Saturday was a very special day because the star of the movie, singing cowboy Jimmy Wakely, was appearing in person.

So after I got out of Daddy's car I bought a cone of frozen custard from a street vendor and worked my way through the throng of children in front of the theater to Jimmy Wakely, and handed my little white pad to the heart-faced cowpoke with the little pointy ears. He smiled at me and swept his fountain pen across the page. As I reached up for my pad, I got a big glob of frozen custard on his coat sleeve. "Careful, son," he whispered. I got the sticky custard on the little notepad and all over me as well. This may have been symbolic of how I would eventually spend my adult life: asking for and receiving little prizes from western-clad men, but often making a mess along the way.

And there goes my life again. Magical childhood, frightful puberty, awkward adolescence, playing in bands, getting married, moving to Nashville, road gig with a superstar, tragedy, wonderful daughter, major publishing deal, hits, divorce, bigger hits, second marriage, second divorce, dry spell and debt, comeback, producing, wonderful grandson, awards and recognition, growing old. And it was almost that fast. If you think life just creeps along, you're either very young or very bored. (In a song called "Time Flies," I tried to explain why time seems to go by faster as we get older: "When you're eight years old, four years is half of your life / When you're forty years old, it's only ten percent.")

When I look back, there are vivid country music scenes that, for some reason or other, have stayed in my mind. When my time comes, maybe these are some of the little snapshots from my life that will flash before me,

> 1965: Marty Robbins's bus driver, Okie Jones, and Johnny Cash's future wife, June Carter, dancing a little jig in a bus-loading area, apparently some kind of a shared country music memory from the days when Okie was a performer, too.
> 1975: Bill Anderson in a recording studio singing into a mic; me in the control room putting the finishing touches on a song that Bill is about to record; and nine-year-old Jeep sitting on the floor working away on her coloring book.
> Around 1980: Guitarist Billy Byrd (immortalized on Ernest Tubb's 1950s hit records when the deep-voiced Texan would introduce Byrd's solos with "Aw, Billy Byrd now") setting the meter in his taxicab and asking me, "Where to?"
> Early 1980s: Running into short and heavily sequined Hank Snow in his later years, accompanied by his tall, glitzy, high-heeled protégé, Kelly Foxton, at Nashville's downtown post office, and Hank saying, in

his Nova Scotia accent, "Bobby, I just don't think they're treating us older artists fairly these days."

Mid-1980s: A female singer, who'd had a couple of Top Ten records, telling me, "I'll give you a blow job for a hit song."

Early 1990s: Songwriter and aspiring producer Byron Gallimore, making the rounds on Music Row with a struggling young singer named Tim McGraw.

Early 1994: Struggling young singer Tim McGraw telling me it's looking like his new single, "Indian Outlaw," might be a hit.

1996: Calling up George Jones's wife, Nancy, and telling her if George changed a line in my song, "Billy B. Bad"—as he insisted on doing— that he would absolutely ruin it, and her saying, "Don't worry, honey, I'll take care of it," which she did.

Around 2000: Up-and-coming Brad Paisley telling me that his favorite song was one of mine that George Strait once recorded, "The Nerve."

2005: Eighty-seven-year-old Eddy Arnold, who had probably been in more recording studios than any other singer in town, at songwriter Ben Peters's funeral, quietly saying to Mrs. Arnold, "This church has good acoustics."

2006: Irving Waugh, the dapper father of the CMA Awards and Opryland theme park, sitting in a barber chair, telling me, "Never ask a ninety-three-year-old man how he's doing."

2011: Jetting from Nashville to San Antonio with Deborah Allen, en route to the royal wedding (Blake and Miranda), my first time in the air in years and a big step toward getting past my old flying phobia.

2012: Tom Douglas, after I suggested that we write a patriotic song for all Americans, singing "America, America," as I think he's saying "America, a miracle," and we decide to call it that.

2014: Sitting onstage at a piano and singing John Anderson's classic "Seminole Wind," at his request, on the night of his induction as artist-writer into the Nashville Songwriters Hall of Fame, as Seminole blood flows through my own veins (on my mother's side from back in the days when Seminole ancestors inhabited South Carolina and Georgia).

Though the famous singers tend to socialize with each other rather than with the people behind the scenes, in the recent years many of the new breed of country music celebrities (like Luke Bryan, Keith Urban, and Dierks Bentley) have been especially nice to me. But in the earlier days, not all of the stars gave me a lot of respect. In the 1990s I told Kix Brooks that I thought a certain legendary singer was a bit of a jerk.

"Why, he's always a sweetheart to us," Kix declared.

"Yeah," I told him, "that's because you're *Brooks & Dunn!*"

I remember being with a songplugger on one long-ago afternoon, playing music for Mickey Gilley who sat through the entire pitch session without once looking at me or even acknowledging my existence. But Gilley was Mr. Nice Guy compared to his cousin Jerry Lee Lewis. Mac Davis told me that before he (Mac) was a singing star, he was in Las Vegas with Elvis Presley, who had recorded some of his songs and was performing there. Mac ran into Jerry Lee, one of his (and my) rock & roll heroes, at the club where Elvis was performing. Mac introduced himself, told Jerry Lee that he was a huge fan, and added that he had written Elvis's big hit, "In the Ghetto."

"Well, that's *your* fuckin' problem," said Jerry Lee as he turned and walked away.

So when I look back over my life, it all comes down to one thing. The ones who mean the most to me are the ones who treated me the best.

I essentially finished *A Life on Nashville's Music Row* in late 2012, and have spent another two-and-a-half years going over everything and making changes—digging up quite a few stumps and planting some new trees. Now it's 2015! This book is about many things, but if I had to say in just a word or two what it's about, I would say, of course, country music. And our country music is going through its biggest transformation—I would say *revolution*—since the early Nashville Sound and crossover days of the late 1950s, or even a couple of years earlier when a part of country branched off into rock & roll. The winds were already blowing from a new direction in the 2000s decade: country boys too proud to cry in their beer like their forerunners—I called it *redneck swagger* (instead of a guy being sad because he got dumped, he's sad because *he* dumped the *girl*, then realized he'd made a mistake). But more often, the dude was partying. We were beginning to hear country words with rock music. A big proponent of this was Jason Aldean, who in 2011 had a country rap monster-hit with "Dirt Road Anthem," but unlike my country rap hit several years earlier, this one started a little bit of a trend. (When country music journalist Peter Cooper playfully proclaimed me "the father of bro-country" in an article he wrote for the *Tennessean*, I got an e-mail from Blake Shelton the next day that read, "You, sir, ARE the father of bro-country . . . asshole.") Then along came Luke Bryan with his romantic, melodic, beer-drinking party songs, and Florida Georgia Line with their catchy hard-rockin' summertime-all-year-long songs. And there's the guy you just heard on the radio, the one I haven't heard yet because he hasn't yet signed his contract as I write these words, This new wave of country is sparser, the rhythm patterns more unconventional, often pieced together with drum loops. Writing in *New York* magazine in August 2013, journalist Jody Rosen named it "*bro-country*: music by and of the tatted, gym-toned, party-hearty young American white dude." I thought *I* had coined a name for it: "hick hop," then found out that a lot of other people were calling it that, too. Among a much younger demographic, the appeal of today's country music seems to be as strong on college campuses as it is in honky-tonks. With the exception of a few female artists, women are largely absent from the country charts, a situation I hope will change before the ink in this book is dry. Contemporary country music isn't leaving anytime soon. To the fans, this is the music of their lives, the music they're growing up with and falling in love to. The fans—and the music—are going to be around for a long, long time. But who knows? The next big thing may come from a pudgy crooner of cheatin' songs, or a blind girl from Canada going viral on the Internet. It won't be like the music of yesterday; it will be the music of tomorrow.

I come from an era when a lot of songs were written solo, sometimes only when inspiration hit, and even the co-writing was often spontaneous and undisciplined, like two guys in a bar and one saying, "Hey, you in the mood to write a song?" Here in the mid-2010s, writers like Rhett Akins, Jessi Alexander, Rodney Clawson, Ross Copperman, Dallas Davidson, Ben Hayslip, Natalie Hemby, Jaren Johnston, Luke Laird, Shane McAnally, Jimmy Robbins, Ashley Worley, and many others (to whom I apologize for not listing) are generally tech savvy (even demoing their songs on their computers as they write them), have a strong work ethic and huge output, and some of them write in groups of three or four or even more.

So how does an old dog like me fit in with this new country? Perhaps by embracing it and writing my own version of it. My best shots never came from being a copycat, but from being original. A songwriter's best chance for survival is to know what's going on. I've always said that to write left of center you have to know where the center *is*. My career obituary has been written many times before, and people always seem to be surprised when I make a comeback, like "Wow, I thought this time you were really through." The day draws nearer, of course, when I really *will* be through, but not yet. I heard a veteran songwriter say many years ago, "There's still a few tricks left in the old whore." I like that philosophy.

I know beyond a doubt what has caused me to keep having successful comebacks even as I've grown older: financial vulnerability. I'm the worst money manager in the world. When the numbers in my ledger start looking scary, I think, "I've got to get more hits and make more money!" Here's an example of where I am, compared to where I should be. Bob McDill and I have had parallel Nashville songwriting careers and similar track records, but I've spent the past twenty-six years in a middle-class neighborhood with college professors living on either side of me, while McDill (who always managed wisely and invested his money) lives in a big mansion and plays croquet with his next-door neighbor, the governor of Tennessee.

The most I ever made in a year was $974,000, in 2003 (writing Toby's big hit and producing Blake). The reality is that a songwriter's income can vary wildly, depending on how well the songs do in a given year. For instance, my income went from $821,000 in 2010 ("People Are Crazy") down to $225,000 just four years later (not counting Social Security). It averages out pretty well, and I'm not complaining, but it pales in comparison to the income of those few lucky writers in Nashville who have a superstar whom they co-write with on a regular basis. Those kinds of relationships give the writers a built-in, on-going outlet into the marketplace and yield earnings of several million dollars a year. It is a great honor to be called a legend and to be inducted into the different halls of fame, but it's never made me rich.

In February 2015, I was thrilled to learn that I would be honored with membership in still another prestigious group, the Songwriters Hall of Fame in New York. The induction usually goes to pop and rock songwriters, so I was feeling all puffed up and proud, but I was also thinking, "Well, I guess that's about *it*." Lauren must have read my mind, because she said, "I'm sorry, Daddy, but I don't think they're going to put you in the Baseball Hall of Fame."

Every story has to end. The Bible concludes with "Amen" and *Gone with the Wind* ends with "The End." Fitzgerald closed *The Great Gatsby* with something about boats against the current. My favorite ending of all endings was in a TV show, the final episode of the great HBO series *Six Feet Under*, in which we are taken on a quick journey through the next eighty years and witness the deaths of each of the show's main characters. But how do you end a memoir? That is, how does one go about ending the story of his life experience while he's still alive? *Is the last text in these pages going to be from whatever keys my nose strikes when I finally keel over?*

I love the wee hours when most of the city is asleep and I have more of the energy to myself. As I sit here, being lulled into tranquility by the hum of the distant late-night traffic, I feel both relief and sadness that this project is coming to a close. Relieved because for several years I have been diverted from my music by what has been the biggest and most overwhelming endeavor of my life (unearthing all this personal history and making sure I tell it right). Sad because I have been revisiting fifty years of my life in Nashville—it's the opposite of amnesia—and have been able to go back to my younger days and relive all the magic moments, and once again be with those who are long gone from my life or from the face of the earth. That part I'll miss.

I think of a memoir as being "the world through my eyes" as opposed to an autobiography, which I think of as "the story of me." Celebrities write autobiographies so this has been a memoir. When I started this many moons and many pages ago, I wanted to write a book about the country music factory through the eyes of one of the workers . . . the country music factory through the years—its bosses, its supervisors, and its laborers . . . the country music factory and its environs, and all the tragedy, comedy, and soap opera that went with it. I promised great characters who were famous, infamous, and unknown; I hope I have fulfilled that promise. So there you have it: a walk down memory lane and back, a guided tour of Nashville's Music Row from 1964 to just now. (Ah, Music Row, growth-obsessed like the rest of

Nashville—and where skyscrapers are beginning to sprout up faster than kudzu, as the old houses come down and music offices move to other parts of the city.)

As I now walk out the door and turn around to wave goodbye, I look forward to the next phase of my life. As long as the higher power allows me to contribute creatively, I plan to keep doing it with a passion. I'll continue living life to the fullest, running this race like Seabiscuit on steroids until fate pulls me off the track.

If we love our jobs—as I have loved mine—we're among the lucky ones. In the introduction to this book, I wrote about feeling as if I had been to the circus. I wrote: "And the ticket didn't cost me much at all. I got it for a song." But after this long journey of walking back through all these years, I see it from a different perspective. I haven't merely been to the circus; I ran off and *joined* it!"

So enough! I just speculated that the last text in the book might be from the keys my nose strikes when I finally keel over. Come to think of it, I'm not feeling so well. zxsd

Blake Shelton and Miranda Lambert cut short their honeymoon to perform at my induction into the Country Music Hall of Fame, 2011.

With the two other 2011 inductees, Jean Shepard and Reba McEntire

At the Medallion Ceremony, singing "He Stopped Loving Her Today"
with the greatest country singer of all time

My best little buddy
doing what he's always
done, kissing me on my
bald head

BMI Awards
with Big Kenny
of Big & Rich

With Luke Bryan

With Keith Urban

On camera at 2011 CMAs with Rebecca Magnuson, as Reba McEntire discusses my Country Music Hall of Fame induction

Congratulations from good friend Shannon McCombs

Bear hug from Blake at Icon ceremony

Owen Bradley's statue waves at passersby on Music Row. In the background are the nude statues that are frozen in frolic on Buddy Killen Circle.

INDEX

Page numbers in **bold** indicate illustrations.
An asterisk (*) indicates a pseudonym.

Illustration Credits

Grateful acknowledgment is made to all the people and organizations who supplied the photos used in this book. Author's private collection: 5, 21, 41 (right), 47, 70, 145, 152, 170, 173 (both), 175, 220, 227, 242, 268, 277, 348; Alan Mayor Photography: 185, 208, 246 (top), 283 (middle), 299, 301 (both); Broadcast Music Incorporated: 91, 190, 246 (bottom), 283 (bottom), 323 (top), 325 (top), 328, 345 (all), 347; Chris Hollo: 343 (bottom); Curly and Bernice Putman: 41 (left), 103, 117; Dennis Carney: 258, 326 (both); Dennis Carney and Donn Jones: 313; Donn Jones: 343 (top), 344 (top); Grand Ole Opry/Gaylord: 191; Laurel Green: 344 (bottom); Leadership Music of Nashville / photo by Steve Lowery: 325 (bottom); Metro Development and Housing Agency: 44, 45; Rebecca Magnuson: 283 (top), 323 (bottom), 346 (top); Ron Newcomer: 279; Shannon McCombs: 346 (bottom); Sony ATV Music: 40 (both), 51, 78, 92 (both), 116, 167 (both), 182, 200, 211, 212, 252, 259, 312, 322; Sparky Reed: 153; *Tennessean* archives: 144